P9-DHT-914

Famous Dave's
LifeSkills
FOR SUCCESS

The Ultimate Manual for Achieving Your Very Best

*Always follow
your dreams
Best Wishes & God Bless
Famous Dave*

Notable Endorsements
See what the experts are saying about Dave's new book!

"This incredible book is so powerful, you could rip out any page and that one page alone could transform your life into a grand adventure of self-discovery and self-improvement!"
> — **Mark Victor Hanson**, *Co-Author Chicken Soup for the Soul and The One Minute Millionaire*

"Famous Dave Anderson is an ordinary guy with an extraordinary message. His heart is solid gold and the information in his book, *LifeSkills* is just as valuable."
> — **Anthony Robbins**, *World's Leading Personal Development Expert*

"Dave's personal life story is nothing less than a real American "rags-to-riches" story come true. In fact, I was so impressed by his life story that I used his experiences to sum up my own best selling book, Failing Forward. Famous Dave's LifeSkills for Success is must reading for anyone looking to jump-start their career."
> — **John C. Maxwell**, *New York Times Best Selling Author and Expert on Leadership*

"Get ready to launch your career or your life! Famous Dave's well-researched book on LifeSkills will teach you the disciplines that will allow you to master yourself before you can master your task. Whether you are launching into space or living life, Failure is NOT an Option!"
> — **Gene Kranz**, *NASA Team Leader Tiger Team Mission Control Apollo 13 and New York Times Best Selling Author, Failure Is Not An Option!*

"America is the Land of Unlimited Opportunity, so…quit coming home empty handed! Just like in fishing, sometimes you need an experienced guide to show you how to get the best results. Famous Dave's LifeSkills for Success is a loaded tackle box of proven techniques that will have you landing the big ones!"
> — **Ray W. Scott, Jr.**, *Horatio Alger Award Recipient, Founder of Bass Anglers Sportsman Society (B.A.S.S.) and Unabashed American Optimist!*

"Learn the secrets of the wealthy for building a massive bank account. You don't have to be a genius; you only need intense desire, passion, and a willingness to go to work! Famous Dave's LifeSkills for Success will teach you winning strategies that will ignite a burning passion in you to achieve phenomenal wealth and success."
> — **Robert G. Allen**, *Author of Multiple Streams of Income and Co-Author of The One Minute Millionaire*

"I am a firm believer in reading inspirational books on self-improvement. Famous Dave's LifeSkills for Success is definitely one of the best! You will want to buy this book by the dozens to give to all your family, business associates, and friends!"
— **Reid E. Evenson**, *President, Eagle Crest Capital Bank*

"I would encourage everyone to read this book. I have witnessed first hand the remarkable growth of Dave's nationally recognized company, Famous Dave's of America, Inc. Study this book over and over again and you too will experience a richly rewarding life. This book is destined to change lives."
— **Michael Wright**, *Sr., Chairman, SUPERVALU*

"Hormel is a major supplier to Famous Dave's of America. We are deeply impressed by the effectiveness of Dave's LifeSkills for Success at work in his own rapidly growing business. A graduate of the "University of Hard-Knocks," Famous Dave Anderson went on to achieve great success. In this book, he shares learnable secrets and methods on thrift and the good life that certify him as a Benjamin Franklin of the 21st century. Just as Ben still is quoted today, Famous Dave will be quoted tomorrow.
— **Joel Johnson**, *Chairman, Hormel Foods Corporation*

"I am the bank president that gave Dave his first start in life, when he was just a teenager, by giving him a bank loan on his signature alone! From the moment I first met Dave, I have been impressed by his industrious work ethic and his willingness to go the extra mile. His enthusiasm for life, positive mental attitude, and his willingness to serve his fellow man is an inspiration for all. I highly recommend everyone to read Famous Dave's LifeSkills for Success."
— **Gerhardt Umlauf**, *President, Advantage National Bank*

"Famous Dave's LifeSkills for Success is a well-researched compilation of amazing, rich, easily readable, practical and useful set of ideas on Success, Work, Health, Motivation, LifeSkills, Wealth, and Careers. Many people will benefit by reading and re-reading this incredible book!"
— **Jack M. Gill, PhD.**, *Horatio Alger Award Recipient, Lecturer Harvard Medical School and MIT, Vanguard Ventures, General Partner*

"Famous Dave Anderson is the most inspiring person I know, especially since he has overcome great personal challenges to get to where he is today! His "can do" philosophy of life has helped him rise above the ordinary. This book is a gold mine—full of treasures that will bring inner wealth to your life."
— **Mark Wilson,** *Senior Pastor, Hayward Wesleyan Church*

"When you read—or, rather, experience!—Famous Dave's enlightening *LifeSkills for Success* you'll learn that the secret to a life well lived is simply a matter of the choices we make each day. As Dave's incredible story proves, it's not just what you choose to do, *but who you choose to be,* that makes all the difference!
— **John Christensen**, *Co-author of FISH!, International Business Bestseller*

"Famous Dave's LifeSkills For Success is the book everyone is waiting for. No nonsense, plain hard facts. Not only a must-read, it's impossible to put down. In his lifetime, Dave Anderson has overcome many adversities to achieve much success. Through God, and with Kathy and his family, he's just getting started. Read with caution. This book is contagious!"
— **Tom Harken**, *Horatio Alger Recipient, Entrepreneur/Literacy Advocate, Author of "The Millionaire's Secret"*

We all can't witness firsthand the enthusiasm and passion of Famous Dave Anderson. But the next best thing is turning to any page in his LifeSkills for Success book and being blown away by his insights into how to live life to the fullest. This book is a daily inspirational calendar you can use every day of every year.
— **Brian Anderson**, *Editor, Minneapolis St. Paul Magazine*

Who or what turns a person's life onto a path of achievement and contribution? For many, the turning point will be Dave's LifeSkills for Success. This book goes right to the heart of what it takes to turn your life and career in the direction of success and satisfaction. And Dave makes it clear that this path is one of adventure and enjoyment, not burden or drudgery.
— **Joseph P. Kalt**, *Ford Foundation Professor of International Political Economy, John F. Kennedy School of Government, Harvard University*

Famous Dave's

LifeSkills
FOR SUCCESS

The Ultimate Manual for Achieving Your Very Best

David W. Anderson

What I learned in 30 years the hard way... you can learn in 30 days!

The Ultimate Manual for Achieving Your Very Best

Published by David W. Anderson

Copyright © 2004 by
David W. Anderson
1508 East Franklin Ave. Suite 200
Minneapolis, MN 55404
www.lifeskillsforsuccess.com
www.famousdaves.com
www.lifeskills-center.org

All rights reserved. No part of this publication may be reproduced in any form or by any means, electronic or mechanical, including photocopy and information storage and retrieval systems, without permission in writing from the publisher.

Library of Congress Control Number: 2003097861
ISBN: 0-9668548-1-0

Edited, Designed, and Manufactured by

FRP.

2451 Atrium Way
Nashville, Tennessee 37214
800-358-0560

Illustrations by Paul Fricke
www.bluemoonstudios.com

Manufactured in the United States of America
First Printing: 2004
15,000 copies

Liability Disclaimer: This book is intended as inspirational reference only. Every effort has been made to ensure that the information contained in this book is complete and accurate. However, neither the author nor the publisher is offering, suggesting, or rendering professional advice or services to the individual reader or interested groups. The ideas, opinions, observations, and suggestions contained in this book are not intended as a substitute for consulting with professional advisors, instructors, physicians, and obtaining medical supervision as to any activity, procedure, or suggestion that might affect your mental health, physical health, or financial condition. Neither the author nor the publisher shall be liable or responsible for any loss, injury, or damage allegedly arising from any information or suggestion in this book.

Disclaimer: Famous Dave's of America, Inc. is a publicly traded company listed on the NASDAQ market. Ticker symbol is DAVE. The views and opinions represented in this book do not necessarily represent Famous Dave's as a company. This book solely represents the thoughts and philosophies of David W. Anderson, Chairman and Founder.

Thank you for buying this book!

All profits from the sale of this book are donated to help people in recovery and to provide leadership training for at-risk youth. My greatest hope is to provide information that will be life-changing to people who need a fresh start in life, who in turn will help others less fortunate than themselves. For more information please check out our website.

Dedication

*This book is dedicated to my parents, whose faith in God has
carried me through many tough times. When I was a child,
my parents prayed with us every night, without fail,
before they tucked us into bed. And they told us, each night,
"We love you, we believe in you, and no matter what happens,
we are always proud of you!" The memory of these words
has meant so much to me over the years.
The effect on me was very powerful.
If all children heard encouraging words like these before
they go to bed, the world would certainly be a better place.*

*This book is also dedicated to my loving wife who has
put up with me for many years. She has stuck with me,
believed in me, and supported me through all the tough times.
Without her help, I would not have accomplished
incredible things in my life. I especially thank her for the
strength to intervene while I was struggling with alcohol.
It was a major turning point in my life, for which I will
always be grateful. Also, I thank God for my two sons,
James and Timothy. Raising them and sharing
their lives has been an incredible learning experience.
It is because of them that I wanted to learn how to become
a better person, able to responsibly and thoughtfully guide them
through childhood and into adulthood.*

Acknowledgements

*I am grateful to Zig Ziglar, who is the first person who
really inspired me to think that I could "go" wherever I wanted,
just "be" whatever I wanted, and "do" whatever I wanted,
if only I would believe strongly enough in my own dreams."
I have practically memorized his books and his audio recordings.
More importantly, I have been influenced by his faith in God.
I am also grateful to John C. Maxwell, who used my
life story in his best selling book Failing Forward.
A special word of thanks goes to Mark Victor Hansen,
co-author of the Chicken Soup for the Soul series of books,
who has befriended me and given me helpful advice
through his inspirational writing seminars.
Tremendous thanks go to all my mentors whose
books and recordings have been a huge part of my daily life:
Jim Rohn, Brian Tracy, Anthony Robbins, Les Brown,
Denis Waitely, Pat Riley, Napoleon Hill, W. Clement Stone,
Norman Vincent Peale, Dr. Wayne Dyer, Harvey Mackay,
Leo Buscaglia, Dale Carnegie, Rick Pitino, Og Mandino,
Cynthia Kersey, Bob Proctor, Earl Nightingale, David J. Schwartz,
Ph.d., Claude M. Bristol, Joe Girard, Tom Hopkins,
Cavett Robert, Robert H. Schuller and Robert G. Allen.*

*I would like to recognize the efforts of Paul Fricke, Blue Moon
Studios, who is responsible for the remarkable drawings that
add life to this text; Mitch Rossow, of Mitch Rossow Design,
who faced the insurmountable challenge of typesetting my notes;
Lance Como, who was available at all hours for technical advice;
David Malone from Malone Creative; and, finally,
all of my editors who have helped to make sense of my notes:
Phil Bolinder, Rebecca Rowland, Graydon Royce,
Leslie Schmeisser, Lynne D'Ascenzo Bucher and Don Jacobs.*

Preface
MY STORY

Writing this LifeSkills book was the result of my personal quest of self-discovery and self-improvement. At a certain point in my life I came to realize that if I was going to become more than I was, I had to take complete responsibility for myself and that all changes had to happen within me first. To become a winner in life, I had to discover the secrets to smashing through all my self-limiting beliefs, and addictive impulsive behaviors, to become a winner in life.

So effective is this information that the results in my own life have been most spectacular, a complete transformation, nothing short of a miracle. I have gone from living a life of drinking to a life of sobriety. I have gone from being a below average student to earning a Harvard Masters Degree without ever getting an undergraduate degree! I have gone from bankruptcy to helping found three publicly traded companies on Wall Street; and now I can count my wealth in the tens of millions!

My beginnings were no different than those of anyone else. I was not born on the right side of the tracks, I am not the most intelligent person that you've ever met and I am not particularly good-looking. I have had my share of setbacks and failures. In fact, there was a time in my life that I was so broke I was selling everything of value just to pay the rent. The bank cancelled my checking accounts, and the credit company repossessed my car.

> **There are many greater advantages to being disadvantaged than there are advantages to being advantaged.**
> — Famous Dave Anderson

I would not be alive if it weren't for the protective hand of God. Without a shadow of a doubt, I believe He has kept me alive because He had a higher purpose for my life. I have survived a heart attack while on drugs; a crash in which my car rolled three times, and I was thrown from the totalled vehicle while I was drunk; and five days in intensive care from pneumonia, which the doctors told me could have been far worse if I had gotten to the hospital two hours later! I have "hit a wall" many times in my life and once I got over being full of myself, I realized my life's higher purpose was to make a positive difference in the lives of others. But most importantly, whatever success I have experienced today, it is only because of the forgiving grace of Almighty God. I have found that it was only when I got my ego out of the way, that I could truly experience the power of God within me.

I have been my own biggest problem. Often, I am asked about my life's greatest challenge, I can truthfully say it has been myself. I was so full of myself, and my self-righteous pride kept from realizing that I was my own worst enemy. Oh, if someone could have whacked me on the head and kicked my rear-end and straightened me out, because I never took responsibility for my behavior. I blamed my American Indian heritage, I blamed my own difficulties in learning, I blamed my parents, I blamed my lack of good luck. I never wanted to take full responsibility for my own actions. I always took the loser's approach and I had an excuse for everything—I was good at lying to myself. Today all that has changed; I am responsible for where I am in life. I fully accept total responsibility for myself, my behavior, and my decisions.

Friends say I shouldn't go running around the country telling people about all the bad things in my life—that it's not necessary and it could be embarrassing. I feel it is important to share the challenges I have overcome, to prove that others can achieve remarkable accomplishments in their lives as well. And many people are ahead of the game because they will never have the unhappy experiences I had; things that were needed to jerk me out of the destructive path I was going down. Although you should not compare your life to mine, if I could overcome my failures and achieve phenomenal success, just think of what you can do. You are incredible in your own right. The things you will accomplish in your life should be your dreams and no one else's. And no matter what happens, don't ever, ever, ever give up on your dreams!

While I have achieved some remarkable successes in my life, I want to make sure everyone realizes that I still have a long way to go on my own journey of self-improvement. I have not completely mastered much of the information you will find in this book. I am still a work in progress.

Today I am devoted to . . .

Lifelong *self-learning*
Lifelong *self-discovery*
Lifelong *self-improvement*
And living an *"excuse-free"* life!

FAMOUS DAVE'S
LifeSkills

These are the personal notes of "Famous Dave" Anderson, your average next door neighbor, whose own personal quest for achievement has led him from a life of frustration and failure to living the American Dream, as a Harvard Graduate and Wall Street Millionaire.

IF I COULD OVERCOME MY FEARS AND ADVERSITIES, JUST THINK WHAT YOU CAN DO WITH YOUR OWN LIFE!

These powerful LifeSkills lessons are jam-packed with "Wisdom Keys," which are the essential lessons in life that everyone should have been taught in school. Unfortunately, our school systems lack the expertise to teach what every millionaire and successful person has learned the hard way. Master these LifeSkills and you can achieve both phenomenal wealth and success. Start now and begin to experience an energized healthy lifestyle that is fulfilling and rewarding to the mind, body, and spirit. The information in this book will keep you from saying, "If only I had known these things when I was younger!" You will also leave the world a better place to live in, because of your contributions!

LifeSkills Lesson One: Mind Dynamics
How to unleash the infinite unstoppable powers of your mind. The first lesson discusses how incredible God has made you. The quest to discover your inner wealth is an amazing journey that unleashes the infinite and unstoppable powers of your mind. Your life's priority should be to learn how to unleash this crackling energy that bubbles within you.

LifeSkills Lesson Two: LifeDesign
How to achieve your maximum potential. This lesson gives you the nuts and bolts for turning your dreams into reality through the process of writing down your personal mission statement, your goals, and your daily to-do list. Instead of just learning how to earn a living, start designing an extraordinary life filled with abundance!

LifeSkills Lesson Three: LifeSkills Mastery
How to live an extraordinary lifestyle. This lesson starts out explaining why life is about change and how everything you accomplish in life is all predicated on your discipline and responsibility for learning these LifeSkills. Jump-start your new life with positive massive action. Positive living is built on a foundation of positive thinking and the development of healthy relationships. All the goodness of the universe will be released to you once you learn how to live a life of service by making others happy first!

WISDOM KEY

WISDOM KEYS are the Keys that open the "Doors of Opportunity!" LifeSkills are the grease that swings these doors open faster. The Doors of Opportunity are not opened by desire. You can stand in front of the door and knock all you want, but unless you have the "Wisdom Keys" the Doors of Opportunity will remain shut. How far you go in life will be determined by how many keys you have. If you are not actively seeking to learn new things and increase your wisdom, you will have few keys to open a limited number of doors of opportunity. Your passion to learn and your industrious work ethic will create the frequency of opportunities that come your way. Sometimes just a little bit of wisdom creates the right magical key that can spring open Big Doors of Opportunity! These "Wisdom Keys" have been proven over time and have been used to change many people's lives for the better.

LifeSkills Lesson Four: Problems

How to turn adversities and failures into opportunity. Probably the most significant lesson in this book is about problems. This lesson provides an eye-opening look at how problems, adversities, and failures in life are really God's gift to you! It's the only way that you can grow to be a better person than you are right now. You will never fear problems and failure again after reading this chapter!

LifeSkills Lesson Five: Total Wellness

How to live an excuse-free, energized, healthy lifestyle. With 61% of all Americans being overweight, this section provides a new healthy look at achieving total wellness for mind, body, and spirit. Control your impulses to live an exciting excuse-free, healthy, energetic, lifestyle full of discovery and achievement!

LifeSkills Lesson Six: A Rewarding Career

How to find your true passion in life and make all your dreams come true. Whether you are just starting out in life, or re-starting your life over again, this lesson will give you the tools to discover the one true passion that will turbo-charge your career. Find out how to never work another day in your life again!

LifeSkills Lesson Seven: Wealth

How to build your own financial empire. If you have never studied wealth, how do you expect to become wealthy? This lesson provides a step-by-step method of turning any income into the "seeds" of a financial empire. The key lesson is that it's not what you earn but what you save and invest that really matters. Regardless of education, gender, or age, anyone can experience great wealth by following this time-tested information. No matter what is happening in the economy, you can start building your financial empire now!

Here's How to Get the Most Out of These Lessons

Memorize the Quotes!

This book is filled with a treasure trove of quotes—brilliant statements by the world's best thinkers, philosophers, writers and famous people. Simple statements that reveal the Aha! moments in life. In order to be successful, you need sound philosophies to guide you, because there are times in your life when you just can't seem to find the right answers. Memorize these quotes and they will "appear" when you need them the most.

Teach It!

There is no way to experience all this book has to offer other than to absorb it, comprehend it, and then most importantly—teach it. When you learn a meaningful **LifeSkill** or **Wisdom Key** from this book—pass it on. Find someone you can mentor. There is nothing more rewarding than to see someone else's life become more meaningful because of your influence. When you teach, it enables you to fully comprehend the meaning of the knowledge you have just learned. The more effective you are in teaching what you have learned, the sooner you will become the master of this knowledge, and knowledge is the powerful key that opens the gates to your destiny.

And Remember!

Become all you can, so that you can give all you can! When you can make the world a better place to live in, God's Universe will provide you with all the financial rewards you need—more than you could have dreamed possible—but don't make greed and the accumulation of material things your priority in life. If your own self-satisfaction, a "what's-in-it-for-me attitude," is your only purpose in life, then the Universe will not recognize your existence. The Universe only recognizes and gives priority to those people who are truly interested in the betterment of others.

Introduction

FAMOUS DAVE'S LifeSkills for Success represents a lifelong study of the greatest lessons in life that can be truly called "The Wisdom of the Ages!" Over thirty years of my life have been dedicated to reading and listening to all of the great masters of self-improvement, personal achievement, motivation, and leadership. I have collected almost every book written on the subject, almost every audio and visual program ever produced, and I have attended hundreds of seminars, lectures and training programs. I have marveled at the wealth of knowledge and life-changing wisdom that is so readily available, if people only knew where to look.

This information is not new and I cannot claim authorship. My goal was to take all the great philosophies of living "a life of abundance," and sift out all but the most meaningful "bits of wisdom." At the end of each chapter is a list of resources, which represent the foundation for the ideas and philosophies of each Lifeskills lesson. I highly recommend you read and re-read these books, as they will positively change your life forever!

I wrote this book as a gift to my family. It was my hope to compile the most comprehensive self-help book ever written so that my sons wouldn't spend a lifetime figuring out what I have learned the hard way. I wanted them to be able to take this information and immediately apply it to their own lives. I also wanted them to experience the thrill of achievement and know that it is all right to fail and make mistakes. I realized that if my sons were going to be successful, they would need to learn lessons about life, and that they weren't going to get this information from their 12 years of formal schooling. As my library and files grew, I wondered how I could condense years of careful study and research into one powerful book for them. Because I love my sons so much, this book represents the best of the best. No expense or commitment of my time was spared in my mission to find the most powerful life-changing information that could be passed on.

While assembling years of notes, clippings and articles, I continued to think about how unfortunate it is that this information—the very essence of success—is not being taught in schools! If schools weren't teaching young people how to succeed, and if parents didn't understand these principles themselves (after all, only 3% of Americans are wealthy), then how could kids ever hope to grow up and live lives filled with achievement and unlimited opportunity? This thought, and the hope of helping all people who are interested in discovering their own untapped potential, became the driving force behind publishing this book.

Seven distinct areas of self-improvement began to emerge from my volumes of notes and personal observations, which became the Lifeskills lessons in this book. It soon became crystal clear to me that these lessons can turn anyone's life into one of exceptional achievement, grand adventure, and great wealth regardless of background, gender, age, or race. This book provides direction to young adults just starting out in their careers, and hope to those who believe life has dealt them a "bad hand." The bottom line is that there is absolutely no excuse for anyone to live a life of mediocrity unless he or she chooses to do so.

How To Use This Book

This book is divided into seven major areas of personal development. These are the key lessons in life that are essential to living an extraordinary lifestyle and will help you achieve all of your wildest dreams and aspirations. Each lesson is broken down so that it is easy to comprehend and memorize. Even though each lesson builds off of the proceeding lesson, you should be able to pick up the book and flip to any page and get something immediately meaningful out of it. I did not want you to read two chapters before you get the point; no mysteries when trying to figure out what earth-shaking idea I am trying to get across. After all, this book is about changing your life. When we are involved in changing lives, we need to get right to the point.

Life is too short to be vague.

I wrote this book as though I was face-to-face with you and you could feel my excitement, enthusiasm, and energy. I wanted every "aha!" moment to be readily apparent. Every paragraph is written in a style that was meant to startle you into wakefulness, jerk you out of your comfort zone, and cause you to start thinking about reassessing your life's goals. These ideas have changed my life: it's time for you to make your dreams a reality too!

ALWAYS BELIEVE IN YOURSELF YOU ARE INCREDIBLE!

Within every individual, there is at least one GREAT IDEA
that can better the world and could be worth millions.
But often, these ideas are never acted upon because of fear.

CONQUERING one small fear every day will eventually EMPOWER
you to TACKLE your bigger fears until finally you can take on that one
BIG OPPORTUNITY that everyone says can't be done.

Don't let your worries give power to your fears.

Instead, let an unwavering belief in yourself, a willingness
to work hard, and unbridled enthusiasm give
POWER TO YOUR DREAMS!

—Famous Dave Anderson

FAMOUS DAVE'S
Table of Contents

Lesson One: Mind Dynamics

Lesson One: Mind Dynamics

Unleash your infinite, unstoppable, and creative mind and discover the awesome powers of your inner wealth!

When you were growing up did you ever feel like your teachers were trying to stuff your head full of meaningless facts? And you had no clue what you were going to do with this information once you grew up? I think that one of the reasons we have a tough time finding our place in the world is we've spent all of our formative years in school trying to master external things rather than learning how to unleash the awesome creative powers of our own minds.

Lesson One: **Mind Dynamics** is the most crucial lesson in beginning your amazing journey of self-discovery and self-improvement. Once you understand your mind's incredible powerhouse of unlimited energy and learn that your thoughts can transcend time and space, you will begin to understand there isn't anything that you can't do once you make up your mind to do it!

PURPOSE:

Many people live a lifetime in frustration because they are searching for answers "out there" when all they have to do is "look within" themselves. The key to all wealth, happiness, and success lies within the incredible powers of your own mind.

We all have a higher purpose here on earth, which can only be realized when we are following the passion of our own dreams. ***Don't live a lifetime fulfilling the dreams of someone else!***

The most powerful force in the world is a fully convicted person with a vision that has been burned into every cell of his or her existence.
— Famous Dave Anderson

AN AMAZING GIFT
Of Self-Discovery!

All great success begins with understanding the awesome powers of your mind.

Your mind's most incredible power is the ability to have faith in a higher power. To accomplish the great achievements and success you would like to experience in life, you should first begin by putting your mind to work through faith! Only humans have been given this incredible gift by God—to harness the powers of faith and unleash the magic of believing. The power of an unshakable faith will open the floodgates of unlimited opportunity, great achievement, and abundant wealth. But before you can even begin to set goals, or achieve great things in life, you must first discover the secret treasures of "mind power."

IT IS NOW ESTIMATED THAT WE USE <u>LESS</u> THAN 10% OF OUR BRAIN'S UNDEVELOPED POTENTIAL!

Our past problem:

> **We haven't fully understood our own inner resources and the incredible power of our minds.** Therefore, in life we tend to focus on and react to what we can see and feel. Simply stated, we have tried to master what is *around us* rather than what is *within us!*

Our new goal:

> **Internal Mastery of Our Minds. This should be our highest priority.**

WISDOM KEY

> **The most important quest in your life should be to understand the enormous potential of your mind.** You can use your mind's awesome energy to: discover your spiritual relationship with God; attain infinite intelligence; make your dreams soar; visualize your future; have greater memory recall; create meaningful relationships and be socially accepted; gain confidence at resolving problems; build the mental resolve to overcome great adversity; and tap into your unlimited creativity. The Powers Of Your Mind Are Unlimited!

Unfortunately, the only education we get in school about our brains is in biology. We are taught that our brain is a chunk of gray matter located in our heads. Rarely do we learn about the amazing resource we are born with and the incredible potential of: our conscious mind (awake mind), our higher conscious mind (subconscious mind), and our divine conscious mind (spiritual mind or soul).

You Are God's Handiwork!

A common excuse for lack of achievement is "Whad'ya expect…I'm only human!" There couldn't be anything more wrong than trying to explain away mediocrity by saying "I'm only human!" In fact, the human brain is the most sophisticated masterpiece in the entire known universe. The power of the mind is infinite, unlimited, and unstoppable.

IF YOU'RE ASKING, "WHAT'S WRONG WITH ME?" YOU'RE ASKING THE WRONG QUESTION. THERE IS NOTHING WRONG WITH YOU, ONLY YOUR THINKING.

We were designed for achievement. Everyone is gifted with unlimited potential. We are all born geniuses and have the same opportunity as anyone else who has ever achieved great things in life. So if we were all born geniuses, why is it that only a few people ever really succeed in life? The real problem is that most of us have never learned just how incredible we really are, or how to unleash these awesome powers, which is what we will be exploring in this book.

First, let's upgrade what you know about your brain.

We are just beginning to understand how the brain works and the amazing potential of mind power. Almost 95% of everything "technical" that we know about the brain has been learned in the last 20 years. And as the technology for scientific discovery increases, we begin to realize that the more we know, the more we don't know. Every time we reach a new level of discovery, we find out that the horizon of our understanding has just begun all over again.

The human brain is a 3½-pound organ made up of tens of billions of brain cells called neurons. Each neuron looks like an octopus with many tiny arms called dendrites. Brain cells communicate through the development of pathways formed by tiny electrochemical pulses exploding from one cell to another across tiny gaps called synapses. Successful repetition of energy passing through these pathways creates learning patterns. It is estimated that 100,000 to 1,000,000 electrochemical reactions occur every second in the brain.

 YOUR BRAIN IS A POWERHOUSE OF ENERGY!

Just how powerful is your brain?

A world renowned Russian doctor, Professor Pyotr Anokhin, says the possible inter-linking connections to create thought are conservatively calculated to be the number one followed by 1,000,000 miles of standard typewritten zeros. Try to imagine what that number looks like— the distance to the moon is 240,000 miles so 1,000,000 miles is over four times this distance. It's incredible what's going on inside your head!

Did you know?

Humans are the only creatures that can store information outside their bodies!

Today, it is scientifically accepted that the power of the brain is limitless. Our ability to innovate ways to store and retrieve information outside our brain is accelerating our learning abilities. Our newest technology becomes an extension of our minds to create new and exponentially-expanding learning horizons. The only boundaries of our minds are the ones we create or let other people impose on us. During our formative years, adults told us what we couldn't do, rather than creating unlimited learning opportunities to satisfy our knowledge-craving minds. This must change. From now on, let your mind be free.

> **Thinking is the hardest work there is, which is probable reason why so few engage in it.**
> — Henry Ford

Use it or lose it! The human brain is like a muscle; to get the most out of it you must challenge it daily. Just like a muscle, your brain will wither away if you are not pushing yourself to learn. To strengthen and develop your brain into the powerhouse it can become, you must challenge it every day to higher levels of comprehension, creativity, and problem solving.

You are constantly losing brain cells just through the process of learning and aging. Learning causes electrical pulses to travel over successful learned pathways created by repetition. Brain cells that are not part of this process die away. So even though you may lose a few brain cells as a result of natural causes and aging, what you have left is infinitely more productive.

DON'T WORRY ABOUT THE BRAIN CELLS YOU LOSE— YOU HAVE A LOT TO SPARE. EVEN THOUGH YOU WILL LOSE ABOUT 10,000 CELLS EVERY DAY, IT IS ESTIMATED YOU WILL LOSE ONLY 3% OF YOUR BRAIN THROUGHOUT YOUR ENTIRE LIFE.

KEEP YOUR BRAIN HEALTHY
Healthy thinking creates a healthy brain.

Good health begins with a positive outlook on life. When your state of mind is cheerful, energetic, playful, and free from worry, your body will respond with good health, longevity, and vitality. A positive outlook on life is directly linked to how the brain produces hormones, which adjusts the biochemical balance affecting overall wellness.

It's not about what happens *to you* but what happens *in you*!

Are you eating enough *Brain Food?* One-fifth of all the food you eat fuels the brain. Consuming more energy than any other organ in the human body, your brain uses about 30% of your available blood supply. Your brain also uses more oxygen than any part of your body—almost 16 times more. Believe it or not, an active brain produces enough energy to illuminate a standard light bulb—giving credence to the term "Bright Ideas!"

There's a lot of truth to the term "hot head!" Because of all the thinking going on in your head, the brain is hotter than any part of your body. Which is one of the reasons we are told to always keep our heads covered in winter—more heat escapes from the head than anywhere else.

WISDOM KEY

What you eat and drink affects the health of your brain. While most people understand the risks of heart disease caused by fatty diets, smoking, alcohol and drug abuse, they don't understand that the same bad things can also affect the plaque buildup in the vessels and capillaries in the brain. Alcohol, drug abuse, and cigarette smoking can destroy the chemical balance needed for "ideal brain functioning" because the "electrochemical energy pulses" have a hard time navigating altered chemical pathways.

Your brain is the ultimate pharmacy. Producing 168 chemicals, the brain can coordinate the production of drugs and hormones and activate your immune system to heal anything that may be wrong with your body. If you alter this delicate bio-system by ingesting toxins—polluted water, polluted air, substance abuse, and killer food—you will overload and shut down your protective system. So...

Don't flood your brain with poisonous toxins. Your brain is like a high performance engine of the most expensive, finely tuned racecar. You wouldn't think of putting sugar water in your racecar, so don't treat your mind with any less care. Your mind is infinitely more valuable than the world's most expensive racecar!

Proper breathing and exercise keeps oxygen flowing to your brain. Your brain cells are so specialized and oxygen dependent that if they are deprived of oxygen, the cells will start to die within three minutes! Rest, proper diet, and exercise do more than just regenerate and renew your mind, body and spirit; they also affect your ability to think positive and live *full-out* in a healthy energetic manner. Your brain is precious—protect it!

Kids' Brains Are Supercharged!

When we are born our brains are turbocharged to learn and master new skills at incredible speed. While we can soak up new information every day of our lives, our greatest potential for learning comes when we are between the ages of 3 and 14. Reading to your children when they are young is one of the greatest gifts you can give them. Reading stimulates their curiosities and imaginations. Reading to your children is also one of the greatest gifts you can give to the world!

Why haven't I learned about this stuff before? Unfortunately, the majority of formal education stresses development of the left brain and generally emphasizes the understanding and perfecting of "technical disciplines." When, in fact, a more rewarding life comes from the development of attitudes, creativity, and emotions, and the cultivation of personal relationships—right brain stuff.

Master the inner mind instead of the external facts. Just think how much more rewarding and enriched our lives would be if we spent our school years learning how to unleash the powers of our higher conscious minds (subconscious) instead of just stuffing our logical minds with facts relating to technical disciplines.

IMAGINE HOW MUCH MORE WE COULD ACCOMPLISH IF **"The Power of the Higher Conscious Mind"** WAS A REQUIRED SUBJECT IN SCHOOL!

KEY LESSON: *Academic achievers* **are no more gifted or higher up on the** *"brainpower totem pole"* **than** *creative achievers*.

Just because you weren't on the honor roll doesn't mean that you can't be successful! We have to transcend many years of negative programming—both from formal education and from our well-meaning families—that conditioned us to believe we're not capable of anything but average achievement. We are all born for great achievement no matter what our test scores may have been. If you are an "A" student, congratulations—you're ahead of the game! However an educator once commented:

YOU WANT TO BE NICE TO YOUR "A" STUDENTS BECAUSE SOMEDAY THEY MAY COME BACK AND TEACH FOR YOU. YOU ALSO WANT TO BE NICE TO YOUR "C" STUDENTS BECAUSE SOMEDAY THEY MAY COME BACK AND FINANCE THE BUILDING OF A NEW ADDITION FOR YOUR SCHOOL!

The point being, you must believe you have the same brainpower as anyone who has ever succeeded in life; that you have an unlimited ability to learn; and that self-discovery, self-improvement, and self-driven learning are your keys to becoming the genius you were born to be.

Develop Good Habits Right from the Start

Want to become more than you are? It's your responsibility! Don't be lazy when you are feeding your mind. If you feed it garbage, your life will end up in the trash. Put the clean, the pure, the powerful, and the positive into your mind and you'll end up with wonderful results. Start today, to learn how to maximize all of your talents and reach your fullest potential. Whether you're trying to master a new skill or memorize a phone number, learning happens in four progressive steps, according to behavior scientist Abraham Maslow:

Thinking Process	Explanation	What it means to you
Unconscious-Incompetent	*You don't know that you don't know.* A baby does not know that it cannot tie its shoes.	*Make sure you listen when you are told that you don't know something.*
Conscious-Incompetent	*You know that you don't know.* A child knows that it cannot tie its shoes.	*Be teachable. Always get the best advice you can.*
Conscious-Competent	*You know that you know.* A child learns how to tie its shoes and knows that he or she can do it.	*Practice at becoming excellent. Good, better, best, never let it rest!*
Unconscious-Competent	*You know how to do things without thinking.* A child has tied its shoes so many times, he can do it without thinking. **The Ultimate Level of Performance**	*When you have reached this level of competency, use your gift to make the world a better place.*

The **Unconscious-Competent** stage is when you are able to excel "instinctively" rather than having to think about what you are going to do next. This is called "being in a zone." Have you ever heard it said about an athlete who's having a great game: "He can't miss, he's playing unconscious today!" This is the level of excellence we want to always be at when we are at the peak of our biorhythms. (See page 69 for discussion on biorhythms.)

KEY LESSON: You will never reach the highest level of performance if you are not doing something you love to do.

Old habits are difficult to break. It is estimated that it takes 21 days to form a new habit. So be careful to imprint only "good" patterns into your memory. Otherwise, you'll have a tough time trying to break your bad habits and that can lead to a lifetime of frustration.

WISDOM KEY

Practice makes perfect—NO! Practice doesn't always make perfect. Only perfect practice makes perfect. If you practice bad form or incorrect procedures, you will only be good at performing "incorrectly." This gives credence to the statement: Only perfect practice makes perfect!

"The Art of Relationships" is Brainwork!

*God has given us a very remarkable brain so
we can become "good friends and neighbors!"*

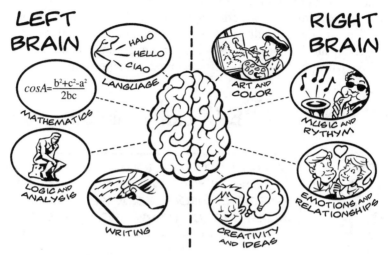

LEFT BRAIN

$$cosA = \frac{b^2 + c^2 - a^2}{2bc}$$

MATHEMATICS

HALO
HELLO
CIAO
LANGUAGE

LOGIC AND ANALYSIS

WRITING

RIGHT BRAIN

ART AND COLOR

MUSIC AND RYTHYM

EMOTIONS AND RELATIONSHIPS

CREATIVITY AND IDEAS

The human brain is divided into two parts:

- The **"left brain"** is the source for logic and reason. Verbal skills, written skills, problem solving abilities, mathematical and analytical reasoning are the priorities of this part of your brain.

- The **"right brain"** is generally thought to be our "creative brain"—the source of our emotions, attitudes, artistic and musical talents. It's larger because it also handles imagination, visual awareness, and personal relationships.

The reason we have larger cerebral hemispheres than any other animal is not so much for being smart or for survival, but for the purpose of creating, maintaining, and mending relationships. Relationships—our bonds with other human beings—will determine how successful we are in making our dreams come true. The area of the brain that controls our "automatic" functions is similar to that of animals. In fact, in some cases the automatic response functions are actually better in animals—an eagle's eyesight or a dog's sense of smell, for instance.

Our faith has a lot to do with the success of our relationships. The greater God's love is within us, the greater our ability to love others. Successful relationships are built on or around our emotions. Strong relationships created through deep emotions are the result of deep thought. Strong faith comes from deep emotions and deep thought; our relationships, like our faith, are built on a foundation of trust. The greater our faith the greater our trust in people. People with histories of failed relationships generally do not have a strong spiritual life and they distrust most everyone. People with strong faith tend to have more successful relationships.

Today, we are just beginning to understand that our "emotional intelligence" is more important than how "technically logical" we can be. Our larger, developed cerebral hemisphere allows us to have thoughts of love; to understand relationships; to interpret information feedback from the thoughts of others; and to solve relationship problems, which affect our emotions. Our emotional intelligence allows us to express, control, or change our emotions which is necessary in developing loving nurturing relationships. The emotional intelligence of the human brain also gives us internal guidance so we can survive successfully with our family, our community, and our environment. We will spend our whole life developing relationships.

WORRYING and FEAR can immobilize your brain!

HAS ANYBODY EVER TOLD YOU, "DON'T WORRY IT'S ONLY IN YOUR IMAGINATION." THIS ADVICE IS TERRIBLY WRONG, BECAUSE WORRY IS THE WORST TYPE OF IMAGINATION THERE IS!

Unchecked worry can stop you in your tracks. Have you ever noticed how ineffective worried people are? Their ability to think has been frozen by worry and fear. If you have ever had a muscle cramp, you know how it just locks you up. Cramps are caused by a chemical imbalance in your system. This cramping is similar to what happens in your brain if you worry too much—it can lock up too!

Worrying is devastating to your mental health. When you worry, you focus all your mental energy on an imagined, fearful event. This "worry" becomes burned into your higher consciousness, which also controls all of your bodily functions.

Worry and fear are "Diseases of the Imagination." Since your higher consciousness does not know the difference between reality and your imagination, it will treat this worry and fear as real. Have you ever gotten to a point where you were so worried that you couldn't think anymore? A fright-filled mind wracked by worry will, in its confusion, become chemically imbalanced and shut down. Worry freezes you in the moment. You've now sabotaged your ability to think! Don't let this happen to you. Learn the difference between "being concerned about something" and "worrying about something."

WISDOM KEY

Worry is actually a form of powerful meditation—the negative kind. Don't negatively preprogram your destiny because what you focus on will manifest into your physical reality. If you focus on the positive, you'll never have worries!

Don't worry—be happy!

— Bobby McFerrin

**When I look back on all these worries I remember the story
of the old man, who said on his deathbed that he had
had a lot of trouble in his life, most of which never happened.**

— Winston Churchill

**A day of worry is more exhausting
than a day of work.**

— John Lubbock

Worry can kill the creativity which could be the answer to your problems.

WHY WORRY?!

There are only 2 things to worry about. Either you are well or you are sick. If you are well, then there is nothing to worry about. But if you are sick, there are 2 things to worry about. Either you will get well or you will die. If you get well, there is nothing to worry about. If you die, there are only 2 things to worry about. Either you will go to heaven or hell. If you go to heaven, there is nothing to worry about. But if you go to hell, you'll be so darn busy shaking hands with friends—you won't have time to worry!

**Now that you have a basic understanding
of your brain, let's start learning about...**

The Awesome Powers of Your Mind!

Discovering the treasures of your inner wealth.

The most important features of the brain, besides those that control your bodily functions, are those that determine your ability to think and believe. These features are collectively known as your "mind." What you think about affects everything—your mental health, your physical wellness, the environment around you, and your future.

It's important to have a "free mind." In order to learn how to tap into this unlimited treasure chest called Mind Power, one must understand how important it is to have a mind that is not bound by ego, guilt, blamefulness, and a lack of self-worth. Forgiveness, complete surrender, and humility are the beginnings of a free mind. Freedom of the mind creates a sense of innocence and innocence leads to childlike curiosity.

**Knowledge and wisdom are the rewards of a free inquisitive mind.
Common sense is the foundation of knowledge and wisdom.**

We are all in this together...

We are connected with everything in God's Universe. Everything vibrates with its own form of energy because everything in the universe is made up of energized atomic particles called atoms. These atoms are in a constant state of motion. This is the Universal Law of Energy. It is for this reason that something that looks stable and hard as a rock like a quartz crystal can vibrate with such perfect precision; it can accurately regulate the timing of a watch! Or something you can't touch, like sunlight, can be turned into energy. We can't see wind, but it is a powerful force. Likewise, we all have our own powerful energy aura around us that transcends time and space.

This field of energy connects us with other people and with nature. Indigenous people like the American Indian have always felt a special connectedness or relationship to Mother Earth, plant and animal life, and the universe. In our "civilized" sophistication we have lost much of this understanding. Earlier peoples worked the land with their hands, which gave them close contact with Mother Earth. They respected the earth and all living things, never took more than they needed, and always shared their good fortune.

Today, our fast-paced urban lives threaten our connection to Mother Nature. When was the last time you dug around in your garden and plunged your hands into fresh earth? We need to have respect for the earth that we live on and regain our sensitivity to nature, because we are all connected, and we all have a responsibility to take care of God's creation.

So...What does this mean to me?

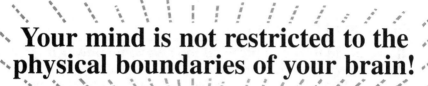

Conscious thought is energy in its most dynamic form. Our minds pulse with electrical energy that creates all thoughts and dreams. This energy transcends time and space, and forms an aura around us that others can sense. Have you ever felt another's presence in a room even though you did not see or hear this person enter the room? All people of great influence who are deeply passionate about their beliefs or causes have mastered the energy of their conscious thoughts. This power is felt instinctively and requires no words to be used to communicate. The people who are around these people immediately sense their passion and influence as if they are spellbound.

Mental energy is the most powerful form of energy that is available to everyone. It is not a supernatural phenomenon that is only enjoyed by a certain few—we all have incredible mind power. **The powers of the mind**—logical thought, memory recall, dreams, moral sense, creative visualization, intuition, inspiration, faith, belief, and sixth sense—**turn internal focused "thought energy" into external reality.**

**There is a powerful driving force within you that,
once unleashed, can make any vision, dream, or desire a reality.**
— Anthony Robbins

Your mind is always trying to manifest what it perceives or imagines as reality, in the outer physical world. Through the power of your faith, repetitive mind programming, deep focused concentration, mental imagery, and visualization, you can achieve all of your grandest dreams.

Napoleon Hill, one of the fathers of positive thinking and who wrote the all-time bestseller *Think and Grow Rich*, said: "Whatever the mind of man can conceive and believe, it can achieve." Whatever you believe yourself to be, you will be. Whatever you can believe in so strongly without easing up, you will accomplish.

Please read this carefully:

WISDOM KEY

If you could fully comprehend the awesome power of your thoughts you would immediately dedicate 100% of your mind to positive thinking. And you would be forever frightened by the consequences of negative thinking. For a better tomorrow, always be positive in your thinking. Your thoughts could change history!

 **If you do not learn about your inner strength and control yourself from within, what's around you will control you!**

To be a champion, you have to believe in yourself when nobody else will.
— Sugar Ray Robinson

If you practice winning habits long enough, you will be a winner!

God's gift to you is more talent and ability than you will ever hope to use in your lifetime. Your gift to God is to develop as much of that talent and ability as you can in your lifetime..
— Steve Bow

Positive Mental Energy
More powerful than we humanly understand.

- Have you ever heard about plants that thrive better in a loving home?
- Have you ever heard that cows, when talked to by a loving farmer, give more milk? This is "positive energy" because cows can't talk or comprehend what the farmer is saying but they feel his energy.
- Have you ever met a stranger and you felt connected, as if you had known this person all of your life?
- Have you ever been in a crowded room and felt the presence of someone unknown staring at you?
- Have you ever passed a stranger on the street and your eyes met by accident and somehow you knew that you had both just made a connection?
- Have you ever been in a conversation with someone and you felt they were reading your mind or you were reading theirs?
- Has someone finished a sentence for you with the same words you would have used?
- Have you ever called someone and were told they were just talking about you?
- Have you ever been in a group setting where everyone is challenged to solve a problem; then all of a sudden several people come up with the same solution?
- Have you ever had a déjà vu experience—like this has happened before?

The power of your mind's energy to transcend time and space can be evidenced by two people deeply in love, separated by oceans, getting an incredible urge to call each other and then both exclaim at the same time, "I was just thinking of you!" Or, the parent who gets a sudden sick feeling that something bad just happened to her children at school. Most often we pass these connective experiences off as coincidences. Don't! These interlinkings of thought, as if "distance" was nonexistent, were meant to happen. It is real evidence of the power of our thoughts overcoming all barriers to reach out across time and space. It is an example of how we are connected to other people and nature through the unbroken interconnectedness of God's great universe.

WISDOM KEY

We are all gifted with intuitive energies and we all have a responsibility to learn how to harness these powers and use them for good.

Believe in yourself.
Believe in the intuition that God has given you.

The Three Parts of Your Mind

To better understand the phenomenon of the mind we first need to understand that the mind is comprised of three distinct parts:

1. THE CONSCIOUS MIND
Your Awake Mind

2. THE HIGHER CONSCIOUS MIND
Your Subconscious Mind

3. THE DIVINE CONSCIOUS MIND
Your Spiritual Mind or Your Soul

The relationship between our three minds is really fascinating!

➤ Unleashing the power of your mind first begins by understanding that it is your conscious mind that is responsible for programming what will take place in your higher conscious mind.

➤ Once your higher conscious mind understands the desires of your conscious mind, it unleashes incredible powers that defy your physical abilities and go way beyond what you "logically" can understand.

➤ The most powerful of your three minds is the divine conscious mind or your "spiritual mind," which instinctively seeks God. Your divine conscious mind interconnects you with God's universe and helps you to fulfill your higher purpose in life.

WISDOM KEY

You have to admit that "you don't know!" One of the strangest secrets to developing a great mind is—at some point you have to give up being full of yourself to admit that "you don't know!" This is not a sign of weakness. People who are always right never learn anything new! Admitting, "you don't know" allows you to have an open, curious mind.
   You have to be teachable! This is the real secret to unlimited growth and prosperity. "Know-it-alls" are dumb. Curiosity is power!

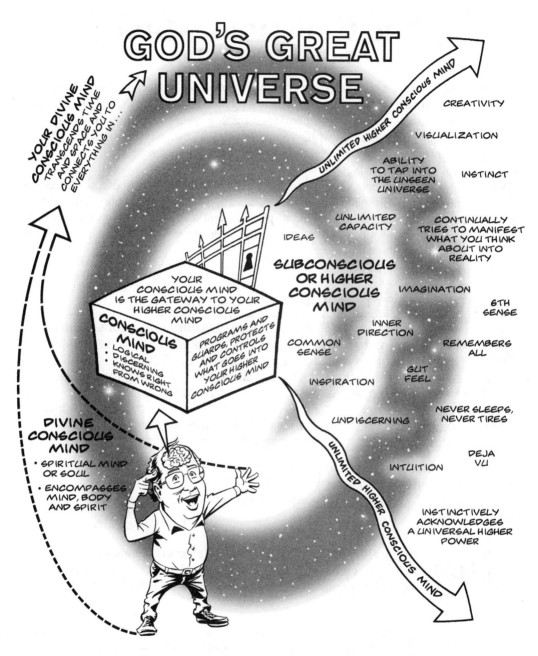

GOD'S GREAT UNIVERSE

YOUR DIVINE CONSCIOUS MIND TRANSCENDS TIME AND SPACE AND CONNECTS YOU TO EVERYTHING IN...

UNLIMITED HIGHER CONSCIOUS MIND

CREATIVITY

VISUALIZATION

ABILITY TO TAP INTO THE UNSEEN UNIVERSE

INSTINCT

UNLIMITED CAPACITY

CONTINUALLY TRIES TO MANIFEST WHAT YOU THINK ABOUT INTO REALITY

IDEAS

SUBCONSCIOUS OR HIGHER CONSCIOUS MIND

IMAGINATION

6TH SENSE

YOUR CONSCIOUS MIND IS THE GATEWAY TO YOUR HIGHER CONSCIOUS MIND

INNER DIRECTION

COMMON SENSE

REMEMBERS ALL

CONSCIOUS MIND
· LOGICAL
· DISCERNING
· KNOWS RIGHT FROM WRONG

PROGRAMS AND GUARDS, PROTECTS AND CONTROLS WHAT GOES INTO YOUR HIGHER CONSCIOUS MIND

GUT FEEL

INSPIRATION

NEVER SLEEPS, NEVER TIRES

UNDISCERNING

UNLIMITED HIGHER CONSCIOUS MIND

DEJA VU

DIVINE CONSCIOUS MIND
· SPIRITUAL MIND OR SOUL
· ENCOMPASSES MIND, BODY AND SPIRIT

INTUITION

INSTINCTIVELY ACKNOWLEDGES A UNIVERSAL HIGHER POWER

Your mind is infinite, unlimited, unstoppable, and has no boundaries!

The Conscious Mind
YOUR AWAKE MIND

You use your conscious mind, your "awake" mind, the most. It's also the part of the brain we know the most about. Your conscious mind is your "logical" mind. It is your discerning mind that knows right from wrong. It is your "reasoning" mind, the source of your thought processes while you are awake. The conscious mind gives you your sense of awareness and is generally where you focus the most time in formal education, stuffing it full of facts.

While your conscious mind plays a very important role in your daily life, the conscious mind's potential can be limited by your attitude. Still, just to show you how remarkable the brain is—the conscious mind, despite its perceived limitations, becomes supercharged and infinitely limitless when it works in harmony with the higher conscious mind and divine conscious mind. More about that later...

THIS IS VERY IMPORTANT TO UNDERSTAND:

WISDOM KEY

Your conscious mind acts as a gate to your higher conscious mind. How you decide to program your conscious mind will determine what goes on in your higher conscious mind. Your conscious mind either controls what goes into your higher conscious mind, or it becomes an open gate letting anything that happens to come along into your higher conscious mind. Your conscious mind has a critical responsibility to protect your higher conscious mind.

Watch what goes into your mind! Do not have the TV or radio on while you are sleeping. You are filling your mind with clutter that distracts your higher conscious mind and keeps it from dreaming freely, working on problems, or being creative for you while you are sleeping.

Be careful what you expose your higher conscious mind to—it's like a giant thirsty sponge waiting to soak up whatever comes its way. Your higher conscious mind is innocent—it is yours to use or abuse.

KEEP YOUR MIND, BODY, AND SPIRIT — PURE. THEY ARE THE PORTAL THROUGH WHICH YOU VISUALIZE YOUR DESTINY IN GOD'S MAGNIFICENT UNIVERSE.

The Higher Conscious Mind
YOUR SUBCONSCIOUS MIND

Your higher conscious mind is more powerful than you can ever imagine! It is always ready to do the work of your conscious mind. While your conscious mind is your source for thought, your higher conscious mind is your source for unlimited power, connecting you to the physical, mental, and spiritual world.

I have chosen to refer to your subconscious mind as your higher conscious mind. I feel that when it's called the subconscious mind, it's viewed as something unseen and unknown. The fact is, your subconscious mind is virtually unlimited in power.

Here's something you must understand...

Even though your higher conscious mind has incredible unlimited power—it is also very fragile. One hint of disbelief will fizzle this energy into thin air! *Pure concentrated thought with complete faith and deep-rooted belief is paramount for the powers of your higher conscious mind to be unleashed.*

Your higher conscious mind is your instinctive mind. It controls physical functions like your blood temperature, blood pressure, digestive process, chemical and hormonal balances, and your emotions. Your higher conscious mind, like your super conscious mind, does not recognize physical boundaries and has the remarkable ability to transcend time or space. It instinctively acknowledges a universal higher power. Found within the higher conscious mind, the sixth sense (instinct or intuition) is connected to the unseen world of God's universe. The energy of this unseen world is what causes seeds to sprout in the spring, birds to fly south, and fish to migrate. It also makes humans emotionally connected. The greatest of these unseen forces is called "love." You can't see it and you can't touch it, yet it can reach across oceans and bring two lovers together! Thought processes are really an immense powerhouse of the quickest, lightest, most transferable form of pure energy, which has the miraculous power to transcend physical boundaries of time and space.

Your higher conscious mind has many miraculous abilities that defy logic:

- Incredible Memory Retention that is virtually unlimited
- Visionary Thoughts
- Intuitive Insight (intuition)
- Premonitions
- Gut Feelings
- Instinct
- Déjà Vu
- Inspiration
- Original Inventive Imagination
- Constant Inquisitive Spirit
- Unrestrained Dreams in Vivid Color and Detail
- Sixth Sense
- Problem Solving Beyond Your Logical Ability
- Inner Wisdom
- Wild and Crazy Ideas
- Unlimited Creativity
- Limitless Potential
- Extraordinary and Phenomenal Healing Powers
- Ability to Transcend Time and Space
- Non-verbal "Radar-like" Ability to Attract Like Passions
- Non-verbal "Radar-like" Ability to Communicate Love
- Connective Ability to Read Other People's Minds

WISDOM KEY

The more in awe of God you are—the more awesome you become! The power of faith exceeds human comprehension. You have to accept that your higher conscious mind can do these wonderful things even though you don't understand how they happen. The powers of faith must be unconditionally believed and accepted.

When you do not have strong faith in a higher power, your ability to access the powers of your mind becomes stunted and limited. You must not try to logically understand what happens in your higher conscious mind. It is like faith. If you try to logically understand the extraordinary phenomena of your higher consciousness, you will actually create barriers that reflect the limitations of your humanity.

Your higher conscious mind is also like your own special "security force" always on call. In times of great emergency, it will become supercharged and spring into urgent action. With supreme command, it will defend and protect. Usually in times of great turmoil, your higher conscious mind working in harmony with your conscious and super conscious minds will find solutions quickly and be alert to opportunities that under normal circumstances would have been difficult to recognize. You see and understand things that you might not normally comprehend because of the sensitive powers of your higher conscious mind. The higher conscious mind's heightened awareness will keep you alert and protect you.

Your higher conscious mind is unlimited in capacity. It remembers everything and is indiscriminate. It does not know right from wrong. It is innocent. Unlike your conscious mind, the higher conscious mind never sleeps and never gets tired. It will work tirelessly for you. It will never give up on you!

THERE ARE **NO** BOUNDARIES FOR THE MIND EXCEPT THE ONES WE CREATE.

KEY LESSON: You can never force your higher conscious mind to do something. It has to have complete freedom. Have you ever forgotten someone's name and tried to remember it? You feel it right on the tip of your tongue, but no matter how hard you try, you can't find the name. Then a while later, after you have given up your quest to remember, out of the blue the name appears. That's your higher conscious mind at work. Once you give your higher conscious mind a command, it will never give up until it finds your answer. It never quits, it never gives up!

May the force be with you!
— Yoda

In Your Wildest Dreams
Your dreams are powerful!

Thinking **is a conscious act and** *dreaming* **is the playground of our higher conscious mind.** Have you ever been in a deep sleep, dreaming a powerful dream full of color, very vivid in detail, and very real…then suddenly get awakened out of your dream? But, because you were "really enjoying" your dream, you couldn't wait to fall asleep again— hoping that you could reconnect where you left off. Why was that? The big question is: Why can't you finish your own dreams while you are awake?

The answer is—you can't. Your conscious mind cannot control the same pathways as your higher conscious mind. Your dreaming occurs in a different realm where only your higher conscious mind and your divine conscious mind travel. You can only enter this realm when you are in deep sleep and you are unconscious to all external influences. You can only enter this realm on a frequent basis when your mind is free from worry and guilt.

WISDOM KEY

Your achievements will never be greater than your dreams. You can never outperform the vision that you have of yourself. So it's important to dream big dreams and never put limitations on how you see yourself. Your dreams are "spiritual seeds" that become your destiny. Dream Positively!

LET YOUR MIND SOAR!

Keep your mind free of garbage, so your higher conscious mind is free to soar! Have you ever had a dream where you were doing something really great that you could never do in reality—like flying? This can only happen in your dreams because your higher conscious mind has no boundaries.

Your higher conscious mind believes it can do anything!

Isn't this incredible? Think about the significance of this—your mind, when it is dreaming, is free from all boundaries! It will always be free. It will explore the unknown. It will always be creative. Your higher conscious mind is on its own constant quest of self-discovery. Your inner mind instinctively seeks to achieve!

Your higher conscious mind is so spectacular that you can dream a whole day's activities in a matter of minutes. In dreaming, your higher conscious mind transcends time. You will feel that you have experienced an actual real life adventure with full details and in full color, but your dream probably lasted no longer than 20 minutes. Your mind has the remarkable ability to compress time.

Daydreams are quick escapes from conscious reality. The conscious mind joins the higher conscious mind in a trance-like state, letting your thoughts wander freely as if you just quickly exited from the reality of your present conscious world. When you leave your daydream, the detailed memory of your dream will last about 30 seconds and then quickly fade back into your unconscious mind.

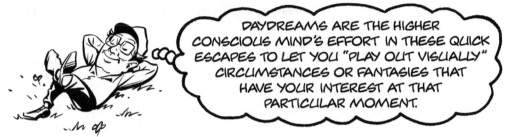

DAYDREAMS ARE THE HIGHER CONSCIOUS MIND'S EFFORT IN THESE QUICK ESCAPES TO LET YOU "PLAY OUT VISUALLY" CIRCUMSTANCES OR FANTASIES THAT HAVE YOUR INTEREST AT THAT PARTICULAR MOMENT.

Daydreams can be powerful tools. If you have programmed your higher conscious mind in the right direction, if you have a positive outlook on life, your daydreams will give you insight, ideas, solutions, and inner wisdom. Your ideas are spiritual seeds that need to be nurtured. But, if you have a cynical and negative outlook on life, then your daydreams will play on your fears and you will play out all the things that can go wrong. Program your inner mind in the positive, so you can dream in the positive!

How to get more out of your dreams:

When an idea or answer to a problem comes to you during your dreams and you are awakened, your higher conscious mind has just transferred this information to your conscious state and it has awakened you. This is your clue that you must write down or record what you just remembered. Don't jump out of bed. Lie there quietly and try to reconstruct your dreams. Try to remember anything significant and visualize it over and over again, and get it transfixed in your memory.

Because your higher conscious mind cannot be controlled, this information is fleeting. Your "awake" mind has just been jolted out of deep sleep and is not fully functional yet—so you have to concentrate on retrieving this information from your dream. Otherwise great ideas, thoughts, and solutions from your dreams can quickly be forgotten. It's a good idea to keep a pencil and paper or a mini-recorder by your bedside.

**Your higher conscious mind will solve problems for you
that your conscious mind cannot solve.**

The powers of faith flee from a doubting mind! This is where faith comes into play. A strong faith in a higher power allows the powers of your higher conscious mind to transcend human frailty and access the unlimited powers of God's universe.

Here's how to turn your problems over to a higher power so you can sleep restfully, "Let go and let God!" At night before you go to bed, you must turn over your problems to God and your higher conscious mind. You must go to bed with the belief that the right answer will be given to you. Then you must relax and get a good night's sleep knowing that you are in God's protective hands. Freeing your mind from worry allows your higher conscious mind to reach out into God's great universe to find the answers that will solve your problems.

"...I think I've done this before!"

Explaining the déjà vu experience. Have you ever felt that something you are experiencing has happened to you before? Sometimes this eerie experience happens when the higher conscious mind understands or comprehends a situation before the conscious mind begins to understand the present reality. This is further evidence of how quick your mind can play out events. The trick is to be able to comprehend what is happening and then harness this phenomenon to make better decisions regarding life. Your intuition is trying to reach out to you.

Autosuggestion or Re-Re-Repetitive Reinforcement

Intensify your Input and Yield greater Output! Repetition creates mind power. Repetition is the mother of all skills. This is why it is so important to know how the brain functions before discussing what it can do.

Repetition creates "known pathways" for your brain's electrochemical energy pulses to travel—increasing your mind power. When you focus your mental energy by repeating positive affirmations constantly throughout the day, you burn a "visual image" into your higher conscious mind that increases exponentially until your dreams manifest themselves in physical reality. Repetition is the fuel for your brain!

This is very similar to the Bible telling you to "Pray without ceasing! *Faith cometh by hearing."* — 1 Thessalonians 5:17, Romans 10:17 (KJV) The more you repeat over and over again the things you believe in, the stronger your faith becomes. Your faith will make your goals become reality. This is God's promise to you.

WISDOM KEY

Conscious, daily repetition of your goals will strengthen the resolve of your higher conscious mind. Reaching out into God's great universe, your mind will unleash a tremendous flow of wild creative ideas and provide you with a heightened awareness of opportunities allowing you to achieve all of your internal goals and aspirations. For example: "Doors of Opportunity" that were previously shut tight to you, will now mysteriously spring open. Great people of influence will seek you out to offer previously unavailable resources to help you in your quest for becoming a person of achievement and leadership. Your higher conscious mind will unleash past information stored in your mind and magically construct it into solutions for difficult problems that you could not solve before.

NOTICE: THE FOLLOWING WISDOM KEY IS POWERFUL!

Read this section over and over again until you fully understand the incredible powers of your higher conscious mind.

WISDOM KEY

Your higher conscious mind does not know the difference between reality and your imagination. Through repetitious visual imagery you can program your higher conscious mind to manifest your positive imaginations into reality. Believe it to achieve it!

How you program your conscious mind determines the output of your higher conscious mind. Your higher conscious mind is a powerful dedicated servant to your conscious mind.

 Your higher conscious mind does not know the difference between right and wrong or between being positive or negative. If you are always negative, your higher conscious mind thinks this is how you want to live your life and will dutifully work hard to create more negative circumstances for you! That's why negative people always seem to have all the bad luck. Negative thinkers don't realize that they are their own worst enemies. They are programming their minds to attract only the negatives of life. They can change all this self-created destructiveness just by starting to think positively. If you want positive results you must fix your conscious mind's resolve to program your higher conscious mind only with positive affirmations and positive experiences.

 Don't let what goes on around you determine how you want to think. Over 90% of what we hear on a daily basis is negative and discouraging; 70% of all diseases are caused by what goes on in our minds. Manifest into reality the quality of life you wish to live by programming your mind with the pure, the clean, the powerful, and the positive!

THE MIND IS LIKE A PARACHUTE; IT DOESN'T WORK UNLESS IT'S OPEN!

The Divine Conscious Mind
YOUR SPIRITUAL MIND OR YOUR SOUL

The greatest miracle signifying the magnificence of God's power is not the enormity of the universe. It is the awesome potential that God gives each of us when we humbly surrender ourselves to a higher faith based on God's love.

FACT: The greatest, untapped mother lode of potential is...your divine conscious mind or your spiritual mind. Your spiritual mind encompasses not only your brain, but everything about you including your heart and soul. It is who you are in your relationship to a higher power.

Even though all civilizations throughout history have known there is a higher power, we sometimes tend to deny God's presence because of our inability to understand this great power within us. No matter how primitive these past civilizations may have been, they were more sophisticated in their understanding of the divine conscious mind. They knew repetitive affirmations—deep meditation, prayers, or mantras—were necessary to expand the mind and reach higher conscious levels in order to connect with a higher power.

This instinctive recognition of a higher power is what makes humans unique. Faith, the ability to believe and to have dreams, is what sets us apart from the rest of the animal world. Questioning if there is a God and stubbornly ignoring your inner need for faith will leave you void of the greatest power available only to humans. *Only humans can have faith.*

Ignorance of your inner strength leaves you vulnerable to external factors such as: self-righteous pride, unhealthy ego, greed, envy, guilt, fear, anger, lack of money, lost love, perversion, and fear of death.

> **When we are not aware of our inner "spiritual strength," we live in the "external material" world. Therefore, we live a "life of reaction" to our physical world.**
>
> **When we begin to understand our inner spiritual strength through the study of God's word, we will start living in an "internal mental world."**

Because of this ignorance of the spiritual side of our consciousness, we need to study spiritual matters. If we do not aggressively pursue a greater understanding of our spiritual side—if we don't address it with the same intensity we bring to our other pursuits and interests—then sadly we are missing the greatest gift God has given us.

WISDOM KEY

Mastery over "mental imagery" in your conscious, higher conscious, and divine conscious minds will allow you to control your external environment. This is where your real power will be found.

Don't wait until you are old to discover the powers of your spirituality!

- **Study and invest in your spirituality with greater determination than you would your career, cooking, music, education, or the development of your physical abilities.**

- **You should have more books on spirituality than you would cookbooks or novels!**

The irony of your spiritual mind is that if you do not acknowledge its existence it will eventually wither away. However, simple unquestioning faith with complete childlike acceptance will jump-start your divine conscious mind to become your strongest force.

So, how do you work on increasing your awareness of your subconscious mind, your spiritual mind, and your inner voice? Through...

Meditation

Most people, when they hear "meditation," have a mental picture of some "spaced out" monk sitting on a mountaintop, contemplating "peace and love." Actually, this is far from the truth. Meditation is the art of focus and deep concentration, not a state of unconsciousness. It leads you to increased awareness and alertness and is a necessary stress reducer in your daily routines. Meditation helps you mentally prepare and focus on what's important in your life without the clutter of a distracted mind.

Meditation helps you accept self-restraint, which is the power over self. Self-restraint is the difference between people who are immature and try to impose power over others and those who have a mastery over themselves and their impulses.

Through meditation, you learn how to control and focus your mind. This increases your ability to concentrate and gives you control over your life. It also gives you strength to say "no" when necessary, so you don't fall prey to peer pressure.

Meditation requires learning "how to breathe" as part of the relaxation process—this frees your mind from stress and brings more oxygen to your brain. Learning powerful breathing techniques helps clear the toxins from your system. A free, uncluttered mind, full of oxygen, is a powerful force.

Life is breath, and he who only half-breathes—half lives.
— Ancient proverb

Meditation allows you to be quiet so you can listen to your inner voice. Getting in touch with your inner voice is similar to learning to pay attention to your dreams. Even though your inner voice is always there, you have to learn how to recognize, expect, and anticipate it when it is trying to communicate with you. You have to be free from external influences in order to fully connect with your inner voice. Scientific research has confirmed that during the regular course of daily activities only individual areas of the brain are being engaged. However, when a person is in deep meditation the entire brain actually becomes more fully aware.

Meditation is an essential part of spiritual life. We all have been taught how to say our prayers, but we have never been taught how to be quiet so that God can talk back to us. Most people after saying their prayers just get up and go. It's almost like they don't expect God to respond! After saying your prayers, you need to allow time to quiet yourself and meditate and give God a chance to talk to you.

There's a very good reason why the Bible says…
"Be still and know that I am God."
— Psalm 46:10 (KJV)

Learn how to meditate and work on creating some quiet time in your busy day for yourself. There are healing and restorative powers in having a daily quiet time. It's good for your heart and good for your soul. Unlike the higher conscious mind, which we cannot control, our divine conscious mind or our "spiritual mind" can guide us, if only we will listen.

WISDOM KEY

A person of great faith will accomplish great things with all of God's resources. A person of little or no faith will only accomplish what is humanly possible.

TO OVERCOME GREAT OBSTACLES YOU NEED TO BE PRAYING GREAT PRAYERS.

YOU CAN'T EXPECT MILLION DOLLAR ANSWERS TO 10¢ PRAYERS!

All great success begins with understanding the awesome powers of your mind!

All great success begins by putting your mind to work!

Unlock the incredible treasures of your mind!

Unleash the unlimited potential of your inner wealth!

The most incredible power of your mind is the ability to have faith in a higher power.

> Once you understand that life's higher purpose is for you to help make the world a better place—you will never ask, "What's in it for me?"

This is the true joy in life, the "being used for a purpose" recognized by yourself as a mighty one; the "being a force of nature" instead of a feverish, selfish little clod of ailments and grievances, complaining that the world will not devote itself to making you happy...

— George Bernard Shaw

The Wise Zen Master

Know Less, Learn More.

Never say, "I know that."
Instead say, "Tell me more."

"Know-it-alls" are dumb!

"I know that" is mental arrogance.

How to Discover and Fire Up Your Own Creative Resourcefulness

How many times have you said...
   "I just wouldn't know where to start?"
   "Where in the world did you ever find that?"
   "How do you come up with all those ideas?"

It's all a matter of being...
   "Creatively Resourceful"

> I PRIDE MYSELF IN FINDING INFORMATION NO ONE ELSE CAN FIND. PEOPLE OFTEN SAY, "I'VE BEEN SEARCHING ALL OVER FOR THAT STUFF, HOW COME YOU WERE ABLE TO FIND IT SO FAST?"
>
> I PRIDE MYSELF IN BEING ABLE TO FIND ANYONE AND ANYTHING IN THE WORLD, AT ANYTIME. OFTEN SOMEONE WILL ASK, "HOW ON EARTH WERE YOU ABLE TO FIND ME?"
>
> I ALSO PRIDE MYSELF ON BEING CREATIVE, ON DEVELOPING IDEAS THAT NO ONE ELSE HAS THOUGHT OF — TO WHICH PEOPLE OFTEN SAY, "I CAN'T BELIEVE THAT YOU CAME UP WITH ALL THOSE IDEAS!"

Everyone can be creative and resourceful. It's a "mind thing!"

When you are following your passion, your mind becomes energized. When you are following your passion, your mind—especially your higher conscious—goes into overdrive, solving problems, puzzles and challenges that would otherwise be unthinkable, unimaginable and unsolvable for most people.

When you are determined to make something happen, your mind starts visualizing, imaging, mapping, going through all sorts of "what if—then this" scenarios. Your mind is actively engaged in dynamic research. You become more alert to new ideas, fresh thoughts and things you see that spark other problem-solving thinking. Incredible insights and creative intuition flow effortlessly through your higher conscious and divine conscious minds, solving problems that you never thought you were capable of solving. Unexpected situations will occur that will provide you with opportunities, ideas and resources. You will be astounded by the creativity and unlimited resources the universe will make available to you.

All this mental energy creates a form of spiritual synergy that "kicks in" the Universal Law of Attraction (see page 41). Your higher conscious mind will reach out to memories that might offer solutions, and to other people of like passion who can mentor you.

You must have an open mind. To attract creative resources, you cannot have a mind that is bound up by ego, nor can you be a "know-it-all!" You must be able to feed off of the creative energy of other people. Seldom is there a brilliant thought that is entirely your own. There is a certain amount of truth to the statement: "There is nothing new in the world." Almost everything new comes from observing what's around you. You see "something here" and "something over there" and take the best of it all to create something new. The more information you can surround yourself with, the more creative you can be.

Don't worry about people stealing your ideas. It's been said, "Imitation is the sincerest form of flattery!" I have always believed that whatever anybody steals of mine is yesterday's old news anyway. What they can't steal is my vision for the future. They can't steal the creativity in my head that is waiting to be unleashed. Don't live in the past by worrying about what others might steal from you; your mind is infinitely more intelligent and creative. Looking will reveal new ideas and new opportunities.

WISDOM KEY

Never quit until you find your answer. You must have faith that you will find your answers. The key is persistent, dogged stick-to-itiveness, never quitting until you find what you're looking for or until you have created a new way to solve your problem. Although you may have never at this point in your life achieved great things, you must continue to believe that you will conquer the unknown. You must believe that you can create new ideas and go where you never thought possible.
   You must confidently believe that you can find anyone in this world at anytime, that you can get to any product or source you need, that you can solve any problem. If you believe this, new and greater ideas will come to you or the information that you need will make itself known to you. Believe that you are creative!

A NEGATIVE MIND WILL SCARE OFF NEW IDEAS. NEGATIVE THINKING DESTROYS CREATIVITY.

Creativity begins with an "I CAN" attitude.

- **Being creative allows you to be independent.**
- **Being creative means you never have to covet someone else's resources.**
- **There is power in knowing that you can find whatever you are looking for.**
- **There is power in knowing that you can always find an answer.**
- **There is power in knowing that you can always create a solution.**
- **You don't need to be born creative to be creative; it's all attitude.**
- **The more positive you are...the greater your creativity!**

How to fire up your creative juices...

LET YOURSELF GO!

- **Be Positive**
- **Be Curious**
- **Explore**
- **Touch Many Things**
- **Don't Prejudge**
- **What You Do—Matters**
- **Open Your Eyes**
- **Open Your Mind**
- **Look Around You**
- **Be Alert**
- **Be Observant**
- **Take Notes**
- **Read Many Things**

- **See Many Things**
- **Do New Things**
- **Travel**
- **Experience New Things**
- **Take Lots of Pictures**
- **Make Many Mistakes**
- **Ask More "What If" Questions**
- **Just Ask More Questions**
- **Live Life Full In the Moment**
- **Change Yourself Often**
- **Believe That You Are a Creative Force**
- **Take Risks**
- **Learn from Others**

How to turn "nothing" into "something!"

- First, determine what it is you would like to create.

- Let your imagination run wild. See all the possibilities. Don't let perceived barriers become real. See the completed vision as reality.

- Have great faith. Faith is the foundation of belief. Faith is a belief in something you cannot see. Believing is the beginning of reality. Faith lets you believe in yourself. Faith allows you to break past all the barriers others get hung up on.

- Believe it is possible. Get consumed by your idea. Visualize your idea into reality.

- Take action. Faith combined with action creates confidence. Action creates reality. There is creative magic in just the act of starting.

- Never quit once you get there. Once you have created something, keep on developing it, expanding it until it has become all it can be.

Become a Wellspring of Ideas!

EVERYTHING GREAT STARTED OUT WITH NOTHING MORE THAN JUST AN IDEA.

THE POWER OF ANY IDEA CAN BE MEASURED BY THE RESISTANCE TO IT.

If people are not laughing at your dreams, your dreams are not big enough. If you are not willing to do that which is ridiculous, you cannot achieve that which is spectacular!

— Willie Jolley

Go to work on your dreams and you'll be amazed at how creative you really are!

DAZZLE YOURSELF!

LET'S SUM THINGS UP!

What does this mean to me?

1. **The mind is unlimited and unstoppable.** The greatest secret power of your mind has nothing to do with intelligence but everything to do with faith and believing. In other words, regardless of your background or where you are right now, you can go forward and achieve a better life filled with accomplishment and success.

   You can accomplish anything you strongly believe in!

2. **All thoughts are the most powerful forms of energy that transcend time and space.** Your mind is not limited by the physical boundaries of your body. All the resources you need are available to you, if you can believe it.

3. **What you focus on intently with internal conviction will become manifested into reality in your external world.** All you need to do is look around you to see where your mind has been! So quit trying to master stuff around you and unleash the power that is within you! Start dreaming bigger dreams.

4. **Your mind instinctively recognizes the power of a higher presence.** You are God's handiwork and your mind has the ability to access the infinite resources of God's great universe.

5. **Your conscious mind programs your higher conscious mind.** Your higher conscious mind never sleeps and will work tirelessly for you once you have a clear vision of your goals. The more in awe of God you are—the more awesome you become!

6. **The powers of your mind are the greatest when it is free of denial, guilt, blamefulness, and ego.** You must have forgiveness and you must be forgiven so you can surrender your past and move forward freely. One of the strangest secrets of your mind is that you must admit that "you don't know." A mind free of ego will allow you to seek help, advice and wisdom from others. It's the only way you can grow.

7. **You must claim ownership of your results, in advance, before your dreams will manifest into reality.** Any doubt will sabotage the outcome and your dreams will fizzle into thin air. Get to know the powers of your faith. Your faith, along with action, will make all your dreams come true.

CALL TO ACTION:

1. Begin a personal quest to explore the powers of your mind. Conquer all of your fears and start living a life of no limits or boundaries.

2. Start believing in yourself so strongly that you will eliminate doubt that you'll achieve your dreams. Start dreaming bigger dreams than you have ever dreamed possible.

3. Create a clear vision in your mind of who you are, where you would like to be, and what you need to do to get there. Envision yourself as already achieving your goals.

WHAT YOU CAN ACCOMPLISH:

If you believe that your mind is unlimited and unstoppable, you can accomplish everything you set your mind to. Your dreams will become your reality. Self-discovery of your inner wealth will energize you to smash through all your self-limiting barriers to phenomenal wealth, great achievement, and success. Start visioning all the possibilities by becoming a positive thinker!

Sources & Inspiration

The information in these books is powerful. I urge you to buy these books and read them over and over again until they become part of your daily life.

GOD, *The King James Study Bible,* (Thomas Nelson, Inc., Nashville, Tenn. 1988)

Claude M. Bristol, *The Magic of Believing,* (Fireside Books, New York, N.Y. 1985)

Arthur and Ruth Winter, *Brain Workout,* (St. Martin's Griffin, New York, N.Y. 1997)

Dr. Joseph Murphy, *The Power of Your Subconscious Mind,* (Prentice Hall, Paramus, N.J. 1963)

James K. Van Fleet, *Hidden Power,* (Prentice Hall, Paramus, N.J. 1987)

Dr. Robert Goldman, Dr. Ronald Klatz, Lisa Berger, *Brain Fitness,* (Doubleday, New York, N.Y. 1999)

Michael J. Gelb, *How To Think Like Leonardo da Vinci,* (Delacorte Press/Bantam Doubleday, New York, N.Y. 1998)

Jean Carper, *Your Miracle Brain,* (Harper Collins, New York, N.Y. 2000)

Sheila Ostrander, Lynn Schroeder, Nancy Ostrander, *Superlearning 2000,* (Dell Publishing, New York, N.Y. 1994)

Doug Hall, with David Wecker, *Jump Start Your Brain,* (Warner Books, New York, N.Y. 1995)

Dr. Gayle Delaney, *Breakthrough Dreaming,* (Bantam Books, New York, N.Y. 1991)

Dr. Lucia Capacchione, *Visioning,* (Tarcher/Putnam, New York, N.Y. 2000)

Lesson Two: LifeDesign

Lesson Two: LifeDesign

Achieve your maximum potential by designing the life of your dreams!

The **LifeDesign** lesson gives you the nuts and bolts for turning your dreams into reality through goal setting. Learn the science of achieving your maximum potential. It's all up to you! Instead of just earning a living, design a life worth living!

PURPOSE:

When is the last time you contemplated what you would like to do with your life? When is the last time you devoted some serious time to creating some incredible goals? Unfortunately only 3% of the people in the world have taken the time to write out goals for their lives. Most people spend more time planning a vacation than they do designing a life plan.

If you can't follow the rules, you'll never be able to follow the plans you have set for your own life! Discipline is the foundation for character and the strength of your character will ultimately determine the extent of your achievements. Success thrives on discipline, so make discipline your friend and not something to be afraid of.

If you don't have a plan for your life, you will become a victim of the plans of the people around you. Don't spend a lifetime as a "wandering generality." Become a "meaningful specific" by designing your destiny through the miraculous powers of written goals.

WAKE UP! THIS IS YOUR LIFE...IT DESERVES BETTER THAN HOW YOU HAVE BEEN TREATING IT. GET A LIFE—BY DESIGNING YOUR LIFE.

THE LAWS OF THE UNIVERSE

<u>**UNIVERSAL LAW NUMBER ONE—THERE ARE LAWS!**</u> It's terribly hard for people to accept the fact that there are laws. There are the Laws of God, the Laws of the Universe, the Laws of Nature, and the Laws of Man. There are principles, values, codes, and ethics. Far from just a list of dos and don'ts, these laws (except those of man) transcend time and space and keep the world from operating in chaos.

WISDOM KEY

Accept the fact that there are laws. Knowledge of these laws will help you become the master of your own destiny instead of living the life of a victim. Ignorance of the laws will cause frustration and failure in your life. Ignorance is not an acceptable excuse for not knowing the rules of this game called "life." It is your responsibility to find out what the rules are and learn how they apply to your life, because there are consequences for breaking the laws.

Mastering the rules and disciplining yourself actually creates freedom!

Like it or not, for the rest of your life, people are always going to tell you what to do. When you are in someone else's ballpark, you must play by their rules. That's life! There are consequences when you are so arrogant to think that you can live by your own rules in someone else's ballpark. Even when you get to the point where you can own your own ballpark, you still have to answer to someone—such as your customers or your shareholders.

No man is an island—you will always have to obey the laws of the land or the rules of whatever game you are playing. So quit with your smart-aleck attitude that no one can tell you what to do. If you are as smart as you think you are, you will listen! There was a time when I was full of myself and thought I had everything figured out. That was also the time when I seemed to have the most problems. The day I surrendered my self-righteous pride and ego is the day my life started turning around for the better. The hardest lesson I had to learn was to respect people in authority.

A complete disregard for the rules will cause the universe to eventually eliminate you. However, mastering the rules of the game will help you design a winning game plan for your life.

YOU'RE NOT PLAYING THE GAME FOR THE MOMENT. YOU'RE PLAYING FOR—FOREVER!

• <u>**The Universal Law of Relativity.**</u> **All laws work together.** All laws are relative to each other. No one law can exist without the others, all laws enhance each other, all laws support each other, and all laws are necessary.

• <u>**The Universal Law of Energy.**</u> **Everything in the universe is made up of energy.** Energy is in a constant state of motion. Even when things die, change continues to take place. All energy manifests itself into reality. Thoughts are the most powerful form of energy–they transcend time and space. Money also is energy and it must be kept moving.

There is positive energy and negative energy. If you do not work to keep positive energy in your life, you will be affected by the negative energy around you. Trying to keep things the same will only cause frustration because when energy clogs up, things get out of whack. This law supports The Law of Constant Change (see below).

• <u>**The Universal Law of Cause and Effect.**</u> **Everything matters.** Nothing is independent. Everything in the universe is connected. Whatever you do—no matter how great or small— affects someone or something else. Whatever you send out will cause something to come back to you. The more you can affect "Cause" the greater your "Effect" will be in the universe.

You are important in the grand scheme of the universe. To fall short of your fullest potential is a tragedy against God's great universe. It is your responsibility to become all that you can be. Remember, everything matters and you matter the most!

• <u>**The Universal Law of Timing, Cycles, and Seasons includes The Laws of Nature.**</u> **Everything has a purpose, a time, and a place.** All living things go through birth, growth, maturity, death, and regeneration. Nature has its seasons—spring, summer, fall, and winter. There is a time to till, a time to plant, a time to weed, a time to nurture, and a time to harvest. Good times and bad times are all part of life, as are times of prosperity and famine, peace and war. There are happy times and sad times. All things ebb and flow.

Every cycle in life has a purpose and helps you grow. Don't complain about the timing or let the downtimes surprise you. Hard as it is to believe, things happen when they're supposed to. It is your responsibility to understand why. Without bad times you could never enjoy the good.

• <u>**The Universal Law of Constant Change.**</u> **The only guaranteed thing in life is change.** In a world that is constantly changing, there is no such thing as security—only opportunity. Don't let "change" just happen to you. Design and plan for the changes in your life. Look for opportunity and become the master of change—not the victim of change.

• <u>**The Universal Law of Nonresistance.**</u> **You must be flexible.** Because everything in nature is changing, we need to learn to be flexible and accommodate change. The reason very young children learn quickly is because they have uncluttered, nonresistant minds that are free of prejudice and emotional obstructions. When we are stubborn and resistant to change we are inflexible and in direct confrontation with the laws of the universe. Even strong, solid trees will bend in the wind and gentle rivers will cut through hard rock.

Go with the flow. Someone will say, "Going with the flow will get you into trouble." Only if you are violating the Laws of Man, the Laws of God, the Laws of Nature, or the Laws of the Universe. When you are in harmony with the laws, "going with the flow" is accommodating change and requires you to put others first!

• **The Universal Law of Increase. You must get better or you will get worse.** If you don't use it, you will lose it. If you don't get more, you will lose what you have. If you don't grow, you will stagnate and die. There is no staying in neutral. There is no such thing as coasting. You must increase or you will decrease. You either get richer or you will get poorer. The Universal Law of Increase is really "survival of the fittest." You must constantly strive to better yourself. Don't stagnate. Revitalize and flourish!

• **The Universal Law of Polarity or the Law of Opposites. This is an interesting law, because if you really understand it, you will see it's the law of opportunity!** While this law seems similar to the Universal Law of Cause and Effect, there's a critical difference—**for every action there is an equal or greater opposite reaction.** For example, every solution creates a problem. Every problem creates an opportunity for a solution. The Chinese call this the Yin and the Yang. Really this is the law of choices. You can say "yes" or you can say "no." There is power in both answers.

Choose to be a positive energizer looking for creative solutions. When others are experiencing bad luck, the smart people (positive energizers) look for opportunity. When the stock market is crashing, someone is always making a killing. When things are going bad, look for the good. When things are going good be prepared for the worst. It's up to you to create the opportunities.

• **The Universal Law of Attraction. Like things will be attracted to like things.** In this attraction the strongest will always prevail. If you are full of positive energy, you will attract other positive people. Together you will all resonate positively and grow by virtue of the strongest energizer in the group. The stronger your passion, the more you will attract others of equal or greater passion. When the "best" attract "other best" the "Power of 2" creates something exponentially even better and stronger. The Universal Law of Attraction creates a very powerful and dynamic synergy that will multiply exponentially the resources the universe will make available to you.

The twist to this law is that negativity has a similar but toxic strength. A negative-thinking person will attract other negative people, and this negative energy will create its own negative synergy of unending negative circumstances. A negative-thinking whiner, worrier, and complainer self-fulfills the misery he or she is always moaning about.

Focus on what you want—not on what you don't want. Only you can decide what kind of energy you will attract. Be a force for good. Living a life full of optimism will attract opportunity and other optimistic people. Together you will attract the abundant resources of the universe.

The strength of your passion is your key to great opportunity. This is an important law for anyone whether you're starting out in life or just starting over. If you are concerned that you don't have the right connections, enough opportunity, enough resources—all you have to be is very passionate about what you love to do, and the strength of your passion will attract all that you lack.

• <u>**The Universal Law of Love.**</u> **All universal laws transcend time and space.** Love is the greatest example of energy passing from one person to another through God's unseen universe. The purest and highest form of internal passionate energy, LOVE, overcomes all barriers. This energy is so strong, it can be communicated without speech. The deeper the love, the greater its impact—not only on all people but also on all living things.

The Universal Law of Love enhances all other laws. The more love you give away, the more it returns to you and in greater abundance. When you work from a foundation of love, you will never run out of energy. Love keeps us healthy because great love is not easy—it demands your all. Great affection is powerful and requires discipline. You must control your desires or impulses to satisfy only yourself. Instead, be a "greater giver of yourself" to others. The person who is hardest to love is the one who needs your love the most. This love creates hope where there is none. After all, "Love will always find a way."

• <u>**The Universal Law of Giving.**</u> **Give first, then you shall receive.** This law doesn't say receive then give. Only when you give with a generous heart, not out of duty, will you always get more in return. However, you should never give with expectation of getting something in return. This is a manipulative tactic that the universe will not acknowledge. The most rewarding approach is to give anonymously.

• <u>**The Universal Law of Return.**</u> **Whatever you send out will always return.** This law is relative to The Universal Law of Timing. The energy you send out doesn't always return when you want it to—the universe has the appropriate time. There is a reason why things happen the way they do and when they do. Seek to discover this purpose.

If you are sending out positive energy it is guaranteed that good things will always happen when you need them the most. However, God will decide what is good for you!

The Universal Law of Return cannot tolerate negative energy. Negative energy always returns immediately. If someone does something bad to you, don't react and send out your own negative energy—it will only come back to you. Instead, step aside and let the negative energy return to the sender. Another way to think of this law is that "what goes around, comes around."

This is an important lesson:

WISDOM KEY

> The "good thing" the universe sends you may be a "growth opportunity" disguised as a "crisis" instead of something fun and easy. You may not have expected this type of answer! Figure out what you are supposed to be learning from this crisis.

• <u>**The Universal Law of Abundance.**</u> **There is more than enough richness, treasure, and goodness for everyone.** No person is poor because there is not enough to go around. According to the Universal Law of Abundance, there is more than enough to satisfy everyone. Good always creates more good. If you are in compliance with all of the laws, the universe will provide abundant resources. You will never have to worry about tapping the resources of someone else.

THE OCEAN OF ABUNDANCE

The abundance of wealth is as plentiful as the water in all of the earth's oceans. So why go to the ocean with just a teaspoon? Even if you went to the Ocean of Abundance with big dump trucks, you could never put a dent in the ocean. Don't be limited by your thinking. There is no limit to the wealth that can be created by an unlimited mind filled with great ideas. A great attitude, a willingness to serve the masses with an industrious work ethic will set you afloat in your own Ocean of Abundance...just don't bring a teaspoon!

Unlimited opportunity exists in abundance for the person who understands and obeys the laws. Someone who swims against the tide and fights the rules is not in compliance with the Laws of the Universe. In this case, greed rules, material thinking causes negative energy, and the Universal Law of Abundance does not exist. In this scenario, one person accumulates only when they deplete someone else's resources. The hardest lesson to learn, sometimes, is that when you follow the natural flow of things according to the rules, abundance will naturally flow to you. This is God's plan.

WHEN YOU ARE IN HARMONY WITH THE LAWS OF GOD, THE LAWS OF THE UNIVERSE, THE LAWS OF NATURE, AND THE LAWS OF MAN, OPPORTUNITY WILL BE IN ABUNDANCE.

**WISDOM
KEY**

The key word is opportunity, because abundance (even though it is there) will not fall out of the sky and hit you. Opportunity is just that—opportunity. It is still up to you to make it happen. *Abundance* and *opportunity* will only manifest into reality according to the strength of your faith. The stronger your faith, the greater your abundance. God's great universe offers unlimited abundance and opportunity—more than we can humanly imagine!

MAJOR LESSON:
Life will be a lot easier when you...

Always respect people in authority and accept the fact that there are laws. Not understanding these laws, or ignorance of these laws, will make your life miserable. Understand the laws and make them work for you! They are not there to make your life full of "dos and don'ts," but to give you freedom. Live in harmony with all the laws, and you will live a rich and exciting life.

Risk more than others think is safe.

Care more than others think wise.

Dream more than others think is practical.

Expect more than others think is possible.

— Cadet Maxim
U.S. Military Academy
West Point, New York

YOUR SUCCESS REFLECTS YOUR CORE VALUES

INTEGRITY AND CHARACTER...Don't leave home without them!

What do you believe in? What values, principles, or standards do you have that guide your daily actions? What guides your thinking when you have a tough decision to make? How committed are you to following your heart in what you believe to be right when your peers are pressuring you to do something that you know is not right? Your values will determine whether you have the integrity to discipline yourself to respect universal laws and whether you will stick to the goals that you have set for your life.

Are you willing to stand up for what is right like a tall powerful skyscraper built on a firm foundation, or are you like a ship without a rudder drifting aimlessly depending on which way the wind is blowing? Not only should you stand tall for what is right, you should also be willing to firmly refuse to go with the flow when you know something is not right.

If you have ever watched a tall skyscraper being built, you would see the builders first digging a deep hole and building a strong foundation. How deep the hole is and how structurally sound the foundation is will determine how high the skyscraper can be built. The same holds true for our lives. If we work on developing a strong foundation we will be able to achieve great things in life. If we do not hold fast to any values, we will drift aimlessly in life falling prey to the corruptness of others. Jim Rohn, a great philosopher on how to live a rich and fulfilling life, gives the following advice...

"DON'T JOIN AN EASY CROWD, YOU WON'T GROW. GO WHERE THE DEMANDS ARE HIGH. LIVE AT THE SUMMIT!"

Always stick to your values no matter what. Never do anything that would cause you to look over your shoulder wondering if you are going to get caught. Never do anything that keeps you awake at night. Never do anything that would make you feel you have to apologize to your family for what you have done. Never say anything that you have to remember, just to keep your story straight—don't lie.

Much of your reputation is built on the values you hold dear to your heart. The more values you have, the greater the depth of your character. Adhering to a set of values is hard because of the peer pressure to go the easy route where everything is not measured by a high standard.

**You can never be moving forward when you are looking over your shoulder.
Once you lose your reputation, it's very hard to get it back.
Your good name is everything; don't ruin it!**

WISDOM KEY

Your integrity and your values determine the strength of your character. Your firm adherence to a standard of emotional, intellectual, moral, and spiritual values that guide your daily decisions, actions, habits, and overall behavior determines the depth and strength of your character. In other words, character is…
What you do when no one is looking!

Some core values include: honesty, loyalty, passion, morality, spirituality, love, forgiveness, respectfulness, fairness, dependability, gratitude, discipline, flexibility, responsibility, honor, optimism, persistence, determination, enthusiasm, industriousness, truthfulness, frugality, dedication and generosity. Build your life on these core values.

LIVE YOUR LIFE TO THE FULLEST BASED ON VALUES AND PRINCIPLES.

Never take the path of least resistance.

**Don't follow where the path may lead. Go instead
where there is no path and leave a trail!**
— Native Wisdom

Be one of the few destined for success. Don't be like the mindless sheep who are content to follow the masses guided by impulse. This choice is up to you. Be a thoroughbred, trained and disciplined for great achievement. Do what others will not do.

YOU HAVE TO SAY, "I AM NOT GOING TO LET THE WRONG PEOPLE INFLUENCE MY LIFE ANYMORE!"

KEY LESSON: You are in control of your life—it's all up to you.

Become one out of a hundred by answering the tough call and making the hard decisions that others are reluctant to make.

Overcome your impulses—do what you know is right. Start building your life's foundation on values and principles that are unquestionable. Don't be afraid of discipline, make it your friend. Understand that the more disciplined you are, the easier life will be on you. ***Become one out of a hundred.***

Be the one person everyone can count on!

Make this your motto:

The Uncommon Man

I do not choose to be a common person. It is my right to be uncommon— if I can. I seek opportunity—not security.

I do not wish to be a kept citizen, humbled and dulled by having the state look after me.

I want to take the calculated risk, to dream and to build, to fail and to succeed.

I refuse to barter incentive for a dole; I prefer the challenges of life to the guaranteed existence: the thrill of fulfillment to the stale calm of Utopia.

I will not trade my freedom for beneficence nor my dignity for a handout. I will never cower before any master nor bend to any threat.

It is my heritage to stand erect, proud and unafraid; to think and act for myself, to enjoy the benefit of my creations and to face the world boldly and say,

This with God's help, I have done.

— Dean Alfange

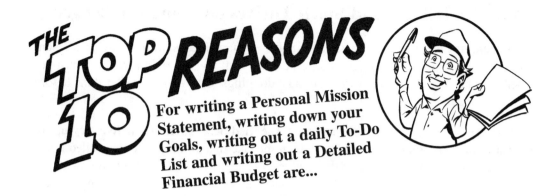

THE TOP 10 REASONS For writing a Personal Mission Statement, writing down your Goals, writing out a daily To-Do List and writing out a Detailed Financial Budget are...

1. You become the person of <u>your</u> dreams.

2. You can design the life you want to live. Your vision becomes your driving force.

3. Your personal mission statement and your goals give your life meaning because you understand what you are committing yourself to achieve.

4. Goals give you hope. They are your plans and not somebody else's plans. You are in control of your destiny.

5. You can stay focused without wasting valuable time and energy, and avoid wandering around aimlessly, wondering what's going to happen next!

6. Your personal mission statement helps you stay committed to the principles and values that are important to you.

7. You are able to make decisions, regarding your life, with clarity.

8. You will never have to look back on your life with regret.

9. You will be able to live a life free of excuses because you have direction.

10. A written mission statement, written goals, a written daily to-do list, and a written financial budget automatically puts you in the top 3% of the people in the world, because the other 97% have no written plans for their lives.

King Solomon said...

"Where there is no vision the people perish."
— Proverbs 29:18 (KJV)

Your Mind, Body, and Spirit Thrives on Being Challenged!

You cannot create a new life with your old ways, attitudes, and behaviors. When you are attempting greater things to become more than you are right now, you must go where you have never been before. You must do things that you have never done before. This is not easy.

Most people of the masses, the average, the mediocre, spend their lives trying to recreate their comfort zones. This is a fatal mistake that you must not get lulled into making! You must become one of the few, one of the elite who have learned how to thrive on the thrill of anticipating the "risk and uneasiness of the unknown" in order to recreate, regenerate, rejuvenate themselves into something greater.

You must force yourself to break out of your comfort zone where it is safe and secure. There is no growth where it is safe and secure! You must break through all your self-imposed and self-limiting barriers. You must abandon your old ways of thinking. You must cast off your old habits, attitudes, and behaviors.

In order to grow, you must risk loss. You must overcome your fear of failure. You must overcome your fear of what others may think of you. You must anticipate feeling uneasy. When you are attempting greater things so you can go where you have never gone before, you will experience frustration and confusion. Don't despair.

It is at this point of confusion that you must never quit or mentally give up because you are about ready to experience an enlightened breakthrough. All major breakthroughs are preceded by moments of frustration and confusion. What is happening is that your old ways, your old thinking, and your old behaviors are being challenged. This is called growth! If you keep rejecting new ideas, you will never grow.

> **Once your mind is stretched by a new idea,**
> **it will never again return to its original size.**
> — Oliver Wendell Holmes

You are growing. You are learning. You are becoming wiser. You are becoming greater than you have ever thought possible. You are no longer the victim of your circumstances but you are now becoming the Master of your destiny!

Your mind, body, and spirit thrive on being challenged. Every thought and cell of your body is energized and operating at heightened levels of awareness, quickness, and intuitiveness. When everything about you is operating at peak levels of performance and top efficiency, you will feel that you are on top of the world. You will feel like the champion you were born to be!

Successful Living Begins With A Great Mission Statement

Nothing in God's magnificent universe is more awesome than the unlimited potential to be discovered within us, once we start taking charge of our own lives.

Do you want to live a more fulfilling life that's exciting and rewarding? All you need is a plan. This plan is called a Mission Statement. While having goals in life is important, just having goals is not enough. A personal mission statement gives you a sense of direction. It is a written summary of how you want to live your life. It details the values and principles that are important to you, and gives purpose to your goals.

This exercise should not be taken lightly. You should give serious thought to the vital areas of your life that will become the blueprint for how you live your life. These areas should include: education, family, spirituality, career, job, financial wealth, health, social life, community, and talents. This is your future. This is your opportunity to become the architect for designing your life's plan. Having a written personal mission statement, written goals, and a daily to-do list will turbocharge the achievements in your life.

GETTING STARTED
Write down the following:

- Think of some people close to you who have made a difference in your life. Think of the best single word that characterizes each person. Next, identify the top five most important characteristics and rank them one through five.

- Think of some public people you admire for leadership, character, achievement, and success in life. These might include: television personalities like Oprah Winfrey, religious leaders like Mother Teresa, sports figures like Michael Jordan and Tiger Woods, business leaders like CEO Bill Gates from Microsoft, political leaders like Abraham Lincoln or Nelson Mandela, science leaders like Albert Einstein. Other people to consider: teachers, authors, musicians, artists, actors, etc. Describe in single words, the best characteristics of these people. Next, identify the top five most important characteristics and rank them one through five.

- If money was not an issue, how would you live your life? Describe the life of your dreams.

- What would you do if you were 10 times more confident, determined, and aggressive?

- If you knew you couldn't fail, what project would you take on and why?

- What are your values? What's important to you?

- When you die, how would you like to be remembered? What would you say were your greatest achievements?

- What are your greatest strengths?
- What do you dream about the most?
- What makes you happy?
- How can you make others happy?
- What qualities of your life would inspire others?
- What things in your life would you like to change?
- What talents, resources, or strengths do you have that would contribute to making the world a better place? Identify the top five and rank them.
- Write down everything that's important to you. Identify the top five and rank them.
- Write down everything that you like to do. Rank the top five.

Take this information and start writing. Clear off your kitchen table and get yourself some big pieces of paper and different color magic markers. Don't worry about format, just write what's on your mind. Next, organize this information into meaningful statements that reflect what's important to you, your values, principles and ideals.

Here's an example of a personal mission statement by a famous author...

> **To laugh often and much;**
> **to win the respect of intelligent people and the affection of children;**
> **to earn the appreciation of honest critics and the betrayal**
> **of false friends;**
> **to appreciate beauty, to find the best in others;**
> **to leave the world a bit better, whether by a healthy child,**
> **a garden patch or a redeemed social condition;**
> **to know even one life breathed easier because you have lived.**
> **This is to have succeeded.**
>
> — Ralph Waldo Emerson

Most mission statement gurus will tell you that a mission statement should be only one or two paragraphs long. My mission statement started out that way but over the years, I have changed it many times and I have kept adding to it as my life grows and matures. There are many things that I still have to work on in my own life—that's probably why it's so lengthy. Perhaps yours will be a lot shorter!

Don't get hung up on rules that tell you what it should look like. The most important thing is that you have started to think about how you are going to live your life and what's really important to you. The second most critical step in this process is that you are finally writing your life's mission and goals down on paper. Just this exercise alone puts you in the top 3% of the people in the world because 97% do not have any written goals for their lives. They are content to be the victims of someone else's goals and plans.

In the following pages you'll read my own personal mission statement. I've developed it over many years— it is the basis for how I live my life. Use it as an example as you begin to develop your own personal mission statement.

WISDOM KEY

You cannot "outperform" the vision that you have of yourself. It's impossible to achieve anything greater than the vision that guides your thinking, language, and behaviors. Every morning, you must create a new bigger and better vision of yourself. Every night before you fall asleep you must prepare your mind to dream bigger dreams. Every day you must become more than you were yesterday. Your mind and body are resilient. They were designed by God to be stretched to new limits by the continued setting of higher goals. This is the only way that you will ever experience the incredible potential God blessed you with!

MY PERSONAL MISSION STATEMENT

Every morning when I get up, I will be happy and joyful. I will freely follow my inner quest to strengthen my spiritual relationship with God. I will free my mind of self-imposed limitations and worldly restraints to experience the greater dynamic energies of God's magnificent universe, yet recognize the importance and unbroken wholeness of all things here on earth.

I will live a healthy lifestyle. I will: breathe deeply, sleep soundly, eat nutritiously, exercise daily, stretch for flexibility, think positively and smile cheerfully. I will sing like no one can hear, dance full-out like no one is watching and love without reservation or prejudice. I will live to make every second count as if there is no tomorrow.

I will live my life soberly. I hate not being in control of myself. I will live a responsible life and be in full control of myself at all times. I will be a role model to my family, others in my close circle of influence, and to my community. I do not wish to put myself in a position where I ever have to apologize to my family for my behavior.

My higher purpose in life is to make a positive difference in the lives of other people. I want to be a breath of fresh air wherever I go, cheerful, energetic, enthusiastic and passionate. I want to be kind, caring, and supportive. I will have a smile for everyone I meet and I will look them in the eyes so they know that I really care. I will listen generously and without judgement to what others have to say.

I vow never to lose my temper. I vow never to get angry again as it serves no purpose. I will not let complete strangers pull me down to their level. I will not allow myself to be suckered into road rage, lost tempers at the checkout line, and I vow never to be mad at the airlines. Right or wrong, I will not live in the past by holding grudges or by being vindictive. My goal is to be more tolerant and patient. I will forgive and forget, quickly moving on to a higher state of positive energy. I will live my life without worry of what others will say or think.

Our home will be a positive and cheerful place. Family and guests will find our home warm, comforting, and inviting. Our home will be filled with music, laughter, and happiness. It will have a sense of security for loved ones, a place where they can always return without being judged. Our kitchen will provide healthy and nourishing meals lovingly prepared for my family, friends, and guests. Nothing out of a box or paper bag!

I will dedicate myself to lifelong learning. I will invest in both my personal and my family's education. My library will be filled with books by great authors and a music collection of great composers and great musicians. I will invest in audio and visual tapes of inspiring speakers and motivating teachers. I will spend at least one hour daily to study my passions. I will attend lectures and seminars. My car will be my "University on Wheels." I will to listen to audiobooks whenever I am in my car.

Every day I will learn something new. I vow never to get stuck in neutral. I vow never to be a "know-it-all" or to say—"I know that." I will approach all this life has to offer with freedom of an open mind and the innocent curiosity of a child. I will be a "living sponge" soaking up all that I can learn and experience. I will commit to self-renewal, reinventing myself many times for growth. Every day, I will meet new people who I can learn from. I will not waste their time trying to impress them with what I know but I will eagerly soak up all they are willing to teach me.

Every day, I will read to satisfy my thirst for knowledge. I will feast on the written wisdom of all the world's great minds. I will be a voracious reader on a rampage of learning! My goal is to become proficient at one new skill every year. I will learn new languages, new art disciplines, and new musical instruments. I will live my life in wonderment and curiosity.

My "learning" will be the legacy that I leave to my children. I will leave the legacy of my library, my writings, my pictures, and my recordings. This treasury of memories will be carefully gathered for my children.

I will never be afraid to ask for help. I will never be so arrogant or naïve to think that I can do it on my own or that I am strong enough to handle my own problems. I understand it is a sign of maturity and wisdom to seek guidance and advice from professionals. I will take inventory of myself with honesty and openness. I will cultivate good habits and replace the bad habits that are killing me.

I will set goals for myself—short-term goals and long-term goals. I will visualize these goals as if they already have been achieved. I will write down my goals with detailed specifics including measurable benchmarks, time and completion dates. I will review them daily and use them to develop my daily to-do lists. I will burn my goals into my memory. I will commit to accomplishing them and I will discipline myself to act on them daily.

"If it's to be, it's up to me." I will not wallow in my comfort zone waiting for things to happen. I will force myself to make things happen, going forward with the understanding that I am responsible for my future. I will not procrastinate. I will get things done when I commit to doing them. I will commit myself to a life of ACTION!

I vow never to be told to go to work. I will stand on my own two feet through hard work. I will always give more than I am paid to do. I will work enthusiastically and without complaint. I vow never to take a handout as long as I am able to work and stand on my own.

I will be thankful for the opportunity to work and I will:

- Work harder than I have ever worked before
- Arrive early and stay late and be available for weekends
- Make it my responsibility to learn all the job skills that I can
- Take great pride in my work and the fact that people can count on me to do the job— right, and on time

Other people will set their standards by my work ethic and I will:

- Never ask anybody to do something that I will not do myself
- Be known as a pacesetter
- Be the first to volunteer for extra assignments and overtime
- Strive every day to learn new job skills, to increase my wisdom and more importantly, to understand my fellow worker
- Share without reservation what I have learned

Honesty and *Integrity* **are the foundations of my character.** I will live the values I believe in. I believe that integrity, honesty, loyalty, trustworthiness, and faith in God are the foundations of who I am. These values are important to me. I will never compromise my values. I will never let people, friends, or family sway me from what is important to me. A man who doesn't stand for something will fall for anything.

I have a responsibility to my community:

- I will stand up for what is right
- I will help the less fortunate, giving of time, money, and myself
- I will defend those who cannot defend themselves

- I will never look down on any man and I will never look up to any man
- I will respect the rights of others and their property
- I will be a "Good Finder"—a builder of people
- I will never engage in gossip or rumors

I will do what I say. I will keep my word. My word is my bond. I will never compromise my integrity by not living up to what I said. I will always follow through without fail. I may lose everything, but I will never tarnish my name or my reputation—it is mine forever!

I understand that problems are part of living and necessary for me to grow and mature. I will not fear problems, nor will I run from them. I will meet them head-on and resolve them with a sense of urgency. I understand that it's all right to fail as long as I admit to my mistakes, correct them, learn from them, and move on. "No Surprises" is my motto. I will not hide from my mistakes or failures. In fact, the more I fail, the more I am learning and I am committed to lifelong learning!

I will not be discouraged, instead I will be encouraging. I will not judge, criticize or condemn others for their mistakes or failures. I will forgive and forget. I will go out of my way to help these people with words of encouragement and personal involvement.

I AM RESPONSIBLE! I will take total responsibility for my life, understanding that where I am in life is a direct result of decisions and choices that I have made. And I am willing to be held accountable for my willingness to accept this responsibility. I will not blame anyone, anything, or any circumstance for problems or adversities that I may face. It is totally up to me to change my circumstances for the better. I will take responsibility for my future.

I will use money wisely and for good. I will work hard to achieve financial independence. I will work hard for my money until my money works hard for me. Money is only a tool to use to better myself and to make the lives of others better. My money will be my servant, not my master. I will not worship money, nor will I be envious of the wealth of others. The accumulation of money is only a measuring stick of how I have been able to satisfy the needs of others first.

I know that having money requires personal discipline and responsibility. I will spend less than I earn. I will not spend more than I earn. Except for car loans, home mortgages and education, I will keep myself debt free. I will respect the use of other people's money and I will pay my debts on time.

I will live on 70% of what I earn after taxes. The remaining 30% will be divided into three parts: 10% for tithing and charity, 10% for building and aggressive investing and 10% for long-term saving.

I will nurture my faith in God. I will develop my spirituality daily. I will seek the gift of faith. I will pray for guidance and strength from my Lord and Savior. I understand that "strong faith" is the foundation for "believing." I need to strongly believe in myself so that I can accomplish all of my goals and ambitions successfully.

I will eagerly look forward to attending worship services and the fellowship of other believers. I will help build vitality and be a generous supporting contributor to this community of faith. With God all things are possible.

I will give God thanks. I believe that God has blessed me with more than I need. I will always be thankful to God for all I have: for my family's good health and safety; for this wonderful country that we live in; and for the opportunity to work.

Carpe Diem—**Seize The Day!** I will live my life to the fullest, experiencing all that I can. I will live my life with meaning. I will try to experience all great moments in history, visiting all interesting, exotic, and exciting places on earth. I will maximize the moment!

My Life's Higher Purpose

I believe that my higher purpose in life is to make a positive difference in the lives of other people. I want to pass on what I have learned and what I have. I want to help grow and facilitate the success of my family and the people who have given me their confidence. My goal is make the lives of others more rewarding.

My desire is that, as my legacy here on earth, I will be remembered as a God-fearing father to my family, a dedicated husband to my wife, a successful businessman, and a God-fearing leader in my community.

WHEN IT IS ALL SAID AND DONE... I WILL HAVE LIVED MY LIFE WITHOUT REGRET, NEVER HAVING TO LOOK BACK AND WONDER — "WHAT IF?"

Far better it is to dare mighty things, to win glorious triumphs, even though checkered by failure, than to rank with those poor spirits who neither enjoy much nor suffer much, because they live in the gray twilight that knows no victory or defeat.

— Theodore Roosevelt

**Keep your sense of humor and
don't take yourself too seriously,
because...
"The higher a monkey climbs,
the more you can see of his behind!"**

**If you're not living on the edge,
you're taking up too much space!**
— Mario Andretti

**From this day forward
I have made my choice:
I will lead not follow.
I will create not destroy.
I will make a difference.
I am a LEADER!**
— LifeSkills Center for Leadership Pledge

MY WHOLE PURPOSE IN LIFE IS JUST TO MAKE YOU HAPPY!

Discover the Life-Changing Power of Setting Goals

Most people spend more time planning their vacations than they do planning their lives.

People generally never set goals because they've never been challenged to set goals. Goal setting is not taught in school and most people have no clue when it comes to creating a life plan. For most people goal setting consists of being told that they have to go to school so they can get a job, get married, raise good children, and then retire. Unfortunately, most people never realize their dreams because they have never taken the time to do any planning for their own lives, much less writing down their goals on paper.

**WISDOM
KEY**

Successful goal setting requires you to stretch to places you have never been before. If the things you dream of achieving push you past your known limits, then they are worthy goals. Anything that does not challenge you to become more, is not worthy of being part of your goals. These are just "things to do" and they can be put on your daily to-do list. Successful goal setting will push you where you're not comfortable. Meaningful growth may be uncomfortable but the feeling of accomplishment is greater. Break out of your comfort zones by taking immediate MASSIVE ACTION.
"Just Do It!"

Who you are right now is the result of the decisions you made 5 to 10 years ago. Who you will become in the next five years is directly dependent on these three things:

1. The books you read
2. The people with whom you associate
3. The choices you make that are consistent with your goals

Your goals, or lack of goals, will determine the choices you make.

Here's a **SCARY** thought…most people's goals are not their own!

IF YOU HAVE NOT PLANNED YOUR LIFE, YOU WILL FALL PREY TO THE PLANS OF THOSE AROUND YOU. YOU WILL BE ACHIEVING THEIR DREAMS!

People without goals are dangerous because they are servants to those who have plans! And not everybody has good plans. That ought to really scare you!

Where are you headed in life?

Lifestory of "The Average"

Most people in the world do not have plans for their life and wonder why life has passed them by.

Lifestory of "All Winners in Life"

All winners have detailed, written plans for their future and experience all the rewards life has to offer.

Invest Your Day Wisely, Your Future Begins Now!

If you want to make God laugh, tell him *your* plans…

In this chapter, you'll find goal setting and daily to-do list strategies that have been developed over many years. I have studied all the great teachers of life, government, religion, and industry. I have taken their systems and come up with a simple goal setting strategy that you can easily put into daily practice.

There are Three Major Goals in life.

1. **LEAVING A LEGACY—knowing that you have made a difference.**

2. **THE RIGHT JOB AND A REWARDING CAREER—being able to get up in the morning and look forward to going to work. Loving what you do for a living because you are following your passion.**

3. **A FULFILLING PERSONAL LIFE—consisting of:**
   - **Spiritual Fulfillment**
   - **Social Acceptance with Good Friendships**
   - **Strong Family Relationships**
   - **Being Healthy**
   - **Financial Security**
   - **Lifelong Learning: career, cooking, music, art and languages, reading, history, government, and travel**
   - **Being able to experience great things or special events of interest**
   - **Having Hope and Being Happy**

Many people only live up to the expectations of their peer group.

WISDOM KEY

Design your life by creating goals based on your life's true passion. The only way that you are going to be really happy in life— and be productive—is by pursuing your passion with all the energy, enthusiasm and persistence you have. And that will only come from doing what you really love to do.

Beginning thoughts about goal setting...

Goal setting is not a foreign concept—we are all goal setters by nature. Have you ever noticed that when you make up your mind to do something and focus all your energy on what is fixed in your mind, that generally you get what you go after? Have you ever noticed how determined kids are when their minds are made up—they never give up! We need to have that same childlike intensity when going after our goals. Use this to your advantage. Start predetermining your goals and go after them.

- **Start by taking responsibility for where you are in life.** Before you can set goals, you have to accept the fact that you are responsible and accountable. Once you have accepted this responsibility then you can start to change your life.

- **Set major time aside to develop your goals.** This is not a half-hour exercise—you may want to dedicate a whole week to designing your life.

 *Abraham Lincoln once said that if he were given eight hours to chop down a tree, he would spend six hours sharpening his axe.*

- **Be serious.** This will be one of the most important exercises you will ever undertake in improving the quality of your life.

A GOAL CASUALLY THOUGHT ABOUT IS QUICKLY ABANDONED AT THE FIRST OBSTACLE.

- **Think about your lifestyle and behavior. If you want to live the good life, you cannot live fast and loose.** A rewarding lifestyle is the result of personal discipline—controlling your impulses. One of the hardest lessons to learn when you are young is that there are rules in this universe. The more you discipline yourself, the easier life will be on you.

- **You cannot expect to achieve great things while thinking, behaving and living like an average person.** If you ever want to become a millionaire you must live your life like a millionaire. Contrary to what you may think, millionaires live lives of responsibility, with great work ethics, high character values and strong personal disciplines that improve them daily. You should desire to be a millionaire—not for the money, but for what you become in the process!

- **There are no shortcuts in life.** Success in the beginning is all about sacrifice and controlling your impulses.

**WISDOM
KEY**

If you cannot control your daily impulses now, you won't be able
to enjoy your big impulses later in life when it really counts.
Discipline is really the key to freedom!

- **Don't be totally materialistic in your goal setting.** It's all right to want the best car and a beautiful home for your family, but don't be shallow in thinking about what's important in your life. Goals based only on material accumulation will lead to a life filled with frustration.

Concentrate your goal setting on what matters most:

➤ **Spiritual fulfillment:** Living a God-centered life
➤ **Physical wellness:** Living a healthy energized lifestyle
➤ **Rewarding career:** Never work another day in your life by finding your true passion
➤ **Strong family relationships:** Close family ties that are nurturing, positive, and enduring
➤ **Social acceptance with strong friendships:** Making a positive difference in your community
➤ **Financial security:** No debt, and knowledgeable in building a strong investment portfolio
➤ **Things you want to achieve or experience:** Climb Mt. Everest, sky dive, be President, run a marathon, bungee jump, etc.
➤ **Lifelong learning:** Career, cooking, music, art, languages, reading, history, government, travel, environment, etc.

To reach your goals, live a meaningful life based on standards.

Standards of *excellence*
Standards of *discipline*
Standards of *values*

WHEN YOU LIVE A LIFE BASED ON STANDARDS, YOU
WON'T HAVE TO FIGHT YOUR WAY TO THE TOP. YOU WILL
ATTRACT OTHER WINNERS IN LIFE WHO WILL OPEN
DOORS THAT ARE OTHERWISE UNAVAILABLE TO
SOMEONE LIVING AN AVERAGE LIFE.

GUIDELINES FOR SETTING GOALS

Stephen Covey says, "Begin with the end in mind." Goal setting is a serious strategy for determining how and where you want to end up in life.

- **What do you know about yourself?** Self-discovery is critical to your quest for lifelong improvement.

- **Take a "Brutal and Honest" Inventory of Yourself.** Before you can begin to set your goals you must first know where you are starting out. You have to ask yourself, "Where am I now?"

Take a legal pad. On the top of each page write these headlines:

- Personal History
- Family History
- Strengths
- Weaknesses
- Talents
- What Interests Me? Things I like
- Things I Dislike
- Things I Would Like To Change

Start filling each page. Take your time. This exercise is important because it will allow you to focus in on your passions.

- **Begin by writing your obituary, as it would appear if you died today!** This is a sobering exercise. If you were to die right now, what would your legacy be? What would they print in the newspaper? Take a newspaper and find the obituary section. Read several of them and then write your own. This exercise should not be taken lightly.

❧ YOU WON'T FIND EXCUSES IN THE OBITUARY COLUMN! ❧

- **Next, write your obituary as you would want it to read.** Where do you want to end up in life? After writing this, compare it to your obituary as it would appear now. You might come to some interesting, eye-opening revelations. Again, take some time to really think this through. How you write your obituary will guide you in developing your goals.

Key thought…
Your obituary is where you want to end up in life.
Goal setting will help you leave a legacy worth remembering here on earth.

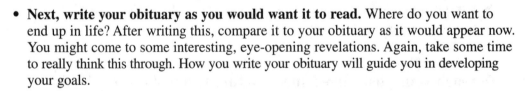

IF THIS WAS YOUR LAST DAY ON EARTH, WHAT WOULD YOU DO? LIVE EVERY DAY LIKE IT WAS YOUR LAST!

Dave's Obituary

This is an example from my own goal setting exercise.

242 Obituaries &
Funerals

Anderson

*David W. Anderson, age 95 of
Edina, Minnesota.*

Surrounded by his loving family, David passed away peacefully in good health to be with his Lord and Savior. David is survived by his wife and two wonderful sons James and Timothy and their beautiful wives and children; his brother Philip of Hayward; and sister Rebecca St. Germaine of Eau Claire, Wisconsin. David was preceded in death by his father an enrolled member of the Great Choctaw Nation from Idabel, Oklahoma and his mother an enrolled member of the Lac Courte Oreilles Lake Superior Band of Ojibwe from Hayward, Wisconsin. David grew up in Chicago where he spent 26 years of his life until moving to Minneapolis. While in Chicago he met his loving wife Kathryn Rynning of Edgerton, Wisconsin. They were married in May of 1976. David was devoted to his family and friends. He was loved and respected by all who knew him and he will be deeply missed.

David was a creative treasure who overcame Attention Deficit Disorder and alcohol abuse to go on to get his Master's Degree from Harvard University's John F. Kennedy School of Government without ever having received an undergraduate degree. David started his first business right out of high school and eventually went on to help found three publicly traded companies on Wall Street, after overcoming several bankruptcies. David readily acknowledged that all his business and personal achievements were only possible once he turned his life over to God.

His attention to detail and constant striving for excellence was rewarded by many regional and national awards, honors, and recognition for his contributions in the areas of leadership, human resources, and product excellence. His commitment to education resulted in a presidential appointment by President George W. Bush. His businesses created tens of thousands of jobs and he was most recognized for his highly successful Famous Dave's Barbeque chain of restaurants and his innovative water parks which revolutionized the way Americans vacationed. The greatest testament to David's success was the thousands of employees who claimed that his philosophies and his example as a role model changed their lives.

David lived his life in gratefulness. Never wanting to forget his roots, he gave generously of his time and money, making a difference in his community. He served on many community boards and spent most of his time speaking to youth groups, community organizations, and helping other substance abusers in recovery. David realized that his higher purpose was to make a positive difference in the lives of the less fortunate.

David was an award winning cookbook and self-help author whose books were number one on the *New York Times* best selling list. He was an avid reader, liked being outdoors, enjoyed music. His hobbies included silversmithing and collecting pigs and antiques.

A Celebration of Life service will be held at Dave's favorite church where there will be joyous singing and happy recitations by family and friends. A party will be held immediately afterwards. We will be happy to receive your flowers but we also encourage you to donate generously to the LifeSkills Center for Leadership.

"Grieve not...nor speak of me with tears...but laugh and talk of me as though I were beside you. I loved you so...'twas heaven here with you!"

**"I always remember an epitaph I saw
in a cemetery at Tombstone, Arizona.
It says,
'Here lies Jack Williams.
He done his damnedest.'
I think that is the greatest epitaph
a man can have."**
— Harry S. Truman

• **Make a dream list.** Write down everything. Brainstorm. Dream Big. Think Big!

This is the fun part. Here's where you "let go!" Don't let anything stop you from dreaming big dreams. This is not where you put conditions on yourself because of where you've been, of where you are, or what you've done in the past. Your present skills or financial condition have nothing to do with where you want to go.

You are no different than anyone who has ever achieved great accomplishments in their lives.

You have a right to dream big dreams.
All the goodness of the universe belongs to you. Believe that.

- **Next, take your list of dreams and turn them into goals by writing them down.** The purpose of goal setting is to realize accomplishments that you normally never would have achieved if you hadn't decided to live a richer and more rewarding life.

See yourself as greater than you ever thought possible.
Don't major in minor things!

- **Prioritize Your Dream List.** After writing down all your dreams, the next step is important to figuring out what takes priority according to your passions. This will help turn your dreams into achievable goals.

- **You must turn your dream list into written goals.**
If you think it—Ink it!

- **This will force you to be clear and realistic.** A dream list without the rigors of turning them into written goals becomes nothing more than a wish list. In fact, God tells you to do three things: 1) Write down your goals, 2) Make them plain, and then 3) Don't delay—ACT on them by running!

  Habakkuk 2:2 (KJV), "Then the Lord answered me and said: 'Write the vision and make it plain on tablets, that he may run who reads it!'" How powerful is that!

  There is something magical about writing down your goals. It's the act of writing down your goals that forces you to think about the specifics needed to develop the action steps necessary to turn your dreams into reality. Writing down your goals and committing yourself to a daily to-do list forces you to follow through. Notice the above verse in the Bible tells you that once you have written your goals, you must take immediate ACTION by running!

- **If it's important to you, write it in a journal. Don't document million-dollar ideas on little pieces of paper.** Get yourself a leather-bound journal for the brilliant masterpieces of your mind! Live a life worth writing about—leave a legacy. Your writings will become treasures!

- **Goal Setting Logistics. Learn the difference between: goals, objectives, strategies, activities, tasks, results, and benefits.** After taking your dream list and ranking it by your priorities, transform your dreams into meaningful goals by fully developing them into the appropriate categories. These are detailed on page 71 in this chapter.

- **The importance of TIME.** In order to accomplish your goals you need to understand the importance of time. There are 168 hours in a week. Make every minute count. Minutes add up to hours and hours up to days. You can never recover wasted time.

MAXIMIZE THE MOMENT!
— T.D. Jakes

HERE'S AN EYE-OPENING EXERCISE! If you were to waste just one hour a day multiplied by 365 days a year then multiplied by what you think you are worth per hour, I think you would be amazed to find out the incredible amount of money that you are throwing away!

Wasted time is the biggest killer of opportunity.

Time is more valuable than money. You can always earn more money, but after today, this day is gone forever, leaving in its place whatever you have traded for it. Plan your time wisely.

The key to successful goal setting is long-term vision with short-term focus!

Goal setting allows you to manage your time effectively.

A person who has goals makes every minute of the day count.

15-MINUTE INCREMENTS ARE IMPORTANT TO HIGH ACHIEVERS. INEFFECTIVE PEOPLE THINK IN DAYS AND WEEKS.

- **VISUALIZE THE SPECIFICS.**

You have to "be there"—to get there!

Have clarity. 80% of the effort is having a clear vision of where you want to go. Be specific.

**Like a vacation, you must first know where you want to go
and how long it will take you to get there.**

WISDOM KEY

YOU MUST BURN INTO YOUR MIND EXACTLY WHAT YOU WANT.
Mental imagery or visualization is a powerful tool of the mind. What you focus on in your mind will become reality. The clearer you can see something in your mind, the clearer you can write down your goals, and the more achievable your goals become.
It's hard to focus on something that's fuzzy!

- **Create a POWER BOOK OF ACHIEVEMENT. This is a visual tool to stimulate your mind.** Put together your personal Achievement Book. Cut out pictures of cars, homes, vacations, and schools you would like to attend. Paste the pictures in your book and then write underneath them describing vividly what you want in full detail. If it's your dream home, describe it in detail. How many square feet? How many rooms? What color is the paint? What kinds of flowers are planted in the garden? Fix in your mind every detail of the things you want.

You must visualize already having achieved your dreams.

You must believe that all good things were meant for you.

- **Set benchmarks.** A fundamental prerequisite for goal setting is establishing benchmarks such as specific times and dates, or deadlines, for accomplishments. The true purpose of goal setting is to hold yourself accountable for decisions to which you have committed.

- **<u>Without accountability your goals are nothing more than fantasy.</u>** A specific date forces you to go all-out to meet your commitment.

- **Be realistic. There are no shortcuts in the game of life.**

LIFE IS HARD BY THE YARD, BUT A CINCH BY THE INCH!

- **Set your goals by your BIORHYTHMS.** Notice how biorhythms affect your productivity. Have you tracked your biorhythms to find out when is your most productive time of the day? Most people haven't. Simply, your *peak* biorhythms are when you are mentally and physically alert and the most productive. The times of the day when you feel drained are your low biorhythms.

- **Everyone has a specific time of the day when biologically they are at their peak.** Figure out your biological peaks. This exercise is important in developing your daily to-do lists, which are critical in meaningful goal achievement. During your peak times you should be doing productive things that will help you achieve your goals. During your low times, you should be getting your hair cut or going grocery shopping.

DON'T SPEND THE MOST PRODUCTIVE TIME OF YOUR DAY DOING THINGS THAT DON'T MATTER.

- **Get Advice.** For some goals, you will need to seek advice from professional advisors. If you've never made a million dollars, how capable are you of creating a plan to make a million dollars? Go to a millionaire financial advisor—find out from an expert. You may need to talk to a physician about your health and physical wellness goals. Members of the clergy can help you with your spiritual goals.

- **If you're serious about your goals, you will seek advice.** How serious you are about accomplishing your goals shows how open you are to getting help in structuring your goal planning.

**Seeking advice from successful experts is a sign of
wisdom and maturity on your part.**

- **Thinking that you can go it alone is immature and foolish.** Don't waste your valuable time and energy making mistakes that you could have avoided. Learn from someone who has traveled your road before and has made all of the mistakes.

- **Keep handy a 3x5 card of your most important goals.** Carry it in your pocket at all times. Burn your goals into your mind daily. If your mind can believe it—it will become reality!

- **Learn something new every day.** You must be constantly improving yourself. Learning something every day will help you achieve your goals.

- **Update your goals.** Continually updating your goals and rewriting them is repetitive reinforcement—a form of positive affirmation. The more you can write down your goals the more you fix or burn them into your mind. You are programming your subconscious through constant positive affirmation.

- **Live in the increase.** Never consume or deplete what you produced yesterday. Be more productive. Be more profitable. Never go backward, always forward.

- **Go for it!** Don't wait for the right time to get started. The right time is right now! Take Action Now! Just do it!

- **From time to time review your personal inventory, evaluate and make changes.**

- **Celebrate your successes.** Anchor the moment by making your achievement memorable.

- **Have Fun!**

- **Be persistent. Don't ever give up on your goals. Never, ever, ever quit!**

SET YOUR GOALS FOR THE FUTURE, BUT LIVE YOUR LIFE IN THE PRESENT OR THERE WILL BE NO FUTURE!

The LOGISTICS of Setting Goals

Most people do not accomplish their dreams because they haven't been taught how to set goals. To set goals you need to understand the difference between *goals, objectives, activities, tasks, results*, and *benefits*. For instance:

> If I said to you, "I am going to walk every day for the next six months," is that a goal? The answer is no. That is a STRATEGY for achieving your goal of Physical Wellness.

> If I said to you, "I am going to live a long and healthy life," is that an objective? No. That is a BENEFIT of achieving your goal of Physical Wellness.

Confused? You're not alone. A major reason why people don't set goals or never achieve their goals is that they haven't been trained in goal setting. They don't understand the process in the first place. The difference between a goal and an objective can be confusing. You really have to think about what you are doing when planning your life.

GOALS—statements defining your desire, which you will direct all of your efforts to achieving. Example: I will achieve Physical Wellness for myself.

OBJECTIVES—what you need to do in order to achieve your overall goals. Examples for Physical Wellness: maintain ideal body weight; replace bad habits with good habits; achieve clean bill of health from doctor.

STRATEGIES—action plans required for each objective. Examples for Physical Wellness: quit smoking; start eating a low fat, high fiber diet; begin a program of exercise; etc.

TASKS—activities that support your action plan. Examples for Physical Wellness: see a doctor for a check-up before starting program; buy new walking shoes; join a health club; read a book on nutrition.

ACTION PLAN—a list of specific measurable activities to be achieved by certain dates. There are three categories of goals: SHORT-TERM GOALS—one month or less, INTERMEDIATE GOALS—six months to a year, and LONG-TERM GOALS—one year or more. Your Action Plan is really part of your daily to-do list. Examples for Physical Wellness: I will walk 30 minutes each day; I will consume only 1500 calories a day; I will reduce my smoking by one cigarette each day.

RESULTS—measurable outcomes. Examples for Physical Wellness: lost 20 pounds and reached my ideal body weight; quit smoking for good; lowered blood pressure to 120/80; reduced cholesterol to 150.

BENEFITS—what achieving your goal means to you. Examples for Physical Wellness: I look better and feel more energized; I have more self-confidence; all my clothes fit better!

The next page is an example of what each goal should look like after you have fully considered the importance of it to your life. You should have a sheet for each of the following: spiritual goals, family goals, reaching full potential of your talents, community and social goals, physical fitness goals, learning and education goals, environmental responsibility goals, financial goals, career goals, play, and fun goals.

YOU MAY THINK THIS IS A LOT OF WORK—BUT THIS IS YOUR LIFE! IT'S WELL WORTH THE EFFORT. YOU SHOULD HAVE A WELL THOUGHT-OUT PLAN FOR YOUR LIFE. YOU DESERVE IT!

WISDOM KEY

Achieving your goals will be easier when you associate with other positive people. It's amazing how often we sabotage ourselves by wasting valuable time trying to please people who don't like us! Don't let the most productive part of your day get wasted by unproductive people.

Hope is not a strategy!

Keep away from people who try to belittle your ambitions, small people do that. But the really great make you feel that you, too, can somehow become great.
— Mark Twain

Worrying is the worst type of goal setting there is!

Here is an example of what you're aiming for:

GOAL
Physical Wellness

OBJECTIVE
Maintain ideal weight and replace bad habits with good habits

STRATEGIES
Quit smoking and drinking
Exercise
Improve diet:
No sugar; less meat; more grains, fruits and veggies

TASKS
See a doctor for a complete physical
Join a health club
Read a book on nutrition
Buy walking shoes

ACTION PLAN
Set benchmarks; coordinate with a daily to-do list

SHORT-TERM (30 Days)	INTERMEDIATE (6 months to a year)	LONG-TERM (1 year or more)
TO-DO Walk 20 minutes before breakfast	**TO-DO** Walk 30 minutes before breakfast	**TO-DO** Walk 45 minutes before breakfast
1000 calories a day	1500 calories a day	2000 calories a day

RESULTS

SHORT-TERM Lose 1 pound per week	INTERMEDIATE Lose 1/2 pound per week	LONG-TERM Maintain ideal body weight

Overall: lowered blood pressure to 120/80, cholesterol to less than 150, lost 20 pounds

BENEFITS
Feel better and look better
Have more self-confidence and better self-esteem
Live a longer, healthier life

Life must be a journey of constantly improving yourself.

Learning something every day will help you achieve your goals. Without goals, life is like a merry-go-round. You simply go in circles and it is hard to get off or to figure out where you are or where you've been.

Don't join the masses that gravitate toward what is easy. Immediate gratification seldom leads to creating growth opportunities that will lead you to a rewarding future.

Without goals you will spend your most productive time doing unproductive things.

The most important aspect of goal setting is that goals keep you productive and not reactive to crisis events. Without goals, you will be reacting to crisis events and urgent matters. If you spend your productive time on your goals, then you will spend less time on crisis events and urgent matters.

Often the things that you should be doing, you are not doing.

If things in your life don't feel right to you, stop and assess where you are in life. Take inventory.

Ask yourself...

> **Why is this?**
>
> **Where am I?**
>
> **Where am I headed?**
>
> **Will I be happy when I get there?**
>
> **What are my goals in life?**
>
> **Are they worthy goals?**
>
> **Is what I am doing right now congruent with my goals?**

Setting a course for your life will be one of the most important things you can do for designing your destiny and taking charge of your future.

Goals keep you moving forward, not backward.

Every evening, write down the six most important things that you must do the next day. Then while you sleep, your subconscious will work on the best ways for you to accomplish them. Your next day will go much more smoothly.

— Tom Hopkins

Your Daily To-Do List

Don't let anything stop you from making your daily to-do list.

Writing out a to-do list is probably the single most important thing you can do daily to change your life. Every morning when you get up, you should already have your day planned. Start the night before by writing down everything you think you might have to do the next day. Next, set priorities based on your goals.

A's are the most important things to do according to your goals. **B**'s are not as important as **A**'s. A "**C**" item might be something like lunch or getting a haircut. Next, rank them by numbers. Some **A**'s are more important than other **A**'s.

Your **A**'s should always be done during your most productive time of the day according to your biorhythms. You should never do a "**B**" item before all your **A**'s have been completed.

A "**D**" is something you should **"D"elegate** or **"D"elay** until it is a higher priority. Don't waste time on **D**'s when there are more important things to do.

Eliminate **E**'s if they have nothing to do with your other goals.

This is how it should look:

A1	B1	C1	D	E
A2	B2	C2		
A3	B3			
	B4			

WISDOM KEY

FIVE SIMPLE KEYS TO DAILY EFFECTIVENESS!

1. Focus your time and energy on one thing at a time.

2. Do the most important things first!

3. Stick with one item until fully completed.
   Don't jump around and leave things unfinished.

4. If it isn't on your list, don't do it!

5. If there are things on your list that are not congruent with your goals, cross them off.

Simply, the best advice still comes from Mom...

1. Eat all your vegetables.
2. Wear clean underwear.
3. Finish whatever you start!

Organization
The discipline of true freedom!

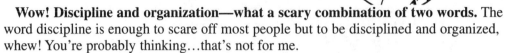

Wow! Discipline and organization—what a scary combination of two words. The word discipline is enough to scare off most people but to be disciplined and organized, whew! You're probably thinking…that's not for me.

For some people, organization is their greatest strength. Organization can be both a blessing and a curse. There are some people who are so disorganized that they are ineffective. Then there are some people who are so overly organized that they are ineffective as well.

Organization is an important life skill that is never taught in school, although it should be the prerequisite for college or any management job. Being organized is fundamental to reaching your fullest potential. It's difficult living life to its fullest potential if you are spending valuable time searching for things that you have misplaced or are late for meetings because you are running around at the last minute trying to get things done.

You can never achieve your fullest potential in life if you cannot organize yourself.

WISDOM KEY

The more organized you are, the greater the teacher you can become. All great success comes from duplicating your efforts through teaching or mentoring. Being organized prevents chaos and facilitates communication on a larger scale. The more people who know what you are doing and can follow what you are doing, the more successful you will be. It's imperative that you get organized.

How organized is your life?
- Are you constantly misplacing things or forgetting where you last left something?
- Have you ever missed an appointment because you forgot about it?
- If you had to produce an important document, how long would it take you?
- What is the general condition of your bedroom?

Major Thought on Living an Organized Life:

I believe that being an organized person is as simple as making your bed in the morning.

The simple task of making your bed in the morning will give you the attitude of being organized throughout your day. Being organized does not mean you have to live your life in a neat-as-a-pin, everything-has-its-place, structured sterile environment. Over the years, I have made it a habit to ask people if they make their beds in the morning. Their answer is generally revealing as to how they live their lives.

Organization is really the art of "being effective," being able to get things done in an efficient manner—quickly and expeditiously.

This was not the easiest chapter for me to write! Anyone who knows me will tell you that I am very creative, smart, and maybe brilliant...but I have to be watched. I am always losing my car keys, my address book, and almost anything that is put in my hands.

So why am I writing about organization? Because it is the only way that you can become successful. Early on in my life, while I was taking inventory of myself—discovering my own strengths and my weaknesses—I came to an understanding that being organized was not one of my greatest strengths.

To this day, every day of my life, I have to work diligently on being organized. So if I can become organized—you can too!

Five things that will keep you from being organized:

1. You can't get started or you don't know where to start.
2. You don't know what to do.
3. Excuses. Not enough time, too busy, etc.
4. You think, "What's the use—it will all get messed up again!"
5. You just can't get yourself psyched up to tackle the project of getting organized!

Man's best friend, aside from the dog, is the wastebasket!
— Business Week

Organization can be learned.
Anything learned can become a habit!

How to get started:

- **Start! There is something magical about the process of just starting.** If you don't know where to begin, start with the priorities you identified in your goal setting program.
- **Whatever you start—you must finish!** Finishing gives you satisfaction and a feeling of accomplishment. Stay focused on each task until it is done.
- **Apply the 80/20 Rule.** Only 20% of whatever is cluttering up your life is important to accomplishing your goals. Identify and start organizing the 20% first. Be really hard on the other 80%. Trash everything that doesn't influence your priorities or goals in life.
- **Group like things together, according to your priorities.** Think in groupings and then organize in groupings. Make these groupings into activity centers and create an inventory sheet for each zone. Sample zones: reading zone, music zone, cooking zone, exercise zone, office zone, and a kid play zone.
- **Plan your day for organizing.** Set aside specific times for cleaning and organizing.

- **Organize your day.** Everything starts by organizing your day. Get a workable calendar system and stick to it.
- **Divide and conquer.** When faced with a large number of unmanageable tasks, "chunk" them into smaller more manageable tasks. The key is to solve each problem one at a time. Take action and move on.
- **Keep a running list of things to do.** Never rely on your memory. Prioritize your daily to-do list.
- **Taming the "Paper Tiger."** Organize the paperwork in your life. In getting started, work on the obvious, don't try and figure out the things that are confusing or on thinking about things you can't see in your files.
- **Don't get sidetracked.** You will be tempted to grab something you forgot to do and you will want to act on it. DON'T! You must not skip around doing a little bit here and a little bit there. This will only cause you to become distracted from your main task at hand—which is to get organized.
- **Sort and File.** Put everything you come across that needs immediate attention into an "ACTION" file. Everything else, file it immediately, delegate it immediately, or trash it immediately. Make a note in your calendar of things that you file but need to follow up.
- **Don't become a paper shuffler.** Your goal should be to handle each paper only one time.
- **Don't open unimportant mail.** At least 25% of your junk mail can be thrown away without ever opening it.
- **Everything needs to be in its own place.** Set up a simple filing system by color. Important categories: home, career, family, auto, personal to-do lists, important documents.
- **Highlight.** When you read documents or books, mark important parts with a highlighter and 3M Post-it Notes™. This will give you quick reference at a later date.
- **When you read letters write your thoughts in the margin.** They will help you to quickly write your response later.
- **KISS—Keep It Simple, Stupid! Don't be a pack rat.** Get rid of stuff you don't need—live your life simply without all the clutter.

WHEN IN DOUBT–THROW IT OUT!

- **Keep "every thing" simple.** Don't write wordy documents. Don't spend your time in mindless chatter on the telephone. Have a purpose to your conversations.
- **Get organized people into your life.** If you are hopelessly disorganized—seek help. Don't give up just because you can't get organized—ask for help.

Organization is a skill that must be learned. Read good books on organization. Emulate people you know who are organized. Ask a friend who is organized to help you. Good organizational habits must be learned. Sticking to your goals will give your life purpose and help you to stay organized and focused.

Organization is the difference between living your life full of purpose, meaning, and contribution or living your life as a victim of whatever happens next without ever being in a position to give back.

Details! Details! Details!

Some say, "The devil's in the details."
I say it's just the opposite, "God is in the details!"

"Attention to details? That's not me!" When I first heard someone say that one of the prerequisites for being successful in life is "paying attention to the details," I thought to myself, "That's not me. How boring! I could never be that detailed. I'll probably never be successful!"

I thought attention to details—dotting all of the i's and crossing all the t's—was loved only by really smart people, like accountants and lawyers. I actually thought people who were that detailed were boring. I never dreamed that one day I would get a reputation for being picky about the details. I was always the dreamer, the creative one. I never thought that "minutia" would excite me.

I didn't realize what a difference "the details" make. Like most people, I did not understand that the difference between "just being average" and "being excellent" has a lot to do with "going the extra mile"—in other words, paying attention to all of the little details. Now I know that the people who become excellent in their careers care enough to pay attention to the small things that really count—it's a "love thing!"

WISDOM KEY

> **Attention to the detail comes naturally when you are following your passion.** It's a lot easier to be concerned about the details when you love what you do. If you take care of the small details, you won't have to worry about the big picture.

When you are following your passion:

- **You fully care about what you are working on**
- **You want everything to be "just right"**
- **You are proud of your work**
- **You become excellent at what you love to do**
- **Excellence naturally heightens your alertness to all the little things that may not be noticeable to others**

❧ YOUR LOVE IS DEMONSTRATED THROUGH YOUR ❧ CARING ABOUT—"EVERY LITTLE LAST THING."

God is in the details. God is love!

Go ahead and sweat the "small" stuff.

Three key fears that keep people away from "the details:"

1. Most people are afraid of asking questions about the little things they don't understand because they are afraid others will judge them for their ignorance.
2. Sometimes they are afraid of saying something because they think no one will care.
3. They think that what they want to bring up is too small to make a difference.

It's really amazing how fear can immobilize a person.

How do you get good at the details? Actually it's as simple as asking:

- **Who's responsible for this?**
- **How does this work?**
- **What does this mean?**
- **When will this happen?**
- **Can this be made better?**
- **Is this right?**

If you don't understand something, ask a question. If you have something to say, say it—no matter how trivial you think it is.

LOOK SMART BY ASKING DUMB QUESTIONS!

It's also about checking your work. Many people are too lazy to check their work. This is how things "fall through the cracks." Making sure you have completed all that's needed and going back over your work to recheck everything requires self-discipline. If you need to, ask someone who is more experienced than you are to check your work.

Here's a statement to live by:

"OK, now let me go over this one more time, until I understand exactly what is going on here!"

Do this, and soon you will be the mastering the details!

Paying attention to simple little things that most men neglect, makes a few men rich!
— Henry Ford, Sr.

LET'S SUM THINGS UP!

What does this mean to me?

1. **Discipline is your friend!** Accept the fact that there are laws. Life would be chaotic without them. Discipline yourself to pay attention to the small details.

2. **No more excuses!** You are totally responsible for where you are in life, so start living your life free of excuses.

3. **Take charge of your life now!** Most people spend more time planning their vacations than they do planning their lives. Become the architect of your destiny!

4. **Create a fulfilling life by dreaming bigger dreams.** Visualize having achieved your dreams and burn that picture into every cell of your body. Create an unquenchable fire in your gut that will force you to overcome any barriers to your success. Never let anyone or anything stop you from achieving your dreams!

5. **You must write down your goals.** There are magical powers in writing out your personal mission statement, your goals, and your daily to-do list. Make sure your goals are challenging goals and not something that belongs on your daily to-do list.

6. **A person with goals makes every minute count.** Fifteen-minute increments are important to high achievers, while ineffective people think in days and weeks. Maximize the moment. Your time is precious—don't waste it!

7. **Your impulses will ruin you and personal discipline will set you free.** Organization is the difference between living your life as a "meaningful specific" or living your life as a "wandering generality!"

CALL TO ACTION:

1. First you must accept the fact that there are laws. Then you must master these laws to create your destiny.

2. Start by being responsible and accountable for yourself. Set aside major time to design the life you've always dreamed about.

3. Start right now: keep a daily to-do list immediately, and commit to completing a mission statement, a dream list, your written goals, and a detailed financial budget.

WHAT YOU CAN ACCOMPLISH:

Going through the exercise of planning your life and writing out your goals will place you in the top 3% of the people in the world—those who have written goals for their life. By designing your destiny and following your passion, your dreams will become reality. Your life's work will be more meaningful because it reflects your plans and not someone else's plans for your life. Your life will be more exciting and fulfilling once you know where you are going and how you will get there.

Sources & Inspiration

The information in these books is powerful. I urge you to buy these books and read them over and over again until they become part of your daily life.

Stephan R. Covey, *The 7 Habits of Highly Effective People,* (Simon & Schuster, New York, N.Y. 1989)

Phillip C. McGraw, Ph.D., *Life Strategies,* (Hyperion, New York, N.Y. 1999)

Brain Tracy, *Maximum Achievement,* (Fireside Books, New York, N.Y. 1993)

Hyrum W. Smith, *The 10 Natural Laws of Successful Time and Life Management,* (Warner Books, New York, N.Y. 1994)

Julie Morgenstern, *Time Management From The Inside Out,* (Owl Books, Henry Holt, New York, N.Y. 2000)

Lisa Rogak, *Smart Guide to Managing Your Time,* (John Wiley and Sons, New York, N.Y. 1999)

Stephanie Winston, *The Organized Executive,* (Warner Books, New York, N.Y. 1994)

Michelle Passoff, *Lighten Up!,* (Harper Perennial, New York, N.Y. 1998)

Julie Morgenstern, *Organizing From The Inside Out,* (Owl Books, Henry Holt, New York, N.Y. 1998)

Ronni Eisenberg with Katie Kelly, *Organize Your Office,* (Hyperion, New York, N.Y. 1998)

Barbara Hemphill, *Kiplinger's Taming the Paper Tiger at Home,* (Kiplinger's Books, Washington, D.C. 1998)

Lesson Three: LifeSkills Mastery

Lesson Three: LifeSkills Mastery

Live an extraordinary lifestyle!

This section explains the importance of change in your life. It also drives home the point that your accomplishments are predicated on your discipline to master these LifeSkills and taking MASSIVE ACTION. Positive living is built on a foundation of positive thinking and the development of healthy nurturing relationships. Your lifestyle will depend on the quality of your thinking, the quality of your language, and the quality of your people skills.

LifeSkills Mastery includes 14 major LifeSkills that are the foundation for living an extraordinary lifestyle. Each lesson builds on the preceding lesson. Mastering these LifeSkills will give you an incredible toolbox of powerful tools to build the life of your dreams.

PURPOSE:

In order for you to become something more than you are right now, you must stretch to places you have never been before. The same thinking and behaviors that got you to where you are now are not the thinking and behaviors that you will need to stretch to where you want to be tomorrow! This requires you to acknowledge the things that are wrong in your life in order for you to change for the better.

Change is the catalyst for all self-improvement. If you don't change, this world is going to pass you by and you are going to be left standing in the dust wondering what happened. LifeSkills will help you master change instead of being the victim of change.

**If we did all the things we are capable of doing,
we would literally astound ourselves!**
— Thomas A. Edison

LifeSkills Mastery

There are 14 powerful LifeSkills, which will let you experience a rich and rewarding life of accomplishment, achievement, and personal fulfillment. I have listed one non-LifeSkill—Gossip, because it is the downfall of many good people. There are three major areas of LifeSkills that will determine the quality of your life: your THINKING SKILLS, your LANGUAGE SKILLS, and your PEOPLE SKILLS.

MASTER THESE LIFESKILLS FOR A MORE POWERFUL YOU!

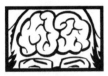 # THINKING SKILLS

THE POWER OF CHOICE: Throughout the day, you are making choices that determine your destiny. You are responsible for these choices. Make sure the choices you make are the right choices!

THE POWER OF PERSONAL RESPONSIBILITY: Before you can do anything, you must accept the fact: **You are responsible for your life.** It's up to you to take charge of your destiny.

THE POWER OF CHANGE: The major lesson to be learned here is that all change doesn't happen "out there," but within you. Change how you think and watch how the world changes.

THE POWER OF LEARNING: Lifelong learning is your key to dealing with change. Curiosity gets you going. Reading is a major part of learning. Being "teachable" opens many doors of opportunity and learning is the opportunity that is available to everyone. Thinking creates knowledge, which is power, and "Positive Thinking" turbocharges your creativity!

THE POWER OF ATTITUDE: Your attitude is the number one quality that makes everything else possible. Positive thinking creates a positive attitude. Attitude determines your outcome.

THE POWER OF POSITIVE ENERGY: For a life filled with vitality and positive results, make sure everything you do is done with positive energy. Energize!

THE POWER OF ACTION: Nothing happens until you take MASSIVE ACTION.

 # LANGUAGE SKILLS

THE POWER OF YOUR VOICE: Everyone has a "voice." What you think matters. Start speaking up and letting the world know that what you have to say is important!

THE POWER OF LANGUAGE: How you talk will determine how successful you are in life. It is one of the building blocks of relationships and a quick indicator of how you think.

THE MAGICAL POWERS OF ASKING: You will never get anywhere in life if you don't ask. Your ability to ask is one of the skills you need to master to open the doors of opportunity.

 # PEOPLE SKILLS

THE POWER OF RELATIONSHIPS: Everything you do is tied to the success of your relationships—your family life, your marriage, your career, and your friends.

THE POWER OF HONESTY: How you relate in your relationships depends on your ability to be honest and say what's on your mind in a way that is constructive, nurturing, and positive.

THE DESTRUCTIVE POWER OF GOSSIP: It is so destructive but yet so tantalizing that many people never know when they are engaged in it. You must get rid of this deadly cancer!

THE POWER OF FORGIVENESS: Part of learning is making many mistakes. Sometimes your mistakes affect other people. Your ability to forgive quickly will allow others to forgive you.

THE POWER OF CHOICE

The power of your decisions, or the choices you make every day, determine the quality of the life you live. From the moment you wake up until you go to bed at night, you are making choices that will affect your present situation and your future.

Things just don't happen to us, we set up our circumstances by the choices we make. Everything that happens to us is the result of our choices. When we get up in the morning we choose our attitudes for the day. We can be positive, encouraging, and uplifting or we can be moody, blameful, and ornery. We choose our friends and choose to be influenced by them whether their motives are good or bad. We choose how we are going to handle our daily challenges. They can defeat us, or we can choose to be proactive in finding solutions. We can choose to be victims or we can choose to be victors.

We all wake up feeling grumpy from time to time. Most people choose to hang onto their grumpiness and then proceed to make everyone else miserable as well. It doesn't need to be like this. You can make up your mind that you are going to be in control of your attitude. Regardless of how down in the dumps you may feel, you can choose to be energetic, positive, and cheerful. If you choose enthusiasm, your day will turn out to be a great one even if it didn't start out that way. If you are going around sucking on lemons, how do you expect your circumstances to change for the better? It's all about choice, and only you can control the choices you make in your life.

> One ship sails east, and another west
> With the same winds that blow.
> 'Tis the set of the sails and not the gales
> That decides the way we go.
> Like the winds of the sea are the ways of fate
> As they voyage along through life.
> 'Tis the will of the soul that decides its goals
> And not the calm or the strife.
>
> — Ella Wheeler Wilcox

WISDOM KEY

Your "voice," or the choices you make, are important! Even not making a choice is making a choice! How you think and the choices you make matter. Everyone is important and the choices they make or don't make affect us all. Never abdicate your responsibility to humanity by not choosing to let your "voice" be heard.

You have an affect on our national economy by the choices you make with your dollars. The restaurants you choose to patronize. The movies you choose to see. The department stores where you choose to spend your money. The cars, groceries, clothes, and everything else you buy are all choices. Business owners and politicians are interested in the choices you make with your dollars and your votes.

The power of choice is an awesome responsibility and you are in total control of your decisions. You can choose to be productive at work or you can choose just to put in your time and complain about having to work. You can choose to persist and doggedly never give up or you can take the easy way out and quit. You can choose a life of mediocrity or you can choose to live at the summit. Choose good not evil. Choose success not failure. Choose to be enthusiastic. Choose to be responsible. Choose to live a life free from excuses. Choose to be a positive difference in your family, at work, and in your community.

The Choice is Yours   —Native Wisdom

One of the most important discoveries made by my generation is that by changing our attitudes, we can change our lives. It's a choice we all have.
— William James

I believe that we are solely responsible for our choices, and we have to accept the consequences of every deed, word, and thought throughout our lifetime.
— Elisabeth Kübler-Ross

THE POWER OF PERSONAL RESPONSIBILITY
"If It's To Be, It's Up To Me!"

The only way you will achieve your dreams is to start taking charge of your life.
I'm not talking about doing whatever you want, because we all have to answer to
someone. I'm talking about taking full responsibility for yourself. If you are to have a
more rewarding lifestyle, you have to understand this very basic philosophy—

It's all up to you…

WISDOM KEY

**One of the hardest lessons for anyone to learn is that you are
100% responsible for yourself.** You are where you are in life
because of the decisions that you have made and actions that you
have taken. Taking responsibility for yourself is not easy. It's always
easier to blame someone else for the bad things that have happened
in your life. Yes, maybe you were a victim but you can't use this as an
excuse for not moving forward. The reason why you can't use excuses
to justify the problems in your life is because you are responsible for
making the decisions to move forward with your life. Living a life as
a successful adult requires you to accept full responsibility for your
actions. **From Now On—No More Excuses.**

YOU WILL NEVER ACHIEVE SUCCESS UNTIL YOU FIRST
UNDERSTAND THE POWER OF RESPONSIBILITY, BECAUSE
IT IS RESPONSIBILITY THAT CREATES SUCCESS
AND THE PRICE OF SUCCESS IS MORE RESPONSIBILITY!

I AM RESPONSIBLE! I AM ACCOUNTABLE!

*From this day forward, I will live my life free of excuses.
I will live my life accepting full responsibility for
my decisions, actions, and behaviors.*

Start Living A Life Free of Excuses!

Achieving your life's dreams is as simple as changing how you think and how you conduct yourself. You need to get rid of your bad habits and start replacing them with good habits. Start believing in yourself and looking forward to your future positively with unrestrained optimism.

Whenever I tell people this, the first thing they say is: "**YEAH BUT,** you don't understand how hard it is to be in my position! You just don't understand." Start by getting rid of the "yeah buts," and quit feeling sorry for yourself...

I AM AMAZED HOW MANY PEOPLE I MEET WHO THINK THAT THEY ARE REGULAR FOLKS MAKING AN HONEST AVERAGE WAGE, BUT CAN'T QUITE UNDERSTAND WHY THEIR LIVES ARE MISERABLE AND UNEVENTFUL. TAKING RESPONSIBILITY FOR THEIR OWN DESTINY WOULD BE UNTHINKABLE.

JUST LISTENING TO THEM TALK, I QUICKLY UNDERSTAND THAT THEY DON'T HAVE ONE NICE WORD TO SAY ABOUT ANYTHING. THEY COMPLAIN ABOUT THE WEATHER. THEY ARE QUICK TO GOSSIP ABOUT THEIR FRIENDS AND NEIGHBORS. THEY COMPLAIN ABOUT THEIR JOBS, THE ECONOMY, INFLATION, AND THEIR HEALTH. THEY ARE VERY HAPPY WALLOWING IN THEIR OWN PITY PARTIES.

WHAT'S EVEN MORE INTERESTING, IS WHEN THEY FIND OUT THAT SOMEONE ELSE'S PITY PARTY IS EVEN MORE DOWN AND OUT THAN THEIRS... THEY'LL GO JOIN THAT ONE!

Sometimes it's our friends, neighbors, and relatives that hold us back. Well-meaning relatives and friends can sabotage our plans to better our lives by their disbelief, nonsupport, and ridicule. How they conduct their own affairs, their habits, and their behaviors can affect how we turn out. Pay close attention to how they talk. What are their ambitions? Are they similar to yours? If not, distance yourself from anyone whose ideas are not congruent with your goals.

In order for you to change, at times it is necessary for you to distance yourself from the negative circumstances and harmful effects of toxic people around you.

There's an old saying–

 IF YOU LAY DOWN WITH DOGS, IT'S ALMOST CERTAIN
THAT YOU WILL END UP WITH FLEAS TOO!

If you are not satisfied with your life as it is right now, all you have to do is take a strong honest look at yourself and answer these questions…

- What are you reading and when is the last time you've pushed yourself to learn something new?
- How often are you watching TV and what are you watching?
- What bad habits do you have? Where did you get these bad habits?
- What kind of goals do you have for yourself? Are they meaningful goals that you have written down or are they just a "wish list" that you keep in your head?
- Does your music make you happy and do the lyrics match your values?
- Just look at who you are hanging around with. Do these people challenge you to become better? Or do they encourage you to engage in destructive behaviors?

I find television very educating. Every time somebody turns on the set I go into the other room and read a book.

— Groucho Marx

If you have friends that are whiners and complainers quit hanging around them. Don't let their negative toxicity pollute your positive thinking. Positive thinking, positive language, and positive behavior are the things you need to do immediately if your life is going to get better.

True friends will always be supportive if you want to change for the better. If they don't, you are hangin' with the wrong crowd.

YOU MAY NOT GET YOUR FRIENDS TO CHANGE,
BUT YOU CAN CHANGE YOUR FRIENDS!

How you see yourself is more important than the opinions of your peer group.
Good friends and positive thinking associates are OK. But if you fall into the habit of
seeking approval from unworthy peers, it will always be difficult to elevate yourself past
their expectations and rise above deceitful value systems. Isn't strange that we often
strive to seek approval from the people who could care less about us, rather than the
people who really love us just for who we are?

**It is dangerous to give in to the notion that the attitudes and opinions of others
are more important than your own!** A desire to emulate may be considered the norm
in given age groups, but do not allow this to sway self-worth or affect your future. Your
dreams and your goals are more important than other people's opinions.

Here's the most important point: When you try to be like everyone else, you no
longer are yourself. And not being yourself keeps you from striving to become all YOU
can be! Another critical point: In a few years, such people will be out of your life, but
their influence can continue to affect your attitude, behavior, integrity, and spirituality.
Negative influences of today's peer group will dog you the rest of your life.

**Never underestimate the negative or positive
influences of your peer group!**

Refuse to belittle yourself because of someone's careless comments. Instead of
seeking approval of others by trying to be like them, your goal should be to discover
how awesome YOU can become. Opinions YOU hold concerning yourself will always
be more valuable than those of any peer group! Visualize yourself as being the most
awesome, brilliant, creative, fun, cheerful and caring person who ever lived! Always feel
good about who YOU are. After all, YOU are the greatest!!!

Personal responsibility means making tough decisions. While it may be hard to
leave your friends, you have to ask yourself, "Are my friends helping me to become a
better person?" If not, then you have to do what's best for your life. If you are going to
change for the better you must make up your mind to start doing things differently.
Personal responsibility is all about you!

You have everything within you, right now, to start living a remarkable life.
Today is the beginning of the rest of your life. What happened yesterday doesn't matter
anymore because today is a brand new day. From this day forward, quit living in the
past. The only thing that matters is that today "God Loves You Forever" and you are
incredibly special.

Take responsibility for yourself. From now on, excuses no longer count. Only you
can do what it takes to better yourself. Only you can make the changes. Start today.

WISDOM KEY

Believe in yourself. Believe in your dreams. Today is "your day." All of the forces are aligned right now in God's Great Universe to bring you unlimited opportunity and fortune. All you have to do is believe this and accept God's gift of blessings and abundance. So pledge to yourself that you will never let anyone hold you down. Pledge to yourself that you will become all that you can be. From the time you were born, you were meant for achievement. God designed you for accomplishment. Start by challenging yourself to have a more positive outlook. Make up your mind to live in the positive.

If it's to be, it's up to me.

This Day Is A Brand New Day

This is the beginning of a brand new day.
God has given you this day to do as you will.
What you do with this day is important.
Because you are exchanging a day of your life for it.
So pledge to yourself
That this day shall be for:
Gain not loss.
Good not evil.
Success not failure.
For when tomorrow comes this day will be gone forever...
Leaving in its place whatever you have traded for it.

— Unknown

Make Today the First Day of the Rest of Your Life.

Today is a brand new day!

Today is a clean slate.

Live it positively!

THE POWER OF CHANGE

> IF YOU ALWAYS DO WHAT YOU ALWAYS DID, YOU'RE ALWAYS GOING TO GET WHAT YOU ALWAYS GOT!

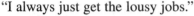

Become the master of change rather than the victim of it. Everybody wants a better lifestyle, but if you ask them how come things aren't getting better for them, they all pretty much have the same responses:

"I always just get the lousy jobs."
"I never have anything but bad luck."
"My boss is out to get me."

Many people wish the world would change. They want their circumstances to change; they want the people around them to change. They complain that nobody understands them. Unfortunately, this complaining and blamefulness only leads to consuming frustration that festers and eventually eats them up. It's as bad as a deadly cancer.

Do you want a happier more rewarding life? Here's the nitty gritty... The world around you isn't going to change until you change!

Be the change you want to see in the world.
— Mahatma Ghandi

And just because you decide to change—things don't happen overnight. The process takes time. You must be patient. The important thing to remember is that you *can* change. The key is to start. Make a decision and act on it.

Bottom line—

It's up to you to change your life for the better.

Change or you're history! The agricultural age lasted for thousands of years. The industrial age lasted for a hundred years. The information age lasted only several decades. Today we are in the communication age where change is happening so fast that what we produce today is obsolete by tomorrow. If you are not willing to change, this world will pass you by so fast you'll be left spinning in the dust wondering what just happened to you!

Today more change happens in one day of your life than in 10 years of your parents' lives. So if you are not committed to learning new things on a daily basis, you are quickly going to become history.

Today change is happening faster!

In fact, change is accelerating so fast that 50% of the Fortune 500 companies listed on the stock exchange in 1980 don't even exist today! 80% of all consumable products that we use today did not exist five years ago.

Before the written word, our knowledge mass doubled every thousand years. Once we had the written word, our knowledge mass started doubling every hundred years. The computer age caused our knowledge mass to double every decade. According to Moore's Law, computer capacity is doubling every 18 months. Today technology and the Internet are causing our knowledge mass to double in months, and soon it will double in just days!

WISDOM KEY

One thing is for certain—you will change. You can't prevent change and things will never be the same—that's guaranteed! Instead of being passive and letting change happen to you, you can become a catalyst for change. <u>You can either be the victim of change or the master of change.</u> Take charge now and design the changes in your life. Become the architect of your destiny!

For many people, change is more threatening than challenging. They see it as the destroyer of what is familiar and comfortable rather than the creator of what is new and exciting.

— Nido Qubein

THE DEFINITION OF "INSANITY" IS DOING THE SAME THING OVER AND OVER AGAIN AND EXPECTING DIFFERENT RESULTS!

Get your own world right by taking charge of the change in your life. Quit frustrating yourself by wishing everyone or everything around you would change—start spending your time and energy changing yourself. If you start thinking more positively and working to better yourself, you'll be amazed at how the world around you will change for the better!

Change your thoughts and you change your world.

— Norman Vincent Peale

Life is about CHANGE!

Getting out of your "comfort zone" is the key to all change!

One of the major laws of the universe is the Universal Law of Constant Change. The only guarantee in life is change. Even if you are not willing to change, **what's around you *will change you*** whether you like it or not. And this is where people get frustrated. They want things to be like they used to be and wonder why life is so difficult. If only they understood that change is good for them, they would start looking for opportunities to grow rather than falling victim to the false security of the "good old days."

Breaking outside of your comfort zone is hard. Many people avoid change because it can be painful. Pushing yourself out of your comfort zone can be challenging and awkward. Going where you have never been before causes uncertainty. In your quest for change, you must be willing to push yourself. In life, there is no security—only opportunity. Successful people don't wait for someone to drag

them out of their comfort zones—they do it themselves. They understand that if they become too content, they're going to stagnate and die.

Doing things that might fail and cause embarrassment is tough. Nobody wants to fail. But staying in your comfort zone dooms you to a life of frustration, mediocrity, and just being average.

Why settle for just being average?

The definition of AVERAGE is being the best of the worst and being the worst of the best! Don't settle for being "just average." God gave us all the same opportunity to accomplish great things. Every one of us has been designed for accomplishment. Believe in yourself! Work to constantly improve yourself. Embrace change.

WISDOM KEY

> People embrace change when it is their decision but fiercely oppose "being changed"!

Good, better, best…never let it rest,
until the good gets better and your better best!

This is a philosophy for life! It's up to you to challenge yourself to improve, to learn more, to raise your own standards of excellence every day of your life. Excellence is not an option—it is a way of life.

Every day in every way, I get better every day!

There Are 5 Ways People Deal With Change:

1. Some people want to change but only think about it.
2. Some people are not ready for change because they are afraid of losing things they are familiar with. They are afraid of the unknown.
3. Some people fight change because they are afraid of losing the things they love to do (impulses or cravings satisfied by not having to think, and a lack of personal discipline).
4. Some people want to change so fast they are impatient. They expect to have overnight success without understanding the process, without preparing for change, and without work—as a result they fail miserably.
5. Some people understand that change is a process, and they prepare for it. Instead of being victims of change, they are proactive—they design the changes in their lives and are willing to take action.

Two major lessons about change:

- **We need to be proficient at change.** It requires flexibility, curiosity, adaptability, quickness, and a willingness to learn.
- **Change requires surrendering old thinking.** We need to be sensitive enough to recognize when change needs to happen and be willing to surrender old thinking and old ways of doing things.

The day you quit changing is the day you die!

Many people's tombstones should read…

DEAD at 30. BURIED at 60!

Today Change is Opportunity

This is an important lesson—everybody has opportunity. And opportunity is created from knowledge. You don't have to be a genius; you just have to be willing to learn. In the old days the wealthy owned things—such as gold, oil, land. Or they owned businesses and factories. Today, the world's richest people own knowledge. Take Bill Gates, the world's richest man. His first priority in growing his company is to hire the world's most brilliant thinkers. He fully understands the power of owning knowledge.

It's no longer about "self"—it's all about "serving others." In the old days, leaders gave orders and demanded respect. Today, leaders serve others and empower others to become better. Anybody can become a leader if they're good at helping others grow.

In the old days, people hoarded knowledge because it gave them job security. Today, your value is determined by how proficient you are at helping others become more knowledgeable. Your greatest hope for job security is to be able to train others or pass on knowledge.

Your ability to "learn and change" is more vital than "seniority." With change happening so fast, seniority can almost be a liability unless you stay current. If you walk into a job interview and say that you have 10 or more years experience, that may mean you are old—a dinosaur!

Think about it. Is it 10 years of constantly learning something new every day and challenging yourself to continually grow and become better every year? Or, is it really 10 years of one years experience? All you have to do is look at where you are in life, and you will get your answer.

Life is about growing and changing yourself, not the world around you. The day you understand that you cannot change the world, but you can change yourself, is the day your life becomes less frustrating and starts changing for the better. Don't wait for someone to tell you how to change. It's your responsibility. You can improve your life just by paying attention to what you put into your mind and by watching those you associate with.

> **All of our dreams come true if we have**
> **the courage and dedication to pursue them.**
> — Walt Disney

> **If you think you have things under control,**
> **you're not going fast enough!**
> — Mario Andretti

THE POWER OF LEARNING
Learning is a Lifelong Adventure.

For most of the world, students spend their formative years
in school learning how to "earn a living." Jump-start your life
by engaging mind, body, and spirit by "designing your destiny."
Learning is your ticket to an amazing journey
of self-discovery and self-improvement.

I AM ON A RAMPAGE OF LEARNING! TWO OF THE THINGS THAT I HATED MOST WHEN I WAS A KID WERE STUDYING AND WORK. LIKE MOST KIDS WHEN I GRADUATED FROM HIGH SCHOOL, I THREW MY BOOKS UP IN THE AIR AND PROCLAIMED THAT I WAS FREE! I ACTUALLY THOUGHT I WAS THROUGH WITH SCHOOLING AND THAT I WOULD NEVER HAVE TO READ AGAIN! I HATED SCHOOL.

I NOW KNOW THAT IGNORANCE IS PRISON AND SERIOUS LEARNING CREATES GREAT FREEDOM. TODAY STUDYING AND WORK ARE MY PASSIONS. I OFTEN TELL PEOPLE THAT I AM ON A RAMPAGE OF LEARNING. I AM A VORACIOUS READER. I READ BETWEEN ONE AND TWO BOOKS A WEEK, AT LEAST 20-30 MAGAZINES A MONTH AND AT LEAST 2-3 NEWSPAPERS DAILY.

I CAN'T EVEN SIT ON THE FAMILY THRONE THESE DAYS WITHOUT A GOOD BOOK IN HAND!

When I was a boy of fourteen,
my father was so ignorant
I could hardly stand to have the
old man around. But when
I got to be twenty-one, I was
astonished at how much he had
learned in seven years.
— Mark Twain

Learning Will Change Your Life

For the first time in history, people can leapfrog into the rarest levels of wealth with only knowledge. Bill Gates' success began as an idea and is built on a foundation of knowledge. No longer is wealth available to a privileged few who own factories, oil wells, real estate, or transportation. Now, anyone with a "willingness to learn" can plunge into the new millennium of unlimited opportunity.

People used to say, "The sky's the limit." Today the sky is no longer the limit! Today, we are witnessing an unprecedented display of accelerated learning and innovation. Smaller, faster, cheaper, more powerful computers are now available to people of all economic and social classes. Teenagers who aren't even old enough to drive around the block are exploring the world's Internet highways.

We are on the forefront of biotechnological wonders that are rewriting our understanding of reproduction, aging, and diseases. We are creating plants that through genetics are immune to diseases and can protect themselves from unfriendly insects. In the future, our medicines will be specifically tailored to our DNA code.

Innovation is everywhere. New products hit the market faster than ever before. It used to take an industry years to bring a new product to the marketplace. Today, any teenager can come up with a new idea and via the Internet be "global" with just one stroke of a keypad! Today, anyone can access the world marketplace from their home.

Reading Will Change Your Life

Developing a passion for learning begins at home at a young age. My parents read books to us kids every night before we went to bed. Even though my passion for the written word started early, reading was difficult for me at first. I often struggled with comprehension and became very frustrated. Finally, I took a course on reading from Evelyn Woods Speed Reading Seminars. What I learned in this course significantly impacted my everyday life. Reading has become easy and enjoyable. I now feed my hunger for knowledge by reading two to three hours a day! That's how committed I am to lifelong learning. And the more I read, the better my comprehension and retention become. Books have the power to change lives.

A PERSON WHO CAN READ, AND DOESN'T, IS JUST AS TRAGIC AS THE PERSON WHO CANNOT READ AT ALL.

How big is your library? You can judge the success of a person by the size of his or her library. What kind of books, if any, do you read? When was the last time you made an all-out effort to learn something new?

Every day you're not learning, you're losing. If you don't have a personal desire to learn each day, you will find the world is passing you by so fast you won't have a clue. When is the last time you reinvented yourself for the better? You need to learn new skills and achieve self-discovery. You have incredible talents that are waiting to be discovered and internal resources that are just waiting to be unleashed. Reading is the key to unlocking your inner wealth.

Learning is the catalyst that stimulates thought...

Thoughts become ideas.
Ideas become dreams.
From dreams a vision is born.
Visions can change the world.

Formal schooling is just the beginning of lifelong learning. For our parents, the "learning experience" was pretty much a one-time affair: go to school—go to work. Today, that is no longer true. With more change happening in one day of your life than in 10 years of your parents' lives, you need to be constantly reinventing yourself through self-learning. Make a personal commitment to daily self-improvement.

Graduation frees you. No longer dictated by what you must study, you will be free to explore your passionate interests. The sooner you realize your true passion in life, the sooner you can begin a daily learning program that will be with you the rest of your life.

TODAY, THE END OF A PERSON'S FORMAL EDUCATION IS REALLY ONLY A JUMP-START TOWARD A MUCH MORE SERIOUS PERSONAL LIFELONG QUEST FOR GREATER UNDERSTANDING AND A MORE REWARDING PERSONAL COMMITMENT TO LIFELONG LEARNING. THE TRUE PURPOSE OF YOUR FORMAL EDUCATION IS NOT TO STUFF YOURSELF FULL OF FACTS BUT TO GAIN THE SKILLS YOU NEED TO SUCCESSFULLY TEACH YOURSELF.

Use it or lose it! Begin a daily discipline of reading to learn. Engage in learning that challenges you. Your mind is like a muscle—if it is not used, it will atrophy. But if you challenge yourself, it will be limitless.

Be childlike in your learning. When children are learning, they recognize no boundaries. They are fearlessly curious. Their minds are free to wander and wonder. With imaginations running at full speed, they aren't embarrassed when it comes to acting out their fantasies. They are flexible in an instant and ready to try something new. Quit pretending to be smart. Sometimes it's better to be childlike—curious and full of wonderment!

Be a student of life and an observer of lifestyle. I study what people wear, what they are eating, what they are driving, what they are listening to and what they are reading. Developing these people-watching skills will help you determine changing trends in society. Understanding trends will help you create both relationships and new opportunities.

Learning stimulates creativity. I have always said, *"I see opportunities that other people do not see."* This creative ability is a direct result of my commitment to reading and lifelong learning.

Isn't it interesting that only the wise seek knowledge!

Knowledge...don't leave school without it!

It's not what you know that makes you smart. One key lesson about learning is that... *What you think you know may already be irrelevant!* Never assume for one second that what you think you know makes you a smart person. The world is changing too fast for anyone to be a "know-it-all."

"Being Right" is one of the most destructive blocks to your personal growth.

Most people overestimate what they think they know. This causes them to think they are "right." Once they think they are right, they set up "walls of defensiveness" to protect their "right to be right." Always thinking you're right blocks out new opportunities for learning and self-discovery.

Practice having an open mind. Never go through life thinking you are the only one who has everything all figured out. Encourage yourself to have an open, inquisitive mind, a mind open to new ideas, new thoughts, and new ways of doing things.

See yourself as a gigantic thirsty sponge eagerly soaking up information, knowledge, wisdom, and new experiences.

Don't be cheap when it comes to feeding your mind!

If you think education is expensive, try ignorance.
— Derek Bok

For the first time in history, we are living in a world where information and knowledge is readily available—make use of it.

WHEN I WAS GROWING UP, LIBRARIES WERE THE MAIN SOURCE OF INFORMATION. BOOKSTORES WERE SMALL STOREFRONTS WITH LIMITED SELECTIONS. BOOKS ON TAPE WERE NONEXISTENT AND SELF-HELP AUDIO/VISUAL TAPES WERE ONLY AVAILABLE TO MAJOR CORPORATIONS THAT COULD AFFORD THE THOUSANDS OF DOLLARS IT COST TO BUY THEM.

TODAY, BOOKSTORES ARE HUGE MEGA-STORES HANDLING MILLIONS OF TITLES, AND THE INTERNET HAS EXPLODED, MAKING GLOBAL INFORMATION AVAILABLE TO ANYONE OLD ENOUGH TO TURN ON A COMPUTER. KNOWLEDGE IS NOW AVAILABLE TO EVERYONE.

- **Learning is unlimited; it has no beginning and no end.**
- **Learning is continuous; therefore your reading should be constant.**

Sixty years ago, I knew everything; now I know nothing. Education is the progressive discovery of our own ignorance.
— Will Durant

There are other benefits to reading...

Reading will improve your vocabulary and writing ability! One of the greatest benefits of reading is that your other communicative skills are further developed almost as if by osmosis! The more you read, the better your vocabulary becomes, and your writing skills may even improve. Whatever you do in life, whether it be business, recreation, or personal—your relationship skills will be greatly enhanced the better you are able to communicate. Plus, reading gives you something to talk about. People who don't read, generally only talk about each other! So read, read, read!

Turn your car into a "University on Wheels!" Every car that I have owned since I was 19 has had a cassette tape player in it. Every time I go somewhere, I listen to books on tape or CDs. Did you know that in three years, just in the amount of time that you spend riding around in your car, if you listened to books on tape you could gain the equivalency of a college education? I am living proof that this works. When I was in high school, I was in the bottom half of the class. But because every day since high school I have listened to books on tape in my car, I have a Master's Degree from Harvard University, even though I don't have an undergraduate degree. So stop looking at your car as just transportation; and start looking at your car as your "University on Wheels!" (Recommended audio books page 479)

Start a daily learning program.

- Read books that challenge you, not just entertain you.
- Reread good books often. You'll learn something new every time and remember more.
- Develop an intense passion and a burning desire to learn success principles.
- Listen to audiobooks in your car. Make your car a "University on Wheels!"
- Buy or rent educational videos.
- Explore the Internet.
- Associate with people who can mentor you. Choose your friends carefully.
- Join community organizations and volunteer for something new.
- Get involved in a church that is "alive," with a spiritual leader who will stimulate your thinking.
- Attend lectures and seminars conducted by successful people in your industry.
- Go back to school. Take evening courses. Always learn from the best.
- Teach. Become a mentor to someone else. Mentoring another person is an awesome responsibility that shouldn't be taken lightly. It will force you to do your homework, but the rewards are priceless.
- Learn how to write. Always keep paper and a pen handy and write down everything.
- Write your own book. Keep a journal of your thoughts, ideas, dreams, goals, and things that you have learned.
- **Start a "Great Idea of the Week" book!** By the end of the year, you will have 52 great ideas about how you can improve your life. That's powerful!

If your life is worth living, your life is worth recording.
— Jim Rohn

**Freedom allows innovation
and inventiveness to flourish.**

The value of learning is freedom.

1. Freedom to learn creates curiosity with a sense of wonderment. This is the beginning of knowledge and wisdom.

2. Freedom to learn allows you to be fearless and courageous so you can go where no one has ever gone before.

3. Freedom to learn allows you to make mistakes so you can really learn!

4. Freedom to learn is being open-minded, not prejudging what you are about to learn.

5. Freedom to learn allows you to see the possibility of something new and great that others cannot or are unwilling to see or accept.

6. Freedom to learn allows you to keep your own sense of purpose when everyone says it can't be done and claims that you are crazy.

7. Freedom to learn is faith in yourself—believing that you are capable of learning how to do innovative and incredible things in life.

8. Freedom to learn is unlimited. Learning is unlimited and keeps you from giving up until your vision has manifested itself into reality. Learning stimulates this driving force within you.

9. Freedom to learn gives you access to resources and opens "Doors of Opportunity."

10. Freedom to learn is the beginning of all creativity.

Learn a New Word Every Day

**The more words you know,
the faster you can comprehend.
The more you can comprehend,
the faster you can read.
The more you can read,
the more knowledgeable you'll become.
Knowledge creates opportunity and freedom.**

**WISDOM
KEY**

You should pursue knowledge with greater intensity than the most exhausting physical labor you do. Your passion for knowledge should be greater than the pursuit of money. However, in the long run, when the passion for learning is at its height, people of great knowledge will attract unlimited wealth.

CURIOSITY IS POWER

Learning Life—Takes a Lifetime!

**Use what talents you possess.
The woods would be silent if only
those birds sang, that sang best.**
— Henry Van Dyke

Read to Achieve!

THE POWER OF A WINNING ATTITUDE!

Being a winner isn't about talent or smarts, it's about how positive and cheerfully determined you are. Your spirit of optimism will turn obstacles into opportunities, adversities into challenges, and fears into confidence.

My Happy, Cheerful, Positive Attitude!

*Attitude is the most valuable quality we possess! Many doors of opportunity have been opened because of my cheerfulness and enthusiasm, and these doors can open for you! Are you dull, or do you **sparkle!** Chunks of coal can become **diamonds!** An attitude of perseverance and determination kept me from quitting when I thought of giving up on my dreams. Now, my attitude of gratefulness keeps me humble and thankful for all God-given blessings. My attitude of hope and a positive outlook have helped me believe in myself when others said it couldn't be done. My attitude is my responsibility. I must constantly be aware that negative attitudes of others do not influence my positive thinking. I refuse to become discouraged, regardless of challenges, adversities or problems that may arise. Wherever I go, and whatever I do, I will strive to be a breath of fresh air to all. My happy cheerful, enthusiastic and encouraging attitude will be my legacy. This is my free-hearted gift to the world!*

— Famous Dave Anderson

Your winning attitude must come from within. Regardless of your past circumstances or failures, if you never ever give up on yourself and continue to strive for achievement, you will win! Your positive mental attitude empowers you to become the person of your dreams!

Success does not happen by accident!

Others can stop you temporarily, but you are the only one who can do it permanently!

— Eleanor Roosevelt

 YOU MUST HAVE UNSHAKABLE BELIEF THAT YOU WILL WIN!

Don't ever let anyone talk you out of your dreams! Most people will never experience the incredible rewards of reaching their fullest potential because someone has talked them out of it! Don't let this happen to you. You must believe in yourself. God meant for you to have nothing but the best in life. Don't let your attitude cheat you out of what you so clearly deserve.

God created us for achievement and accomplishment. Your destiny is to do great things. We were all born with an unlimited curiosity and an eagerness to try anything—the concept of failure is foreign. As time goes by, we learn boundaries and the sense of limitation through well-intentioned directives from parents and teachers. While we can't change our past, we can change our approach to learning. Instead of concentrating on boundaries, we need to shift our focus to our unlimited potential and ability to achieve by developing a winning attitude. A positive, confident, winning attitude is something we can learn.

What are you really afraid of...Failure? Success?

The biggest roadblock to developing a winning attitude is the fear of failure. Ironically, failures are actually building blocks in developing a winning attitude. If you never attempted to overcome what you feared, you would never achieve anything great. Failure creates experience. Don't be afraid of it. Learn from it. Turn your fears into your strengths.

WISDOM KEY

If you fail, quickly try again. The difference between winners and losers is how fast they get back into the game. Quitting is the easy way out. Winners are not quitters. Winners are determined and persistent. By not giving in and quitting, you will begin to conquer your own fears. Once you have conquered your fears, you will wonder, "Why didn't I try this sooner?" Determination conquers fear. Persistence conquers fear. Your attitude conquers fear.

Fear exists only in your mind.

Remember...worry is actually a form of intense meditation.
What you focus on will become your reality!

Don't make your fears come true! Constant worrying programs your mind to focus on something negative. Your higher conscious mind, not knowing the difference between right and wrong, will misunderstand your preoccupation with this fear and think it is something you really would like to see come true. In the spirit of trying to serve you, it will vigilantly do everything it can to help your fears become reality! To overcome your fears, it's important to quit worrying about things that have never happened.

For the thing which I greatly feared is come upon me,
and that which I was afraid of is come unto me.

— Job 3:25 (KJV)

The only way you can conquer your fears is to face them head-on. Remember, many people have gone down the same road before and conquered the very thing you fear the most. If they can do it, so can you. You have everything you need to conquer your fears. You can do it. In fact, you must do it! Conquering your fears helps build your self-esteem, which builds your self-confidence. You are now starting to build a winning attitude! It's really easier than you think.

What you can walk away from ...you have conquered.

What you cannot walk away from ...has conquered you.

WISDOM KEY

The most important step to overcoming your fears is to take action. Don't play into your fears. Doing what you fear the most is the only way to get rid of your fears. Repeating positive affirmations will help you mentally prepare yourself before you take action against your fears.

Just suck it up and go for it!

ONCE YOU START TO TAKE ACTION, YOU WILL FIND THAT JUST BY "STARTING THE PROCESS," YOUR FEARS WILL BEGIN TO MELT AWAY!

GET RID OF YOUR FEAR BY DOING SOMETHING YOU FEAR EVERY DAY.

Persistence

Nothing in the world can take the place of persistence.

Talent will not,
Nothing in the world is more common
than unsuccessful men with talent.

Genius will not,
Un-rewarded genius is almost a proverb.

Education will not,
The world is full of educated derelicts.

Persistence and determination alone is omnipotent.
— Calvin Coolidge

You Can't Stop Someone Who Won't Quit!
A winning mental attitude is the key to your future.

Your positive attitude will get you anything you want. Consider the important things in your life: career, family, good health, financial well-being, and the relationships within your community. Then ask yourself, "What are my goals in each of these areas?" Next, with complete honesty, take inventory of your current attitude. Is your attitude where it should be for you to achieve your goals? If you are going to have great goals, you must have a great, positive, enthusiastic attitude.

You will have to work on your attitude every single day of your life. When's the last time you consciously worked on developing a positive winning attitude? A great positive mental attitude just doesn't happen. You have to work at it…

DEVELOPING YOUR POSITIVE WINNING ATTITUDE IS JUST LIKE BATHING—YOU DON'T DO IT JUST WHEN YOU FEEL LIKE IT, YOU MUST DO IT EVERY DAY—AND CREATING A GREAT ATTITUDE IS SO MUCH MORE IMPORTANT THAN BATHING.

 THE DAY WE SAY WE DON'T CARE ABOUT WINNING IS THE DAY WE START BELIEVING THAT MEDIOCRITY IS ACCEPTABLE.

We must seek the positive. We are constantly surrounded with trash. Every day, we are bombarded by negativity—from the gossip of people we run into, to gratuitous programming on TV, and endless tragedies in the newspapers. Quit filling your mind with other people's nonsense!

The positive attitude you are nourishing and cultivating should be protected. It's the most valuable thing you possess. <u>From now on, start practicing selective listening.</u> Don't let others pollute your mind with their negative garbage.

Don't let other people's opinions determine your reality.

Negative thinking keeps you from succeeding in life. Negative thinkers consistently deny their lives are in a mess. They want everyone to think that their lives are just fine when actually they are dying inside. They truly want a better life, but in reality they don't believe they deserve the good things in life. They tend to find fault in, and gossip about, other people because they aren't happy with their own lives. Steer clear of people who have nothing good to say. Stay away from people who do nothing but gossip and complain. Your mind is too valuable; you must protect your mind at all times.

Negative thinkers are the first ones to give up. They have every so-called "good excuse" and justification why they can't get themselves out of bed to take on the world. They don't believe they have what it takes to win. When you don't believe in yourself and you don't have a clear picture of your future, you generally don't have hope for yourself.

Don't be a negative thinker. Live your life free from excuses. Don't justify why you can't do something—instead figure out how you can do something productive. Never compromise your values. Believe in yourself. Believe that God meant for you to experience a full and rewarding life. Cleanse your mind of all negativity.

WHAT YOU THINK ABOUT IS WHAT YOU WILL BECOME!

Feed your mind the pure, the clean, the powerful, and the positive. Don't feed your mind junk.

Believe that you are the most important person who has ever lived.

Believing that you are the "best" will attract other "best" people into your life, and together your output will be even greater!

**Whatever the mind of man can
conceive and believe, it can achieve.**
— Napoleon Hill

HAVE YOU EVER NOTICED WHEN KIDS' MINDS ARE MADE UP—THEY NEVER GIVE UP!

How I think determines my destiny!
A mind full of great ideas has no room for little ideas.

Success is something you have to work on every day. You need to read every day, because you can't cram a whole week's worth of reading into one Sunday night session. You need to exercise every day, because you can't squeeze a whole week's exercise program into one Saturday afternoon. You need to eat an apple a day, because you can't eat seven apples on Sunday night and expect the same healthy results. The same thing holds true for positive thinking. You need to work on creating a "healthy positive thinking mind" every day of your life.

How is your thinking? Don't have a clue? Record your thoughts. For one day, try to write down every thought. Next, look at what you've written and see if your thoughts are consistent with your dreams, goals, and aspirations in life.

You may be surprised at how you are thinking. If your thinking is not consistent with how you would like to be and where you want to end up in life, then you need to change. Start cultivating and nourishing your own positive winning attitude.

Start focusing on positive things:

- **Repeat positive affirmations many times a day**
- **Read positive mental attitude books, self-help books, and feel-good books**
- **Listen to motivational audio books on tape or CD**
- **Attend seminars and lectures by motivational speakers**
- **Be active in your local church**
- **Associate with other positive people who are trying to do good**
- **Practice thinking "no negative" thoughts**

Positive attitudes are related to positive relationships. Much of your success will be determined by the winning relationships you create. And the quality of those relationships will be determined by your attitude. Many people get this backward—they think the other person determines the quality of a relationship, and they always think it's the other person who has to change. The fact is: it's your attitude that determines the quality of your relationships. Get your attitude right and you'll be amazed how quickly the people around you seem to change!

The Golden Rule says, "Do unto others as you would have them do unto you." If you treat everyone you meet as the most important person in your life, you will be amazed at how people will respond to you.

In fact, there's an updated version of The Golden Rule: "Do unto others *'better'* than you would have them do unto you!"

WISDOM KEY

Positive relationships depend on really caring about people.
I believe our higher purpose in life is to make a positive difference in the world. By putting the welfare of others first, we can achieve so much more. The foundation of all winning relationships is how much people think you care about them. It's not, "What can I get?" Success is all about, "What can I give?" Give of yourself!

I have a personal greeting that has produced some pretty amazing results. When I meet people I tell them…

MY WHOLE PURPOSE IN LIFE IS JUST TO MAKE YOU HAPPY!

When you have cultivated a positive attitude, everyone will know. Your positive attitude will be evident in your facial expressions, your body language and the way you talk. Self-confidence will make you stand taller. You will glow with enthusiasm. This is called charisma.

Have you ever noticed when some people walk into a room, everything stops and everyone turns to see who just captured everyone's attention? That person seems to have a glow about them, and there is electricity flowing throughout the room. That person has charisma.

Charisma is catchy.
Charisma is the product of enthusiasm!

Enthusiasm!

It's one of the most awesome forces in the world.

All of us enjoy being around passionate people who bubble over with meaningful purpose. We look for something to believe in, and we crave positive change. Therefore, we are drawn to those with positive, winning attitudes, people who have fun living and make us feel good! Such enthusiastic, cheerful individuals exist, and YOU can be that person!

One man has enthusiasm for 30 minutes, another for 30 days, but it is the man who has it for 30 years who makes a success of his life.
— Edward B. Butler

YOU CAN'T START A FIRE WITHOUT A SPARK!
— Bruce Springsteen

WISDOM KEY

It's up to you to start thinking and behaving like a winner. You will never enjoy a more rewarding and exciting life with your old thinking!

If you aren't already...

Start Living Like a Winner Today!

Don't Negatively Forecast Your Own Future:

- Don't read horoscopes
- Don't listen to economic analysts
- Don't read tragic newspaper stories
- Don't listen to the negative trash talk of others

Don't Do The Things Losers Do:

- Don't think like a loser
- Don't talk like a loser
- Don't act like a loser
- Don't worry like a loser
- Don't dress like a loser
- Don't hang around losers
- Don't quit like a loser
- Don't be a loser

Do The Things Winners Do:

- Think like a winner
- Talk like a winner
- Act like a winner
- Dress like a winner
- Hang around winners
- Believe that you are a winner
- And never, ever, ever give up!

Man who said "It can't be done"
should not interrupt man who is doing it!
— Old Chinese Proverb

Successful Traits of Winners:

- Every day winners work on having a positive, cheerful, enthusiastic outlook on life.
- Winners live lives of integrity and values. Their word is their bond. Their reputation is everything.
- Winners realize it's up to them to make things happen. They are committed to action. They don't wait for things to happen, they make things happen. They refuse to procrastinate!
- Winners take full responsibility for their actions.
- Winners dream big dreams and they believe them.
- Winners are "decision makers."
- Winners overcome fear to take on risks.
- Winners face adversities and problems as nothing more than challenges and they meet them head-on.
- Winners are committed to lifelong learning.
- Winners are willing to ask for advice or help—quickly when needed. They choose successful mentors and they listen to them.
- Winners want constructive criticism. They thrive on the feedback because it helps them achieve higher standards. Constructive criticism is the "Breakfast of Champions!"
- Winners speak with projection, force, and conviction. They don't use wimpy powerless words or phrases.
- Winners are not mavericks. They understand that success can only happen with other people and they are committed to building strong relationships.
- Winners are quick to admit their mistakes.
- Winners are quick to forgive and forget when others make mistakes.
- Winners are industrious. They are willing to work hard and do more than they are paid to do.
- Winners are "solution conscious" not "problem conscious."
- Winners recognize change and adapt, or they create change.
- Winners only do productive important things during their most productive time of day according to their biorhythms.
- Winners have found their true passion in life.
- Winners are determined, persistent, and have vowed never to quit.
- Winners understand that success is a long-term process and they never compromise their standards by looking for shortcuts.
- Winners are clean and organized.
- Winners lives are free from excuses.
- Winners are grateful, appreciative, and thankful.
- Winners always put others ahead of themselves.
- Winners believe in God. They understand their spirituality is a gift from a higher power that allows them to achieve things greater than humanly possible.

Make up your mind that every day of your life you are going to live like a winner. Get determined to live your life like that of a successful person. Think as though you are the most successful person on earth.

Success and achievement will only come to those who think and behave like winners!

How have you been thinking?
Just look around you and see...

The Man Who Thinks He Can

If you think you are beaten, you are.
If you think you dare not, you don't.
If you like to win, but you think you can't,
It is almost certain, you won't.
If you think you'll lose, you're lost.
For out in the world, we find...
Success begins with a person's will...
It's all in your state of mind.

If you think you are outclassed, you are.
You've got to think high to rise.
You've got to be sure of yourself before
You can ever win a prize.

Life's battles don't always go
To the stronger or faster man.
But soon or late the man who wins
Is the man who thinks he can!

— Author Unknown

All of us are self-made, but only the successful will admit it!
— Earl Nightingale

Climb the Ladder to SUCCESS!

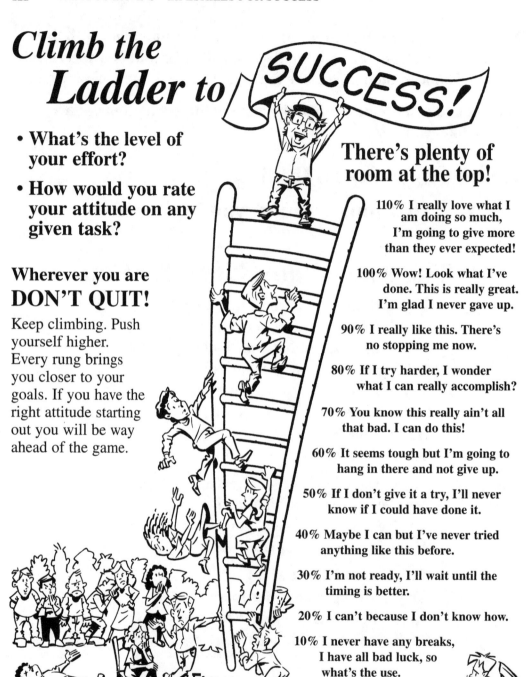

- **What's the level of your effort?**
- **How would you rate your attitude on any given task?**

Wherever you are
DON'T QUIT!

Keep climbing. Push yourself higher. Every rung brings you closer to your goals. If you have the right attitude starting out you will be way ahead of the game.

There's plenty of room at the top!

110% I really love what I am doing so much, I'm going to give more than they ever expected!

100% Wow! Look what I've done. This is really great. I'm glad I never gave up.

90% I really like this. There's no stopping me now.

80% If I try harder, I wonder what I can really accomplish?

70% You know this really ain't all that bad. I can do this!

60% It seems tough but I'm going to hang in there and not give up.

50% If I don't give it a try, I'll never know if I could have done it.

40% Maybe I can but I've never tried anything like this before.

30% I'm not ready, I'll wait until the timing is better.

20% I can't because I don't know how.

10% I never have any breaks, I have all bad luck, so what's the use.

0% It won't work so I won't waste my time.

ANGER   FAILURE   FRUSTRATION

IT'S ALWAYS CROWDED AT THE BOTTOM.

You Are A Winner!

Believe That You Are A Winner!

Act Like A Winner!

Start Right Now,
You Have No Time To Lose!

THE POWER OF POSITIVE ENERGY

You can either live your life positively charged, giving energy to everything you come into contact with, or you can be like a dead battery—always draining.

Have you ever noticed how some people can brighten up a room just by leaving it? Do you know if you are one of these people? Don't let this happen to you.

How you live your life is all about energy—the vitality of your lifeforce energy! Think about this concept carefully:

> **You should always be giving energy or you should be getting energy from the people around you.**

Check the quality of your lifeforce energy by asking the following questions:

1. **When you meet someone, does your presence energize them?**
2. **Do you leave them feeling energized because they have met you?**
3. **How are you affected by other people's energy?**
4. **Do you feel drained or charged up?**

People are divided into two types of energy forces: *Positive Forces* (energizers) and *Negative Forces* (devitalizers). <u>There are no neutral positions.</u> You are either creating and giving energy or you are using up your energy and draining others of theirs.

The energy you create is strictly a matter of choice.

WISDOM KEY

To be a force for good, you must create positive energy. You must give positive energy and you must feed off of other people's positive energy. To create positive energy, you must think positively, you must live healthy, eat foods that cleanse you not clog you, exercise so you function at optimum levels, and associate with other positive people. Get charged up to energize others!

The benefit of being around other positive people is that positive people can feed off of each other's positive energy without depleting their own energy. This combined energy actually creates "excess positive energy" of exponential proportions. The opposite is not true. Negative energy is always draining. Two negative people consorting together will never create anything good and they will drain the energy from everything that is around them. Stay away from negative people. Understanding these life forces is necessary to understand why some groups of people can build and other groups of people seem to do nothing but destroy. It comes down to the differences of energy within these groups.

Too many people approach disagreements with the sole intention of crushing the energy of the other person or group. Not only is this wrong, it wastes energy. Instead of feeling energized, people leave that kind of confrontation drained of precious lifeforce energy because it was used it to crush another person. By not approaching a confrontation positively, a chance is missed to get any reinforcing energy in return. This is "negative, draining energy," and no good ever comes of it for either party.

How to solve problems in a positive manner using positive energy:

1. **Dynamic synergy is created and problems are solved only when the positive energies of both parties are used to resolve the situation.**

2. **If you have confronted the problem positively, you will leave the confrontation feeling energized.**

3. **The person you have confronted should feel energized by your positive influence. In return, this person will give you back positive energy because you have reinforced and recharged their energy.**

STAY AWAY FROM PEOPLE WHO DRAIN YOU OF YOUR ENERGY AND GIVE YOU NOTHING IN RETURN.

The energy already within you is powerful! Your quest is not figuring out how to gain more energy but learning how to unleash the incredible unlimited and powerful energy that is already within you!

WISDOM KEY

Determine that you will be a force for good and a person of positive energy. The next time you confront a "people problem," approach it with the intention of having a positively energized outcome.

- Be solution positive, not problem negative.
- Focus on the solution.
- Keep the outcome a win/win situation for both parties.
- Keep it a learning experience.
- Leave the other person feeling energized because of the positive energy radiating from your spirit.

Conduct yourself with:
- Positive Energy
- Spiritual Energy
- Productive Energy
- Creative Energy
- Physical Energy

How you get up in the morning will determine how successful you will be in life!

- Begin your day by thinking positively.

- Send out only positive thought waves.

- Work for a body that radiates health.

- Have eyes that sparkle and electric smiles.

- Get fired up, speak with enthusiasm.

- Give glowing compliments to everyone.

- Associate with brilliant, passionate people.

- Live an energetic life full of spirit and vitality.

- Be a force for good.

This is the day which the Lord hath made; we will rejoice and be glad in it.
— Psalm 118:24 (KJV)

Your life will be far more rewarding, if the energy you give or the energy you receive is always... "positive revitalizing energy."

"Sparkle" when you are around other people!

THE POWER OF
ACTION!

"The road to hell is paved with good intentions"

WISDOM KEY

> **I don't care how good your intentions are—they don't count. YOU MUST TAKE ACTION.** Nothing in this book matters if you don't commit to taking decisive and immediate ACTION! Goals and ambitions are nothing more than wishful thinking, if you don't make a committed decision to ACT. Don't be like the rest of the world, waiting for things to happen. It's up to you to make things happen. <u>The magic is in you!</u>

Don't wait for the right time—
The right time is always RIGHT NOW!

The first magical key to all success is simply STARTING.

When you begin to take action, something magical happens. Just getting out of your chair, rolling up your sleeves, making up your mind to begin, puts in motion a force of energy that attracts other positive forces around you. You'll find that momentum will start to carry you. The majority of a rocket's fuel is consumed just in taking off and reaching altitude. Once airborne, the rest of the journey is almost effortless. Success begins the same way, a majority of your hard work is needed up front just in getting started. Get going. **Start taking MASSIVE ACTION now!**

Don't let self-doubt keep you from taking the first step. Clear your head of everything except your determination to go after the one thing in your life that makes everything worthwhile.

Focus, Concentrate, Pump Yourself Up! Your focus should be so fixed on your goal that you're not distracted by whatever else is going on around you. Everything that is not congruent <u>to taking action</u> must be completely shut out. Everything that is not congruent <u>to your goals</u> must be shut out.

Your mind and every cell of your body must be so tightly pulled together by concentration that any slight hint of fear or self-doubt cannot penetrate your resolve to taking action.

Then once you've started, you can't let yourself get distracted. Repeat affirmations, keep your goals firmly planted in your mind and constantly visualize yourself successfully completing every step of your task. This will keep you moving forward.

GET RID OF SAYING, "AS SOON AS..."

A journey of a thousand miles begins with just one step.
— Old Chinese Proverb

Make this your motto and repeat it to yourself throughout the day...

**Every moment of my life is precious.
I must do the most productive thing possible
at every given moment.**

ACTION is a state of mind.

ACTION begins right now.

ACTION is simply taking the first step.

ACTION is being proactive.

ACTION is being "solution conscious" not "problem conscious."

ACTION is living a life free of excuses.

ACTION is believing in yourself.

ACTION is being a "front-row seater."

ACTION is speaking up first.

ACTION is doing what others won't do.

ACTION is breaking out of your comfort zone.

ACTION is making something happen instead of waiting to see what happens.

ACTION is taking control of your destiny!

JUST DO IT.
— Nike

THE POWER OF YOUR VOICE

No one has ever succeeded in life by being shy or timid. Right now you may be thinking to yourself, "I will never get the job I want because I am too afraid of selling myself" or "I could never be a leader because I am too afraid to speak in front of groups. I even have a hard time expressing myself in small groups!" Guess what—you're not alone.

Don't be afraid to toot your own whistle! You must step up to get up! If you don't let the world know what you're about…who will? When you go to meetings, do you find yourself sitting in the back-row seats? Why? What are you ashamed of? Are you afraid someone will call on you? You may have gotten away with this in school but in the real world this reluctance to be a "front-row seater" is unacceptable. If you are going to hold any type of management or leadership position, you must be able to speak to people and get your point across with conviction.

YOU HAVE A VOICE. Who you are and what you have to say is important.

BUT…

I'm not a born speaker.
I have a lousy voice for speaking.
No one wants to listen to me anyway.
I get so nervous I forget my lines.

I have nothing important to say.
I'm afraid of crowds.
I'll make a fool of myself.
I'm not a born salesman.

Our excuses hold us back in life. How many times when you were in school did you "miss out" being selected for the class project you wanted to be on because you were too afraid to speak up? How many times did you "miss out" going on the date you wanted to go on because you were too afraid to approach the love of your dreams? As you have grown older, how many times have you been passed up for promotions because you were too timid to express your opinions although you were highly experienced and qualified?

Here are some reasons why you must be able to express yourself:

- You have great ideas that need to be expressed.
- You have important concerns that need to be addressed.
- You need to ace an important job interview.
- You want to date the person of your dreams with confidence.
- You need to be able to ask what you think are dumb questions because you really need to know the answers.
- You want to be able to answer tough questions with confidence.
- You have to be able to address and resolve tough issues with people.

We all have to conquer our own fears. Often, when I am speaking to a business or community group, I will challenge people to get more aggressive and take action in their lives. Someone will always counter and say, "that's easy for you to say. I could never stand in front of a group and talk like you do!" I will always reply, "There is no one in this room that is more deathly afraid of speaking in front of groups than me."

I have spent most of my life sitting on the sidelines watching other kids fight to be first or compete to be front-and-center. Given this, it's not surprising that public speaking did not come naturally for me. Even today, despite having given hundreds of speeches, I still get nervous and weak in the knees!

In fact, my first speech was before a group of 300. I was so nervous that the sweat rolling off of my forehead soaked my notes until I couldn't read them, and the suit coat I was wearing was wringing wet in the armpits. I never once looked at my audience, and the 45-minute speech I was supposed to give lasted only 10 minutes. When I was done, I practically ran out the door without talking to the people who had invited me and vowed I would never speak in public again. For weeks after this experience, I avoided all the people I knew because I was so sure they were still laughing at my speech and at me!

Sheer determination changed my life. This was the most embarrassing moment of my life. I had made a fool of myself in front of hundreds of people. But I knew if I ever was going to achieve success in life, I had to conquer my fears of speaking in public. That day, I determined I was going to be a great public speaker. I started to visualize hundreds of people giving me a standing ovation, clapping, and cheering over a heartfelt speech that I had just given. I pictured this over and over again in my mind.

My family and friends know I have a very "airy" light voice—not the voice for public speaking. But the first thing I did was to go buy Dale Carnegie's book *How to Develop Self-Confidence and Influence People by Public Speaking.* And for years, after my family had left the house, I would stand in my basement in front of a $5 mirror that I bought from K-Mart, reading books out loud to myself. I repeated the ABCs and numbers over and over again out loud at the top of my voice, practicing diction and enunciating the sounds of each letter. I practiced deep breathing using the fullness of my belly, letting my diaphragm project my voice. Next I practiced how I looked to other people. I smiled thousands of smiles at myself. I wiggled my eyebrows, winked at myself, and practiced smiling at myself with big wide-open eyes. I even shook hands with myself.

I wrote out my speeches in 10-minute segments that I memorized, and recorded these speeches so I could critique myself. Next, I memorized several poems just to give me something to repeat over and over again when I was alone in my car driving around. I can't tell you how many times I would find myself waiting at a stop light still in the midst of a rip-roaring speech including extreme facial gestures and waving arms only to realize someone in another car was watching me. When I turned and looked, I often would find amused, surprised wide-eyed people staring back at me. But you know what? I didn't care because I was working at improving myself. The most important thing about all of this was that I had gotten over my fear of what others thought of me.

Join Toastmasters. The next most important thing I did was to join Toastmasters. Toastmasters is an international organization made up of people just like you and me for the common purpose of improving their speech making skills. It is a nonprofit organization that only charges for materials you use. It is the most valuable thing I can recommend to any young person or mid-career person interested in making a significant improvement in their career. You can find a local chapter of Toastmasters in the community event section of your local newspaper. They understand your predicament, having been in the same situation, and would love to have you join their group.

You don't have to be a natural born speaker. The reason I have shared these very embarrassing moments of my life with you is because if I can conquer my fears, you can conquer yours. In fact, many people enjoy my talks because they feel that what they are hearing is passion coming directly from my heart and not just some prepared speech coming from a polished speaker. It has taken years for me to get to where I am today, and I am still working even harder at becoming better at my craft.

Tips for improving your voice and your public speaking:

- **Get a burning passion in your gut. Start letting the world know what you've got to say is important!** Believe that God put you on this earth for a reason. Your higher purpose is to make a difference by what you have to say.

- **Talk about things you are passionate about.** When you speak from the heart, people will listen intently to what you have to say.

- **Speak with enthusiasm.** Nothing is more powerful than a person with attitude!

- **Speak with confidence.** Speak with more volume. Speaking louder will hide any fear you may have.

- **Practice, Practice, Practice.** Practice speaking at the top of your voice whenever you are alone. Practice in front of a mirror. Watch your facial expressions and your body movements. Practice your speeches when you are driving in your car and make up your mind that you couldn't care less about what other people think!

- **Record yourself.** Most people have never heard themselves talk. Be prepared to get grossed-out, as most people do not like the sound of their voice when they hear it for the first time.

- **Smile when you talk.** You'll be amazed at how different your voice sounds when you have a smile in your voice. A little added enthusiasm to your voice makes people want to hear what you have to say.

- **Memorize your speech.** Chunk your speech into memorable ten-minute highlights that can be identified by a single "trigger" word. Memorizing your speech in chunks takes the fear away from thinking you have to memorize a whole 45-minute speech. Speaking from the heart about things you are passionate about will keep you from having to use notes. Whatever you do—**don't read your speech.**

- **Get good at telling your own stories.** Some of the world's best speech makers were storytellers like Mark Twain and Will Rogers. Never get caught giving someone else's speech. People know immediately, and it's embarrassing. Talk about the experiences that have impacted your own life—they'll be more meaningful and interesting to your audience.

- **Paint a picture when telling your stories.** Don't just state boring facts. When making a point, tell it visually. Use descriptive words, colorful words, words that make sounds, words that stimulate interest, words that paint pictures in the minds of your listener's mind. You want them to hear with their eyes not just their ears. When you have captured their imagination, you will see it in their eyes.

- **Start speaking 25% louder all the time.** Consciously start projecting your voice in your everyday speech. Every time you say something, make your voice fill the room.

- **Slow down!** Most people are so nervous that they rattle off everything they have to say within minutes. Slow down and concentrate on delivering a great speech.

- **Practice your diction.** Enunciate your words very clearly and with force. Hold a candle one foot from your mouth and try to put out the flame when you speak.

- **Change your pitch or the tone of your voice.** Create vocal contrasts so your speech doesn't come out in a boring monotone voice. Highlight vital areas of your speech with enthusiasm, passion, excitement, and silence. Sometimes the tone of your voice will more accurately reflect your true feelings and the depth of your passion than your ability to choose the right words.

- **Include pauses and moments of silence.** Pauses can be just as effective as enthusiasm to highlight something of importance. Count to three and then begin again. It may seem like an eternity, but it isn't—try it.

- **Establish eye contact with your audience.** Pick out several friendly faces in the audience who are actively engaged in your speech. Alternate between them. If in the beginning you are having a difficult time looking people in the eye, look slightly above them at the wall. They will think you are looking directly at them even though you are not!

- **Body language and movement.** A passionate speech requires parallel body movement. Your body movements should act as punctuation marks highlighting your speech. Most people don't know what to do with their hands. This is something that must be practiced in front of a mirror, or have a friend critique your speech. Better yet, join Toastmasters and your peer group will help you immensely.

- **Don't let your audience distract you!** Many times when you are giving a speech, you may encounter wait staff serving or cleaning up. You may see several people holding their own conversations, people sleeping, or even people getting up and leaving. Don't let these things bother you! Make a renewed effort to pump up your energy level and keep going. Don't let a few people throw you off especially when you have the attention of 99% of the rest of your audience.

- **Practice your breathing.** Speak from your gut. Let your diaphragm do your work. Using your diaphragm to project your voice will save your vocal chords.

- **When your are walking on the street look people in the eye, smile and say, "Hi!" to everyone you meet.** See if you can get them to respond. Don't worry if they look at you like you are nuts! This simple exercise will help you to break out of your shell.

- **Start being a "front-row seater" and start asking questions even if you think they are dumb.**

- **Start volunteering for speaking assignments.** Your local Toastmasters group is an excellent place to start. Also get involved at your church by teaching Sunday School classes. Get involved with your local community. Join the PTA, the local Chamber of Commerce, the Rotary, the United Way, or other civic groups and volunteer to get on a committee where you have to give reports. These civic groups are always looking for volunteers and would actively welcome you. In addition, your community participation is great for your career, your family, and your community. Get Involved!

WISDOM KEY

Live your life out loud! Be proud of who you are. If you have something to say, stand up and say what's on you mind. You have a voice. Speak up! Taking action is the only way to overcome your fears. There is magic in standing up and just starting. The key is to take ACTION. Being able to speak in public will give you great pride and a wonderful sense of accomplishment.

A speaker's confession...

Two minutes before I begin,
I would rather be whipped than start;
but two minutes before I finish,
I would rather be shot than stop!

— Unknown

I'M LOUD AND I'M PROUD!

When I encourage you to be Loud and Proud,
I am not suggesting that you start "grandstanding."
It's one thing to be proud of who you are and what
you stand for…but it is a mistake to try and pretend
to be something you are not! Never call attention
to yourself for the purposes of satisfying your own ego!

LIVE LARGE!
THINK LARGE!
GIVE LARGE!

THE POWER OF LANGUAGE

Happy Smiles—Happy Talk!

Creating a Positive Attitude Begins with Positive Speech And a Cheerful Smile!

Being cheerful is really a form of being thankful you're alive— What a wonderful way to be!

Smile when you talk! If you want to really enjoy life, start speaking positively. You can't help but feel better about yourself and your world when everything that comes out of your smiling mouth is encouraging, uplifting, and refreshing.

MOST PEOPLE ARE UNAWARE OF HOW THEY TALK. IF THEY EVER STOPPED TO LISTEN TO THEMSELVES, THEY REALLY WOULD BE SURPRISED WHAT COMES OUT OF THEIR MOUTHS!

WISDOM KEY

How you talk can make you feel down or make you feel on top of the world. Your language will determine the good or bad that comes into your life. The quality of your day obeys your talk. If you whine, complain, rumor, and gossip, then you will attract only negative things into your life. If you talk positively, speak of hope, spread encouragement, and say only good things, then you will attract all the positive things into your life. Your future obeys how you talk today. To determine how you have been thinking and talking, just look around you and see!

Start paying attention to how you talk. Record how you talk. For one day, write down everything you say. Highlight all the negative things you say, and then make a conscious effort to rid your speech of these negatives. Is your speech consistent with your goals and the person you want to become? Ask a friend you trust to tell you what he or she thinks of your speech patterns. The answer could be very revealing! Your friends' answer may surprise you. Don't get defensive or argumentative— just listen and learn.

Get rid of all the negative words in your vocabulary and avoid talking down about yourself. Have you ever caught yourself saying:

I can't...	I'm so embarrassed.
I won't...	I'll probably fail if I try.
I should have...	What if I can't make it?
I could have...	What's the use, I'll never catch up.
I would have...	I have all the bad luck.
I'm always getting sick!	I was going to, but...
I never have enough money.	I hate going to work.

This is wimpy talk using "powerless" phrases. Talk like this undermines how terrific you are. Talk like this is fatalistic and mirrors what is going on in your head. You are prophesying your own future. How can you ever expect to be successful if this is how you talk? Start turning your negative speech into *positive power talk*!

From now on become a "positive power-talker" and only use phases like:

I can...	I am a winner!
I will...	I can make this happen!
I shall...	I'm never going to give up!
I'm the best!	I feel great!
I feel Super Good!	I do what others won't do!
I feel fantastic!	I feel terrific!

Every day in every way, I get better every day!

Smile whenever you talk. When you answer the phone—SMILE! Practice keeping a smile on your face at all times—even when no one is around. Keeping a smile on your face will always keep you in the positive. You can't get angry when you are smiling!

Talk like a winner. Speak with confidence. Project your voice at all times. Talk forcefully with conviction. Speak from your heart. Be passionate about what you are saying. People react positively to someone who is passionate even if they don't necessarily agree with what is being said.

An "I can" beats out an "I can't" every time!

Positive speech requires you to think positively. When you think positively you will also act positively and enthusiastically.

Positive Thinking will lead to:	Positive Speech
Positive Thinking will create:	Positive Decision Making
Positive Thinking will lead to:	Positive Action
Positive Thinking will encourage:	Positive Persistence
Positive Thinking will promote:	Positive Living

BE A POSITIVE THINKER! BE A POSITIVE POWER-TALKER! SPEAK WITH FORCE AND CONVICTION. SPEAK FROM YOUR HEART. SPEAK WITH CONFIDENCE, CHEERFULNESS, AND OPTIMISM—AND WATCH THE WORLD AROUND YOU CHANGE FOR THE BETTER! SMILE AS MUCH AS YOU CAN WHEN YOU TALK AND WATCH HOW MANY PEOPLE AROUND YOU WILL START TO LOVE YOU!

Practice using a tape recorder. Most people have no idea how they sound. Practice in front of a mirror. Talk confidently and look confident when you talk. Smile when you talk!

HERE'S A SPECIAL MESSAGE FOR PARENTS:

The way you talk to your kids makes a huge difference. It's so unfortunate that we subject our children to negative talk almost from the time they are born. We are responsible for how our kids talk—what they say is a direct reflection of the way we talk at home. If you are always griping and complaining, your kids are going to grow up to be complainers. Start talking positively. Be uplifting and encouraging when you are around your children.

Unconsciously, parents negatively program their children's thinking by saying:

"No, don't do that!"

"Don't touch that!"

"Get away from there—you'll hurt yourself!"

"Don't get near the street—you'll get run over!"

I really cringe when I hear parents telling their children:

"What's the matter with you? Are you stupid?"

"Why can't you be good? What's wrong with you?"

"Shame on you. You're naughty!"

"How come you never listen to me? Are you deaf?"

"If you don't behave, I'm going to give you a good whipping!"

"Why can't you ever do anything right?"

"Why are you always watching TV?"

DON'T MAKE ACCUSATIONS. Get rid of saying, "You always…" or "You never…" or "How come you…"

Talk like this is so devastating to young minds—it's really verbal child abuse and equally as bad as physical abuse.

Verbal abuse kills a child's ability to dream and sets the course for the rest of his/her adult life. Is it any wonder that children grow up thinking they can't be achievers? Remember, from the moment your children are born, to age 14, they have the greatest learning potential they will ever have in their entire lives.

Children remember everything they hear.
What you say is critically important.

Early affirmations reinforce a child's development. Your positive affirmations are the building blocks for all their future achievements and successes. Here are a few for starters:

- You look really happy today!
- I'm so proud of you!
- You did a really great job!
- Way to go, you're terrific!
- You look so beautiful!
- You're one in a million!
- Congratulations, keep up the good work!
- You're very special!
- You mean a lot to me!
- You keep getting better all the time—don't give up! Hang in there!!
- You are really precious!
- God loves you!

WRONG

RIGHT

Over-reacting to early stumbles makes a child afraid to fail. How an adult handles failure reflects how his parents responded to his childhood mistakes. If a child thinks he is bad because he made a mistake, he will think he is bad whenever he makes mistakes as an adult.

THE REASON WE ALWAYS EXPECT THE WORST FROM OUR CHILDREN IS BECAUSE WE KNOW THEY HAVE SO MUCH OF US IN THEM!

Start treating failures and mistakes as learning opportunities. Failure is only an event and should never be considered a personal fault. If children make mistakes, show them the difference between right and wrong. Don't punish them for their mistakes. Instead, give them praise for trying. Children need to be recognized for their effort, attitude, and willingness to learn something new.

Tell your children that you love them. Tell them that you are proud of them. Tell them that they are wonderful children of God. Smile when you talk to your children. Always have good things to say about your children.

How you talk to the people around you is critically important as well. Be encouraging. Be a "breath of fresh air." Wherever you go, be happy, smile, and be cheerful. Be a "Good Finder," always have something good to say about the people you meet. Make them feel good!

Quit making people feel bad. Quit making people feel wrong. I wish I could buy back all the times I tried to make someone feel inferior because I wanted to prove how right I was. Take my advice, there is absolutely no good reason why you should ever have to prove how big or important you think you are. This type of behavior is nothing more than pure immaturity and selfishness.

Do you sparkle? Are you effervescent, energetic, and enthusiastic when you talk? Try to be and just watch how your world changes because of your positive speech! People will be more inclined to help you when you are positive. If you are cheerful and always have something positive to say, people naturally will respond to you likewise.

HAVE YOU EVER NOTICED SOME PEOPLE ARE SO SOUR ON LIFE THAT THEY NEVER A HAVE A GOOD THING TO SAY ABOUT ANYTHING? HAPPY PEOPLE TEND TO STAY AWAY FROM THE NEGATIVE PEOPLE.

Ask yourself, "How do people see me?" It doesn't matter how tough things may be at times, if you stay enthusiastic and positive you will have a less stressful time getting through the challenges of life. Positive thinking may not solve your problems, but having a positive attitude will sure help you solve your problems with a better frame of mind. Positive speech will make a difference in how people react to what you say.

But most importantly...

By being positive all the time, you will attract great people into your life. A group of great people can create a dynamic synergy that attracts all the goodness that God's great universe has to offer!

The best way to cheer yourself up is to cheer everybody else up!
— Mark Twain

**Smile, and the whole world smiles with you.
Cry, and you cry alone.**

Speak with clarity not cleverness.

This Chapter really should be titled...

How to Look Smart
By Asking Dumb Questions!

Ask, and it shall be given you.
— Matthew 7:7 (KJV)

You have been ordained by God to ask questions! Wow, how powerful! If God has boldly declared that if we ask a question...it shall be given, then who are we to be afraid of asking questions! But how many times have we sat timidly without asking for what we really wanted to know because we were too afraid of how ignorant we might look?

IT'S UNFORTUNATE THAT WE LIVE OUR LIVES IN IGNORANCE BECAUSE WE ARE AFRAID OF LOOKING STUPID FOR ASKING A DUMB QUESTION!

If you don't know something, don't be afraid to ask a question.
We have all heard the familiar...

**THERE IS NO SUCH THING AS A DUMB QUESTION.
THE ONLY DUMB QUESTION IS THE ONE YOU DIDN'T ASK!**

Avoid looking dumb by pleading ignorance. Trying to conceal what you don't know only reveals your foolishness to the world in all its glory! I never really understood the power of asking questions in the classroom until much later in life when I was going back to college to get a degree. I remember a young lady who kept asking simple questions such as, "Could you please repeat that? I didn't quite understand it." And I thought to myself, I wondered about the same thing but I was afraid to ask. Because of this "A" student's questions, the teacher thought she was very interested in the class, which motivated the teacher to pay special attention to her.

So why was I afraid to ask a simple question? We were all born with an unlimited appetite to ask questions. We were fearless until our parents put the kibosh on our questions by saying, "Why are you always asking so many questions? Are you stupid?"

Anthony Robbins, the world's leading personal development trainer, says, "The quality of the life we live is the result of the quality of questions that we ask." If we want to change our life for the better, all we have to do is change the quality of our questions.

WISDOM KEY

Powerful questions are: "How can I get better? How can I improve myself?" Powerless and wimpy questions are "What's wrong with me? Why do I have all the bad luck?" Question asking is so fundamental to everyday living that it's unfortunate that we are not taught in school how to properly ask questions. When you only ask, "What's wrong with me?," you are living in the past. Your focus on the negative prevents you from developing the positive thoughts you need to move forward. Start asking positive questions for positive results.

You must become good at asking questions if you are going to experience the life you have dreamed about. Every day you ask questions just to live:

- You ask questions of your parents because you want to know something.
- You ask your parents for permission to do things.
- You must ask questions in school so you understand the material.
- You must ask for dates.
- You have to ask for your first job.
- You have to ask to get married.
- You have to ask for raises or promotions.
- You must ask for forgiveness.
- You need to ask for help.
- You need to ask for advice.

YOU WILL NEVER GET ANSWERS TO THE QUESTIONS YOU DON'T ASK!

If you ask weak questions you will get weak answers and weak results. It never hurts to ask. The worst that can happen is that the answer is NO. But if you never ask, the answer is always NO! The more effective and persistent you are at asking questions will determine the quality of your dating life, the size of your raise, and the quality of the advice you get. Insecurity keeps people from asking powerful questions. This is confirmed by the statement, "Be careful what you ask for—because you just might get it!" Many people are afraid of success. They might have to be accountable!

Why are we afraid of asking questions?

1. **Fear of Rejection.** We are afraid of getting rejected, and our egos can't handle the fact that we may not be liked. We must understand that just because our question got turned down, the world is not going to end. Everything is a numbers game; <u>we must keep asking until someone says yes or gives us what we want.</u> Success rewards persistence.

2. **Fear of Our Own Ignorance.** The last thing we want people to think is that we are stupid. We fail to realize that everyone is ignorant of some things and a genius in other things. It's all right not to know. It's <u>not</u> all right not to ask the question.

3. **Fear of the Unknown.** Many times we fail to get out of our comfort zones because we are afraid of the unknown. We can overcome our fears by having a stronger faith. Strong faith in God and in ourselves gives us the confidence to overcome our strongest fears.

4. **Fear Caused by Low Self-esteem.** We are afraid to bother someone with our insignificant requests. When we ask, we apologize for bothering them. It's almost like we are begging.

5. **Pride.** We are afraid to ask for help because of our pride. We don't want to look weak. Men are famous for not asking for something as simple as directions. The fact is, asking for help only shows how mature and wise you are in asking for good advice. Ignorance is showing how immature and foolish you are by <u>not</u> asking for help.

FEAR DOES NOT EXIST UNTIL YOU CREATE IT IN YOUR MIND! ONLY YOUR WORRY GIVES FEAR ITS POWER.

How to become a better question asker:

- **Never be afraid to ask for anything.** You will never find out unless you ask. If anything, your questions will give you better information. The more information you have, the more knowledge you have, and knowledge is power.
- **Be specific in your request.** Your request can never be answered if you are vague. Being specific shows how serious you are about getting more information.

- **Believe that you are worthy of receiving what you ask for.** You will never receive what you don't deserve. The worst consequence of fear is believing that you don't deserve an answer and you are supposed to be satisfied with what life is dishing out to you.
- **Never beg.** When you ask for something, you need to feel that you absolutely deserve what you are asking for. When you beg, you are sending a message that you are not worthy and that you are hoping someone will pity you. Always ask with confidence.
- **Ask as if you have already received. Claim ownership over your request.** You must ask with confidence, as if you are already in possession of your request. You must believe that your request will be granted. Anticipate with conviction. Envision your ownership.

**Therefore I tell you, whatever you ask in prayer,
<u>believe that you have received it</u>, and it will be yours.**
— Mark 11:24 (NIV)

- **Thank God in advance for providing for all of your needs.** Notice I said "needs" not "wants." When you thank God in advance you demonstrate your confidence in getting your needs met. God will give you that for which you are grateful.
- **Make sure what you ask for is congruent with your values and your goals.** Outrageous requests only for personal gain fall on deaf ears. However, if you are living your life to make the world a better place, you will receive more than you ask for!

**Delight thyself in the Lord, and he shall
give thee the desires of thine heart.**
— Psalms 37:4 (KJV)

- **Make sure you are asking the right question.** Many requests never get answered because you are asking the wrong question. Never ask God to take away your problems but instead ask God to give you wisdom so you can handle the problems on your own.
- **Make sure you are asking the right person.** Make sure you are asking someone who is qualified to answer your question. You can't ask a naked man to give you the shirt off his back! Neither can you ask your poor uncle Bob how to become a millionaire.
- **You must be persistent.** If you don't get a positive response the first time, keep trying. Never give up. The universe rewards persistence. However, if you keep asking and you are getting nothing, check to see if you are following the above criteria. You may have to change what you are asking for or take another look at the validity of what you are asking for. Sometimes it's all about timing. God's time may not be your time.
- **Now is the time to ask for what you want.** Don't wait for the "right time." The right time is now. Go ahead and ask! The answer you get will be a reference point for your next question.

Develop the powerful skill of asking open-ended questions.

There is magic in becoming skillful in the fine art of asking open-ended questions. You can find out everything you want to know, have all the friends you want to have, and be very successful in your career. Know the difference between a close-ended question and an open-ended question. Unsuccessful people ask close-ended questions and wonder why they are poor conversationalists.

Here's an example of a close-ended question, "Can I have a raise?" The answer is very easy to give in a single-word sentence—Yes or No.

Here's another close-ended question, "Did you enjoy your vacation?" They can respond Yes or No and your conversation has just ended.

An example of an open-ended question is, "What criteria do I have to meet in order to qualify for a raise?" or "What did you enjoy most on your vacation?" Neither of these open-ended questions can be answered with just a simple one-word sentence. Rather, these types of questions encourage the person to actually tell you something.

If you have nothing to say, you can keep the conversation going on forever by asking only open-ended questions and the other person will do all the talking! People love hearing themselves talk and they will think you are a brilliant conversationalist! The key is to let the other person talk after you've asked the question.

There is magic in asking.

If you want to get something done, ask—don't order people around. For example:

"SON, I WANT THE FAMILY CAR WASHED BY THIS AFTERNOON, I HAVE AN IMPORTANT MEETING TO GO TO AND I WANT THE CAR LOOKING ITS BEST."

Instead, ask…

"SON, I HAVE AN IMPORTANT MEETING THIS AFTERNOON, CAN YOU HELP ME BY WASHING THE FAMILY CAR, I WOULD CERTAINLY APPRECIATE YOUR HELP… THANKS!"

Phrase your questions to get a positive reply. For example:

"DAD CAN YOU LET US USE THE BOAT THIS AFTERNOON?" THIS QUESTION CAN BE ANSWERED YES OR NO.

Instead, ask...

"DAD, HOW LONG ARE YOU GOING TO LET US USE THE BOAT THIS AFTERNOON?" THIS QUESTION ALREADY ASSUMES A POSITIVE RESPONSE.

How can you better your life by asking other people the right questions? For example:

"WHAT ARE THE REQUIREMENTS I NEED TO ACHIEVE TO QUALIFY FOR A PROMOTION?"

As opposed to...

"HOW SOON CAN I GET PROMOTED?"

Or...

"HOW CAN I BE OF MORE SERVICE TO YOUR COMPANY AND HELP YOU ACHIEVE YOUR COMPANY'S GOALS?"

As opposed to...

"OUR COMPANY IS HAVING A SALES CONTEST, CAN YOU INCREASE YOUR ORDER WITH ME?"

Or...

"HONEY, HOW CAN I MAKE YOUR LIFE MORE HAPPY?"

As opposed to...

"HOW COME YOU NEVER (FILL IN THE BLANK) WITH ME ANYMORE?"

Your life will <u>never</u> get better if you are only asking, "What's in it for me?" Your life will get infinitely better once you start asking how you can be of service to others. That's really what life is all about.

Others have seen what is and asked why.
I have seen what could be and asked why not?
— Robert Kennedy

Dealing with NO answers. When you get a NO for an answer, don't accept it as personal rejection. People may still like you, but may have different ideas about your question. For example, if you are asking for a raise and the answer is NO…don't take this to mean they don't appreciate your efforts. Instead, use this as a learning opportunity to ask another question. Ask what you can do to gain more experience so you can become more valuable. You may need to change your question or change your approach. Again, a NO answer should be considered a reference point for your next question.

> **All NO answers can be turned into learning opportunities by asking more open-ended questions!**

WISDOM KEY

> YOUR "ASK LIST" SHOULD BE JUST AS IMPORTANT AS YOUR GOALS LIST.

Here are the powerful questions you should be asking to better your life:

- Am I doing the right thing?
- Am I giving it my best effort?
- How can I improve my_____?
- What are my values?
- Am I following God's will for my life?
- If I could become the happiest person in the world how would I live my life?
- If I could marry the right person what would this person be like?
- How do I need to change myself to attract the right person for me?
- In a perfect world, how would I be living my life and what do I need to change to start living this life now?
- How can I improve myself to make my career more rewarding?

Let your requests be made known unto God.
— Philippians 4:6 (KJV)

The most innocent dumb question can be rocket fuel for the imagination!
— Famous Dave Anderson

ALL WINNERS ARE POWERFUL QUESTION-ASKERS!

- Winners ask good powerful questions.
- Winners ask to be first.
- Winners ask other winners for advice.
- Winners ask for help when they need it instead of demanding it.
- Winners ask for positive results and they expect them.
- Winners ask for forgiveness.
- Winners ask God for His blessings.

ASK. YOU MUST ASK.
YOU WON'T GET ANYWHERE BY WISHING!

Become an unstoppable question-asker.

What have you been asking for?
Just look around you and see!

Ask for wisdom.
It's a smart thing to do...

Miracles Happen When You Ask!

THE POWER OF RELATIONSHIPS

The real game of life is "People Power!"

Have you ever heard somebody say, "I am a self-made success?"
The fact is that there's no such thing. Sure, someone may have put
in a lot of individual effort, but it just isn't possible to become a
success all by yourself.

You need people to be successful. Winning in the game of life takes help from people—a lot of people. No one has ever achieved great success without first developing successful relationships.

If you want one year of prosperity, grow grain.
If you want ten years of prosperity, grow trees.
If you want one hundred years of prosperity, grow people!
                                    — Chinese Proverb

Life is really all about relationships. Everything we do involves people. The art of developing winning relationships takes a great deal of work and understanding on our part. People are different—we all have our own set of individual idiosyncrasies—that's what makes people so special.

IF WE WERE ALL THE SAME,
SOME OF US WOULDN'T BE NECESSARY!

It's not always what you think that matters, it's what <u>they</u> think that matters. External circumstances and the environment people live in have a lot to do with their perspective. The key to effectively communicating with people is understanding how they think. Your success is dependent on your ability to successfully communicate with the greatest number of people possible. This can't be accomplished if you are only thinking about what matters to you.

Values determine the quality of a relationship. Rewarding relationships are built over time, and based on a foundation of values. Personal character values include: trust, integrity, honesty, loyalty, compassion, caring, sharing, generosity, forgiveness, dependability, responsibility, and patience.

<u>Trust</u> **is the number one value that people treasure in a relationship.**

WISDOM KEY

Major question to ask yourself... Is there anything in your life, that if people found out, would keep them from trusting you? If you answered yes, you need to stop these behaviors right now or seek help or counseling. It is very hard to rebuild trust, once it is broken.

Life is nothing but relationships, both good and bad.

Good relationships are giving. Bad relationships are draining. The most important thing in all relationships, both good and bad, is honesty. You have to be true to yourself. Never compromise your values just to satisfy toxic relationships.

Even though everyone needs to be loved, it's a fact of life that not everyone is going to like you. Unfortunately, some people will even hate you! It's not easy to accept or understand this. As heartless as it sounds, the reality is people generally couldn't care less whether you exist unless they have some very pressing need to get something out of you. This is why it's so critical to develop relationships. However, you'll soon find that the greater your success, the more difficult it will be to influence and maintain your relationship with a wider body of people of different opinions. This is one reason why so many people have become distrusting—the people they gave their trust to failed them.

It's natural for people to have different opinions. Not everyone is going to understand your point of view. More often than not, people think their beliefs and opinions are more important than yours.

IF YOU LAID ALL OF MAN'S OPINIONS END TO END, THERE WOULD BE NO END.

You may be thinking to yourself, "What's with this negative stuff about people not liking me? I thought this chapter was about developing "winning relationships!"

The truth is—to create winning relationships you must prevent misunderstandings that turn into disagreements and prepare yourself for the pain that's sure to come when others resent or reject you.

The true value of winning relationships is discovered during times of great disagreement. The true problems in life do not come from breaking your leg or crashing your car, but from "people problems;" people who have let you down, people who are plotting against you, people who lie to and cheat on you. These are the real problems that will wrench your gut and keep you awake at night thinking that your world is crashing in on you. Only your positive mental attitude will help you overcome any difficulties from "soured" relationships. Maintaining your own cheerful and positive outlook on life will help others put aside their differences.

Everyone wants to be loved. And love is forgiving. Have you ever noticed how difficult it is to stay mad at a puppy that just peed all over your best carpet, especially a puppy with big eyes, a smiling face, and a tail that's wagging its whole body?

One important thing to remember is that people are fundamentally forgiving.

It's amazing how much healing power there is in a smile, a warm handshake, and a friendly hug. Work on forgiveness in a relationship and forget about whether somebody did you wrong—it's not important. Five years from now, chances are you'll never remember the incident.

The harder it is to love someone, the more that person needs your love!

Great relationships begin with a great attitude. Having a great attitude and a positive outlook will help attract other cheerful people—people you will want in your life. What you get out of a relationship begins with what you put into it. You will reap whatever you sow. The quality of your relationships directly reflects who you are as a person. Unfortunately, many people in difficult relationships take the easy road by blaming the other person and never questioning their own responsibility.

WISDOM KEY

If you enter relationships expecting to get things just to make you feel good, you will have lousy relationships, and you will probably blame the other person. But if you go into a relationship without expectation and are willing to give it all you can, you will experience the rewards and joy of a great relationship.

To change others, you must first change yourself.

If you are kind, generous, and loving, you will attract other kind, generous, and loving people into your life. If you are pessimistic (or just being "realistic," as some people call it), down on life, and ornery, you will attract other pessimistic, down on life, and ornery people.

Your relationships are a direct mirror of your attitudes, thinking, and behavior.

IF YOU WANT BETTER RELATIONSHIPS IN YOUR LIFE, WORK ON BEING A BETTER YOU. AND FORGET ABOUT TRYING TO CHANGE OTHER PEOPLE. WHEN YOU WORK ON BECOMING A BETTER YOU, YOUR RELATIONSHIPS WILL MAGICALLY BECOME BETTER.

WISDOM KEY

It's been said that if you want the perfect wife—you have to be the perfect husband. In other words, don't go into a relationship trying to change the other person. *Work on changing yourself first.*

As you become better, the quality of your peer group will become better. There are some people in your life who will drop away when you start working on yourself. You won't miss these so-called friends. Instead, as you continually work on becoming better, you will notice a whole new peer group developing around you—people who believe in you and support you.

Enthusiasm is valuable in any group relationship. The most valuable people who go to the top in any organization, are the ones who can inspire enthusiasm and passion in other people. They are cheerful and always have something good to say about their friends and coworkers. They can brighten a room just by entering it. People gravitate toward these people and are willing to follow their leadership because they want to share in their enthusiasm.

These people have learned that great relationships are built on what they can give to people—not what they can take. What makes these people so special? They have discovered and mastered the art of developing winning relationships with other people.

WISDOM KEY

> As a role model and leader, you must commit yourself to a higher standard than the people you wish to influence—commit to developing stronger relationships.

Enthusiasm is the highest paid quality on earth!

— Frank Bettger

The Golden Rules for Developing Winning Relationships

There are many golden rules for a life filled with great relationships, but there are two major rules that are above all others.

Major Rule #1:

- **Treat other people better than you treat yourself.** The old golden rule, "Do unto others as you would have done unto you," has been updated. Just treating others as you would yourself is not good enough. Go out of your way to make other people feel "special." They should feel "delighted" after meeting you. "Wow" them with your hospitality.

Major Rule #2:

- **Get rid of your ego.** Don't be self-centered. It's hard because it's only natural to constantly think about yourself. But, the real winners in life have learned that great success comes only from teamwork. It's an old cliché but there is a lot of powerful philosophy to the acronym **T.E.A.M.—T**ogether **E**veryone **A**chieves **M**ore. Learn how to be a team player. Start by removing the word "**I**" from your conversation.

Start using "we" and "our" more often in your conversation. Consciously listen to yourself and catch yourself every time you use the word "I."

The world does not revolve around you. By putting others first and being an active contributing team player, other people will recognize your value. Even in sports, the most talented athletes like Michael Jordan used their talents not for their own glory but to increase the effectiveness of the whole team. Don't be self-centered—be team conscious. **T**ogether **E**veryone **A**chieves **M**ore.

- **Be Yourself.** It is important to "be yourself" in any relationship. Don't try to become somebody else to satisfy the perceived ideals of another person. Over the years, I have both said and done dumb things because I was trying to be somebody I wasn't. Remain true to yourself and you'll never get frustrated or embarrassed.

- **Remember names.** The sweetest sound on earth is the sound of a person's name. Everyone feels special when you remember his or her name. Weave the other person's name into your conversation and use it often. It's like magic and will capture attention.

- **Make people feel important.** Show them that you care by looking them in the eye when you talk to them. Your eyes often say more than your words.

- **Be a generous listener.** People want to feel that you are listening to them. Practice listening to find out what interests them. And then repeat it back to them in your conversation. Don't finish their sentences—it's rude. Let them talk—it will make them feel more important.

- **Get to know the other person.** Find out what's important to them. Find out their likes and dislikes. What turns their crank? Open-ended questions are an important tool to use.

- **Develop the skill of open-ended questions.** As we discussed in the Magical Powers of Asking section, open-ended questions will get people talking about themselves.

- **Talk about what they want to talk about.** Don't use your conversations to talk about yourself. It's human nature to want to talk only about your own life. Resist the temptation and put a tight rein on your ego. Let someone else talk about you—it's more effective.

- **Be engaged.** Your body language says a lot. Nod your head in agreement, even if you don't agree. Nodding tells the other person that at least you are listening.

- **Think before speaking.** Don't react if they say something you don't agree with. Think and then respond. You can never take back hastily offered comments.

- **Learn to understand and appreciate the other person's point of view.** You will be highly successful once you understand what the other person thinks about and what's important to them. Forcing a person to only understand your point of view disregards the other person's thoughts and feelings. Understanding the other person's point of view is the difference between success and failure. The skill of inviting opposing points of view to your dinner table makes you invaluable!

- **Be dependable.** Be on time. Better yet—be early. Live up to all your commitments. If you can't, call right away and let people know what's happening. Don't promise anything you can't deliver. "<u>No Surprises</u>" is a good motto.

- **Be a "Good Finder."** Never get in the habit of criticizing your neighbors. Speak only good of people. Critics are everywhere. "Good Finders" are rare. Gossip is the easiest form of conversation but also the most destructive form of conversation. Don't get yourself involved in vicious gossip or rumor mongering. If anyone approaches you with a good "juicy one," stop him or her immediately and tell them you're not interested.

- **Remember, what goes around comes around!** Finding the good in people takes work, but the rewards are tremendous.

- **Be complimentary and generous with your praise**. People love to be recognized through small sincere compliments. Know the difference between honest and sincere appreciation and off-the-cuff flattery. People know when you are not sincere. It's better not to say anything if your compliment isn't sincere. Praise people in front of their peers—it will make you seem very wise!

When you praise them—you raise them!

- **Be a "breath of fresh air."** Wherever you go, be enthusiastic, cheerful and positive. Give a big smile to everyone you greet. Treat everyone you meet like long lost friends. When you enter a room, consciously pump yourself up so you can energize everyone you come in contact with. A cheerful smile is catchy and really warms the room.

- **Give great handshakes.** When you shake hands with people make sure it's a warm, friendly, firm handshake. There's nothing worse than shaking hands with a cold fish!

- **Be encouraging in your greeting.** When people ask you how you are, give an enthusiastic response. People love a positive response. It's refreshing.

- **Don't be a whiner and complainer.** If you are always complaining about something, people will eventually start avoiding you. If you find people who are actually interested in your whining and complaining, you are hanging out with the wrong crowd!

- **Don't bore others with your problems or sicknesses.** When people ask, "How are <u>you really</u>?" don't tell them! Never tell people your problems. 80% of the people couldn't care less and the other 20% are actually glad! Only confide in your mastermind group of close advisors—the ones who can really help you.

- **Give credit to other people.** No man is an island; it takes many people to create successes in life. When something good happens, make sure you recognize all the people who have helped you get there. When the spotlight is turned on, remember the others first and then humbly acknowledge your contribution.

- **Be "Solution Conscious" not "Problem Conscious."** Many relationships are destroyed or sabotaged when one party concentrates too much on the problems. Most of the time you can't go back and change things. What has happened, has happened. What's important is determining how you are going to move forward. Being able to find solutions is the only way to progress. Great relationships are strengthened during times of crisis when all are involved in solving problems.

- **Develop an "Attitude of Gratitude."** Always be thankful. Don't ever take anything for granted. Be generous with your appreciation. If people think you are ungrateful, they will soon avoid you.

- **Call people on the phone—just to keep in touch.** Don't wait until people call you. Take the initiative to call and tell them you were thinking of them. There's a lot of magic in calling people and letting them know that you were thinking of them.

- **Call people just to build them up.** Be a morale booster. Make them feel good. Have a smile in your voice when you talk to them. You will be surprised how much you can make this world a better place.

- **Write letters of appreciation daily.** Develop the habit of writing letters every chance you get and write them right away. If you meet someone interesting, write them a letter telling them how much you appreciated meeting them. If someone does you a favor, write and tell them how much you appreciated them going out of their way for you. If you are patronizing a business and one of the employees gives you excellent service, write their supervisor and let them know about this employee's outstanding performance. An unsolicited letter of praise and testimony can really make someone's day!

- **Be a friend.** In order to have strong relationships you must love people—all people. You have to let them know that you care. Be supportive. Once people know that you care, they will appreciate you and support you in return. When people feel they have somebody who really listens to them and understands them, they will loyally guard this friendship forever.

- **Go out of your way to help someone.** Always be first to give a helping hand to someone in need. Give of yourself; give of your money, give of your time.

YOU GET THE BEST OUT OF OTHERS WHEN YOU GIVE THE BEST OF YOURSELF!

- **Be tolerant.** Everyone is different. We all come from a distinctive upbringing and environment, and have experienced different circumstances. As a result, everyone has different behaviors and opinions, some you may not understand or agree with. Regardless, no one should be "superior" to anyone based on race, religion, education, or gender. You should never look down on anyone, nor should you look up to anyone.

- **Give up your need to be "right."** Many relationships are destroyed when one person cannot give up a perceived need to be right. Your "right" to be right makes you defensive. Once you start defending your need to be right—you start living in the past. Your need to be right means someone has to be wrong. Your goal should be to create win/win situations for everyone.

- **Give up ownership.** Often it's best to let the other person have ownership of an idea. People have an easier time accepting a new idea if they feel like they are part of the process.

- **Be forgiving, patient and nonjudgmental.** We all make mistakes. Failures are part of the process of growing and learning. Forgiving yourself and others removes guilt and blame. You can't move forward when you are blameful and bound to the past.

YOU CAN NEVER GET AHEAD BY GETTING EVEN!

- **Don't be vindictive.** Don't hold grudges. Be the first to forgive, because everyone needs forgiveness—some more than others! <u>Even God will not judge a man until life is over.</u> <u>Don't put yourself ahead of God.</u> It's best to forgive, forget, and quickly move on.

- **Admit when you are wrong.** One of the biggest tragedies of life is when people just don't have it in them to say they are wrong. They stubbornly stick their chins out and move on without admitting to their mistakes. They have to be willing to say that they are truly sorry. Anything less than true admittance and repentance is dishonesty and everyone knows it. As soon as you realize you are wrong, admit it right away. Be the first to say that you are sorry.

- **Admit when you don't know something.** Admitting your ignorance is the best thing you can do for yourself. "Fake it 'till you make it" is not a wise policy. Faking what you don't know is always found out.

- **Get help.** Getting help when you need it shows maturity and wisdom. Refusing to get help, or resisting it, not only shows ignorance on your part, but also shows a lack of respect for others who are counting on you.

- **Be someone people can trust.** Strong relationships are built on trust, honesty and integrity. Your reputation is everything. Once you have lost your integrity, your word will always be suspect. Never compromise your values and never ever lie. Once you have told a little white lie, it grows out of control. When you always tell the truth, you won't need to remember what you've said to someone. Honesty is always the best policy.

- **Keep confidences.** If people confide in you, it's because they trust you. Don't ever violate this trust. People will respect your discretion and will honor you for it.

- **Trust everyone.** The best policy is to trust everyone. Only 3% of the people will let you down. If you suspect everyone—you will be right 3% of the time and wrong 97% of the time. Everyone wants to be trusted. Err on the side of trust. It's better to be trusting and have peace of mind. Don't worry about the other 3%—the universe will make sure they get what's coming to them.

- **Play by the rules.** When you are in somebody else's ballpark, play by their rules. One of the hardest lessons for some people to understand is that there are rules to follow in this game of life. You just can't "do as you please." Understanding and following the rules—whether it's family rules, school rules, sports rules, company policies, or government laws—shows respect for the guidelines that people have set up to make our world less chaotic. Mavericks who want to do their "own thing" stick out like sore thumbs.

- **Chaos happens when someone thinks the rules don't apply to them.** If you want to succeed in the game of life—don't fight the rules or look for shortcuts. Become good at following the rules. It's easier than trying to fight the system. Great relationships are created when everyone is playing by the same rules.

- **Don't get mad.** Getting mad and throwing temper tantrums just shows your immaturity and your inability to handle frustrations when things don't go your way. Get out of your pity party and quit feeling sorry for yourself. You're living in the past and wasting energy that could be used for going forward and doing something positive with your life. If someone else is mad, don't let them pull you down to their level.

- **Never get angry again.** Everyone can get angry, it's a weakness not a strength. Never use anger to crush the spirit of another person. Use anger to correct injustice. Use anger to protect our environment. Use your anger in a good way!

- **Don't argue.** No one ever wins an argument. If you win an argument, all you did was prove the other person was wrong. Nobody wants to be wrong. You shouldn't have to win every battle. Learn to be flexible. Relationships are based on flexibility and negotiation. The best outcome is a win/win situation for everyone.

What is right is important—not who is right!

- **If you find yourself in an argument, don't lose your temper.** You'll say things you may not mean and can never buy back. Volunteer to be wrong first by saying, "You know I'm not always right. Let's take another look at this."

- **Examine the facts again together.** Try to understand the other person's point of view. Find common ground you can both agree on first. Save the areas you can't agree on for later. Negotiate where you can. Be prepared to sacrifice. If something is really a deal breaker, be prepared to walk away to give it some time. But always leave the conversation with appreciation for the other person's attempts to try and work things out.

- **Respect the other person's rights.** Don't argue your own agenda all the time. It's OK to disagree. You will not always be able to agree on everything—that's life. Don't take it personally. Most importantly, respect the other person's right to disagree.

- **Make dissenters part of the process.** Even though you know some people will never support your ideas, sometimes it's better to invite them to be part of the process rather than ignoring them. Even if they don't agree with you, at least they will have respect for you when you invite them to join you.

- **Find the good first.** If you must disagree, don't belittle others or put them down. First find good things to praise. Tell the other person how valuable they are to the process. Point out all the good things that are right. This will get more results than going in and pointing out everything that's wrong. When you only point out what's wrong, others will get defensive and never hear what you are saying. Instead, they will concentrate on constructing "their" arguments to defend "their" position. Eventually, they will switch to being on the offensive and start pointing out everything that's wrong with you.

- **You may not agree ever!** Close relationships and friendships are too valuable to your support system to lose because of a disagreement. Sometimes it's better to realize that you will never see eye-to-eye on some things and that it's all right to agree to disagree!

Do not use a hatchet to remove a fly from your friend's forehead!
— Old Chinese Proverb

- **Start the healing process.** Always take the high road, never hold grudges and don't wait for the other person to say he's sorry first, no matter who is at fault. Winners don't wait for the other person; they always initiate the healing process. Don't let one day go by without committing yourself to the golden rules of developing "winning relationships."

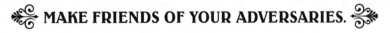 **MAKE FRIENDS OF YOUR ADVERSARIES.**

- **Don't burn bridges.** No matter how angry you may be, don't ever kill a relationship because of one disagreement. You will never know when you might need that person again sometime in your life. Life has many strange twists. Who knows, one day you may need that person's approval for something that affects your life.

- **Be honest.** Honesty is critical in any relationship, but it starts with you. You can't have a meaningful relationship if you are not honest with yourself. Complete understanding in a relationship will never happen until you first understand yourself.

- **Don't be a bank.** Don't lend money unless you are prepared never to get it back. Nonpayment of debts has destroyed many wonderful relationships. Don't lend money to friends, and don't ask friends for money.

IF YOU'RE EVER RUNNING SHORT OF ENEMIES JUST GIVE SOME MONEY TO ONE OF YOUR FRIENDS!

- **If you must help a friend in time of extreme emergency, do so with the understanding you will never get your money back.** This will help you keep your sanity and your relationship with your friends intact. Sometimes friendships are worth more than money. Decide which is more important to you.

A WORD TO THE WISE!
- **At all times conduct your affairs with integrity.**
- **Never make promises you can't keep.**
- **Your reputation is more valuable than money. Protect it!**

Successful relationships don't come easy.

They are built over time and with a lot of work. The rewards of a successful relationship don't come from what you get, but from what you freely give to the development of your friendship.

Because relationships are so necessary in your success journey, don't hold anything back. Give more than 100% of your effort to develop relationships. Approach everything with great attitude and enthusiasm. Always be grateful and appreciative of your friends and teammates.

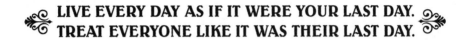

GIVE YOUR RELATIONSHIPS EVERYTHING YOU'VE GOT. A GOOD RELATIONSHIP IS WORTH THE BEST OF YOUR TIME AND EFFORT.

LIVE EVERY DAY AS IF IT WERE YOUR LAST DAY. TREAT EVERYONE LIKE IT WAS THEIR LAST DAY.

True friendship and loyalty are priceless.

Do you make the people around you better?

Let no one ever come to you without leaving better and happier. Be the living expression of God's kindness: kindness in your face, kindness in your eyes, kindness in your smile.
— Mother Teresa

Always remember, others may hate you, but those who hate you don't win unless you hate them...and then you destroy yourself.
— Richard M. Nixon

THE POWER OF HONESTY

Honesty is the first chapter in the book of wisdom.
— Thomas Jefferson

Many relationships are destroyed through deceit and a lack of honesty. Sometimes people fail to communicate because they are afraid of what the other person will think. Arguments are never put to rest and people harbor resentments. Valuable time and energy are wasted on festering misunderstandings. Give the gift of honesty.

Dealing with problems honestly and directly is a valuable gift.

Honesty is one of the most important character traits and a fundamental building block in your quest for self-development. In your relationships, honesty is a gift both to yourself and to others. By putting your fears aside and being honest and tactfully direct, you will avoid much stress, anxiety, and bureaucracy.

Dishonesty is a waste of time and energy. It's tough when you are always looking over your shoulder, worrying about who's going to "find you out." Always conduct your personal affairs with honesty and truthfulness, and you will never have to question yourself about something you might have said or done. Be honest. If it isn't right, don't get involved. It's that simple.

"How can I be more direct without hurting people's feelings?"

Focus on solving the problem and not trying to place blame. There are times when somebody just needs to get to "the heart of the matter." If you approach the issue with a genuine desire to resolve the problem in a positive manner, you will get mutual respect and the other person's help.

> **You can be very direct if the other person knows you genuinely care.** When dealing with tough issues the other person must not feel that you are being blameful or condescending.

WISDOM KEY

Make the other person your ally. By making the other person part of the solution you get better results. Try saying: "I need your help on this problem" or "Here's what I think is going on—if I am wrong please correct me" or "If I am right, how can I help?"

MANY PEOPLE FAIL TO COMMUNICATE BECAUSE THEY ARE AFRAID OF WHAT THE OTHER PERSON WILL THINK.

While it may be tough to "break the ice," it must be done. When it comes to resolving conflicts, your best guides for creating an atmosphere of trust are openness, honesty, and directness. Once you achieve trust, barriers will come down and the real issues will surface.

There is no wisdom like frankness.
— Benjamin Disraeli

PEOPLE ARE OFTEN RELIEVED ONCE THEY ARE ABLE TO BRING THEIR PROBLEMS OUT INTO THE OPEN AND DEAL WITH THEM.

Once you get everyone's opinion on the table, it's easier. Personalities and misunderstandings are major roadblocks to problem solving. Being forthright lets you get to the real issues of the problem. You will never get to the solutions fast enough when others are afraid of saying what's on their mind.

When something needs to be solved, it's important that you act on it. You must be direct in asking what you need to know and just as direct in explaining what you don't know. The respectful way to approach solving a misunderstanding is to be tactful and recognize the needs and feelings of the other person while still being honest and direct.

Being direct is even more important when someone has made a clear mistake. If the situation really is a problem and the other person is at fault, it's important that you are direct in dealing with the problem. You need to tell them, "Look, you have gotten yourself in a jam here. You need to own up to it. Let's figure out a way that we can get this thing right."

"What about people who won't be honest with me?"
If people won't be honest with you, it's honestly time to end it.

People with low self-esteem often have many things that have not been addressed in their lives. They live in fear and are constantly looking over their shoulder. People who are not honest with themselves will be defensive and blameful of others.

WISDOM KEY

Honesty allows you to look the other person in the eye. It also allows them to look back at you. If they cannot look you in the eye, they have something to hide. Dealing with problems honestly and directly is a gift you must work on in your relationships.

THE DESTRUCTIVE POWER OF GOSSIP

Whoever gossips to you will gossip about you!

HAVE YOU EVER STARTED A CONVERSATION, "DON'T TELL ANYBODY THIS, BUT HAVE YOU HEARD...?"

Your mind is not a dump and your ears are not garbage cans to be filled with trash about other people! Some people allow anything to be dumped into their minds—that's why they have "stinking thinking!" One of the most destructive habits, that people unconsciously find themselves engaged in, is perpetuating rumors and gossip. It's human nature to compare yourself with someone else and talk about their problems. Unfortunately, many people actually find comfort and joy in other people's problems. Somehow it makes them feel better to know someone else is worse off than them!

> LOSERS TALK ABOUT OTHER PEOPLE. AVERAGE PEOPLE TALK ABOUT THINGS. WINNERS TALK ABOUT GREAT IDEAS.

The best rule of thumb is to...Mind Your Own Business! Most of the rumors you hear aren't true anyway. Don't become part of the problem by spreading gossip, especially when you don't know all the facts about what really happened. There are always two sides to every story. If it isn't your business—stay out of it.

Never gossip. Gossip can really tear apart a family, social group, organization, or business. It's really a form of insecurity and shows a lack of conversation skills. Most people can't figure out what to talk about so they find it easier to point out all the faults in other people. They are delighted if they know all the latest details; they feel like they are "in the know" and in a sick way, it makes them feel important!

Gossip is a form of one-sided criticism. If given in the proper format—on a one-to-one basis for the sole purpose of helping someone better themselves—criticism can be good and very helpful. However, criticism, when shared with others for the sole purpose of just talking about someone, is merely destructive and harmful gossip.

Why spend your time and energy being a critic? There are all kinds of critics these days. You have music critics, food critics, movie critics, newspaper critics, radio and TV critics, and they all get paid for it. So if you're not getting paid to be a critic—why do it? If you're not honorable and courageous enough to talk with the victim directly—don't criticize.

Gossip is a waste of your time. Instead of talking about other people's problems and wallowing around in their tragedies, you should be spending every waking hour and minute of your day doing things that will help you better yourself and help you achieve your goals in life. It's a waste of your precious time to gossip about other people.

Practice selective listening. Your mind is your most precious possession. Only fill it with the pure, the clean, the powerful, and the positive. Be aware of what you are listening to!

Gossiping is destructive talk—no good ever comes from it. From now on, promise yourself you will never get involved in rumors or gossip. I don't care how interesting or juicy they are. If someone comes to you and says, "Did you hear about so-and-so?", tell them you are not interested in their negative trash talk. Tell them you are only interested if what they have to say is positive and uplifting.

Don't take your enjoyment from other people's misfortunes. When we find the good in others it elevates us and promotes a higher living standard. Start being a "Good Finder." Look for the good things to say about people. We are all human, and we all are going to have our good days and our bad days. So, "Don't judge lest ye be judged!"

A LOT OF PEOPLE HAVE GONE FURTHER THAN THEY THOUGHT THEY COULD BECAUSE SOMEONE ELSE THOUGHT THEY COULD

Remember, "What goes around comes around." If you are involved in the spreading of untruths, then sooner or later you are going to be the subject of rumors and gossip. However, if you are always talking positive and finding the good in others, then you can be sure that not only will goodness come back to you, but it will be multiplied.

STOP MAKING THE OTHER PERSON WRONG!

IF YOU ALWAYS HAVE A KIND WORD AND ALWAYS LOOK FOR THE GOOD IN OTHERS, YOU WILL FIND THAT PEOPLE WILL ONLY HAVE THE BEST THINGS TO SAY ABOUT YOU.

Don't get even! Don't be vindictive. Even if you find yourself to be the brunt of a vicious rumor that is absolutely not true, don't react. Many would want to get even. Don't! You only continue the vicious circle, and you lose your momentum to go forward with your life.

THE ONLY WAY YOU CAN GET EVEN IS BY FORGIVENESS.

WISDOM KEY

Always take the high road. Don't let others pull you down to their level. Forget, forgive, and move on with your life. Losers rely on gossip and rumors for their entertainment and have a hard time figuring out how to say good things about other people. Don't be a loser. Be a winner! Say only good things about other people; be a "Good Finder." Be a builder of people and your life will be more rewarding.

Here's a poem I have become very fond of...

The Builder

I saw a gang of men from my hometown.
I saw a gang of men tearing a building down. With a heave and a ho and a yes, yes yell...they swung a beam and a side-wall fell.
I went up to the foreman and asked, "Are these men skilled as the one's you'd use if you had to build?" He looked at me and laughed,
"Common labor is all I need for I can destroy in a day, what it's taken a builder 10 years to build." And I asked myself as I went my way,
"Which one of these roads am I going to take? Am I one who's always tearing things down, as I carelessly make my way around, or am I one whose community will be a little bit better... just because I was there."
— Unknown

Live your life so that no one would ever believe the gossip!

THE POWER OF FORGIVENESS

The weak can never forgive.
Forgiveness is the attribute of the strong.
— Mahatma Gandhi

Forgiving becomes easier when you surrender your "need to be right" and your sick need to prove someone else wrong. The need to be right is almost a pity party in reverse and just as devastating to yourself. You want somebody else to hurt because you hurt. You want them to be wrong. You want them to be sorry. Your "need to be right" is more important than doing "what's right." If this is how you feel—You're in trouble!

The most important lesson to be learned here is that when you can't forgive, you have just become your own worst enemy. When you cannot find it in yourself to forgive, then you become the one in the wrong. This is devastating behavior to yourself and counterproductive—no matter how right you think you are.

Even if the other person is wrong, the real question to ask yourself is, "Why is it so important that you exhaust your positive energy on an already negative situation?" Give it up. And quit spending your valuable time and energy dealing with something that is in the past.

The best advice is always to forgive, forget, and move forward.

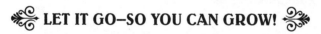 **LET IT GO–SO YOU CAN GROW!**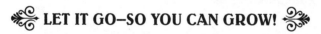

WISDOM KEY

> **The quicker you can forgive, the more productive you can become again.** Your ability to move forward and to become full of positive energy again will overcome any wrongs that have happened to you. The past is the past—keep it there!

Don't carry a grudge. While you're carrying the grudge, the other guy's out dancing!
— Buddy Hackett

The real benefit of forgiving is that the other person can heal as well. Your forgiveness will allow people to get on with life without having to constantly be looking over their shoulder wondering what you are going to do to them. Forgiveness fosters healing and your forgiveness will create positive energy around you. Most importantly, your forgiveness will allow others to forgive you.

If you cannot forgive, don't expect to be forgiven yourself.

I'M SORRY, I MUST APOLOGIZE...

The flip side of forgiveness is your willingness to apologize when you have wronged someone or done something stupid. Just as the inability to forgive is a character flaw, so is the inability to apologize when you are wrong. Some people can never find it in themselves to apologize. They think it is beneath them or a sign of weakness. Most often it is because they are arrogant and stubborn. People who cannot apologize show how shallow they are and eventually the people around them will go out of their way to avoid them.

The best time to apologize is immediately and with sincerity. The longer you wait to apologize, the less meaning it has. When you know that you should apologize for something you have done, it bothers you and you don't feel good about yourself. So quit worrying about what the other person will think of you—go ahead and apologize. If the other person will not forgive you, that's OK. Just feel good that you know in your heart you have attempted to do the right thing.

There are awesome healing powers in the words...

"I forgive you."
and
"I'm sorry."

Finally, forgive yourself. To complete the healing process of forgiveness, you must be able to forgive yourself. We have all done things of which we're not proud. Unfortunately, what's done is done and there is nothing we can do but to move forward. The past is the past.

Don't get hung up asking yourself, "What's wrong with me?" Questions like this are destructive and keep you reliving your past mistakes. "What can I learn from this so I can be a better person?" is a more appropriate question to start becoming a better you.

Forgive yourself...God already has!

LET'S SUM THINGS UP!

What does this mean to me?

1. **Anybody can learn and learning is your opportunity.** Lifelong learning is one of the keys to living a rewarding and fulfilling life of adventure and achievement. Starting today, commit to a plan of reading and writing.

2. **Change doesn't happen "out there."** All meaningful change happens within you. Decide how you are going to change your life for the better.

3. **Positive thinking and a big cheerful smile will open any door.** A positive attitude and an unshakable belief that you will win is the key to unlimited opportunity. From now on commit yourself to thinking only in the "positive."

4. **There are magical powers in "asking!"** Don't live a life of ignorance because you were too afraid to ask a dumb question! The most powerful question is an open-ended question. Become the master of open-ended questions.

5. **Ask for help.** Don't be arrogant in thinking you can manage your life without help. There is wisdom in asking for help when you need it.

6. **Life is really about relationships.** Everything we do involves people. The success of your relationships reflects the depth of your values and character.

7. **Your attitude will determine your relationships.** The quality of your life will be dependent on the quality of your relationships. If you want to change the quality of the people who are around you, begin by changing yourself.

CALL TO ACTION:

1. Reading will turbocharge your ability to change yourself for the better. Commit yourself to a daily program of reading, self-discovery and self-development.

2. Become a "better you" to attract better relationships into your life. Don't worry about the other person. Work on building a better "you!'

3. Develop an unshakable positive mental attitude and live every day to its fullest as a winner!

WHAT YOU CAN ACCOMPLISH:

A few simple LifeSkills, a willingness to change, and a positive cheerful attitude will help you achieve peace and success. Develop a lifelong hunger for knowledge and an unquenchable thirst for wisdom and you will experience great rewards—more than you could ever imagine! Surrendering your self-righteous ego to put the other person first and staying true to your values will help you attract winning relationships into your life. The greater your relationships—the greater your success!

Sources & Inspiration

The information in these books is powerful. I urge you to buy these books and read them over and over again until they become part of your daily life.

Napoleon Hill, *Think and Grow Rich,* (Wilshire Book Co., North Hollywood, Calif. 1966)

Zig Ziglar, *See You At The Top,* (Pelican Publishing, Gretna, La. 1998)

Og Mandino, *The Greatest Salesman in the World,* (Bantam Books, New York, N.Y. 1968)

Anthony Robbins, *Awaken The Giant Within,* (Fireside Books, New York, N.Y. 1991)

Napoleon Hill and W. Clement Stone, *Success Through A Positive Mental Attitude,* (Pocket Books, New York, N.Y. 1977)

Norman Vincent Peale, *The Power of Positive Thinking,* (Fawcett Columbine, New York, N.Y. 1996)

Samuel A. Cypert, *Believe and Achieve,* (Avon Books, New York, N.Y. 1991)

Dr. David J. Schwartz, *The Magic of Thinking Big,* (Fireside Books, New York, N.Y. 1987)

Dale Carnegie, *How To Win Friends & Influence People,* (Pocket Books, New York, N.Y. 1982)

George Shinn, *The Miracle of Motivation,* (Living Books, Wheaton, Ill. 1981)

Napolean Hill and E. Harold Keown, *Succeed and Grow Rich Through Persuasion,* (Fawcett Publications, Greenwich, Conn. 1971)

Dale Carnegie, *How To Develop Self-Confidence and Influence People by Public Speaking,* (Pocket Books, New York, N.Y. 1956)

Dottie Walters and Lilly Walters, *Speak and Grow Rich,* (Prentice Hall, Paramus, N.J. 1997)

John C. Maxwell, *The Winning Attitude,* (Thomas Nelson Publishers, Nashville, Tenn. 1993)

Jack Canfield and Mark Victor Hansen, *The Aladdin Factor,* (Berkley Books, New York, N.Y. 1995)

Jim Rohn, *7 Strategies for Wealth & Happiness,* (Prima Publishing, Rocklin, Calif. 1996)

Rick Pitino with Bill Reynolds, *Success Is A Choice,* (Broadway Books, New York, N.Y. 1997)

John C. Maxwell, *Failing Forward,* (Thomas Nelson Publishers, Nashville, Tenn. 2000)

Lesson Four: Problems

Lesson Four: Problems

Overcome the problems, adversities and failures in your life and turn them into opportunities!

Have you ever felt like you didn't want to get out of bed because you dreaded having to face a problem that you just didn't want to deal with? Have you ever felt like the whole world was crashing in on you and you didn't want to live another day? Have you ever felt like things were so hopeless that you didn't know which way to turn?

Why is it some people just seem to have all the luck while you keep getting hit with nothing but problems, adversities, and failures? Probably the most significant lesson in this book is the lesson on **Problems**. This lesson provides an eye-opening look at how problems are actually God's gift to you—so you can grow to be a better person.

PURPOSE:

This chapter is the smallest of all the LifeSkills lessons, but I felt it was necessary to give this discussion on problems its own chapter because as much as we try to avoid problems, all of us are confronted with difficult situations, adversities, and gut-wrenching challenges almost every day of our lives. More often than not, not only are we dealing with our own problems but we are deeply affected by the problems of our friends and family, even though we are not in a position to help them.

Until you fully understand that problems, adversities, and failures are your keys to creating great opportunities, you won't accept responsibility for what's wrong in your life. You will run from problems and you will be afraid to fail. You will never experience the exhilaration of overcoming great adversities and the triumph of a winning spirit. When you grasp this concept you will start looking for problems. You will realize what a great God we have, to have given you all these opportunities. This is your chance to show the world what you can do. Go after problems, learn from them, so you can grow into the person you were really meant to be!

You will never fear failure again after reading this chapter!

Problems Are Your Opportunities!

You cannot grow without problems.
Problems are the universe's way of testing you
to see how much you have grown.
Immature people are afraid of problems—they wish
their problems would somehow just go away.
Only your fear gives power to your problems.
The thinking and behavior that created your problems
is not the thinking and behavior you will need
to overcome your problems.
You must grow to become bigger, better,
and greater than your problems.
Remember, people who have never given up,
have always outlasted and overcome their problems.
And you can do it too. Believe it!

Above all...
Never, Ever, Ever let your problems become your excuses!

— Famous Dave Anderson

Fail Your Way to Success!

Only those who dare to fail miserably can achieve greatly.
— Robert Kennedy

Why are we so afraid of failing? As toddlers, failure was an inconsequential event—it didn't bother us. Once parental disapproval and peer ridicule started causing us discomfort, we became sensitive to embarrassment and to what others thought of us and began to fear failure. Then—and only then—did failure become a negative experience.

Although success makes us feel good, we learn more from failing than we can ever learn from success!

Unfortunately, we become conditioned to avoiding failure, as if it were death itself. We let our embarrassment and silly pride keep us from experiencing the exhilaration of great accomplishments because we are afraid of what others will think if we fail. Once you understand that failure is one of the major building blocks to experiential learning—in fact, it's the most effective way to learn—then you begin to ask yourself, "Why am I so afraid of failure? Why am I so afraid to take risks?"

Here's an interesting thought...

If you want to double your rate of success... You must double your rate of failure!

Just look at the failures of this great American hero:

1831—Failed in business	1843—Defeated for Congress
1832—Defeated for the Legislature	1848—Defeated for Congress
1833—Second failure in business	1855—Defeated for the Senate
1836—Suffered a nervous breakdown	1856—Defeated for Vice President
1838—Defeated for Speaker	1858—Defeated for the Senate
1840—Defeated for Elector	1860—Elected President

Who was this determined famous American failure? —Abraham Lincoln.

IN SPITE OF ALL THESE FAILURES, HE MANAGED TO ACHIEVE THE HIGHEST OFFICE IN THE LAND. IT JUST GOES TO SHOW WHAT ANYBODY CAN DO IF THEY NEVER GIVE UP.

Success is moving from failure to failure with no loss of enthusiasm.
— Winston Churchill

When we are born, we all start out in life out as geniuses. As children we are creative prodigies with unlimited curiosity—we are nonstop seekers of new knowledge. We have the greatest learning potential we will ever have when we are very young—for instance, the incredible ability to learn many languages easily.

Why? Because as children we are not afraid of failure.

We are innocent, nonjudgmental and fearless—we recognize no bounds.

Consider a baby, learning to walk. The baby falls many times before walking becomes natural. Often the baby squeals in delight as it continually falls. Failure is actually fun to the baby! The key to the baby's success is that it gets right back up and tries again. The baby doesn't lie there making up excuses or being blameful.

"But what about when failure marks the end of success?"
It's important to understand this truth: <u>Failure is not final!</u>

> *Consider the pole-vaulter who keeps raising the bar, constantly achieving greater heights until he can no longer reach any higher. The same is true of the weight-lifter who keeps adding weight until he can no longer lift it. But where these athletes last failed, this mark becomes the goal for their next effort. Failure is not final!*

- **You keep succeeding until you fail. But you are never really a failure.**
- **You are always recognized for your last successfully completed attempt.**
- **Your last failure becomes your next goal. It's a starting point for you to try again.**

It's not your failures that people care most about!

*While it is natural for people to be curious about your failures, they are actually more interested in how you **react to** and **handle** your failures.*

People have respect for those who pick themselves up, who step out of their self-pity and get right back into the game. The greater the adversity, the greater the hero. And people love heroes! Once people see that you are determined not to let your failures dictate your future, I have learned that they are generally very forgiving. They will actually help you get back on the road to achievement! Your past failures will be long forgotten. So, don't get hung up on people's first reaction to your failures. Instead, show them how determined you are to move forward with your life in a positive cheerful manner. This is how you want them to remember you, not as a spoiled sore-loser!

Show me a thoroughly satisfied man—
and I will show you a failure!
— Thomas Edison

We need to become childlike in our acceptance of failure, and unafraid to take risks. Like an athlete, we must constantly keep raising our standard of excellence. An athlete could never set new records by being satisfied where he or she is comfortable. Any athlete stuck in a comfort zone is quickly cut from the team. We must get out of our comfort zones and take risks. Every failure is a step toward success.

Failure does not have to be feared
or cause embarrassment.

WISDOM KEY

Failure is the natural evolution of learning. There would be no new ideas, fresh concepts, innovative products or solutions without mistakes and failures. If you're not failing, you're not learning. The greater the failure, the greater the lesson! And remember, failure is not final; it's only the beginning point for your next achievement!

You will be moving in and out
of crisis the rest of your life!
— Og Mandino

"Failing your way to success"—It's a powerful concept!

Failure is the beginning of learning and the hallmark of success.
— Famous Dave Anderson

He who never fails will never grow rich.

Never give up. Never, never give up.
— Winston Churchill

You can't stop someone who won't quit.

**Each success only buys an admission
ticket to a more difficult problem!**
— Henry Kissinger

**Show me someone who has done something worthwhile,
and I'll show you someone who has overcome adversity.**
— Lou Holtz

**Tough times never last,
But tough people do!**
— Robert H. Schuller

PROBLEMS—A Fact of Life!

You don't become a good sailor by sailing smooth seas!

A ship in harbor is safe, but that's not what ships are built for.

Problems are critical building blocks for success. Some of the most incredible opportunities for learning in life are often the most debilitating and devastating roadblocks for people—PROBLEMS! Unfortunately, throughout our adolescence, we were never taught the real truth about life. We were never told that every day of our lives, we would be bombarded with problems, setbacks, failures, mistakes, tough times, and adversities.

*How come we were never warned that
the seas of life could be so rough?*

In fact, "the true reality of life" is that every day the possibility of getting whacked by problems is enormous. Then there are the times when we really get thumped. But you know what? That's OK! This is what life is about—problems, lots of problems, little problems, big problems and ones that jackhammer us. It's normal to have problems and life isn't just targeting you. So shrug off the "poor me" attitude and sail on!

Everybody has problems. Poor people have problems. Wealthy people have problems. Ugly people have problems. Pretty people have problems. Skinny people have problems. Fat people have problems. Kids have problems. Old people have problems. Everyone has problems.

Life might have been simpler if there was a required course in school called **Problems 101**. Maybe then we would see early on that problems are great learning opportunities, the building blocks of experience. Plus, when dealing with problems, you get the fringe benefit of building character. By persevering in the face of overwhelming odds when everyone else is giving up, you are building a solid foundation of integrity and accomplishment.

Here's a real good reason why you should never give up when faced with adversities and problems in life...

WE ALL HAVE OUR BIG ROCK (PROBLEMS) WE THEY PUSH UP THE MOUNTAIN OF LIFE. IF YOU QUIT PUSHING, YOUR BIG ROCK DOESN'T JUST STAY THERE, IT COMES ROLLING BACK DOWN THE MOUNTAIN, CRASHING ON TOP OF YOU.

IF YOU DECIDE TO GET BACK IN THE GAME, IT WILL BE HARDER TO START TO PUSH IT BACK UP AGAIN. HOWEVER, IF YOU NEVER QUIT AND YOU KEEP PUSHING YOUR BIG ROCK UP THE MOUNTAIN OF LIFE—YOU WILL MAKE IT!

AND ONCE YOU GET TO THE TOP, EVEN THOUGH YOU WILL NEVER GET RID OF YOUR ROCK TO PUSH AROUND—IT'S A LOT EASIER TO PUSH ONCE YOU'RE ON TOP. THE GOOD NEWS IS THAT THERE IS ALWAYS ROOM AT THE TOP BECAUSE MOST PEOPLE HAVE GIVEN UP—THEY ARE AFRAID OF PROBLEMS.

So why is it that only a few ever experience a wildly successful and prosperous life? A lot of nice people work hard to earn a living but they rarely earn more than just a living. They just "get by" despite all their hard work.

> *Truly successful people who earn above-average incomes have come to the realization somewhere in their careers that "shouldering responsibility for solving problems" is the true key to untold fortunes and a more rewarding lifestyle.*

The more successful you become, the more problems you will have! In fact, you don't climb the ladder by working harder, but rather by taking on more responsibility for more problems. Most people have the wrong impression of being at the top. They think life there is easy when in reality every promotion is only an entitlement for more problems and the higher up you go, the bigger your problems. Sounds exciting, doesn't it?

> *In fact, the more problems you face, the easier and more rewarding life will be to you.*

What's so interesting is the strange fact that the more successful you are, the more problems you are entitled to—Wow! Nobody ever really explained life to us in this context before. Remember, "To whom much is given—much is expected," including getting more than your fair share of problems! Most people are afraid of becoming successful for this very reason.

Quit avoiding problems! The sad truth is that most people have never experienced the sheer exhilaration of fighting through the real thumpers that really whack them. They give up before the fight even begins. Instead they go through life running away from problems. They avoid problems. They don't want to think about problems. All they want is for life to be nice to them. How cute. Actually, how sad. They wish all their problems would just disappear.

Everyone has heard... **"Hey! don't lay that one on me—it's not my problem!" or "Go see Joe— it's his problem. I'm not involved, don't blame me!" or "Don't come to me with your problems, I ain't your mother!" or "You're not paying me enough to handle those problems!" Sound familiar?**

Don't ever think your company is taking advantage of you.
Just think about it this way—your extra effort is an investment in your future.
People who run around complaining about their problems and that the "higher-ups" are somehow responsible, often say, "They're taking advantage of me. I work too hard for them and they don't pay me enough," etc. etc. etc… They think the "higher-ups" could solve all their problems if only they would pay them more money, promote them, or give them more responsibility.

Actually the reverse is the major key. The more people "higher up the ladder" you can resolve problems for and the greater the number of people you can solve problems for, the more readily the forces in the Universe will come to your aid in solving these problems! So quit thinking about your own problems and wallowing around in your own self-absorption. Try to figure out how you can help a "bigger person" or figure out how you can help a lot of "smaller people" first, then the universe will immediately and exponentially reward you.

WISDOM KEY

There are four key lessons about PROBLEMS:
- The "<u>bigger the problems</u>" you are able to tackle and resolve, the higher the quality of your life and your value to the marketplace.
- The greater the "<u>quantity of people</u>" that you are able to resolve problems for, the greater your value to the marketplace.
- The greater the problems that "<u>you are able to lead your people through</u>," the stronger your leadership and your value to the marketplace.
- Your ability to resolve problems for people "<u>higher up the ladder</u>" will determine how successful you are within your company, organization, or community.

When's the last time you asked for your fair share of some really sticky problems? I challenge you to go to your boss and volunteer yourself for some problems!

Tell your boss..."GIVE ME SOME PROBLEMS! Give me the tough ones nobody else wants!" I'll guarantee you, you'll get her attention real fast because she's never heard that one before. Asking for problems will change your life forever—YES, you read this right. **Asking for problems is your key to unbelievable and unlimited opportunity!** Going after problems can make you the most valuable person in your company.

When dealing with problems never be blameful or point fingers. There's always a time and a place for finding out who is responsible and then determining a course for corrective action. The most important step is to get all the facts. Then determine what's really "the issue." Focus on the issue, deal with it, quickly move forward, and don't dwell on the past.

THIS IS IMPORTANT. Problems are nothing more than great opportunities for you to demonstrate how responsible you are under pressure and how effective you are as a leader. Problems create opportunity for a significant career and a meaningful life!

The most important thing about problems is that when you face up to them and do your best to try and resolve them, things will get better. The old saying—that no matter how tough things may seem today, tomorrow will always be better—is very true. Most often, just sleeping on a problem and letting your higher conscious mind work on your problems will provide the answers you need. Sleep allows the higher conscious mind to work on providing you with solutions without being pressured. These answers are generally the best answers.

Sometimes when the problem is really difficult, the best thing to do is admit that you can't handle this one by yourself.

Put your ego aside and get help! There are times when no matter how tough or strong you think you are—it's best to get help. Go talk to someone who you know has been down the same road. Put your ego and pride aside and ask for help. Asking for help and admitting that you can't handle your own problems is not a sign of weakness. It's actually a sign of maturity and wisdom.

In life we all need people we can talk to, who can guide us through the difficult times. There are a number of key people in our lives: 1) parents, 2) clergy, 3) doctors, 4) accountants, 5) financial advisors, 6) teachers, 7) insurance specialists, 8) real estate advisors, 9) attorneys, and maybe even 10) close friends.

BE CAREFUL WHO YOU TELL YOUR PROBLEMS TO BECAUSE 80% OF THE PEOPLE YOU TELL COULDN'T CARE LESS AND THE OTHER 20% ARE ACTUALLY GLAD!

Spiritual help is highly recommended. Just talking to someone like your clergy will often lighten your load. It's amazing how comforting it is to have someone praying for you. Having faith in a higher power will make your life here on earth a whole lot easier.

GOD DOES NOT RESPOND TO YOUR TEARS, BUT TO THE STRENGTH OF YOUR FAITH!

WISDOM KEY

Don't ask God to take your problems away, but pray for wisdom and strength to weather the storms. Asking God to take away your problems only weakens you. Asking for wisdom and strength to overcome your problems, gives you confidence and experience to take on even greater problems the next time. This is called "growth."

During these times of adversity you must never give up. You see, when you are in a comfort zone and everything is going along smoothly...God comes along and smacks you right out of your comfort zone with a "confidence crushing problem" that makes you think your whole world is caving in on you. These challenges are very necessary for your growth. The fire of adversity forges our character and strengthens our resolve to fight through our problems.

Quit thinking that problems are cruel punishment from God. The common response is to think that God is punishing us, when actually He loves us so much that He finds it necessary from time to time to jolt us out of our comfort zones. You cannot grow and be successful in a comfort zone.

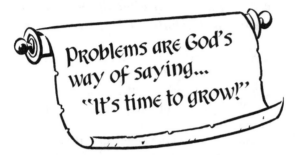

Problems are God's way of saying... "It's time to grow!"

You cannot grow without problems! God knows that we can handle the problems we face. It's our own self-doubt that troubles us, which really has nothing to do with the challenge God has sent our way.

WISDOM KEY

The most common and misunderstood belief is that God will never give you anything you can't handle. The fact is that God gives you challenges and adversities <u>you can't handle</u> so through your faith He can demonstrate the wisdom and unlimited power of an almighty God.

HERE'S THE LESSON: If you had problems you could handle, you wouldn't grow. The strength of your character can only be forged through adversity and problems. People who don't experience great adversity cannot test the resolve of their character or the strength of their leadership abilities.

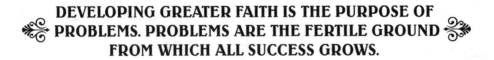

DEVELOPING GREATER FAITH IS THE PURPOSE OF PROBLEMS. PROBLEMS ARE THE FERTILE GROUND FROM WHICH ALL SUCCESS GROWS.

There are two major ways to approach a problem. You can either think God is punishing you or you can think God is rewarding you with opportunity! *How you think about your problems will determine the quality of the life you live.*

Problems are God's ultimate challenge for you to grow. To run from problems is wasteful of the opportunities God has given you!

THE SIZE OF THE PROBLEM WE FACE — ONLY REVEALS THE DEPTH OF OUR CHARACTER.

KEY THOUGHT:
Great heroes were never made without great problems!

Don't have any problems? If you are so smug to think you ain't got problems, you better get down on your hands and knees and ask the good Lord to give you some…ask Him, "What's the matter Lord? Don't you trust me? Give me some problems!" Because if you don't have problems, you're on your way out. The only people without problems are buried six feet under.

From now on stop running away from problems. In fact, I am challenging you, if you haven't got problems—go ask for some! Going after problems instead of running from them will dramatically change your life for the better.

WISDOM KEY

- When dealing with problems—be "solution conscious" not "problem conscious."
- Develop a reputation for being the one everyone can count on during times of crisis.
- Start seeing problems as great opportunities to make you a better person.

Are you a "diamond in the rough" or nothing but crushed rock? Problems are like a grindstone. They will either grind you down or they will polish you up to become the best you can be. It all depends on what you're made of.

> **The strength of your character is directly mirrored by the size of the challenges you strive to conquer.**
> — Famous Dave Anderson

You cannot help these kinds of people with their problems:

- People who don't think they have problems.
- People who think that you are the problem.
- People who "know it all."
- People who do not have a good self-image and believe they deserve their bad luck!
- People who live in the past and refuse to change.
- People who think that the world owes them.
- People who can't forgive and hold grudges.
- People who are full of excuses and are blameful.
- People who think negatively.
- People who talk negatively.
- People who won't take action to help themselves.
- People who want something for nothing.
- People who don't have a clear vision for their future.
- People who are only out for themselves.
- People who are not grateful.
- People who do not respect those in authority.

You cannot solve problems with the same thinking, attitude, and behavior that created them. You must rise above your problem by becoming better. You need greater thinking, a super improved attitude, and positive behavior. You have to be "solution conscious" not "problem conscious."

**Strength does not come from winning.
Your struggles develop your strength. When you go through
hardships and decide not to surrender, that is strength.**
— Arnold Schwarzenegger

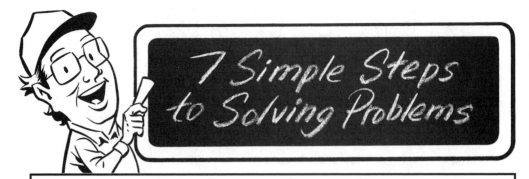

7 Simple Steps to Solving Problems

1. **Accept responsibility for your mistakes immediately. Don't shy away from dealing with your problem. Deal with it, learn from it, and then move forward with your life.**

2. **Don't be the one to point fingers. Fixing the problem is more important than placing blame.**

3. **Find out the issues and remove your emotions from the process. Pride, anger, or embarrassment are selfish attitudes that have never solved any problem.**

4. **You cannot solve problems with the same thinking, attitude, and behavior that created them. You must rise above your problems with greater thinking, a super improved attitude, and positive behavior.**

5. **Decide quickly what issues are the most important. Focus your energy on the solution, not on the problem.**

6. **A positive attitude is necessary to attract solutions.**

7. **As soon as you realize that you are in over your head, put your ego aside and get help.**

Dealing with problems is a little like wrestling a gorilla. You don't quit when you are tired, you quit when the gorilla is tired!
— Robert Strauss

ALL SHOOK UP!

Throughout life, we will experience bone-jarring teeth-grinding problems that shake us to the very core of our existence.

We get so shook up that we run to God, only to find out that it is God who is doing the shaking!

He has shaken us out of our comfort zones, and he is telling us…"It's time to grow!"

The small-minded only see the adversities in opportunities. Great minds find the opportunities in adversity!

— Famous Dave Anderson

Learn the Real Secrets of
"Screwing Up!"

IF YOU DON'T LEARN FROM
YOUR MISTAKES, THERE'S NO
SENSE IN MAKING THEM.

The secret of screwing up is an interesting concept. I used to wonder why I had all bad luck. Whenever I messed up, I usually suffered terrible consequences, while others seemed to go through life unscathed even though they messed up too. It was only later in life that I learned the real secrets to "screwing up!"

Today, I have come to understand that there is a big difference between "screwing up" because of my bad habits and "messing up" because I was trying to better myself. That's when I learned I didn't have to be afraid of making mistakes.

Making mistakes is all part of living life.

Try! Reach higher than you have ever reached! Go for it! Make some mistakes! Your greatest learning opportunities will come from getting "out there" and "getting it on." When this happens, not all your decisions or all the things you do will be right. Your inexperience or lack of being prepared will cause you to fail. You cannot get out of your comfort zone and go where you have never gone before without making some mistakes. You cannot attempt things you have never done before without some failures.

We all make mistakes and screw up—that's OK! This is how we learn. The more mistakes we make, the more we are pushing ourselves out of our comfort zones. People who are really good at something understand this and allow for mistakes and failures.

PEOPLE WHO GET REALLY GOOD AT SOMETHING
HAVE FAILED MANY TIMES. PEOPLE WHO NEVER
FAIL ARE NEVER REALLY GOOD AT ANYTHING.

Everyone has been there before and survived—so don't feel that you are being singled out. If you're not making mistakes you're not growing, and you start stagnating. Go ahead, make some mistakes—it's the only way you're going to grow!

Always make your own mistakes! This is how you learn. However, ignorance comes from not learning from the mistakes of others.

The only time a problem becomes a problem is when you keep making the same mistakes. When you repeat the same mistake over and over again, you are not learning. This pattern of failure is just plain carelessness, and consistent carelessness eventually warrants consequences. If you continue in careless behavior, those consequences become more severe. Quit being so ignorant. Sooner or later you are going to have to wise up, learn from your mistakes and make the necessary corrections!

Why do some people go through life without major defeats while others have all the bad luck?

Think of it as being given "Screwing Up Opportunities." We are all given a certain number of times to screw up without consequences. We need to screw up once in a while if we are going to take risks. But when we keep screwing up and we are not learning from our screw-ups, then we are in big trouble.

WISDOM KEY

There are two major differences in the ways to screw up.

1. If you screw up while attempting to do a good job or while trying to better yourself, your "opportunities for screwing up" will be renewed, because these are the mistakes you learn from. If you learn something, these types of screw-ups will actually turn into opportunities!

2. When screw-ups are the result of bad habits: mistakes caused by the effects of alcohol, smoking or drug abuse; carelessness; bad habits; or from continued negative attitudes, you are "using up" your opportunities to screw up and these types of "screw-up opportunities" don't get renewed. Bad habit screw-ups always have consequences.

---

*Remember, if you're going to screw up,
do it because you are trying to better yourself.*

Don't screw up because of your bad habits!

The world knows the difference between your screw-ups ... and gets sick of it! If your mistakes and failures are continually the results of your bad habits, you start to become a pollutant or toxin to the universe. The universe will say, "Enough is enough" and start penalizing you for your bad mistakes or bad habits. If you continue, the universe will eventually start to treat you like the toxin you are and try to expel you from its system. So some of us can't screw up any more because we are over our limit. Our screw-up opportunities are gone forever. For all future violations we will have to suffer the consequences.

But here's the deal—you're going to have to change. Only by a change of heart, a change of mind, and a commitment to dedicating yourself to becoming a better person can you make a positive difference in the world and redeem yourself.

When you screw up, admit it. I am amazed at how many people try to get by without admitting their mistakes. They seem to think that people have not noticed. You can count on people finding you out! Be "up front" when you have messed up, admit it immediately! You will be relieved to have everything out in the open. Offer to do whatever it takes to right the situation. Never hope that the problem will go away or that people will forget about it.

Beware...your sins will find you out!

Be sincere about your apologies and accept total responsibility for your actions. Don't spend time worrying about who else is wrong. The only thing that matters is for you to be forgiven, so your mind can be free again.

Quit feeling sorry for yourself and get back in the game as soon as possible. The most important thing to remember is that, for the most part, people are forgiving and will allow you to start over. Whatever happened has happened, it's over and done with. The sooner you can become an enthusiastic, productive person again the sooner people will start believing in you again. It's important to remember that people are forgiving if they believe that you are truly sorry for your behavior and are trying to do the right thing.

IT'S OK TO SCREW UP,
BUT...
DON'T BE SCREWED UP!

REMEMBER:

You can never be a big failure unless you are trying
something very big! People who never achieve
greatness are afraid of failing. Surprisingly, the
effort between trying something big and trying
something small...is not much.

However, when you do fail, deal with it immediately.
All of our most embarrassing mistakes are easily forgiven
when they are honestly and openly dealt with...
rather than the unforgivable behavior we use to
deceive and conceal our failures.

So, if you are going to do something—Do it BIG!
Make your effort worthwhile because the success
you will achieve, will be very rewarding.
If you fail, the lessons you learn
will be very meaningful.

LET'S SUM THINGS UP!

What does this mean to me?

1. **Problems are God's gift to you!** Problems are nothing more than opportunities.

2. **You must come clean.** You must acknowledge what is wrong in your life in order to become better. You must not fall into the habit of believing your own lies.

3. **Learn how to ask for help.** Never ask God to take away your problems but ask for wisdom and strength to handle your problems. It's the only way you can grow into a better person.

4. **It's OK to fail and make mistakes.** But you can't dwell on what's in the past. You need to learn from your failures, make corrections, forgive, forget, and then move forward.

5. **Problems define you as a person.** How you act under pressure reveals what you are made of. The amount of adversity you are able to handle directly reflects the strength of your character. The greater the problems, the greater the person you become.

6. **Become the one person everyone can count on.** The adversities you are able to lead people through determine your value as a leader in the community and what the marketplace is willing to pay you.

7. **Live a life free of excuses.** You alone are responsible for the outcome of your destiny, so live your life without blame and excuses. Remember, never let your problems become your excuses!

CALL TO ACTION:

1. Acknowledge what's wrong in your life. Accept full responsibility for your actions, attitude, habits, and behavior.

2. Only you can change your life for the better by changing your attitude. Become "solution conscious" instead of "problem conscious."

3. Start going after problems instead of running away from them. Become the one person everyone can count on to handle problems during a time of crisis.

WHAT YOU CAN ACCOMPLISH:

Once you realize that problems are only great opportunities, the weight of the world will lift from your shoulders and you will never fear problems again. You will experience freedom. An amazing thing will happen—you will start looking for problems to resolve once you understand that they are your keys to personal achievement and great financial wealth. People will look up to you once they realize that they can count on you to lead them through times of crisis, because of your problem solving abilities. Instead of fear, you will have hope.

Sources & Inspiration

The information in these books is powerful. I urge you to buy these books and read them over and over again until they become part of your daily life.

Robert H. Schuller, *Tough Times Never Last, But Tough People Do!,* (Bantam Books New York, N.Y. 1984)

Willie Jolley, *A Setback Is A Setup For A Comeback,* (St. Martin's Press, New York, N.Y. 1999)

John C. Maxwell, *Failing Forward,* (Thomas Nelson Publishers, Nashville, Tenn. 2000)

Zig Ziglar, *See You At The Top,* (Pelican Publishing, Gretna, La. 1998)

Napoleon Hill and W. Clement Stone, *Success Through A Positive Mental Attitude,* (Pocket Books, New York, N.Y. 1977)

Norman Vincent Peale, *The Power of Positive Thinking,* (Fawcett Columbine, New York, N.Y. 1996)

Lesson Five: Total Wellness

Lesson Five: Total Wellness

Live an excuse-free, energized, healthy lifestyle!

D o you feel more fatigued than you should? Have you ever struggled with your weight? Are you plagued with colds, headaches, and minor pains? Have you ever struggled with an addiction, whether it is eating, drugs, alcohol, smoking, or other things you can't control in your life?

61% of all Americans are seriously overweight due to bad eating habits. And our children are gaining 10 pounds more every ten years than the previous generation. We are eating out more often and eating more processed and refined foods than ever before. We spend more time watching TV than we do engaging in physical activity. Our ancestors died from sickness and old age; today we are dying from our lifestyle. Heart attacks, strokes, cancer, diabetes, obesity, and AIDS are all "lifestyle" diseases. But we can change our lifestyle.

PURPOSE:

All success in life begins with having a healthy attitude, a physically fit body, and freedom from addictions. The discipline of eating properly, and not gorging as a result of your impulses, is a major key to finding the magic in living a healthy lifestyle. In addition, if you are not exercising, don't expect to reach your maximum potential. The discipline of exercise carries over to all other habits of achievement. Start living an excuse-free, energized, healthy lifestyle today!

ADDICTIONS

What you can walk away from
…you have conquered.

What you cannot walk away from
…has conquered you.

White sugar and pop are two of the most destructive substances you can give to a child!

One of the greatest gifts you can give to your child
…is to keep them off of white sugar.

I have chosen to start with sugar because I wanted to catch your attention right away. Most people, when then see the word, addiction, will want to skip this section because they believe "addictions" have nothing to do with them. Nothing could be further from the truth.

Addictions affect all of us in one way or another. I believe that giving candy to babies is one of the most destructive things you can do to create addictions in children. Sugar causes mood swings and creates "cravings." Unchecked cravings will eventually lead to other addictions and behavior problems. I especially cringe when I see parents putting various forms of pop and soft-drinks into their babies' bottles. Chocolate is a double whammy because it contains both caffeine and sugar!

The average American consumes 124 pounds of sugar a year, <u>or 1 pound of sugar every 3 days</u>! The average can of pop contains ten teaspoons of sugar!

Think twice about Halloween! Once it's moving, the sugar train doesn't stop. As our children grow older, we continue, "stoking of the fire" with a sick tradition of giving out candy at Halloween. I can remember coming home with big huge bags of candy! What loving parents would purposely give five pounds of sugar to their child to eat? Is Halloween candy any different?

Sugar in itself is not that bad—sugar is energy. Your body needs sugar to function optimally. The problem with sugar is the amount and the fact that it's generally found in food products that are high in fat; this creates a lose/lose situation for kids and adults alike.

Sugar highs and lows are a very real thing and the primary cause of mood swings in children. A candy bar can really get a kid going—then the bottom drops out. The answer for many kids and adults? More sugar! We start learning how to self-medicate at a very early age with sweets, candy, and pop. This is the beginning of a very vicious cycle of reliance and addiction—sugar really isn't very sweet, is it?

Sugar is a "gateway drug" to all other addictions!

Instead of sugary desserts, give them fruit. Instead of pop, give them pure clean water and fresh fruit juices. The longer you can keep your children from indulging in sweets, the healthier their lives will be as they grow.

WISDOM KEY

Your children do not need man-made white sugar or pop in their diets. There is enough natural sugar in food to satisfy their daily requirements. Children will never miss white sugar. Besides, it's very bad for their teeth.

I am speaking from experience. For most of this book, I have drawn on wisdom, proven strategies, and lifeskills from all the great teachers living today and throughout history. However, when it comes to the topic of addictions, I can, unfortunately, share with you my own life experience of dealing with addictions and the resulting devastation of family, friends and business associates.

As parents, the biggest worries we have are keeping our kids from drinking, smoking, drugs, and sex. Yet we are afraid to discuss these issues with our children, primarily because we either don't know how or we are afraid to admit the failure in our own lives.

This is a touchy subject because it is human nature not to admit having any weaknesses that we cannot control.

Who gives a rip about what others think…this is your life! We are so sensitive about what others may think of us that we tend to sweep as much as we can under the rug, hoping they will never find out. We feel that others will think less of us because we have certain behaviors in our lives that are out of control. Other people's opinions are not precious—your life is what's precious.

Having an addiction is basically being out of balance. If you have ever said, "I need to go on a diet," something is out of balance in your life. Being able to say this is an indication of how mature you are, and not an indictment that you are a criminal from the seedy side of town.

The truth is, everyone has skeletons in their closets.
The truth is, everyone *knows* about our skeletons (addictions).

The real tragedy in life is never admitting to what is destroying us so we can get help. I know from first-hand experience that you can overcome the destructive behaviors in your life. If I can help you open your eyes to see the early signs of addictions and encourage you to realize you can quit them before they destroy you, I will feel grateful that my own experiences have made a positive difference by helping to better the lives of other people.

To those of you who refuse to discuss these issues, I hope I can pull your heads out of the sand and help you face the realities of life.

This stuff is all around us and it greets our kids every day with open arms.

Addictions Affect Everyone!

No one is exempt. You don't have to be born on the wrong side of the tracks to be an alcoholic, drug addict, or a sexual abuser. People from all walks of life and of all ages are susceptible to addictions. You can be rich, middle class, poor, educated, ignorant, talented, physically fit, or a couch potato. It doesn't matter—anyone can become addicted.

If you think this could never happen to you—you better be careful <u>because you have just committed your first denial</u>!

There is an unjust stigma about addictions. The worst thing we can do is pass judgment on people with addictions. They aren't bad—they have a disease. They can recover, and they can go on to lead very productive and rewarding lives.

To be free from addictions is a blessing!

Many people who are successful in recovery lead rewarding lives and have been "enlightened" by the true meaning of surrender and forgiveness. They are thankful to a higher power for their recovery and generally get a deeper understanding of spirituality. In my own life, I reached a point where I needed help from a higher power.

It has often been said…

"**Religion** is for those who don't want to go
to hell and *Spirituality* is for those of us…
who have been there!"

Somebody has to talk about this stuff…

So sensitive is this subject of Addictions that I have had well-meaning people come up to me and say, "You know, Anderson, you don't have to tell people about all the bad things in your life. Just share with them all the good stuff. That's really what people want to hear!"

I BELIEVE THAT I WOULD NOT BE HONEST WITH YOU IF I LED YOU TO BELIEVE THAT MY LIFE HAS BEEN NOTHING BUT ONE BIG POSITIVE "LIVING THE AMERICAN DREAM" LIFE. I HAVE ACHIEVED INCREDIBLE SUCCESS BUT I BELIEVE THE STRENGTH I'VE GAINED FROM OVERCOMING MY PERSONAL FAILURES AND MY WILLINGNESS TO TALK ABOUT THEM — ARE WHAT MAKE MY MESSAGE AND THIS BOOK SO VERY VALUABLE.

I believe God has had His hand over my life. Otherwise, I would not be alive today to share this hope that everyone can have a better life. Most importantly, it doesn't matter what has happened before, or how tough things may seem right now; things can get better if you are willing to change. I am so grateful to be living a sober life, free from addictions, that I want to share this message of healing and the gift of recovery with others who are in need of help.

Change can only happen if you acknowledge there might be things in your life you can't control.

Admitting there are things in your life that you can't control does not mean you are a bad person. I truly believe that if I did not talk to you about *addictions* and *denial*, I would be doing you a terrible disservice. Addictive behavior is so widespread that anyone who reads this book is probably either addicted themselves or has experienced the ravaging devastation of addictions with family members, friends, or fellow business associates.

The greatest gift to an addicted person is "the gift of reality."

If someone in your life is struggling with addiction and denial, give them the "gift of truth." If you love these people, you need to do everything in your power to get them to face up to the realities of what is happening to their lives. You can't look the other way. You can't ignore what is happening.

In the first stages of youthful addiction, parents and loved ones often try to protect their kids by shielding them from the truth. They use the excuse...

"OH, THEY'RE JUST KIDS SOWING A LITTLE WILD OATS — NOBODY GOT HURT, NO HARM DONE!"

I WANT TO WARN YOU...

If your kids are young or you are young and just starting out in life and you take an occasional drink, I want to warn you: there is a very good chance that your drinking will start to progress very slowly over many years into a full-fledged drinking problem. The odds of you controlling your drinking are very slim.

The odds of you developing other addictions are very great.

That's just the way it is...

This is very serious stuff.

TAKE AN HONEST LOOK AT YOUR FAMILY OR YOUR FRIENDS AND SEE HOW MANY OF THEM ARE STRUGGLING WITH ADDICTIONS OR HAVE SUFFERED GREAT TRAGEDIES BECAUSE OF SOME ADDICTIVE BEHAVIOR. I THINK IF YOU TOOK A GOOD HARD AND HONEST LOOK, WHAT YOU WOULD FIND WOULD BE EYE-OPENING. YOU MIGHT FIND THAT ALL MAJOR PROBLEMS IN YOUR LIFE, YOUR FAMILY'S LIFE, OR THOSE AROUND YOU CAN BE TRACED BACK TO SOME FORM OF SUBSTANCE ABUSE.

You could be very fortunate...
If you have had loving parents who did everything they could to raise you right— you might be one of the lucky ones who has escaped acquiring any personal addictions yourself. If that's the case, thank God profusely for your freedom from the bondage of substance abuse.

However, just because you don't have an addiction doesn't mean that you don't have to bother yourself with this touchy subject. The truth is, in your career you will have exposure to many people who are addicted and like it or not, you will have to deal with the consequences of their addictions. So you better have an open mind about this stuff and you better understand it.

All addictions start out with innocent curiosity.

Peer pressure in school makes you want to be part of the fun crowd. If you have parents who have addictions, there is a good chance you will have them too. Big business and the media make it appear that smoking and drinking are the only ways to have fun. Don't become a puppet of big business. You have a mind—make a decision to be substance-free.

Addictions come in many forms.

Addictive substances and behaviors include:

- White sugar and pop
- Alcohol abuse
- Drug or chemical abuse
- Smoking
- Caffeine
- Chocolate
- Overeating
- Gambling
- Sex abuse/Pornography
- Surfing the Internet
- Handheld electronic games
- Being a workaholic
- Using vulgar language
- Uncontrollable anger
- Soaps/Watching TV to an excess
- Gossiping
- Negative attitudes/thinking
- Telling "little" lies

Basically, an addictive substance or behavior is something you cannot control that is slowly destroying you. People with one addiction generally have more. People who abuse alcohol probably also smoke cigarettes, overeat, swear, and get angry when they are frustrated.

If you smoke, you probably will try other substances.
If you drink, you probably will try other substances.

Smoking is a "gateway drug."

Avoid smoking at all costs. Smoking is one of the few habits that is almost certain to lead to other addictions. Immediately, from the first inhalation that you take, it affects your lungs—depleting oxygen to your heart, brain, and all cells and tissues. Smoking hurts your stomach and digestive system and severely weakens your immune system. It also affects the quality of your skin and makes you look older than you really are.

Smoking depletes the body of vital nutrients and is a major contributor to cancer and heart disease. Smoking is a dirty habit—beyond the burn holes in your clothes, it leaves your clothes, your home, your car, and your mouth smelling like a dirty old ashtray.

Smoking is not a cool thing to do...
Don't smoke. Don't even start.

SMOKING COMBINED WITH ANY OTHER ADDICTIONS, LIKE ALCOHOLISM AND DRUG ABUSE, INCREASES THE TOXIC LEVELS IN YOUR BODY, WHICH WILL KILL YOU EVEN FASTER.

One addiction generally leads to other addictions. People who have addictive behaviors often trade one addiction for another. For example, someone who gives up smoking may turn to overeating. Someone who gives up drinking may start gambling. Someone who quits overeating may start smoking.

Denial is the single biggest reason why people don't get help. The second biggest reason why we don't get help is our own self-righteous pride—we are afraid of what other people may think if we seek help.

THOSE WHO WILL LIE ABOUT THEIR ADDICTION WILL ALSO LIE ABOUT EVERYTHING ELSE!

The most important question regarding our addictions:

Why do we stubbornly deny, creatively scheme, justify to no end, and protect with everything we've got...

Our right to destroy ourselves?

Why do we refuse to give up...
THE THINGS THAT ARE KILLING US?

The answer is that our addictions are "devious" and "instinctively defensive." They twist our thinking so out of whack that we will do anything to believe our own lies and deny we have a problem.

IF YOU THINK LIKE THIS, YOU MAY BE IN DENIAL...WATCH OUT!

- You start believing after a long week of work, you deserve to "let loose!"
- You deserve your "night out with the boys!" (or girls!)
- You start believing that your addictions are your own little pleasures.
- You start believing your addictions don't hurt anyone else.
- You believe that you are actually having fun, despite how sick you feel the next morning.

Most people who have addictions live double lives. First, there is the life where they want everyone to believe everything is OK. And then there is the other life, where they drop all their values—anything goes as long as they are able to enjoy their addictions.

Addictions love company. People who are addicted go out of their way to help other people get addicted, "Here try this, you'll like it!" or "Come on, let me buy you a drink." Have you ever noticed people who smoke all hang out together in the same places? Have you ever noticed fat people are always with other fat people?

There's a lot of truth to the old saying...
"Misery loves company!"

PLEASE READ THIS VERY CAREFULLY:

WISDOM KEY

> **Addictions are devious in protecting their right to exist.** The first clue that you have an addiction is when you deny you have a problem. Another indication is when you start telling yourself that you are in control and you can stop anytime you feel like it. As soon as the words come out of your mouth, "I am in control," you are not in control! You are addicted! The moment you think you probably should quit—you are addicted!

The truth is that _all_ addictions are progressive, addictions will always get worse. You may quit for a time. But every time you relapse, your addiction will come back with a vengeance. You never go back to the level of substance abuse you were at before you quit. After you quit and you start again, your addiction always progresses to a higher level. People who have quit for a while will often think they have things under control. They do not!

Once addicted, always addicted. One little relapse, and old addictions are back in full force immediately. You may not want to think that—but that's the way it is. Accept this as fact.

The consequences of addictions get worse. The consequences of your addictions get progressively worse as well. Whether it's legal problems, financial problems, or health problems, your situation will eventually get to a point of helplessness.

Your whole day will be planned around your cravings to indulge your addiction. Your whole life starts to revolve around your addictions. You can't wait to get to the bar where you can see your friends and have a drink. Or you can't wait until break time so you can go have a cigarette.

Pretty soon you are on a merry-go-round that is out of control and you can't get off.

Next...
You begin to lose what's important to you.

Gradually, people with addictive behaviors start losing the values that were once important to them. When addictions progress to the point where they consume your every thought, you begin to lose all integrity in your life. You start by compromising your values and get to the point where you actually can start justifying your addictions and behavior.

Once addicted people can justify their actions, they start to believe they are no longer doing anything wrong. Since they no longer hold themselves responsible, they need to place the blame somewhere.

People who are addicted have a tough time taking responsibility for the consequences of their addictions. They blame everything and everyone around them. These people are miserable to be around because they are always finding fault in other people. <u>They are like the little kid who got caught with his hand in the cookie jar who said, "Looky over there!"</u> They hope that by pointing out the faults of others the attention will be taken off of them.

"Looky Over There!"

Addicted people become so twisted in their thinking that they truly believe they don't have a problem, and they resent anyone who tries to help them. This eventually leads to resenting all people in authority. They are so convinced that they are right and the whole world is wrong, and they wonder why on earth nobody is intelligent enough to understand them!

Watch who you are hanging out with!

Don't kid yourself. You will pick up the habits of the people you are around. Don't ever blind yourself to what's happening around you. Take a good hard look at who you are associating with and honestly ask yourself if there are any redeeming character values these people have that will help you become a better person. If not, run for the hills!

YOU CAN'T BE SOARING WITH THE EAGLES IN THE MORNING...
WHEN YOU'VE BEEN OUT ALL NIGHT SCRATCHING WITH THE TURKEYS!

It's almost certain that you will pick up habits—good or bad—from the people you are hanging around with. If you associate with people who are abusing alcohol or drugs you will pick up their bad habits. It's a fact of life. These addictive influences affect you.

WISDOM KEY

Don't ever fool yourself into thinking that just "one little try" won't hurt. The fact is you will like what it does to you. Then you think, "that wasn't all that bad!" and sooner or later you will try it again. It may take years, but pretty soon you're hooked.

> Don't hang around with people whose financial
> and emotional thinking is on a lower level than yours.
> You want to grow. They don't. So they won't help you
> expand your horizons, and they can't inspire you.
> — Tom Hopkins

Don't kid yourself. If you have friends who are starting to drink or do drugs—do yourself a big favor...distance yourself from them—now!

> *Nobody can:*
> *Hold you down,*
> *Beat you down,*
> *Keep you down,*
> *Unless you give them permission!*
> — Sign at the LifeSkills Center for Leadership

No one addiction is safer than the other.

Don't fool yourself into thinking that just because you drink wine
it isn't as addictive as whiskey...It is!

Don't fool yourself into thinking that just because you smoke a "little grass"
it isn't as addictive as cocaine...It is!

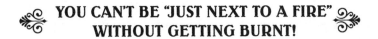

YOU CAN'T BE "JUST NEXT TO A FIRE" WITHOUT GETTING BURNT!

Don't get to the point where your addictions have to drop you to your knees
before you will admit to having a problem. Quit now.

There is nothing you will miss. You can still have fun without your
addictions. Once you quit, you won't believe how rewarding your life will be.

The fun you do have will be real fun, without the substance abuse. If you
can't imagine your life without your addiction, then your addiction is
stronger than you can handle by yourself. You need to get professional help.

YOUR LIFE IS A GIFT—DON'T TRASH IT!
— John Alston

DENIAL

"Da Nile" is not some big river in Africa!

YOU CANNOT CHANGE FOR THE BETTER WHEN YOU START BELIEVING YOUR OWN STUPID LIES.

There are four major reasons why people won't change to better themselves:

1. **Lack of knowledge or ignorance**
2. **Plain laziness**
3. **They haven't been knocked down far enough to want to change**
4. **Denial (know-it-all stubbornness—or, they just don't get it!)**

Out of the four, **DENIAL is probably the most destructive.** <u>You cannot change what you will not acknowledge.</u> If someone won't admit to being wrong or needing help—how can they change? Denial is probably one of the most damaging personal traits that keeps people from making positive changes in their lives and getting better.

Our stubbornness, self-righteous ego, false pride, and addictions keep us defensive and protective of the bad things in our lives that are slowly destroying us.

We are afraid of admitting we may have weaknesses.

We lie to cover up our weaknesses. We don't want anyone to know there are areas in our lives that are not working. We want everyone to think we are OK. We lie to them, and we lie to ourselves. But when things are not right in our lives, other people know it. We are not hiding anything. We are only harming ourselves when we lie and refuse to face up to reality—what is so clearly evident to everyone else.

We are only kidding ourselves if we think our self-destructive behaviors are our own "little secrets."

Denial is a gradual process—like a disease that keeps getting worse. If the disease gets worse, no amount of medicine can stop it from destroying the victim. The symptoms of denial are very similar. At some point, the lies become so pervasive that it's like being on a merry-go-round that's out of control. The momentum is so strong you can't get off. Your life is spinning out of control.

The Traits of Denial are:

- Not admitting to addictive habits and saying you can quit anytime you want even though you haven't been able to
- Not willing to accept the truth about your circumstances
- Not willing to listen
- Not being able to admit to personal failure
- Feeling misunderstood
- Being unreceptive and resentful of people trying to help you
- Being resistant to higher authorities and supervision

Symptoms of Denial:

- Failed relationships
- Constant legal trouble
- Financial trouble
- Not being able to keep a job for any length of time
- Lack of hope for the future

As denial progresses, we go from being accountable for our actions to blaming others.

WE BECOME SO CALLOUSED THAT OUR BEHAVIOR NO LONGER OFFENDS US.

Once our addictive behavior becomes acceptable to us, we actually start believing our own lies and that's when denial really becomes dangerous because we no longer feel guilty. At that point, we no longer have respect for authority. In fact, we resent authority. We delude ourselves to the point that we are able to justify our actions and beliefs. The danger is that we start believing we are right and everyone else is wrong—or they just don't understand.

While at first these little "white lies" seem like no big deal, the law of denial dictates that things will get worse. Not only will circumstances get worse but so too will the consequences, which feed the momentum of your decline. Your life is in a tailspin.

People who have gotten to this point can't figure out what went wrong. They cannot accept the fact that they need to change—they can only blame others. Ever since Adam lied about eating the fruit and then blamed Eve, mankind has denied guilt.

❧ WE HAVE A HARD TIME DEALING WITH THE TRUTH. ❧

I believe people who have dedicated themselves to a lifetime of self-improvement and positive living will be more receptive to changing the bad behaviors and bad attitudes in their life.

For the hard-headed ones, the ones who just don't get it, reality needs to get knocked into them! Those in deep denial sometimes need a very traumatic failure in their lives that brings them down to their knees before they will accept both the responsibility for their actions and the need to change. Only then can they begin to conquer the ill effects of denial.

The Miracle Of "Surrendering!"

Don't let yourself get to the point where you have to suffer some great setback or failure in your life to wake up and find out what everyone around you already knows about you!

So quit kidding yourself that this is your own little secret.

When people in your life are trying to help you, don't fight them by denying there is nothing wrong. Rather than looking at this advice as a threat to your self-righteous pride, perhaps you should listen with an open mind. Accepting help when it is needed is a sign of maturity and wisdom.

Surrender is VICTORY! The "miracle of complete surrender" is that it allows you to conquer the things that have blinded and deceived you and made you feel out of control and headed for disaster. Surrender is a very powerful concept. People who have a hard time surrendering actually have given in to their weaknesses. Any time you can conquer your weaknesses, you are the VICTOR!

Quit being "full of yourself!" Self-righteous pride and misplaced ego keep us from understanding and dealing with our addictions. Thinking you are in control of your addiction will keep you from totally recovering, and relapse is "a given." Change can only happen if you are willing to surrender your self-righteous pride. Surrender allows you to have an open mind so you can get help.

➢ **"The truth will set you free."**

➢ **Taking responsibility for your actions will set you free.**

➢ **There is freedom in surrendering—go ahead and give it up!**

➢ **Surrender, in its purest form, is finally achieving "peace of mind."**

➢ **Surrendering yourself to the truth and admitting the "wrongness" in your life will overcome the pains of a lifetime of denial.**

> **You must be totally honest with yourself.** No more believing your own lies. Without complete surrender, you are still hanging onto the disease of denial. Without totally coming clean, even the littlest seed of denial will always be there—hiding and ready to pounce back with a vengeance when given the first opportunity. If you are not willing to go all the way—to do whatever it takes—you will never fully recover from your addiction.

Surrender allows you to forgive. Surrender allows you to release all the mental barriers that are binding you and causing stress in your life. Forgiveness helps remove the stressful "knots" buried in your mind. Forgiveness also helps you accept responsibility for your actions. Unconditional forgiveness lets you acknowledge that you can never right what's happened, but you are free to move forward and focus on the future.

Have Faith In A Higher Power

When you surrender, you are free to admit that you need help from a higher power. Having faith in a power greater than yourself will help you through the tough times of recovery. Forgiveness from God will give you comfort in knowing that your past has been forgiven and that you can go forward with a clear conscience. Surrender will help you overcome your weaknesses and allow you to deal with powerful addictions you can't humanly control.

There is great strength in surrendering to the truth. The weight of the world will lift from your shoulders when you come clean and you will never again have to look over your shoulder!

Start living a life based on Integrity and Honesty. These values are the very foundation for building a richer and more rewarding life. Don't ever lie to yourself. Don't ever compromise your values.

> **You will never change what you stubbornly refuse to acknowledge.** Your life really starts going downhill once you start believing your own stupid lies. Get totally honest with yourself by dealing with the truth. There is real strength in surrendering. "Let Go and Let God!"

WE ARE ONLY AS SICK AS OUR DEEPEST SECRETS!

THE ROAD TO RECOVERY
You Deserve a Better Life!

How do I get better?
- **You must have an open mind.**
- **You must be willing to get help.**
- **You must take responsibility for yourself.**
- **You must work at your recovery daily.**

First, you must believe that your life can get better. You are not the only one who has ever encountered an addiction. People recover and go on to live successful rewarding lives. You can overcome your addictions too. Believe it!

Then you must acknowledge that you have a problem and you need help. You will never turn your life around unless you are willing to acknowledge that you need help. Once you have acknowledged your addiction, you have to make a committed decision that you are willing to do whatever it takes to overcome your addiction.

Overcoming your addiction must be a serious endeavor on your part. Not taking your recovery as serious business will only yield a halfhearted effort and you will not be successful.

You must hate what is killing you! A major step in recovery is to learn how to hate what your addiction is doing to you. You must reach a point where you are no longer willing to put up with all of the grief your addiction causes. You must get tired of being sick. You must get tired of being broke. You must no longer tolerate your life as it is. You must get disgusted with what your addiction is doing to you and hate it so much that you are willing to change. Just saying that you'd like to quit is not enough. Talk is cheap. It doesn't mean anything if you still really like what you're doing to yourself.

You have to get disgusted with your addiction. It must repulse you. You must believe that continued use will kill you! You must program your conscious mind and your higher conscious mind to the realities of your addiction. You must program your mind to recognize that your addiction is killing you. You have to learn how to hate the very thing that you have enjoyed for so many years.

Only when you hate what your addiction has been doing to you— can you begin to really concentrate on changing your life.

TURN YOUR STUMBLING BLOCKS INTO STEPPING STONES!

WISDOM KEY

> **Willpower is not good enough. You must change how you think.** For example, let's say you make up your mind to quit drinking. Every day you tell yourself over and over again that you need to quit. The problem with this is that your higher conscious mind still enjoys your former addiction and is quietly telling you how tasty a good drink would be right now. You must burn into your mind the idea that your substance abuse is going to kill you and you hate what it is doing to you. See yourself in your mind as healthy, energetic, and sober!

Don't live in the past. Focus on the positive. Focus on the future. Start painting a picture in your mind of how much better your life will be without your addiction. When you can see yourself living a healthy life free from the bondage of the thing that was killing you, it will be easier for you to quit.

Recovery Happens One Day At A Time

Recovery is a daily project. You cannot change overnight. To rid yourself of an addiction that has taken many years to develop, you have to work at it minute-by-minute, hour-by-hour, and day-by-day. Like it or not, here's the "straight skinny." You will have to fight the urge to indulge every day for the rest of your life. Hopefully, you'll understand this while you are young and you'll make a decision never to start.

Don't let "TREATMENT" be a scary word to you. Many people with addictions are afraid to get help because "treatment" sounds like something terrifying that doctors do to you. Having spent 30 days at Hazelden in Center City, Minnesota, myself, I have come to know differently. **Recovery is really a gift, a "Gift of Healing!"**

Today, I tell people the time I spent at Hazelden was the most profound, enlightening 30 days of my life. It's so unfortunate that people who really need help will aggressively argue and fight against getting the help that they so desperately need. What's even stranger is when I have helped other people get their lives turned around and they are entering the program, they often say, "Don't tell anyone where I am!" Can you imagine…they are terrified that someone might find out they are doing something positive for themselves. These are the same people who never gave it a second thought how embarrassing they were while they were abusing! If you decide to get help, be thankful and proud that you are doing something positive for yourself. There is nothing embarrassing about getting your life back on track.

Today, I even tell my sober friends that everyone should take a 30-day time-out just to reassess their priorities in life and get their feet back on the ground again. Don't let the fear of the unknown keep you from getting help. Remember, recovery is a gift of healing.

What you can walk away from …you have conquered.
What you cannot walk away from …has conquered you!

Be A Bigger Person Than You Are By Getting Help!

People fail in their recovery when they try to change on their own terms and conditions. When addicted people start dictating the terms by which they will change, you can tell they never fully "surrendered to getting well." Self-righteous pride and misplaced ego are big hindrances to people who need to make a change in their lives. Pride and ego keep people from total surrender. They are afraid of what other people will think of them if they get help. They think it's a sign of weakness or a character flaw to get help. Surrender helps you get rid of any preconceived ideas that hinder your recovery, and allows you to listen to people who can help you.

It's arrogant and naïve to think you can do it yourself.

The real weakness is being ignorant and stubborn and refusing to get help.
The real strength of a person is to admit helplessness.
It is wisdom and maturity to get help.

IF YOU WANT TO START FEELING BETTER, PUT YOUR EGO ASIDE AND GET HELP.

YOU WILL STILL HAVE PROBLEMS.

If you have made a decision to turn your life around, you are to be congratulated. But, just because you are on the road to recovery doesn't mean your problems will evaporate without consequences. Many times through years of abuse, there is a history of financial and legal problems, and failed relationships. You will still have problems—that's OK. Dealing with your problems one day at a time will help you start living in the real world.

Many times the consequences are compounded because while you were "using," you swept problems under the rug and left them to fester. Your saving grace is that now you can deal with problems and consequences <u>soberly</u>.

Live An Excuse-Free Life!

Turning your life around requires you to be responsible for yourself and to learn how to stand on your own without some chemical to prop you up—in other words, live an excuse-free life. This means that you can no longer blame other people for where you are in life. It's up to you now to start standing on your own.

Change Who You Are Hanging With...VERY IMPORTANT.

Living a different lifestyle—one that is positive, healthy, and constantly improving—may require you to change your associations. It's human nature to not want to be left out. But if you have friends who drink, do drugs, or indulge in any other addictions that you are fighting, you will have to distance yourself from them.

If they really care about you, they will understand because they wish they could quit too. If they only want to know you while you are abusing, then they were never your friends in the first place. A toxic peer group that is still abusing will eventually cause you to start indulging again just to be part of the group. Don't be afraid that you'll "miss out" when you separate yourself from your negative influences. Once you make your break, you won't believe how much better your life will be when you get rid of the toxic relationships in your life!

Start Living Positively!

Don't Worry, Be Happy! Developing a positive attitude and a willingness to better yourself will help immensely in recovery. Starting your day with enthusiasm will help you face the negative situations found every day in life. Being able to laugh at yourself will help you cut the stress. Get rid of the baggage in your life. Set yourself free!

WISDOM KEY

Practice positive thinking and no negative thoughts. Practice being positive at all times. If you catch yourself thinking something negative, find a way to turn your thoughts into positive ones. You'll be amazed how much better your world will become—you won't want to mess it up by ingesting poisonous toxins. Positive thinkers have an easier time making the adjustment to a sober life.

If you don't believe right, you won't live right!
— John Wesley

Relax and "Go With the Flow!" Be flexible. Not everything is going to go your way. You have to learn to go with the flow and to be flexible. This will reduce the stress in your life and keep you from getting "angry at the world."

Get Some Balance In Your Life

Commit yourself to doing whatever it takes to get healthy. Striking a balance in your life will help keep the stress at a minimum.

- **Instead of drinking—try reading.**
- **Instead of smoking—try exercising.**

People who have been living addictive lifestyles generally are in poor health. See a doctor for a complete physical. Your successful recovery is dependent on your commitment to good health and total wellness. Instead of feeling polluted, you'll feel like a fresh, sunny, spring day.

Exercise is important to the recovery process. Exercise helps stimulate the pituitary gland which releases endorphins that are 100 times more powerful than morphine. When you exercise regularly your body won't crave your former addictions as much. Plus, you will feel better about yourself and you won't want to trash yourself with damaging addictions.

Get proper rest. Getting a good night's sleep helps restore your body's balance. Plenty of rest also helps in dealing with everyday problems and stressful situations.

Eat Right

A balanced nutritious diet is also necessary to a healthy recovery. When you are healthy, your attitude is better. Remove sugar (except for fruit) and caffeine from your diet and you will have an easier time conquering your addictions. Sugar, pop, and caffeine cause mood swings, which aggravate and perpetuate your addictive behaviors. Alcohol is turned into sugar by our bodies. Our bodies crave sugar, which contributes over time to our addiction to alcohol.

In recovery, we would be better off removing sugar from our diets. Generally the addictive lifestyle is high in junk foods, which leave you feeling lethargic. By eating whole grains, fresh fruit, and vegetables, you will help heal your cardiovascular system, nervous system, and digestive system. You will start feeling better and your outlook on life will improve.

Start taking control of your life by getting rid of your addictions.

Remember:
Life is a gift—don't trash it!

You can do it!
Believe you can do it!

The Serenity Prayer
Oh Lord, grant me the serenity to accept the things I cannot change, the courage to change the things I can, and the wisdom to know the difference.
— Reinhold Niebuhr

TOTAL WELLNESS
The Essence of Exceptional Living!

Learn the difference between being *"Physically Fit"* and *"Total Wellness."* It could save your life!

Total Wellness is one of the magical keys to the kingdom. The wisdom of long-term thinking not only applies to learning and wealth, but also to health. Preventing disease when you are older begins today. Never be sick or tired again! Learn how to live optimally and you will have vitality, stamina, and limitless energy for peak performance. Feel better. Think better. Eat better. Sleep better. Love better. Look better and feel fit by training your body to burn fat, not sugar. Never be hungry or go on a diet again. Control insulin levels by maintaining stable levels of blood sugar.

Learn how to jump-start your metabolism by feeding it, rather than starving it and shutting it down. Simple aerobic exercise, like walking, will flood your system with life-energizing oxygen. Good health is characterized by an energetic outlook on life, vigor and vitality, emotional and social well-being, and freedom from sickness and life threatening diseases.

Our health is America's number one cause of worry.

Quit worrying about your health. If you are busy living a positive, full and productive life, you won't have time to get sick. We need to quit worrying about our health and start enjoying it!

WISDOM KEY

Our bodies are remarkable "fountains of youth." Within every one of us are amazing powers of rejuvenation and healing. Every second our bodies are in constant change: fine-tuning, balancing, and adjusting automatically to our environment and our emotions. Don't sabotage this incredible miracle that is happening in your body by clogging it up with grease and polluting it with toxic substances. Your body is not a dump for junk food!

Where do we start?

Let's start by understanding what total wellness means. It includes your:

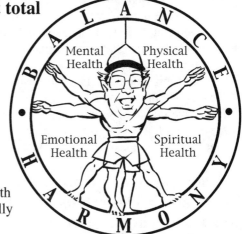

- **Mental health**
- **Emotional health**
- **Spiritual health**
- **Physical health**

Balancing all four areas of wellness are essential for you to be in harmony with yourself. Focusing only on your physical health leaves you emotionally, mentally, and spiritually malnourished.

Being healthy and physically fit are not the same. You can be physically fit from a muscular point of view and look good but your life can be completely out of balance. You are "walking tired" and sooner or later you're going to crash and burn.

Just because you have no outward signs of illness doesn't mean you are healthy. There is a big difference between being aware of your health and adopting an attitude of ignorant bliss—some people think if they're not on their deathbed, everything must be all right. Being healthy is not the same thing as not being sick!

≡Life in the Fast Lane!

Have you ever experienced any of the following?

- No time for exercise
- Troubled and irregular sleeping patterns (not enough rest; don't know how to relax.)
- Tension in your personal relationships
- Marital problems or divorce
- Weight problems and constant dieting
- Dissatisfaction with work
- Impatience or a short fuse
- Money problems and financial worries
- Concern and worry about what others think
- Preoccupation with immediate personal gratification and accumulation of material things
- One or more addictions, generally: smoking, drinking, or overeating
- Chronic bouts of fatigue during the day
- Frequent "sick leave" days at work

- High incidence of headaches, infections, and sore throats (Your immune system is not performing at optimal levels.)
- Sore muscles, tendons, cartilage, and a stressed back because of the wear and tear of high impact sports or work (e.g. construction)
- A negative attitude with occasional bouts of loneliness and depression
- A suspect heart and cardiovascular system because of improper diet and addictive behaviors such as smoking
- A diet of junk food and fast food usually eaten under stress
- No clue about nutrition
- Excessive intake of sugar, pop, and coffee, and hardly any water
- A stressed digestive system with symptoms of heartburn and upset stomach due to a diet high in red meat and sugar, fast food, and frequent alcohol binges

If you can relate to any or many of the above symptoms, you better take a closer look at how you are living your life, because you are quickly heading for disaster.

Your body is supposed to be a temple. Quit treating it like a shack!

"I treat mine like it's an amusement park!"
— Famous Dave Anderson

Life in the fast lane—creates high levels of stress, doubt and poor self-esteem, and a lack of confidence that continues to feed off the never-ending problems associated with this type of lifestyle.

IT'S A MERRY-GO-ROUND YOU CAN'T GET OFF. THINGS NEVER GET BETTER—THEY ONLY GET WORSE.

Heart attacks, strokes, cancer, obesity, and diabetes are the diseases of an unhealthy lifestyle.

People who get angry, slam doors, and swear have increased chances for heart disease. Negative attitudes incubate stress and play havoc on a worn-out immune system. Instead of being flexible and agreeable, most people are controlling and confrontational. Uneven temperaments cause erratic eating behaviors. Try to smooth out your temperaments. Start controlling your impulses. You must control your impulses if you expect to live a healthy life.

How's your health...really?

Most people don't have a clue. Just because they show no outward signs of sickness doesn't mean they aren't slowly dying inside.

IT'S <u>NOT</u> NATURAL TO HAVE ANY OF THESE SYMPTOMS FREQUENTLY...

Symptoms of an unhealthy system are: chronic fatigue, being overweight, dry skin, heartburn and indigestion, frequent colds and sore throats, headaches, and body aches.

Most of the time, we "unknowingly" sabotage the miracles that are taking place within us by exposing our bodies to environmental toxins such as air pollution, smoke, and other sick people. Or we purposely destroy our highly complex internal control systems through the use of alcohol, nicotine, sugar-rich foods, fatty foods, and a lack of exercise.

Complete mind-flushing of old misguided thinking and drastic behavior changes is necessary to break this vicious cycle of unhealthy living!

TO LIVE POSITIVELY, YOU MUST BEHAVE POSITIVELY.

TO BEHAVE POSITIVELY, YOU MUST THINK POSITIVELY.

GOOD HEALTH STARTS BY THINKING POSITIVELY!

EXERCISE DAILY
Walk with God!

The Benefits of Good Health

Being healthy is a state of physical, mental, emotional, and spiritual wellness where all systems are performing at optimum efficiency.

- Your diet should consist of whole grains, legumes, fruits, nuts, veggies, fish, some chicken, and very little red meat.
- You should drink plenty of purified water and natural fruit juices.
- You should exercise and stretch regularly.
- You should get plenty of restful sleep and relaxation.

Which results in:

- A great positive mental attitude
- A joyous spirit and free emotions
- A healthy heart and strong cardiovascular system
- An oxygen-energizing respiratory system
- An aggressive immune system
- Strong healthy bones
- A problem-free digestive system
- The ability to eliminate toxins and waste successfully
- A good nervous system
- Freedom from dieting because of proper and nutritious eating habits
- Freedom from addictions

Start by taking inventory of your health.

1. Get a complete physical check-up.
2. Learn how to eat right.
3. Be prepared to make lifetime behavior changes.

   Good preventative health care is your daily responsibility. Many people have the idea that seeing a doctor on a regular basis is preventative maintenance. NO! Just seeing a doctor is not preventative! If something is wrong with you—it's already happened! The doctor is only identifying what is wrong with you and giving you a prescription to remedy the disease.

   The fact is, some doctors don't take the time to educate you on how to live a healthy, balanced life. You need to learn about total wellness, and like everything else in this book—the learning part is your responsibility!

Surrender your ignorance! You need to learn about your body, your mind, and your spirit. Spending 10 minutes in the doctor's office while he taps you on the knee and tells you to cough is not enough. Get a good health-conscious doctor who can guide you in your efforts to building a better you!

Don't just focus on being physically fit—which generally refers to a high degree of athletic ability and toned muscular definition. Your goal should be good overall health —total wellness.

You Must Keep Your Own Health Records!

Why do we take better care of our cars than we do of ourselves?

Humans are the most sophisticated miracle of life, yet we fail to keep our own maintenance records like we would our cars. Every car, even the cheapest car, comes with a "maintenance schedule" book. Every 10,000 miles or so certain things need to be done or the manufacturer will not honor the warranty. Everything that needs to be done for your car is recorded for future reference. You are no different!

GOD MADE US IN HIS OWN IMAGE, BUT JUST LIKE A CAR MANUFACTURER, EVEN GOD WON'T WARRANTY US IF WE DON'T KEEP UP PROPER MAINTENANCE OF OURSELVES!

It's important to start keeping your own health journal. You need to start keeping records of all maintenance and tests needed at certain years as you age. When you visit the doctor's office you need to be prepared to ask questions and be truthful about things that you have experienced with your body. Bring a journal and be prepared to take notes. Start keeping a record of your blood pressure, pulse, cholesterol levels, blood sugar levels, and triglycerides. For more information, ask your doctor about these health indicators and start keeping track of them.

Your health is affected by:
- **Mental attitude**
- **Your environment**
- **Stress**
- **Diet and nutrition (what you eat)**
- **Sleep**
- **Exercise**
- **Genetic history**

Everything except your genetic predisposition, you can control. So…what do you know about these things? Living an energetic healthy lifestyle depends on your commitment to studying proper diet and nutrition. One of the biggest detriments to good health is a general lack of knowledge. Misinformation and a lack of understanding can be more harmful to our health than getting hit by a car. For instance, I have watched people turn down a wonderful grilled lean steak only to turn around and eat a loaded, butter-soaked, baked potato—all in the pursuit of good health! They would have been better-off eating the lean steak.

Start learning about your health, your body, and your mind.

All of us should read books on wellness, nutrition, exercise, stretching, meditation, and breathing. We spend more time reading manuals on how to work our computer than we spend learning about our body, mind, emotions, and spiritual needs. We have incredible bodies with almost miraculous recuperative powers; our minds are more complex than any computer. It makes sense to find out how we can unleash these incredible healing powers.

Our lack of health information began when we were children. Parents will say…"Eat a well balanced meal" but then have no clue what that means. You have to study and learn about diet, nutrition, exercise, and how your body functions.

You must be responsible for learning how to take care of yourself!

Good Health is About Change

If you always do what you always did…
You're always going to get what you always got!

Like all things in life, you are constantly changing. We need to treat our bodies differently as we age. What we do as teenagers is not always appropriate behavior for us as we approach middle age and our senior years. Even more importantly, how we ate in our teenage years is not appropriate as we get older.

Change does not mean going on a diet. Diets are really ineffective because at some point you go off of them. Living a healthy lifestyle requires a lifelong behavior change and generally a whole new way of thinking. As you reach new seasons of your life, learn how to take care of your changing body.

The mind and the body are one. How you think determines a lot about how you feel. Good health is a general state of well-being that includes the mind, body, emotions, and spirituality. Simply, it is balance.

BALANCE IS A TOUGH WORD FOR MOST PEOPLE. DESPITE THE GOODNESS IT REPRESENTS, PEOPLE AVOID THE WORD LIKE IT WAS THE PLAGUE! MAINTAINING BALANCE REQUIRES A CONSCIOUS EFFORT, DAILY PLANNING, AND LOTS OF WORK.

Balance requires a behavior change for most people. Balance requires maintaining ideal body weight, having a positive outlook on life, supportive relationships, and inner peace coming from a relationship with a higher power. Balance requires personal discipline.

PEOPLE DON'T LIKE THE WORD "BALANCE" BECAUSE THEY DON'T LIKE BOUNDARIES.

Change requires work, but you should enjoy your life changes. Look forward to change. The worst thing you can do is to dread change. Don't concentrate on what you are sacrificing—concentrate on how great your life will be after you have made the changes for the better.

**When you quit looking for the changes outside yourself...
you will discover the strength within yourself to change.**

Change for the better starts from within.

Our bodies are continually regenerating and reconstructing. You are continually growing new hair, new fingernails. Your stomach gets a new lining every five days and your skin is replaced every five weeks. Every two years, you have completely regenerated yourself, except for your brain. Don't sabotage the miracles that are taking place every second by polluting your system with toxic bad habits. Here's an interesting question, "Why not regenerate a healthier body?"

HELP YOUR BODY REGENERATE ITSELF. GIVE YOURSELF A FRESH START ON LIFE.

Achieving Optimum Health

There are 3 major health distinctions that will change your life forever:

1. The difference between being "Physically Fit" (pure strength) and "Total Wellness" (balance of mind, body, and spirit)
2. The difference between "Aerobic Exercise" and "Anaerobic Exercise"
3. The difference between a dangerous "High Sugar and High Fat Diet" and a healthy "Low Fat, High Fiber, Low Density Carbohydrate Diet"

<u>You</u> must be responsible for learning how to take care of yourself!

For example, a football player may be physically fit and strong but doesn't have the endurance strength of a swimmer.

Technically this is the difference between <u>aerobic</u> and <u>anaerobic</u> exercise:

Anaerobic exercise is typical of the "no pain—no gain" philosophy. It is often associated with high impact power sports and intense physical fitness activities. Anaerobic exercise pushes your limits with intense bursts of physical exertion until you deplete your body's supply of oxygen and sugar. You feel out of breath and you are exhausted.

Aerobic simply means **with** oxygen (the swimmer).

Anaerobic simply means **without** oxygen (the football player).

Unlike aerobic exercise, which burns fat, in anaerobic exercise you are burning glycogen which is stored in your muscles. When the sugar in your muscles is burned up and the oxygen in your circulatory system is depleted, you are physically worn out.

Anaerobic exercise only burns oxygen and sugar...not fat! This is the reason why those who are physically active, may still have trouble losing the little tire around their mid-section—despite all of their activity, they are burning oxygen and sugar and not fat.

You can't be out of breath and expect to lose weight!

Aerobic means maintaining consistent moderate exercise sustained over a period of time for the purposes of strengthening your cardiovascular system, improving your breathing, and stimulating your digestive system. Aerobic literally means to elevate or increase the oxygen in your system.

FOR PEOPLE TRYING TO LOSE WEIGHT, AEROBIC EXERCISE COMBINED WITH RESISTIVE WEIGHT TRAINING, IS THE MOST EFFICIENT WAY TO BURN FAT.

You will only burn fat when oxygen is present in your muscles. This is one of the fundamental reasons why even construction workers who are physically active all day need to exercise aerobically on a daily basis.

Have you ever watched a professional football game? These players are physically fit and are playing hard, but some are not the best examples of trim and healthy athletes. In fact, they have to keep oxygen on the sidelines—just so they can breathe!

A complete, balanced, training program focuses on aerobic training with a more holistic approach that includes:

- Mind focus and concentration
- Healthy emotions and relaxation
- Cardiovascular and respiratory development or aerobic strength
- Body, mind, emotional and spiritual development
- Breath training and respiratory development
- Stretching to promote flexibility
- Low-impact strength training
- Being more balanced
- Creating heightened awareness, sensitivity, and alertness

If you are past the age of 25 and not trying out for the Olympics or you are out of school and no longer active in organized sports, you need to learn the difference between...

"Maximum Conditioning"
and
"Peak Performance"

Maximum Conditioning is pushing yourself to your limits, which could be stressful to your system and you could suffer injury. Your new goal should be preservation.

Peak Performance is a balance of physical fitness, diet and nutrition, and a healthy positive emotional state; always being able to perform at your very best.

WISDOM KEY

> **Peak Performance is really Total Wellness.** Once you are out of any team sports in school…your number one priority should be to keep your body free from wear and tear. Keep yourself free from injury; preservation, not destruction. When you are in your 60s, you will appreciate this advice.

Enjoy your exercise but don't get fanatical about it. The best exercise is one that is balanced and is both aerobic for your cardiovascular system and anaerobic for muscle development. If you have a sedentary lifestyle you are losing muscle mass over time.

- **You need muscle maintenance and development to help burn fat.**
- **You burn 75 calories to maintain every pound of muscle you add to your body.**
- **Almost all of the fat energy that is burned up in your body takes place in your muscles.**

Strength and power characterized by big muscles is not necessarily better than feeling your best and living longer.

Improved cardiovascular capacity, total health, vitality, an energetic mind, and an optimistic outlook on life should be your goals. A person who walks and swims could be in better health than someone who only lifts weights for bigger muscles.

There is a difference between maintaining muscle mass and keeping your muscles toned through sustained aerobic training and some anaerobic muscle development. The key factor is balance. Don't overdevelop. This depletes your muscles of their vital oxygen.

Remember, your muscles will not burn fat when there is no oxygen present.

Instead of heavy power lifting characterized by short bursts of "<u>oxygen burning</u>" and "<u>glycogen burning</u>," a muscle development program should use more repetitions of smaller weights to tone muscles through "<u>oxygen building</u>" and "<u>fat burning</u>."

USE IT OR LOSE IT!

Lost Muscles Kill Your Metabolism! As you age, your metabolism—basically the rate you convert calories into energy—slows down because you are naturally losing muscle mass. It's estimated that your metabolism changes somewhere between your mid-20s and your 30s.
All adults after the age of 25 start to lose a half pound of muscle every year due to muscular atrophy. For sedentary people the rate is three times faster! The danger of this is that you begin to trade muscle mass for fat. Even though your weight may stay the same, your metabolism is slowing down, which means you're not burning calories as fast. Every pound of muscle burns 75 calories. You lose 5-7 pounds of muscle every 10 years. That means every 10 years, your metabolism keeps losing the ability to burn another 500 calories a day.

The higher your muscle mass, the greater your ability to burn calories, even at rest. The average 25-year-old can burn 3000 calories a day without much problem. By age 30 your metabolism is starting to decline due to the loss of muscle. By the time you are age 40 you can only burn off 2000 calories a day depending on how much muscle mass you have lost. That means every time you eat, you have 1000 calories floating around without a home. But not for long, because your body will quickly find a home for these calories by packing them on as fat!

25% of all Americans live a sedentary lifestyle. The American College of Sports Medicine recommends 30 minutes of daily aerobic exercise to reduce the risk of cardiovascular disease.

But aerobic exercise is not enough. After age 25, you need to start a program of regular weight training to keep your muscle mass. For both males and females, weight training is the only way that you can keep muscle mass.

Here's a startling statistic—more people are in nursing homes because of a lack of muscle strength than as a result of illness. They don't have the muscle strength to take care of themselves. They can't go grocery shopping or lift themselves out of chairs or bathtubs. They put on weight because they don't have the muscle to burn calories.

Whether you are female or male, if you don't want to end up in a nursing home having other people feed you and wipe your butt— you'd better start a program of resistive weight training NOW!

WISDOM KEY

Here's an interesting thought…
Plan on being a trim and fit 80-year-old weight lifter!

Weight Lifting Maintains Bone Density. There are other side benefits of a regular weight training regimen. Muscle development maintains bone density. When there is no pressure on the bones, they become brittle. When muscles are strained by weight training, they put pressure on the bones. This pressure causes the bones to build up mass, which promotes density and strength.

Other Benefits of Exercise and Weight lifting. Balanced muscle development helps you maintain correct posture, muscle tone, and body alignment, reducing your risk of back pain and other joint aches. Proper posture will cure most body pains and joint aches.

When you are healthy, you feel better, you look better, you sleep better, and you are able to deal with everyday pressures and stress. Exercise and strength training help your immune system stay strong and your ability to recover from sickness becomes quicker. Improved flexibility will help prevent injuries.

Understanding the effects of aerobic and anaerobic exercise is very important to your overall health, especially in fighting diseases.

Life Giving OXYGEN

Aerobic exercise builds strong immune systems. Aerobic exercise, along with deep-breathing exercises, elevates the oxygen levels in your blood stream. This is important because your immune system needs lots of oxygen to effectively fight diseases. Anaerobic cells that are deficient in oxygen create the perfect environments for *disease causing* bacteria, viruses and cancer. Bacteria, viruses, and cancer are "anaerobic loving"—they hate oxygen.

When you "aerobically" increase the oxygen going into your blood stream, you destroy parasites, germs, bacteria, and fungi that are thriving in an "anaerobic," oxygen deficient environment. In fact, through aerobic exercise and deep breathing exercises you flood your blood stream with "life giving" oxygen. You also rejuvenate anaerobic cells into healthy aerobic cells with strengthened healing powers and strong immune systems.

Your body without oxygen is similar to a stagnant pond. Lack of oxygen has killed every living thing and the water is full of bacteria, slimly fungi, and parasites. If you bubble oxygen into the water, the pond will heal itself over time and host new plant and fish life.

DISEASE CANNOT LIVE IN AN OXYGEN-RICH ENVIRONMENT! THE BEST THING YOU CAN DO FOR YOUR IMMUNE SYSTEM IS LEARN HOW TO BREATHE DEEPLY AND EXERCISE.

Drink Lots of PURE, Cool and Refreshing,

Fountain of Youth

Your body is 70% water, the earth is 70% water and the best fruits and vegetables for your diet are 70% water—that ought to tell you something. The earth is not 70% pop or 70% coffee…there's a big difference. Drinking pop, juices, or coffee is not the same as drinking water! Pop and coffee will dehydrate you. Don't fool yourself—drink plenty of water.

Throughout the day and throughout the night you are dehydrating. Water is eliminated through urination, perspiration, and evaporation. Water is lost through your skin and through breathing.

Besides drinking lots of water, it is good to limit your intake of salt. Salt causes dehydration in your system, and your body must work extra hard to retain excess water to dilute the salt. Excessive water causes an imbalance in your system and is hard on your cardiovascular system, causing your heart to work overtime.

Don't let your body become dehydrated. The best rule of thumb is to drink all the water you can until your urine turns clear. Even the smallest amount of water lost will cause biological imbalances in your body.

Your body does not know the difference between <u>thirst</u> and <u>hunger</u>. This is a very important concept to understand because when your body needs water you will feel hungry and irritable. You might have headaches, and your stomach may growl. Your body sends signals to your brain saying that you need something to get you energized again. These signals confuse your brain because it doesn't know if you are hungry or thirsty. Most often, you are dehydrated more than you are hungry. Most of us probably are not starving because our beltlines tell us different. What happens is that dehydration causes your blood to become thicker and it becomes very inefficient at removing the toxins from your system, which further aggravates your uneasiness. This makes you feel fatigued and sluggish and far from your best.

Drink plenty of water before and after your meals. The best thing you can do for yourself is to fill yourself up with water a good hour before you eat. Not only will you eat fewer calories, but water helps in absorption, digestion, and elimination. However, you really don't want to drink fluids during your meal. Drinking ice-cold water, in particular, will slow the digestive process.

Dehydration will slow you down. For athletes, drinking water is very important because dehydrated muscles will cause you to lose significant muscle strength and speed. Dehydration causes your blood viscosity to thicken, reducing oxygen to your system and causing you to become fatigued and sluggish.

How much water should you drink? Drinking ten 12-ounce glasses of water every day is just maintenance—the minimum no matter what your weight.

Make sure you are drinking purified water. The Department of Health has estimated that 85% of the water in America is not good. Increasingly, our water supply is becoming polluted through industrialization, fertilization, and waste toxins from farms. Even communities far out in the country have polluted lakes caused by toxic rain fallout from clouds that have passed over cities. This acid rain falls into the lakes and eventually seeps into our aquifers.

The best water you can drink is pure, distilled water or water purified through reverse osmosis. Don't fall prey to claims that you need minerals in your water. You will get everything you need from your fruits and vegetables. Use your tap water for bathing only.

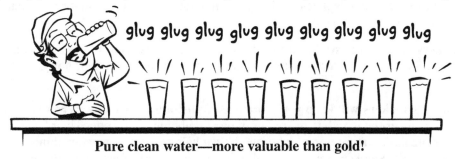

glug glug glug glug glug glug glug glug glug

Pure clean water—more valuable than gold!

You would puke if you saw the pipes that city water travels through! Have you ever seen the mineral buildup that sometimes gathers at the base of your faucet or colors your sink or toilet bowl? That stuff also goes into your body!

Where is your water coming from? Make it your responsibility to know how good your house water is and what kind of pipes are in your house. Drinking water from old lead pipes is just as bad as eating lead paint chips. If you have bad water, get yourself water filters for the faucets you drink from. For your health and for your family's health, they are worth the investment.

Don't put toxins into your body.

Life is a gift—don't trash it.

WISDOM KEY

Pure clean water that is full of oxygen can truly be called the "fountain of youth."

WARNING! DON'T SMOKE. PLEASE DON'T SMOKE!

Smoking is a "gateway drug." If you have never smoked, don't even get near a cigarette! Smoking is the number one cause of lung cancer and it is one of the worst things you can do to yourself. It is the only drug that will lead to other addictions. If you drink, it doesn't necessarily mean you will smoke or do drugs. If you smoke, it's almost certain you will try drinking and other drugs. Again, don't smoke. I don't think I can say too many times.

Avoid smoking at all costs—it is one of the most damaging addictions, it costs major amounts of money, it affects your health for the rest of your life, and it is almost impossible to quit. It affects your lungs (depleting oxygen to your heart, all tissues, and brain), your stomach and digestive system, your immune system, and the quality of your skin and hair. Smoking depletes the body of vital nutrients and is a major contributor to cancer and heart disease. Don't smoke!

Smokers have bad nasty breath and their clothes, cars, and homes smell like ashtrays. Smokers burn things—their clothes, furniture, and even their houses at times! Don't smoke!

At work, smokers will keep you from accomplishing your goals. When you are ready to conquer the world, they are out in back grabbing a cigarette. Their "negative" cigarette breaks are more important to them than helping you to get something "positive" done. Smokers are prone to illness because of the effects that smoke has on their immune system, so they run up company expenses because they have a greater number of sick days. Don't smoke!

Smoking is Nasty!

61% of Americans
Are OVERWEIGHT!

According to the 1999 National Health and Nutrition Examination Survey by the National Center for Health Statistics/Center for Disease Control and Prevention, 61% of Americans are overweight or obese. This is drastically up from the early 1990s. <u>Even more alarming is the fact that children are 10 pounds heavier than they were 10 years ago and this is becoming a trend!</u>

And the problem is going to get worse if we don't...
LEARN HOW TO EAT!

IT'S AMAZING THAT WE WILL FORCE OURSELVES TO EXERCISE, PUMP WEIGHTS, RUN FOR MILES AND THEN SAY "WATCHING WHAT WE EAT IS HARD WORK!"

Changing your eating habits shouldn't be agonizing. Relying on willpower to avoid fatty foods is not the answer. Willpower alone will not work. If you are eating a low fat diet, but your higher conscious mind is busy telling you how much you would like a greasy cheeseburger, french fries, and a milkshake—you will fail. You need to change your attitude about eating so you can start enjoying living your life with energy and vitality—not being frail and susceptible to every virus that comes along.

**WISDOM
KEY**

Eating right is critical because everything that goes into your mouth will affect the health of every cell in your body, either positively or negatively.

Eating right is a "lifelong change." Eating a balanced diet is a lifelong pursuit that requires you to learn about your body, your diet, your thought patterns, and your eating habits.

When you understand the reasons why you must do something, you can plan how you are going to eat, rather than falling prey to eating impulses. When you give in to your impulses you are only eating what you crave. Eating impulses generally are caused by addictive cravings for foods high in sugar, high in fat, high in cholesterol, and high in calories.

Your most important goal is to pay attention to how you feel after you have eaten a complete meal versus eating to satisfy your cravings. Not every meal should be eaten just to satisfy cravings. Meals should be designed and planned to provide your body with the "right fuel."

WISDOM KEY

The secret to dieting is not to diet. The key is to develop lifelong healthier eating habits—eat less meat, no processed fats, and no refined sugar. Then feast on all the whole grains, fruits and vegetables you want.

THIS IS VERY IMPORTANT!
When you are about to eat something—

ASK YOURSELF,
"WILL THIS <u>CLEANSE</u> ME OR WILL THIS <u>CLOG</u> ME?"

WE ARE WHAT WE EAT!

One of the main reasons we get fat is because—we eat fat! Our bodies are very efficient at storing fat. Our ancient survival instincts to preserve fat are protecting us from long, cold, hard winters, famines, starvation, and traumatic emergencies. Today, we live in a country that is full of food and we don't need to fight saber-toothed tigers to survive.

We need to train our bodies to burn fat—not sugar.

A diet high in sugar and fat will cause your body to burn the sugar first and store the fat. So the more high fat and sugar rich foods you eat, the less your body has to work at burning fat—it will burn sugar and readily store the fat. High fat foods include all meats, fish and chicken. All dairy products: whole milk, 2% milk, 1% milk, cheeses of all kinds, ice cream, butter, margarine, salad dressings, mayonnaise, and desserts. We need to drink milk because of the vital nutrients and vitamins found in milk. But milk is very high in fat—the only way to cut down the fat is to start drinking skim milk and eating nonfat yogurt and soy dairy products.

One out every three Americans is overweight.
"…that's because we eat a lot of fat!"

Bad cholesterol or Low Density Lipoprotein (LDL) is elevated by *saturated fats* found in all animal products. These fats are solid at room temperature. LDL can form hard deposits of plaque in the arteries. They also will reduce the good cholesterol or High Density Lipoproteins (HDL) found in the blood stream. HDL is good cholesterol because it carries the bad cholesterol LDL from the blood stream to the liver where it can leave the body. An easy way to remember which is healthy cholesterol and the stuff that's bad for you is to think that <u>L</u>DL stands for <u>L</u>ousy cholesterol and <u>H</u>DL stands for <u>H</u>appy cholesterol.

Hydrogenated Fat is man-made fat from liquid oils. By adding hydrogen to fat you create a solid fat like margarine or shortening. These fats also increase LDL levels. *Polyunsaturated fats* are liquid at room temperature and can spoil. Examples are corn oil, sunflower seed oil, and soybean oil. These fats will not raise blood cholesterol but they are still fats and if you ingest them, you will get fat!

The best fats are *Monounsaturated Fats,* which are found in peanut oil, canola oil, or olive oil. Monounsaturated fats help to reduce LDL cholesterol without affecting your HDL cholesterol.

The average American takes in 30-40% of the wrong kind of fat. Your daily fat intake goal should be no more than 20%, and it should come from monounsaturated fats. Reducing your fat intake means you should limit your intake of animal products.

Unless used immediately by your body through physical exercise, <u>ingested fat will turn to body fat.</u> Whether you are using olive oil, canola oil, butter, or margarine—these are all fats.

Omega-3 fatty acids are a form of polyunsaturated fatty acid. Examples include cold-water fish such as salmon, tuna, and sardines. Omega-3 fatty acids reduce triglycerides in the blood and have anti-clotting properties. Triglycerides are fats in the blood, which cause plaque build-up. Omega-3 fatty acids are also found in soybean products such as tofu and soymilk.

**Daily exercise and deliberate increase of activity
increases your HDL levels or good cholesterol.**

**WISDOM
KEY**

> **Reduce your dietary cholesterol intake by eating less meat, and when you do eat meat choose lean cuts and remove the skin from chicken.** Eat more fruits and vegetables. Drink non-fat milk, or better yet, soymilk, and choose egg substitutes or egg whites. Use fresh homemade jams made with only fresh fruit on your toast instead of butter or margarine.

SUGAR!

Americans are "sugar happy!" The average American consumes 150 pounds of sugar a year or one pound of sugar every 3 days. The average can of pop contains ten teaspoons of sugar. The body consumes simple sugars very quickly, then wants more. You get chemical highs and lows from sugars, which are direct causes of mood swings.

Sugar is a very addictive substance. Once you taste it, you will always want more. Sugar is one of the reasons why it is hard for alcoholics to quit drinking. Our bodies turn alcohol into blood sugar. Our bodies crave sugar. In fact, most drinkers when they are trying to quit, trade one addiction for another. Many say that once they quit drinking, they ate ice cream by the gallons.

Still, biologically, we need sugar to function. However, what's so destructive is the fact that sugar is often found in foods that are also high in fats like candy, cakes, and ice cream. This deadly combination of sugar and fat makes a pretty dangerous toxin that causes all sorts of chemical and hormonal imbalances in your system.

A diet high in refined sugar and high in animal fat is tough on your digestive system. Refined sugar is a simple carbohydrate and has no fiber. An apple, a natural complex carbohydrate, is full of fiber. Your digestive system will absorb an apple with better results than simple sugar. Simple sugar enters your system quickly and gets used up quickly. Complex low-density carbohydrates take longer to get absorbed into your system. This is important to your health because it influences the production of insulin. Insulin helps turn calories into fat and helps remove sugar from the blood.

When simple sugar or high-density starchy carbohydrates enter your digestive system, they are immediately absorbed and your body releases insulin to deal with all this sugar. The yo-yo effect caused by the need for all this insulin is hard on your system and leads to chemical imbalances. It's also one of the major causes of diabetes, a disease related to sugar levels in your blood.

Complex low-density carbohydrates, such as fruits and vegetables, are much nicer to your system. The sugars in these foods are released slowly over time as nature intended so you don't get the highs and the lows caused from simple sugar or high-density starchy carbohydrates, which drastically increase the body's production of insulin.

To give you an idea how serious this is in today's society...

Our bodies produce more insulin in one day than was produced during a whole lifetime in one of our "hunter/gatherer" ancestors!

Your stomach does not know the difference between a candy bar and an apple— they are both carbohydrates. The big difference is that the candy bar is high in fat and the apple is high in fiber. Candy bars and potatoes are both excellent sources of sugar. If I were to take a baked potato and scoop out the inside and fill it up with sugar—would you eat it? Of course not, but did you know that only two ounces of potato is equal to 1/4 cup of sugar to your stomach! Am I saying to give up on potatoes? Again, of course not. But the secret to all nutrition is control and moderation. Potatoes are an excellent source of vitamin C and fiber but they are fattening if they are fried or piled high with condiments like butter, sour cream, cheese, and bacon bits.

The best sources of good carbohydrates are low-glycemic index foods. Biologically some carbohydrates are called "hypoglycemic," which means they have a higher effect on increasing the insulin levels in your blood compared to other complex carbohydrates. Certain complex, starchy carbohydrates like potatoes, white rice, and corn have a high glycemic index and are not the best foods for diabetic people who have to watch their insulin and blood sugar levels. Low glycemic foods like certain fruits and vegetables get turned into blood sugar over a longer period of time, which controls the ups and downs of insulin production.

Do we really need sugar?

Yes! Absolutely...sugar is an excellent form of energy. If you are healthy and physically fit, you need sugar for energy. Health-wise, when I refer to sugar, I am really referring to natural complex carbohydrates such as whole wheat, grains, fruits, vegetables, and beans. Your body is very efficient at turning these carbohydrates into **glucose** and **glycogen**—blood sugar for energy.

Glucose is one of the most important energy providers in your system. Your brain, which is the largest single user of oxygen and sugar in your body, thrives off of glucose—30% of all your body's available blood supply, is used by your brain. The rest of the glucose is used to energize your immune system, aid in healing, give strength to your lungs for optimum breathing, help maintain body temperature, power your digestive system, and provide for a top performing cardiovascular system.

Glycogen is stored in your muscles and your liver. When you are engaged in anaerobic exercise you are burning up glycogen. When you use up all the sugar in your muscles, you can't exercise anymore. You are physically all worn-out and have depleted your oxygen and sugar supply.

WISDOM KEY

Don't be fooled into substituting honey for table sugar thinking that honey is more natural or less refined, and therefore better for you. The truth is that sugar is sugar! Whether it's brown sugar, raw sugar, honey, corn syrup, or white table sugar—sugar is sugar. In fact, honey may be worse for you, if you have to watch calories. Because a tablespoon of honey is liquid, it has a higher density of calories than a tablespoon of loose granular sugar.

Start eating whole grain breads with high fiber contents. Control your carbohydrate intake by focusing on low density carbohydrates like fruits and fiber rich vegetables. Eat only brown rice. You may have to cook it longer, but it will still have all its vitamins and nutrients. You can still have pasta, but find pasta that has been made with whole grains and is high in fiber. Eat natural whole grain cereals and hot cereals like natural oatmeal. Never eat *instant* anything!

Avoid all refined foods like:

- **instant potatoes**
- **instant oatmeal**
- **instant rice**
- **instant anything**

All refined instant foods have a high glycemic index and are quickly turned into sugar that opens the insulin floodgates. Your body needs sugar but it doesn't need man-made refined foods that turn almost instantly into blood sugar. There are plenty of carbohydrates found naturally in the foods we eat that are a lot better for you and will keep your insulin levels stable.

WISDOM KEY

Enjoy yourself. Don't diet to satisfy someone else's standards. Life was not meant to be lived miserably. Eating should be enjoyed. Great tasting meals are one of life's great pleasures. Good health does not require you to suffer bland boring food.

Throw Out
Your Salt Shaker

The Silent Killer!

Most of us do not know what good food tastes like, because we are constantly altering the natural flavors of food with salt. Removing the salt from our diets will allow us to taste our food the way it should be. After two weeks of doing without salt, you'll be amazed at how much better your food tastes! Salt is bad for the cardiovascular system because your body regulates how much salt you should have in your system. When there is too much salt in your system, your body retains fluids to dilute the salt content, which puts a strain on your cardiovascular system and causes high blood pressure or hypertension.

High blood pressure means that your heart is working harder to pump blood through your system. The harder it works, the faster it weakens and deteriorates. You then become susceptible to a higher risk of heart failure. Other problems caused by hypertension include kidney damage and blindness.

According to *USA Today***,** January 4, 2001 in the Health and Behavior section, the average American consumes 3,300 milligrams of salt a day (about 1-1/2 teaspoons). The study showed that the greatest drop in blood pressure came when salt intake dropped below 1,500 grams a day.

WISDOM KEY

Flavor your foods with fresh garlic, fresh onions, fresh herbs, fresh lemons and fresh pepper. If you absolutely must use a little salt, use sea salt or kosher salt. The stuff in the round blue box has everything taken out of it—what is left is pure chemical. The only place it may be useful is in baking.

Learn the Difference Between
"Good" foods and "Bad" foods

GOOD "nature friendly" foods include: vegetables, beans, fruits, some whole grains, skim milk and nonfat products.

BAD "industrially manufactured" foods include: refined, processed, genetically altered, artificially preserved, and some packaged products.

Some helpful advice...

When you go grocery shopping only buy foods found on the outside perimeter of the store and avoid everything in the center! The outside perimeter is where you will find all the fresh foods and everything in the center of the store is processed, refined, preserved and packaged.

There is a major reason why the wise proverb says:

"Eating an apple a day keeps the doctor away."

The major reason is that—eating an apple is very healthy for you. It is a good "nature friendly" food.

That's why the proverb doesn't say:

"Eating a candy bar a day keeps the doctor away!"

Candy bars are bad, "industrially manufactured" or refined foods.

By the way...you can't eat **7** apples on Sunday and expect to get the same healthy results as eating one apple every day.

EAT FRUIT DURING THE DAY

Fruit sugar, or fructose, is biologically better than simple sugar because it does not quickly stimulate higher production of insulin. And fruit is better for you because it also provides fiber and vitamins unlike refined sugar.

The best way to eat fruit is on an empty stomach. When eaten alone, it efficiently works its way through your small intestine faster than high fiber foods. When mixed with high fiber foods, fruit will stay in your system longer and begin to ferment and cause other digestive problems.

WHY IS FIBER SO IMPORTANT?

A diet high in fiber is the best thing for a very efficient digestive system. Whole grains, fruits, and vegetables are high in fiber, which provides "bulk", or roughage. Your body does not absorb non-soluble fiber, but fiber provides a very valuable function by bulking up in your intestines.

There are two types of fiber—***Non-soluble fiber*** and ***Water-soluble fiber***. Non-soluble fiber is never absorbed into your body. It goes right through and is more commonly known as roughage. If you removed the water from celery, the roughage that is left is non-soluble fiber. Water-soluble fiber is the slimy stuff found in oatmeal, whole grains or beans. Water-soluble fiber is absorbed into your blood stream and attaches to fat and removes it through your system. Fiber is nature's broom.

Sugar rich and fatty foods encourage gluttony. High fiber diets do not.

Sugary and fatty foods turn to fat faster and create cravings so strong that you won't know when to quit! One of the problems of diets that are high in fat and sugar is that they trigger cravings—that's why even if you just stuffed yourself, hours later you will be craving fat and sugar again. This is the major difference between high fat, high sugar diets and high fiber diets.

High fiber foods make you feel full sooner. High fiber diets trip a hormonal trigger in the brain that tells you that you are full. High fat, high sugar diets, on the other hand, do not tell your system you are full but work instead to fuel the craving for sugar and fat. This is one of the reasons why you will eat high fat and high sugar foods until you are literally stuffed.

There's another good reason why you need fiber rich foods.

Fiber rich foods are hard to turn into fat. Foods that are rich in complex carbohydrates like vegetables, fruits, beans, and grains are difficult to turn into fat. It takes eight times the effort for your body to turn high fiber diets into stored fat compared to high fat diets.

However, just because you eat a high fiber diet doesn't mean that your body can't turn this food into fat. If you ignore the natural signals that tell you to stop eating and you go ahead and stuff yourself—your body will eventually turn even high fiber food into fat.

The other part of eating healthy is just not to overeat...

Push yourself away from the table!

Overeating is not healthy for you. Your stomach needs to be at least 1/3 to 1/4 empty just for it to properly digest your food. Remember all foods have calories. A high fiber diet has calories and the more calories that you stuff yourself with, the more they will eventually be turned into fat. That's why even cows that eat nothing but grass— eventually get fat!

Do you really know how many calories you are consuming a day? Generally, if you can keep yourself around 500 hundred calories per meal, you will be OK. Anything over 500 calories, and your body will go from "calorie burning" to "fat forming," getting the excess calories ready for "fat storage." Brush your teeth after eating whenever possible. This will help you to realize that your dining is done.

Be accountable to yourself:

1. **Maintaining a record of what you eat will heighten your awareness of your calorie intake and fat intake. Remember, high density, no fiber, simple carbohydrate fatty foods elevate the level of triglycerides or fat in the blood.**

2. **Reduce intake of high density, no fiber, and simple carbohydrates: pastries, candy, milkshakes, honey, sugar, and no-pulp fruit juices.**

3. **Reduce intake of high density, no fiber, and fatty foods like: cheeseburgers, butter, fried cheese sticks, fried chicken, and marbled steaks.**

Old USDA Food Pyramid

Fats, Oils, and Sweets
(use sparingly)

Milk, Yogurt, and Cheese Group
(2–3 servings)

Meat, Poultry, Fish, Dry Beans, Eggs,
and Nuts Group
(2–3 servings)

Vegetable Group
(3–5 servings)

Fruit Group
(2–4 servings)

Bread, Cereal, Rice, and
Pasta Group
(6–11 servings)

Source: US Department of Agriculture

New Holistic Food Pyramid
for Mind, Body, and Soul

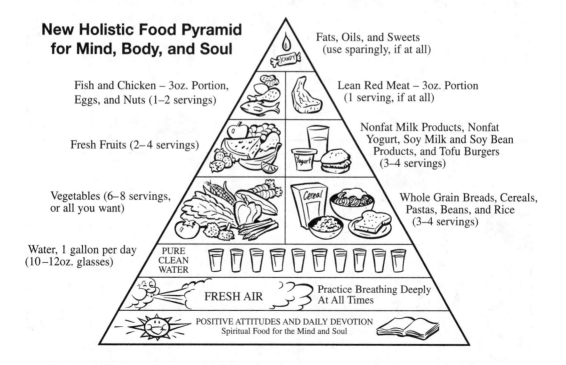

Fats, Oils, and Sweets
(use sparingly, if at all)

Fish and Chicken – 3oz. Portion,
Eggs, and Nuts (1–2 servings)

Lean Red Meat – 3oz. Portion
(1 serving, if at all)

Fresh Fruits (2–4 servings)

Nonfat Milk Products, Nonfat
Yogurt, Soy Milk and Soy Bean
Products, and Tofu Burgers
(3–4 servings)

Vegetables (6–8 servings,
or all you want)

Whole Grain Breads, Cereals,
Pastas, Beans, and Rice
(3–4 servings)

Water, 1 gallon per day
(10–12oz. glasses)

PURE
CLEAN
WATER

FRESH AIR

Practice Breathing Deeply
At All Times

POSITIVE ATTITUDES AND DAILY DEVOTION
Spiritual Food for the Mind and Soul

The Typical All-American Diet

GET UP AND SMOKE A CIGARETTE.

BREAKFAST

GO TO WORK, SIT IN MEETINGS, DRINK COFFEE AND SMOKE CIGARETTES ON BREAKS.

LUNCH

GO BACK TO WORK, SIT IN MEETINGS, DRINK MORE COFFEE AND GET STRESSED OUT. HAVE A SODA POP AND A CANDY BAR DURING A CIGARETTE BREAK. GO HOME AFTER WORK, GRAB A BEER, SMOKE MORE CIGARETTES, WATCH TV, YELL AT THE WIFE AND KIDS, THEN LATER GO OUT TO EAT.

SWIG A COUPLE COCKTAILS TO WASH DOWN SOME SALTED PEANUTS.

DINNER

COME HOME, WATCH MORE TV, DRINK A FEW MORE BEERS AND SMOKE CIGS BEFORE GOING TO BED WITH TIRED AND ACHY JOINTS. WAKE UP THE NEXT MORNING STILL TIRED AFTER A RESTLESS SLEEP AND START THE VICIOUS CYCLE ALL OVER AGAIN.

Take a look at the following daily menu and ask yourself...
"How many times have I eaten like this?"

TYPICAL AMERICAN DIET

	Cal	Prot Grams	Carbs Grams	Fat Grams	Chol Mg	Sod Mg	Fiber Grams
BREAKFAST							
2 Eggs Fried in Butter	184	12.6	1.2	13.8	436	353	0
6 oz. Hash Browns	240	4	30	11	30	410	2
3 Slices Bacon	120	7.5	0	11	20	510	0
Buttered White Toast with Jelly	240	3	30	14	30	290	1
(chemically flavored sugar water)							
Coffee with Half & Half and Sugar	154	1	30.1	3.5	15	24	0
TOTAL BREAKFAST	**938**	**28.1**	**91.3**	**53.3**	**531**	**1587**	**3**
LUNCH							
8 oz. Cheeseburger	1010	55	47	67	180	1460	3
Large Order Fries	590	5	74	30	0	300	5
Chocolate Milk Shake	570	14	105	10	30	520	3
TOTAL LUNCH	**2170**	**74**	**226**	**107**	**210**	**2280**	**11**
SNACK							
Candy Bar	280	4	35	14	5	140	1
Soft Drink	140	0	39	0	0	50	0
TOTAL SNACK	**420**	**4**	**74**	**14**	**5**	**190**	**1**
DINNER							
2 Mixed Cocktails	180	0	22	0	0	30	0
1/4 Cup Salted Peanuts	170	7	7	14	0	80	0
Dinner Salad with Dressing	312	10	2	28	75	690	1
Egg Crumbles, Bleu Cheese Crumbles, Bacon Bits, Croutons							
1 Slice Buttered Garlic Bread	170	2	16	10	0	260	1
2 Beers with Dinner	292	1.8	26.4	0	0	38	0
16oz. Seasoned Porterhouse Steak	1038	84.6	0	75.1	282	880	0
1/2 cup Sautéed Mushrooms	209	.7	1.6	22.2	60	161	.4
Fully Loaded Baked Potato	630	15.7	53	39.7	110	641	4.8
Cheesecake	350	7	37	19	85	300	.5
TOTAL DINNER	**3351**	**128.8**	**165**	**208**	**612**	**3080**	**7.7**
DAILY TOTALS	**6879**	**234.9**	**556.3**	**382.3**	**1358**	**7137**	**22.7**

See comparison on top of Page 260.

An Ideal Healthy American Diet

GET UP REFRESHED AFTER A RESTFUL NIGHT OF SLEEP.

DRINK A GLASS OF WATER AND EXERCISE FOR 30 TO 45 MINUTES.

BREAKFAST

GO TO WORK, DRINK A COUPLE GLASSES OF WATER AND MUNCH ON AN APPLE.

LUNCH

GO BACK TO WORK, DRINK MORE WATER, SNACK ON SOME RASPBERRIES WITH NON-FAT YOGURT.

GO HOME, KISS THE WIFE, READ AND PLAY WITH THE KIDS, EAT TOGETHER AS A FAMILY.

DINNER

SLEEP SOUNDLY AND WAKE UP ENERGIZED AND READY FOR ANOTHER GREAT DAY!

NEW HEALTHY DIET

	Cal	Prot Grams	Carb Grams	Fat Grams	Chol Mg	Sod Mg	Fiber Grams
BREAKFAST							
1 Slice Whole Grain Bread	90	5	17	1	0	170	3
1 Tbls. of Fresh Homemade Jam	50	0	13	0	0	10	0
1 Cup Oatmeal	300	10	54	6	0	0	15
1/2 Banana	50	.5	23	.3	0	.5	1.3
4 oz. Skim Milk	40	4	6	0	0	62	0
TOTAL BREAKFAST	**530**	**19.5**	**113**	**7.3**	**0**	**242.5**	**19.3**
SNACK							
1 Apple	80	0	21	.5	0	0	3
TOTAL SNACK	**80**	**0**	**21**	**.5**	**0**	**0**	**3**
LUNCH							
1 Cup Bowl Mixed Fruit	180	0	44	0	0	20	0
1-1/2 Tomato Vegetable Soup	100	3	19	1.5	0	100	4
2 Slices Whole Grain Bread	160	8	36	2	0	340	6
4 oz. Roast Lean Turkey	178	33.9	0	3.7	78	73	0
Lettuce	3	.2	.4	0	0	2	.3
Tomato	8	.2	.7	0	0	0	.2
TOTAL LUNCH	**629**	**45.3**	**100.1**	**7.2**	**78**	**535**	**10.5**
SNACK Non-Fat Yogurt Mixed with Fresh Raspberries							
2 oz. Raspberries	15.5	.3	3.5	.1	0	0	2.1
6 oz. Non-Fat Yogurt	100	8	16	0	5	130	0
TOTAL SNACK	**115.5**	**8.3**	**19.5**	**.1**	**5**	**130**	**2.1**
DINNER							
Shrimp Cocktail (4 Shrimp)	30	5.7	.3	.5	43	42	0
Cocktail Sauce	50	1	8	0	0	150	.2
Dinner Salad	80	1.8	19.3	.2	0	339.3	2.6
served with Fat Free Salad Dressing							
4 oz. Salmon	206	28.8	0	9.2	81	64	0
4 oz. New Potatoes	86	2.4	19.4	.1	0	3	0
1 Cup String Beans	44	2.4	9.8	.2	0	2	2
2 Large Chocolate Dipped Strawberries	82	1.2	13.2	2.6	0	37	1.3
TOTAL DINNER	**578**	**43.3**	**70**	**12.8**	**124**	**637.3**	**3.3**
DAILY TOTAL	**1932.5**	**116**	**313.6**	**27.9**	**207**	**1544.8**	**41**

See comparison on top of Page 260.

COMPARE THESE TWO DIETS:

	Cal	Prot Grams	Carbs Grams	Fat Grams	Chol Mg	Sod Mg	Fiber Grams
Typical American Diet	6879	234	556	382	1358	7137	22
New Healthy Diet	1932	116	313	27	297	1544	41

Look at the huge difference—major reductions in all critical areas and a needed increase in fiber! Learn how to properly plan your meals to feel more energetic and live healthier!

Remember:
The most important question you can ask yourself is—

"Will this cleanse me or will this clog me?"

Your daily diet is a destructive toxic bomb that is slowly killing you!

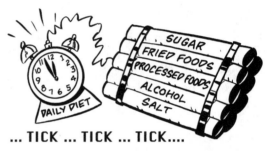

... TICK ... TICK ... TICK....

Fried Foods: High in fat that clogs your arteries as it travels through your blood stream, causing your blood to thicken and making you feel lethargic. Primary cause of obesity.

Red Meat: High in fat and cholesterol, red meat rots in your digestive system very slowly compared to fresh foods. The fat clogs you and the cholesterol builds up in your arteries.

Salt: Causes water dehydration, so the body responds by retaining extra water. You feel bloated and the extra water causes your heart to pump under pressure, which could lead to heart and other organ failure.

Sugar and Pop: High in calories, these are chemicals with no fiber or nutritional value. They give you a quick high but then just as fast, bottom-you-out into depression. Sugar and pop cause tooth decay, obesity, and diabetes.

Dairy Desserts: High in animal fat and cholesterol; when these are combined with sugar they create a destructive toxic cocktail and are addictive to your system.

Alcohol: Turns into blood sugar, which raises your insulin levels. Causes euphoria, which diminishes over time and your tolerance keeps building until you have to ingest large destructive amounts of this chemical. Causes you to lose control of yourself. Highly addictive.

Caffeine: Another quick pick-me-upper that slams you down with a crash. Addictive.

Nicotine: Kills your immune system. Destroys your ability to get precious oxygen to your brain and body. Heavy long-term use causes a prolonged painful death and you look like crap. You stink, and so do your clothes. Nasty, highly addictive, and a gateway drug to other substance abuse.

How to fill your plate with the right stuff!

Here's a good rule of thumb. Most plates are about 9" to 10" with a one-inch rim. Make sure your food fits only on the inside rim, and never eat seconds. Drink a whole 16-ounce glass of water one hour before you eat. Eat a salad dressed with fat-free dressing before your meal. Your meat or protein should fit in the palm of your hand or be about the size of a deck of cards. Fill up the rest of your plate with vegetables and beans. If you do this, you will never have to count calories.

The best diet includes lots of low calorie/low density foods, high fiber, and complex carbohydrates (basically fruits and vegetables).

WISDOM KEY

Low calorie/low density foods fill up your stomach faster than high calorie/high density foods. Low calorie/low density foods have a higher water content, higher fiber content and are low in calories. If you want to reduce your calorie intake, fill up on low calorie/low density foods first, before you eat high calorie/high density foods. For example, eat some fruit, a salad and vegetable soup before you eat a steak. The higher the water content is in your food, the fewer calories you will be eating.

Corn Niblets, Corn Flakes, Corn Oil
The Lower the Density—The Lower the Calories
The Higher the Density—The Higher the Calories

A good example of a lower density complex carbohydrate is fresh corn, which has about **490 calories** per pound. Corn flakes are an example of a higher density complex carbohydrate where all the water has been removed. A pound of corn flakes has about **1600 calories**! The highest density example would be corn oil, which has almost **4000 calories** per pound!

The closer to nature your food is, the better it is for you! The more processed your food is, the higher the calorie concentration will be.

WISDOM KEY

Have you ever felt like you were "just tired" all of the time and couldn't quite figure out why? Research has shown that people with high fat and high sugar diets are susceptible to higher incidences of depression, anger, and hostility.

The fat in high-fat diets causes both mental and physical fatigue.

After high-fat meals your blood viscosity turns thicker, causing sluggishness. High sugar foods cause mood swings that can crash you into depression, anger, and hostility.

This roller coaster effect causes extreme fatigue, which is one of the reasons why you fight sleepiness during certain times at work or while driving. Often, people who experience these effects will grab a cup of coffee, a candy bar, and a cigarette to pick them up again. These quick pick-me-ups, combined with fatigue and the emotional highs and depression, damage the immune system. People who engage in this behavior are susceptible to colds, flus, headaches, muscle aches, infections, and sore throats.

Removing refined sugar and the fat from your diet
will help you to be emotionally stable and in better health.

A Clean Colon is A Happy Colon!

Digestive problems are the third largest category of illness in the United States. Some of you right now are probably thinking, "How disgusting—can we please change the subject!" But did you know that most causes of disease and death begin in our digestive system? Unfortunately, discussing colon health, defecation, and someone's stools is almost a "taboo" in the United States. As a result, Americans are the most uneducated, constipated people on earth.

Understand the ill effects of the typical American diet. When you have a diet rich in fatty foods such as meat, eggs, cheese, milk, ice cream—bad "inefficient visitors" to your digestive system—your system breaks down this food into a fatty, greasy sludge with zero fiber. Your digestive system—all thirty feet of it—doesn't like this stuff and collapses almost like a "flat garden hose," and the villi are extremely unhappy. Villi are little hairy-like projections inside the small intestine that help move waste and fiber efficiently through your system and assist in the absorption of nutrients. Because the villi are unhappy and your intestines have collapsed, this fatty waste travels very slowly through your digestive system, taking almost 48 hours—two whole days—to get through!

You may have daily bowel movements but not because your system has voluntarily moved it through—it's more the result of being packed in one end and then forced out the other. Bottom line, this toxic waste has been in your system far too long, which is one of the reasons why a high-fat diet often leads to a high incidence of colon cancer.

Get Healthy! High fiber food quickly moves through your system in about 8-10 hours. When you have a diet that is high in fiber your intestines are expanded and the villi are happy, happy, happy! And when they're happy—you're happy. So, for both stable emotional vitality and a healthier digestive system, cut down on meats, dairy products, and refined sugar products.

Instead, eat all the whole grains, vegetables, fruits, and beans you can. You will get all the nutrients from your food, and high fiber waste will exit your system quickly. After all, no one wants to be full of _ _ _ _!

Here's an interesting question...

> IF YOU EAT 2-3 MEALS A DAY AND ONLY DEFECATE ONCE, WHERE DO YOU THINK THE OTHER 2 MEALS ARE?

You should eliminate or defecate at least *once* or *twice* a day. If you are eating a healthy diet and you are properly hydrating with water, you should have a transit time from mouth to rectum of 12-24 hours. However, today's processed foods are very strenuous on the digestive system. Eating cheeseburgers and fries and hydrating with pop, milkshakes, or coffee will result in a backed up transit time of 48 hours. Many Americans eliminate every 2-3 days. This is very unhealthy and could be prevented if people knew how to determine the health of their colon by a quick look at their stools. Education is an important weapon in the battle against digestive illness.

Can you pass the "turd test?"

You're probably thinking, "Is this a joke?" But seriously, how many people do you think actually know if their stools are healthy? It's a matter of life or death! According to Edgar Cayce's *Guide to Colon Care*, "Fecal matter, or stool, is composed of about 75% water; the rest is solid, indigestible material. A normal stool is soft, firm, breaks up easily, is light, or medium brown, and floats on water. If it stinks, it is loaded with mucus, and is thought to be a constipated stool even if there is a daily elimination. Since mucus is sticky and slimy, it packs the stool more tightly and lengthens the time it takes to pass through the colon. Consequently, more pushing and straining may be necessary to having an elimination. A healthy stool is quickly eliminated and fully formed. It should not be hard and round, or thin, like a pencil." A flat stool signifies that there is relatively low fiber in the diet and the colon has collapsed like a flat garden hose.

When it comes to the health of your stools remember the 4 Fs!

- Firm
- Fluffy
- Foot-long
- Floats

The health of your colon affects everything in the body. Toxins can be produced in the body through improper food combinations, overeating, poor digestion caused by eating too fast and not chewing your food slowly and completely. Problems start occurring when old fecal matter builds up in the colon and prevents proper elimination. Waste that moves sluggishly through the digestive system will ferment and create an acidic, poisonous environment in the digestive tract. This toxic buildup will be reabsorbed back into our bodies. We literally die a slow death from poisoning ourselves! Not to mention the fact that an enlarged colon caused by constipation or buildup can put pressure on and irritate the nerves in the lumbar area of the back, causing chronic back pain.

Bodily waste products should not be toxic. Waste will become toxic in your body only when your digestive system is not functioning optimally. For example, foul smelling body odor, bad breath, underarm and foot odor is not entirely normal if the body is able to optimally eliminate its wastes and toxins. Babies smell fresh, sweet and clean because of good eliminations and a simple diet of mother's milk. They are getting nourished with what they are supposed to be getting nourished with as designed by God. A good indicator of internal cleanliness is when you no longer have any underarm odor and no foul-smelling stools.

If everything about you stinks, what in the world do you think is going on inside you?

Digestive Problems Caused By A Clogged-Up Colon Include:

Feeling tired and sluggish	Stiffness in the joints
Swelling and stiffness in the hands	Headaches/migraines
Muscle aches and pains	Joint aches
Foul-smelling stools	Body odor
Undigested food in stools	Anemia
Bad breath	Depression
Gum disease	Dizziness
Coated Tongue	Indigestion
Heartburn	Constipation
Allergies/food allergies	Skin rashes
Over-abundant nasal mucus	Roaring in the ears
Restless sleeping	Belching and gas
Diarrhea	Bloating
Moodiness	Poor memory
Hypertension	Nervousness
Easily angered	Shakiness
Ulcers	Gout
Itchy hemorrhoids	Arthritis
Eczema	Psoriasis
Yeast infections	Gallbladder problems
Hiatal hernia	Prostate cancer
Eye problems	Dark circles under the eyes
Brown blotches on the face	Obesity
Colon cancer	Sore feet

While not all of these are necessarily caused by toxicity, isn't it surprising how familiar these symptoms and problems are when you look at your daily life?

The American diet is slowly destroying this country. In this country of fast food drive-throughs, where everything is "biggie sized," is it any wonder that we are experiencing unprecedented increases in road rage, depression, and workplace shootings? And now even kids are going berserk and shooting up their schools! Is it any wonder, since our children are fatter than ever before?

The old statement, "You are what you eat," is only partially correct. The more accurate statement would be, "You are what you eat, digest, and absorb."

The three stages of digestion are:

Absorption: when food crosses through your intestinal wall into bloodstream
Assimilation: when nutrients enter the cells
Elimination: when your body gets rid of waste products

The digestive system has three major functions: 1) To digest the right food; 2) To protect you from unfriendly attackers; 3) To move your waste through your system at the appropriate rate.

A healthy intestine will naturally clean and rejuvenate itself. A properly functioning colon improves the health of every cell in our bodies. 80% of the body's lymph nodes that host white blood cells are found in the digestive tract, creating the most powerful immune system in your body. The colon contains approximately 500 varieties of bacteria, fungi, yeast, and viruses.

Here's how messed up we have become… There are about 3½ pounds of bacteria— 80% friendly and 20% bad—in the colon. The typical American diet and overuse of antibiotics dramatically *reverses* nature's perfect balance to 80% bad bacteria and only 20% friendly bacteria.

There's more truth to following your "gut feeling" than you realize!

Your digestive system is your "second brain!" Isn't it interesting that your brain weighs 3½ pounds and the bacteria in your gut also weighs 3½ pounds? Did you know there are more nerve cells in your digestive tract than your spine? In fact, the digestive tract has been called "the second brain!" because it can operate many bodily functions independently of your brain. In other words, your gut has "a mind of its own!"

WISDOM KEY

The largest supply of blood is found in your intestinal tract and your brain is the largest user of blood. There is a direct correlation between your brain and your gut! When your body is free of toxins and every cell is healthy and pure, you are more keenly aware and sensitive to what is going on around you.

A Toxic Gut Affects Your Outlook on Life.

When you eat excellent foods and drink pure water you will have an easier time thinking excellent thoughts. A toxic gut can result in negative attitudes, anxiety, nervousness, and depression. Have you ever noticed that junk food eaters and alcohol drinkers have the greatest mood swings and the "sourest" attitudes on life!

Toxins build up in the body over time and become difficult for the body to naturally eliminate. Most problems caused by a toxic digestive system will magically disappear if we routinely fast and cleanse. Removing old fecal matter from our colon allows our natural filters to clean the blood, which in turn cleanses all of the rest of the cells in our body.

Many of the above symptoms and illnesses are not always caused by toxicity—fasting and cleansing are not always the answer. You should always consult with your doctor before beginning any detoxification process. However, detoxification and eliminating dietary abuses are generally nature's ideal first steps to improving your health.

The Closer Your Food Is To Nature The Healthier You Will Be.

Progress has created unhealthy eating habits. Digestive problems, depression, and chronic fatigue were almost unheard of before the introduction of refined flour, which provides no benefits nutritionally or digestively. Stone ground whole grains of earlier civilizations provided the benefits of high fiber and were nutritionally superior. High fiber foods act as nature's brush to cleanse and refresh the colon. This allows better nutrient absorption and facilitates waste elimination.

> **Myth:** We assume that just because we eat something that we automatically digest it.
>
> **The Truth:** We often overeat while our cells starve, and instead create backed-up toxins that poison us.

WISDOM KEY

Better digestive health can be achieved without the use of processed or refined foods. Eating refined grains—white bread, white rice, and white pasta—can create vitamin B deficiencies which can make you fatigued, irritable, and depressed. Chronic fatigue is one of the most common ailments caused by poor digestive health as a result of the highly processed foods we eat.

Don't look for a quick fix when it comes to your health. Unfortunately, modern medicine is quick to prescribe pills to address the symptoms of illness. We seldom take the time or we are too lazy to correct the problems that are causing our illnesses. Our goal should be to follow a "natural" way of healing before we resort to man-made manufactured prescriptions that generally mask the symptoms and the discomfort of the illness until the body can eventually heal itself.

Fasting and Cleansing

Fasting and cleansing allow our bodies to rest and refocus the energy normally used for digestion. This energy is then used for healing, regeneration, and rejuvenation. Colon cleansing, or colonics, should be considered as important as fasting. A regular cleansing of the colon to remove old built-up fecal matter will also help tone the colon muscles and help purify the blood and lymph. Please seek advice from your physician when starting a fasting or cleansing program.

Simple Tips to Help Your Colon

- **Drinking enough pure water is vital to colon health.** Liquids should be taken up to one hour before a meal or two hours afterwards, so the digestive enzymes will not be diluted. Ice-cold beverages slow down the digestive process.
- **Chew foods twenty times before swallowing.** Instead of chewing our food thoroughly, we have a tendency to wash it down with liquids. Proper chewing allows your digestive system to operate at peak performance and helps conserve your valuable energy. Have you ever felt tired after you gulped down a big meal? It takes a lot of energy to digest unchewed food.
- **Variety is the spice of life!** It is best to eat small amounts of a lot of different types of food than to eat a lot of only a few types of food. Your colon needs variety and excitement! Otherwise it becomes lazy from processing the same foods.
- **Pure fresh lemon juice, the natural grease cutter.** To aid digestion, alkalinize the system, help eliminations, and prevent poisons from accumulating in the system, add pure fresh lemon juice to body temperature water and drink 30 minutes before breakfast.
- **Early walking gets your juices flowing!** Brisk walking in the morning stimulates the digestive system for better elimination of toxins built up overnight and also helps stimulate the lymph glands for better blood cleansing.

Hopefully the next time you look in the toilet and you see a nice big fluffy, firm, foot-long floater—you won't find it disgusting but the most beautiful thing you ever saw because you will be tickled pink to know that you are healthy inside!

Why is it hard for fat people to lose weight?

One of the reasons it is difficult for obese people to lose weight is because over time the body has stored toxins in fat. Obese people's toxic and abusive eating habits over-impact the bowels and overload the body's ability to eliminate these toxins efficiently. When the digestive system overloads, the body starts storing toxins in fat.

During dieting, the body fights to keep the toxins safely stored in the fat reserves and instead starts burning muscle tissue. So while it seems that dieting is helping burn fat, the body is actually fighting to keep the fat!

One answer? Weight training. It not only builds muscle but also helps burn the fat. This is the main reason why resistive weight training is highly recommended as an important part of losing weight. Another fringe benefit is that weight training also stimulates the digestive system for optimal waste elimination.

Have you ever wondered why you feel so awful at the end of your diet? Often, at the end of a fast or the diet process when the fat is eventually burned off and the embodied toxins are turned loose, they overwhelm the body's ability to eliminate them naturally and temporary inflammations, mucus buildup, viral colds, headaches, and joint aches are often the result. This is the reason why people sometimes feel bad toward the end of a fast or diet. But this is only a minor setback for the long-term gain of being healthy and toxin free!

The Secret of Eating for Nourishment and Rejuvenation and Not Eating Out of Impulse Just to Stuff Your Face!

Eating should be spiritual, joyous, and a time of thankfulness. The groceries we have worked so hard to buy should be lovingly cooked and eaten with a spirit of peacefulness, harmony, thankfulness, and an understanding of the food's importance to the health of our bodies.

The process of getting ready to say grace before a meal relaxes you. Prayer gives you peace of mind. Asking God to bless your food and thanking God for your food causes you to momentarily remove all outside stress and helps you relax so you can enjoy your food. Prayer gives you a sense of well-being, which aids in the digestive process. Meals eaten under stress have many negative and detrimental side-effects to your emotions and overall health.

When we eat, we are not only consuming food but also absorbing whatever is going on around us. If we eat our meals in a frenetic environment of stress and hurriedness, with the TV blaring, people bustling about, and outside traffic zooming by, our digestive system will not be in a peaceful state to welcome the nourishment that we need. Instead of being nourishing, our meal will turn acidic, poisonous and toxic.

Slow Down! Enjoy Your Food

"BEING GRATEFUL"
**will help your stomach
to be happy!**

According to Edgar Cayce's *Guide to Colon Care*, "We not only absorb the life force and vitality of the food itself, but the energy of everyone who has handled it: the seed company, the farmer, the harvester, the trucker, grocery store employees, and those who do the shopping, cooking, and serving. Their state of mind has a tremendous impact on the food and, ultimately, on us. Therefore, we should take a few moments to quietly bless and give thanks for our food by holding our hands over it. This not only helps to uplift our conscious awareness, but also clears any negative emotions, and makes the food more compatible with the assimilation process at the cellular level. A time of quietness should be honored after meals."

- Clean out your pantry and refrigerator of all high-fat and high-sugar food items.
- Avoid the "3 Killers"—White Sugar, White Flour, and White Salt.
- Eat fresh, natural, and unprocessed foods. Eat fresh locally grown foods in season. Buy "organically" grown foods as much as you can.
- Shop at community co-ops and farmers markets whenever you can.
- Eat slower and chew everything 20 times before swallowing.
- Bake your own whole grain breads. Use applesauce instead of oil. Use extra egg whites instead of whole eggs.
- Avoid all fatty foods high in saturated fat and cholesterol, such as butter, margarine, lard, all vegetable oils, whole milk, and high-fat cheeses.
- Never consume more lean protein than can fit in the palm of your hand; about 3 ounces or the size of a deck of cards. Preferably lean steak, skinless poultry, and fish.
- Stay away from ground meats that are high in fat and have a high chance of bacteria contamination. If you do eat burgers, always order them well-done just to be on the safe side.
- Avoid all processed meats that may be high in nitrates or fat, like sausages and hot dogs.
- Drink skim milk; avoid cream and ice cream. Try nonfat yogurt or soy products instead.
- Cut out high cholesterol egg yolks, or eat eggs only a few times a week.
- Steam, boil, roast, or grill instead of frying.
- Use fresh ground pepper, garlic, onion, or lemon juice to flavor your foods. Or try using mustard and red pepper hot sauce—excellent condiments without the sugar, fat, or calories.
- Throw out your saltshaker. If you must use some salt, use sea salt or kosher salt. The stuff in the round blue box has everything taken out of it and what is left is pure chemical. The only place it may be useful is baking.
- Get healthy Omega-3 oils from sardines packed in sardine oil or olive oil, fresh albacore tuna, or tuna packed in spring water.

- Eat more high calcium foods such as low-fat dairy products like nonfat yogurt and skim milk. Sardines are high in calcium too! Plant sources include broccoli, spinach and tofu.

- Eat Romaine lettuce instead of Iceberg lettuce. Romaine is healthier for you. Iceberg lettuce is nothing more than water, which isn't bad, but Romaine has more vitamins, fiber, and is more nutritious for you.

- Make your own jams, by taking raw fruit and pulverizing them with a food processor. Leave it natural. Don't add sugar. Just keep it in the refrigerator until it goes bad. Use this on toast instead of butter.

- Learn to read food labels so you know how many calories, cholesterol, fat, fiber, and carbohydrates you are eating.

- Don't stuff yourself. Your stomach needs to be at least 1/3 to 1/4 empty to properly digest your food.

- Practice diet diversity. Don't get into a rut eating the same foods every day. Your colon will grow lazy from processing the same foods.

- Increase your intake of fruits and vegetables. Buy yourself some good health cookbooks. Identify 10 good recipes that meet your low-fat, high-fiber, low-density, and complex carbohydrate diet requirements.

- Don't skip breakfast—it kick-starts your metabolism in the morning. Missing a meal puts your metabolism into a "starvation mode," where your body is afraid it's going to starve, so instead of having calories available for energy-burning it stores them into fat.

- Eating smaller meals more often keeps your metabolism fires burning. It's easier to burn calories on a fired-up metabolism. A perfect example is when you add a log to a burning fire it is consumed immediately. But if you add a log to a bed of ashes it takes a long time for the log to catch fire and get consumed. The same thing happens to your metabolism. Putting food into a system that's in a starvation mode makes it hard on your metabolism to get back into calorie burning mode and it takes longer.

- Eat smaller meals during the day. Three major meals and two snacks, making breakfast and lunch your larger meals and dinner a lighter meal. Besides keeping your metabolism fired up, smaller meals help keep your insulin levels more stable than one or two big meals, which flood your system with higher excessive levels of insulin.

- Don't eat after 6 o'clock in the evening. You are not as active in the evening and all those calories that are not burned are stored as fat.

- If you have cholesterol problems, don't eat heavy meat items late at night. Most cholesterol is formed during your sleep. Best rule of thumb: don't eat anything dead after 6p.m.!

How to Live an Energized Healthy Lifestyle

- Exercise 30 minutes at least 5-6 times weekly. The more, the better!
- Exercise creates positive hormonal changes, brings more oxygen to the brain, and invigorates the cardiovascular and respiratory systems.
- Spend time outside every day as much as you can.
- Protect yourself from overexposure to direct sunlight and use sunscreen when you are outside.
- Get full-spectrum lighting for your house.
- Drink ten 12-oz. glasses of pure clean water every day.
- Drinking plenty of water helps flush toxins out of your system.
- Practice deep breathing and meditation.
- Relax and stretch.
- Sit-up straight, don't slouch.
- While standing or walking, pull your shoulders back and don't slump.
- Wear loose-fitting clothes and shoes that fit properly.
- Fast and detoxify yourself (check with physician first).
- Reduce your exposure to toxins.
- Avoid "coughers" and "sneezers."
- Wash your hands frequently and don't touch your face.
- For people living in winter climates, make sure you have a humidifier in your house. Dry air is bad for your respiratory system and increases your chances of getting sick. Mucous surrounds the bacteria and gets eliminated when you blow your nose. Bacteria in a dry nose stays around longer.
- Go to a health spa and sweat out the toxins.
- Walk 25% faster whenever you can or just move more often and more quickly during the day.
- Join the YMCA or a health club.
- Sleep in a totally dark room.
- Take frequent short naps as needed. Long naps will sabotage your sleeping pattern.
- Get rid of all electrical clocks by your head. You may not hear the electrical buzz, but subliminally it can be disturbing to your mind while you are sleeping.
- Do not have TVs or radios turned on while you are sleeping. It is dangerous to your overall physical and mental health, because:
  -You are unconsciously programming your mind.
  -You are not free to dream.
  -Your subconscious mind cannot work on problems or be creative for you.

- Invest in a good mattress and good pillows.
- Avoid heavy consumption of alcohol.
- Protect your back by lifting heavy things correctly. Bend your knees and use your leg muscles to lift up.
- Get regular dental checkups. Good dental care is essential for overall health.
- Floss!
- Get regular medical check-ups and be prepared to ask questions.
- Stay away from antibiotics unless they are absolutely necessary. Continued use of them over time reduces the effectiveness of your immune system.
- Reduce risk of injuries and wear-and-tear on your body.
- Maintain ideal body weight to reduce the risk of backaches.
- Wear your seat belt!

Things to Do to Make You Feel Better!

- Start your day off with energetic music.
- "Dress up to go up!"
- Say "Hi!" to everyone your eyes come into contact with.
- Treat everyone like they are your long-lost friends.
- Always smile as much as you can throughout the day.
- Give sincere compliments to everyone you come in contact with.
- Give more hugs.
- Tell more jokes (clean ones)—make someone laugh, even if it's at your expense!
- Clean up your language!
- Call someone you haven't talked to in awhile.
- Join *classmates.com* and find your old school friends.
- Write short notes and thank-yous to as many people as often as you can.

- Send people birthday cards…it's so neat to be remembered!
- Find a lone elderly person in a restaurant and pay for his or her meal.
- Take dance lessons and dance like no one is watching!
- Start a "great idea of the week" book. Every week add a new idea about how to improve yourself. At the end of the year, you will have 52 great ideas to better yourself!
- Make a "Victory List" of all your accomplishments.
- Live every day like it was Christmas!
- Have your friends over for a potluck supper and play board games.
- Keep photo albums and take lots of pictures.
- Learn how to give massages. Use exotic scented oils.
- Clean your house and organize your closets.

- Quit being a "pack rat." Hold a garage sale, then donate or throw out what's left.
- Grow plants in your house.
- Buy flowers for as many rooms as you can, as often as you can.
- Burn scented candles.
- Send flowers to others whenever you get the urge.
- Get involved at church. Teach Sunday School, help out at special events, bake sales, etc.
- Get involved in your community. Volunteer! Attend planning meetings, fund raisers, etc.
- Get involved politically and vote. The future of our country needs your input.
- Go listen to a visiting author at your local bookstore.
- Take an art class.
- Take music lessons.
- Take cooking classes.
- Learn a new language and visit that country.
- Start using natural handmade soaps.
- Use eco-friendly soaps and cleaning agents throughout your household.
- Be earth conscious; recycle and pick up trash whenever and wherever you see it.
- Plant some trees every year, wherever you can.
- Float down a scenic river in an old inner-tube.
- Make a compilation of your favorite music.
- Give your time and money to the less fortunate.
- Do something out of the ordinary to experience more of life—like bungee-jumping!
- Take a balloon ride.
- Color and perfume your bubble bath water. It's more relaxing.
- Every once in awhile, let your hair down, let loose and have a good cry if it is needed. Get the tension out of your system. The release will make you feel better.
- Make your pleasures healthy and memorable.
- Pamper yourself—go to a spa.
- Go out and have a good time. Enjoy yourself!
- **Do something frivolous, something just for fun. Recreation means RE-CREATE!**
- Live your life out loud! Live it full out!
- Celebrate life every day.

THERE ARE 52 ITEMS ON THIS LIST. I CHALLENGE YOU TO CREATE YOUR OWN "FEEL GOOD" LIST OF AT LEAST 20 DIFFERENT FUN AND CREATIVE THINGS TO DO AND ADD THEM TO THESE. ON JANUARY 1ST START ALL OVER AND CREATE A BRAND NEW LIST — I GUARANTEE...
YOU WILL NEVER BE BORED AGAIN!

Learn to Relax!

Suppleness and flexibility is better than being "bound up" and "tight." Being relaxed and loose, free from tension is better for you. Trying too hard causes resistance and errors.

WISDOM KEY

> Being in a relaxed state of mind or "being in a zone" does not cause you to focus on "trying" but rather on being relaxed and letting your instincts take over without thinking. Peak performance comes from being in a zone. You must be in a totally relaxed state of mind.

Ease Up. Trying too hard causes stress and tension. In order to become stronger with better effectiveness and efficiency, you must learn better relaxation techniques. When you are tense, you lose energy, you lose coordination, and you become prone to making more errors, which leads to your becoming frustrated. When you are relaxed you are more efficient in learning and refining your skills. You have heightened awareness and sensitivity to imitating or apprenticing from your teachers or masters. You can achieve greater excellence with greater ease when you are relaxed and alert. Mind and body naturally resist change. Relaxation eases change.

Relaxation creates greater ease of concentrated focus. Taking repeated breaks facilitates the learning process and retention. After every break, your mind retains new input with greater comprehension than if you just slug it out over long periods without needed breaks. Don't think you're tough just because you're hangin' in there when your body says you need a break.

At first all new things seem hard to master—they are. It takes work to learn. Repetition eventually leads to "unconscious mastery" at the high end of your comfort zone. When what you are doing comes naturally and effortlessly—you are "in a zone." There is no hesitancy caused by stress from doubt. Your mind is working in harmony with your body and emotions. Preparation, practice, and learning from your mistakes are paying off. You are at the top of your game. The secret is not to give up before you get there!

Learn how to breathe!

To repeat the ancient proverb...
LIFE IS BREATH, AND HE WHO ONLY HALF-BREATHES, HALF-LIVES.

I have been amazed at the thought of learning how to breathe. I thought it just
came naturally. Yet, many of us do not know that there are actually breathing techniques
that can maximize the life-giving oxygen circulated throughout our respiratory and
cardiovascular systems. Learn how to breathe more deeply, utilizing your whole lungs.
Breathe more fully from your stomach. Attend classes based on ancient breathing
techniques. You'll be refreshed!

Learn how to meditate.

**Meditation requires learning how to breathe as part of a relaxation process to
free your mind from stress and bring more oxygen to the brain.** It helps clear the
toxins from your system. Meditation allows you to listen to your inner voice. Your inner
voice, like a dream at night, is there but you have to expect it. Just like when you dream, to
hear your inner voice you have to be in a state of mind that is free from external influences.

Learn how to stretch!

Proper stretching helps position your body, muscles, and skeletal framework.
Actually, stretching should be part of your daily routine even if you don't find time to
exercise. Gravity is constantly pulling at us and throwing our skeletal structure out of whack.

Do you know that man is the only mammal that does not stretch automatically?
Observe any family pet or farm animal, whether it is a dog, cat, horse or cow—they all
stretch constantly. Many of our pains, joint aches, headaches, and other bodily
discomforts would be eliminated if we regularly stretched at least 20 minutes every day.
Stretching reduces muscle tension, relaxes your body, promotes better circulation and
makes you feel good all over!

HEY, WE NEED TO TALK ABOUT SOMETHING REALLY IMPORTANT!

DON'T BE EMBARRASSED ABOUT HAVING A HEALTHY *SEX LIFE*!

Openness is the key to a good healthy sex life. Everyone likes to fantasize about being the world's best lover, but in reality, many relationships are sexually dysfunctional because of our puritanical attitudes and unwillingness to talk about sex or even learn about it.

A good attitude promotes a fundamental enjoyment that is both healthful and natural. A good healthy sex life is God-ordained. There are few physical functions that provide more enjoyment than a great orgasm.

Good sex requires education, a willingness to discuss, and openness to practice. In other words, you have to work at it—it just doesn't come naturally as most young people think. Because of this fact, monogamous sex is better, besides being morally right. One-night stands do not provide the time to learn about each other's likes or dislikes. Monogamous sex becomes better over time because the partners have learned how to provide mutual satisfaction with openness.

Now that I have broken the ice on this publicly forbidden subject, let me also strongly caution you. Like anything else that is physically stimulating, sex can be addicting and abuse can be harmful. Perverse over-indulgence is not healthy. Stay away from pornography and web-site pornography. While it seems harmless at first, it is addicting. Exposure to unnatural sexual situations will destroy the "innocence of pleasure" experience found between partners God has brought together.

WISDOM KEY

If you are determined to have sex, practice SAFE SEX. This is not a plea for moral integrity more than it is a realization that healthy individuals with healthy attractions tend to follow their impulses. Don't ruin your life or place your partner's life in jeopardy by taking chances— it isn't worth it. Don't take chances. Know what you are getting into and ask questions!

Safe sex starts with education. Don't be ignorant by pretending that you know everything. You have a responsibility to learn about sexually-transmitted diseases and learn about the consequences of taking chances with other sexually active partners.

Good sex promotes good health. Biologically and physiologically, an active sex life helps you stay fit. It's an excellent aerobic exercise that encourages strong healthy rhythmic breathing during orgasm and floods your body with life-energizing oxygen. Partners who practice healthy, vigorous sex will often find that it not only energizes their relationship, but also gives them a positive healthy outlook on life.

Your partner comes first! Like everything else in this book, give of yourself first. Good sex is all about healthy relationships and giving of yourself first to satisfy your partner. All winners in life enjoy a good healthy sex life and have overcome the barriers about being able to talk about it freely with their partners. A healthy sex life also creates overall well-being, an emotional sense of security, and confidence in your marital relationship. Don't "miss out" on one of God's greatest gifts between two married people because you are afraid to talk about it! Learn about it, and get committed to work at it. Like everything else in life that is worth having, good sex takes practice!

"The sleep of a laborer is sweet..."
— Ecclesiastes 5:12 (NIV)

EVERY MORNING WHEN YOU GET UP, YOU SHOULD BE WELL RESTED AND EXCITED THAT GOD HAS GIVEN YOU ANOTHER DAY TO BE ALIVE! WAKING UP CHEERFUL AND READY TO TAKE ON THE WORLD REQUIRES A GOOD NIGHT'S SLEEP.

Sleep doesn't come easy. When you are fully engaged in living a productive life you will naturally be subjected to your fair share of failures, adversities, stress and challenges. Sometimes, when you think the world is caving in around you and discouragement and disillusionment have filled your day, it's difficult to get a full night's rest.

Here's how to get the rest you need. First, if you are distracted by a problem, you must acknowledge the fact that there is nothing you can do about it overnight. Worrying about things that you cannot do anything about, only works against you. You cannot handle adversities the next day if you are tired and all stressed-out.

Your mind needs rest for it to heal and to grow. You must recognize that it's important for you to be well-rested to meet the challenges again tomorrow. Being fully rested helps conquer your deepest fears.

WISDOM KEY

There is power in prayer. For a good night's rest, give your problems to the Almighty and your higher conscious mind. Give thanks that God has watched over you and your family. Give thanks for all that He has done for you. If you have done anything wrong, ask for forgiveness. There are tremendous healing powers in forgiveness. Ask for God's help and wisdom. Give your problems to Him and ask Him to give you the answers. Go to sleep knowing that you are safe and secure in God's hands.

Having faith in God is important to having a well-rested mind and body. If you don't believe in a higher power, who can you turn to in times of need? Who can forgive you?

Yesterday's mistakes and yesterday's failures are in the past. You must not relive them in your mind. Negative things that already have happened are over and done. Being forgiven will help you look forward. Just think to yourself that many people have survived far worse problems than yours. You will live through these tough times as well. Tomorrow is always a better day, after a good night's sleep. Hope conquers fear.

Coach Vince Lombardi said...

"FATIGUE MAKES COWARDS OUT OF US ALL!"

WISDOM KEY

> **Here's how to properly pray about your problems...**Don't ask for God to get rid of your problems. Instead, ask Him to give you the wisdom and strength to conquer your challenges in life. You have to remember that God has allowed you to have these problems so that you can grow. It's the only way you can become a bigger and better person!

Ask your higher conscious mind to find solutions to your problems with God's help. Your higher conscious mind is amazing. It is tireless and it will find solutions to many of your problems while you sleep. But it's important to remember that you cannot force your mind to work on your problems. Once you have handed them over to God and your higher conscious, you must not worry about them. Relax and go to bed with the comfort that your higher powers are now in control. Sleep with peace of mind, knowing that God will take care of you.

Remember...

"If God is before you, who can be against you?"

Prepare yourself to fall asleep by repeating positive affirmations to yourself over and over again. These will take the place of filling your mind with self-doubt and worries. Instead, repeat to yourself, "I will wake up happy, cheerful and enthusiastic. I will rejoice in this day that the Lord has made! I will face all my problems and challenges with a positive attitude. I will overcome them with God's help. I will win! I will succeed! Tomorrow will be a better day."

Go to sleep being thankful. Put a smile on your face while you are going to sleep. It's pretty amazing how much this will help. Memorize Psalm 23 (KJV). If you are ever having a difficult time going to sleep, say this comforting prayer over and over again until you fall asleep.

The Lord is my shepherd; I shall not want. He maketh me to lie down in green pastures: he leadeth me beside the still waters. He restoreth my soul: he leadeth me in the paths of righteousness for his name's sake.

Yea, though I walk through the valley of the shadow of death, I will fear no evil: for thou art with me: thy rod and thy staff they comfort me.

Thou preparest a table before me in the presence of mine enemies: thou anointest my head with oil; my cup runneth over.

Surely goodness and mercy shall follow me all the days of my life: and I will dwell in the house of the Lord forever. Amen.

— King David

In the morning...

Before you get out of bed, while you are still awakening, visualize to yourself how beautiful and positive your day will be. Start programming your mind for a positive successful day. See yourself as being positive, cheerful and enthusiastic. Visualization is useful in seeing yourself successfully handling your problems. Envision what you want the results to be. Even though you may not have all the answers, see yourself having handled the problem successfully. You must claim your victory in advance!

Then start your morning by thanking God for being alive. Get happy. Put on some snappy happy music. Repeat positive affirmations over and over again to yourself while you are getting ready to start your day. Listen to positive mental attitude tapes while you are driving to work. Make up your mind that nothing will get you down.

Do this and I guarantee—*You will have a great day!*

The benefits of total wellness:

- Positive outlook on life
- Energy, vitality, vigor, enthusiasm
- Restful sleep
- Healthy immune system
- Better digestion
- Healthy cardiovascular system
- Less stress
- Reduced wear and tear on the body
- Less pain in your joints
- Lower risk of developing varicose veins
- Ideal body weight
- Reduced risk of backaches
- Healthy relationships
- Healthy sex life
- Life free from addictions
- Rewarding career
- More alert, aware and observant

Change Your Eating Habits.

Start Exercising More.

Eat more High Fiber, High Water Content, Low Calorie Density, Complex Carbohydrates.

ACHIEVE TOTAL WELLNESS!

No More Fatigue!

Feel Better!

Look Better!

Sleep Better!

Love Better!

Eat Better!

Life is a Gift— Don't trash it!

This chapter on Total Wellness wouldn't be complete without a discussion on spirituality. It's all part of mind, body, and spirit.

DON'T BE SHY ABOUT YOUR FAITH
Be Spiritually Awake!

I don't know why it is that we Americans are either shy or embarrassed to admit that we worship an almighty living God. Many religions in other countries are very aggressive in letting the world know how strongly they feel about their faith. Just look at the Jews in Israel, the Muslims in the Middle East, the Hindus in India, the Catholics and Protestants in Ireland, and the Buddhists in Japan—there is no doubt as to the conviction of their faith.

I find it disturbing for a country that was built on a foundation of faith that today we find it "politically incorrect" to suggest to anyone, even a hint, that we may worship an almighty living God. We are so sensitive, that we are afraid of infringing on their civil rights! It is unfortunate that people who refuse to acknowledge that there is a God have more influence on what we do—than we do as God-fearing citizens. This is not right!

I have re-dedicated myself to letting everyone who is willing to listen know that I am grateful, humble, and proud to say that I am a fully-devoted follower of Jesus.

Having a strong personal relationship with a power greater than ourselves is very important to healthy living and raising families. Start going to church regularly if you are not doing so already.

There's a lot of healing power in being part of a group that worships together. According to the Reader's Digest, May 2001 article *Faith Heals* by Elena Serocki, hundreds of research studies document the link between faith and healing:

Longer Life. A nationwide study of 21,000 people from 1987 to 1995 found a seven-year difference in life expectancy between those who never attend religious services and those who attend more than once a week. A similar study reported by Lydia Strohl, cites a 1998 research project by Duke University Medical Center, which found that people who attended church weekly were not as likely to be hospitalized, and when they were, they did not spend as much time in the hospital as those who went to church less frequently.

Overall Well-Being. In research co-conducted by epidemiologist Jeff Levin, author of God, Faith, and Health, older adults who considered themselves religious had fewer health problems and functioned better than the nonreligious.

Better Recovery. Patients comforted by their faith had three times the chance of being alive six months after open-heart surgery than patients who found no comfort in religion, a 1995 Dartmouth Medical School study found.

Lower Blood Pressure. In a 1989 study of 400 Caucasian men in Evans County, Georgia, Duke researchers found a significant protective effect against high blood pressure among those who considered religion very important and who attended church regularly.

Good Mental Health. Attendance at a house of worship is related to lower rates of depression and anxiety, reported a 1999 Duke University study of nearly 4,000 older adults.

Reduced Stress. Humans under psychological stress experience higher blood pressure and heart and breathing rates, straining the body and lowering immunity, according to Dr. Herber Benson of Harvard Medical School and author of *The Relaxation Response*. In many studies, Benson has found that an opposite response can be elicited by combining two steps: repeating a prayer and disregarding other thoughts.

Spirituality helps maintain your sense of balance during times of crisis.

Participation in religious activities and community involvement helps prevent depression. It gives people a sense of belonging, a sense of contribution, and a sense of being wanted. This sense of belonging also helps develop social skills. Just going to church for one hour is not enough. You need to get involved.

Often it's the greetings that you get from interacting with other churchgoers that are more beneficial than the sermons! Being around happy, cheerful people who are full of thankfulness, praise, and hope will bring peace and well-being to your soul.

Sometimes when I invite people to worship, I get the comment, "I really don't want to go because church is full of hypocrites!" This has to be the lousiest excuse. Like my friend Zig Ziglar says, "If the hypocrites in church are the only thing keeping you from attending, all that means is that the hypocrite is closer to God than you are!" In my own life, I have done many things that I have not been proud of, and I tell my non-churchgoing friends that church isn't for saints, church is for sinners and hypocrites just like me! It's the only reason they let people like me in the front door!

Often, people will tell me that they get their "God moments" from just being out in the country. I am sure that you can definitely appreciate God's handiwork, but the healing benefits of fellowship and being part of a social group are not fully experienced when you are out alone in the middle of some field.

A worshipful community is similar to a roaring fire made up of many burning sticks. If you take one of these sticks out of the fire, it will glow by itself for a short while before it smolders and eventually goes out. All people need to be part of something larger than just themselves or the fire in them will fade out. Standing alone in the middle of a field may be peaceful, but it is not edifying in the long-term and you will not grow as a person because you are not engaged in a regular process of creating relationships.

Don't underestimate the healing powers of being part of a church body. We all have times when we get depressed, when we are faced with problems that seem bigger than ourselves, and it's during these times that having a support group to lean on is necessary for your well-being.

Isolation is one of the leading factors of stress and loneliness, and eventually causes heart disease. Mayo Clinic doctors have stated, "People that are filled with hope and

ANYONE CAN ATTEND CHURCH ON SUNDAYS, BUT IT TAKES A WHOLE WEEK OF LIVING YOUR FAITH TO MAKE IT MEANINGFUL.

It takes a whole community to raise a child. It takes education, government, business, church, and other God-fearing families to raise children. Our children need to be raised around other children in Sunday Schools, who are learning values, principles, and developing character.

What is happening in our public schools today is appalling. The lack of discipline, respect, personal responsibility, dress codes, and manners needs to be balanced by children learning these important lifeskills in Sunday School. When I attend church, I am encouraged to see families bringing their children to Sunday School. Children who have grown up in a Sunday School environment are better equipped to deal with moral issues as they grow older. Parents—don't be lazy on Sunday mornings. Get yourself out of bed, get your kids dressed up and take them to church!

> **Unquestioning faith in a power greater than ourselves is the key to lifelong spiritual fulfillment.**

WISDOM KEY

We have an unbroken connection to the laws of nature through our mind, body, and spirit. Developing stronger spirituality helps complete the natural circle of life that we need in our lives. Involvement in a local church is important to family values and critical to building a strong foundation for the problems that all families face in everyday living. Every one of us has a responsibility to our communities to be the building blocks of the American dream.

In closing...

I BELIEVE THERE ISN'T ANY GREATER GOAL MORE MEANINGFUL FOR MY LIFE THAN TO BE RECOGNIZED AS A GOD-FEARING LOVING FATHER TO MY CHILDREN, A GOD-FEARING DEDICATED HUSBAND TO MY WIFE, A GOD-FEARING BUSINESSMAN, AND A GOD-FEARING LEADER IN MY COMMUNITY.

Attend a church of your faith—it's the best thing you can do for yourself and your family!

"**Religion** is for those who don't want to go to hell and *Spirituality* is for those of us...who have been there!"

"**Religion** is man's attempt to get to God...
Spirituality is God's attempt to get to man!

LET'S SUM THINGS UP!

What does this mean to me?

1. **Be honest about your health problems.** Acknowledge the power of your addictions. What you can walk away from, you have conquered. What you cannot walk away from, has conquered you.

2. **We cannot eat with reckless abandon.** We do not have stomachs made out of lead and arteries made out of steel pipe. We must start eating a low-density, high-color, high-fiber, nonfat, and sugar-free diet. Eat more legumes, whole grains, leafy greens, fruits and all the vegetables you want. Eat more fish and reduce your intake of chicken and red meat. The closer your food is to nature the healthier it is for you.

3. **Avoid these three killers: White Flour, White Sugar, and White Salt.**

4. **Water is the fountain of youth:** Drink at least ten 12-ounce glasses a day.

5. **Strive for Total Wellness.** There is a big difference between being just "physically fit" and having "total wellness!" We should be building bigger physical fitness centers and smaller hospitals!

6. **Use it or Lose it!** Daily exercise and resistive weight training is important to maintaining muscle mass. After age 25, you start losing a half-pound of muscle each year. Muscle mass is one of the keys to burning the calories, sugar, and fat that you eat. In addition, active muscles keep your bones healthy.

7. **Learn the health importance of your colon and stools.** It is estimated that 80% of all of our sickness, aches, and pains can be avoided if we have healthy colons.

8. **Jump-start your faith!** Start going to church regularly and take your family. Your faith in God is the key to all success in life. Spiritual fulfillment is the ultimate quest for a richer, more rewarding life.

CALL TO ACTION:

1. **Get knowledgeable about your health and start keeping your own life records. Make it your goal to live within your ideal body weight. It's a matter of life and death.**

2. **Start eating properly and banish fast food from your life. Start exercising at least 5-6 days a week. Breathe deeply.**

3. **Begin a daily commitment to a personal time of devotion and prayer. Find an alive place to worship and start attending faithfully.**

WHAT YOU CAN ACCOMPLISH:

Live an energetic life full of vitality, optimism, and adventure. It's refreshing to the mind, body, and spirit to be in good health. Quit walking around tired; eat foods that cleanse you— not clog you. A healthy lifestyle will result in fewer doctor bills and you will look great, have better sex, and radiate with a great attitude!

Sources & Inspiration

The information in these books is powerful. I urge you to buy these books and read them over and over again until they become part of your daily life.

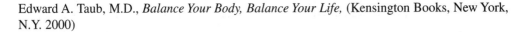

Anthony Smith, *The Intimate Universe/The Human Body,* (Discovery Channel Books/BBC, Great Britain, 1998)

Dr. Ken Cooper, *The Aerobics Program for Total Well-Being,* (Bantam Books, New York, N.Y. 1982)

Edward A. Taub, M.D., *Balance Your Body, Balance Your Life,* (Kensington Books, New York, N.Y. 2000)

Dr. Ken Cooper, *Overcoming Hypertension,* (Bantam Books, New York, N.Y. 1990)

Dr. Ken Cooper, *Controlling Cholesterol the Natural Way,* (Bantam Books, New York, N.Y. 1999)

Andrew Weil, M.D., *Natural Health, Natural Medicine,* (Houghton Mifflin Company, New York, N.Y. 1998)

Robert Pritikin, Pritikin Longevity Center, *The Pritikin Principle,* (Time/Life Books, Alexandria, Va. 2000)

Barbara Rolls, Ph.D., and Robert A. Barnett, *Volumetrics Weight Control,* (Quill/HarperCollins, New York, N.Y. 2000)

Miriam E. Nelson, Ph.D. with Sarah Wernick, Ph.D., *Strong Women, Strong Bones,* (Penguin Putnam Inc., New York, N.Y. 2000)

James M. Rippe, M.D. with Sean McCarthy, M.S. and Mary Abbott Waite, Ph.D., *The Joint Health Prescription,* (Rodale/St. Martin's Press, 2001)

Dean Ornish, M.D., *Eat More, Weigh Less,* (HarperCollins, New York, N.Y. 1993)

Rex Russell, M.D., *What the Bible Says About Healthy Living,* (Gospel Light, Ventura, Calif. 1996)

Don R. Powell, *365 Health Hints,* (Galahad Books, New York, N.Y. 1999)

Covert Bailey, *Smart Exercise,* (Houghton Mifflin, New York, N.Y. 1994)

Covert Bailey & Rhonda Gates, *Smart Eating,* (Houghton Mifflin, New York, N.Y. 1996)

Dr. Howard M. Shapiro, *Picture Perfect Weight Loss,* (Rodale/St. Martin's Press, 2000)

Sandra Duggan, R.N., *Edgar Cayce's Guide To Colon Care,* (Inner Vision Publishing Co. Virginia Beach, Va. 1995)

Elizabeth Lipski, M.S., C.C.N., *Digestive Wellness,* (Keats Publishing, Los Angeles, Calif. 2000)

Trent W. Nichols, M.D. and Nancy Faass, MSW, MPH, *Optimal Digestion,* (Avon Books, New York, N.Y. 1999)

Peter Bennett, N.D., Stephan Barrie, N.D., with Sara Faye, *7-Day Detox Miracle,* (Prima Health, Rocklin, Calif. 1999)

Bruce Fife, N.D., *The Detox Book,* (Health Wise Publications, Colorado Springs, Calif. 1997)

Kenneth M. Wright, *Miracles Of Internal Cleansing,* (P.O. Box 889. Morton Grove, Ill. 60053)

Lesson Six: A Rewarding Career

Lesson Six: A Rewarding Career

> Never work another day in your life by following your passion and making your dreams come true.

Do you hate when Monday mornings roll around and you have to restart your daily grind all over again? Do you look forward to Fridays? Do you feel trapped in a career that is going nowhere? Do you feel taken advantage of at work? Do you think your gender, race, looks, or education are holding you back from a better paying job?

If you have ever asked these questions of yourself, you have not figured out how to follow your dreams by doing what you love to do. You are just like 85% of all people who think that they are "working for a living" instead of "living for their work."

PURPOSE:

Life is too short to spend a lifetime becoming good at something you don't love to do. Learn how to never work another day in your life by having all of your dreams come true following your one true passion in life. The greatest satisfaction in life comes from knowing that what you do for a living is making a positive difference in the lives of others.

Whether you're just beginning your career or starting over, this lesson, A **Rewarding Career**, will give you the tools to find your one true passion in life and turbocharge your career.

JUMP-START YOUR WORK LIFE!

**Whatsoever Thy Hand Findth To Do…
Do It With All Thy Might!**
— Ecclesiastes 9:10 (KJV)

Don't have enough experience? Never put yourself down just because you may think you don't have any experience compared to others around you. It's scary to think that you have to compete with millions of other people looking for work. Here's how to never be concerned about your future again while doing what you love to do by following your dreams and getting paid big bucks.

> **The closest to perfection a person ever becomes
> is when he fills out a job application form.**
> — Stanley J. Randall

KEY THOUGHT:
You should never have to apply for but one job in your life!

Remember, everyone starts out inexperienced. Inexperience can quickly be overcome through your willingness to learn and by keeping a cheerful positive attitude while doing even the least desirous job, like cleaning the toilets. Do what others won't do and you will quickly become the one person everyone can count on.

NEVER BE SO ARROGANT AS TO BE ABOVE DOING MENIAL TASKS. THEY ALL NEED TO BE DONE.

Here's how to jump-start your career!

Rule Number One: Start with your best foot forward. When you are first starting out in life, make up your mind that whatever job you get you are going to go all-out. You'll never get a second chance for a first impression. Right from day one you are developing your reputation. Make it a great reputation.

Rule Number Two: Always keep busy. If you are quickly done with the job you were just given and you can't find something else to do, start cleaning up! Pick up a broom and start sweeping.

WISDOM KEY

Jump-start your career by being industrious. People who are industrious, get invited into the circles or confidences of other industrious people. Knowing all the right people is not a function of being in the right place at the right time or being born on the right side of the tracks. It is the result of having an industrious work ethic. Opportunity is the resulting benefit of "being industrious with a great attitude" that fosters all great success in life.

Opportunity is available to all who are industrious.

Here's an important truth to remember:

Working 40 hours a week will only let you survive!

Rule Number Three: Great fortunes were never made working only 40 hours. A 40-hour paycheck is only subsistence pay. Consider the time you spend before and after work as an investment in your future. <u>The time you spend "over" 40 hours is where you will earn your fortune.</u>

Rule Number Four: Whatever you do, great or small, give it your all. Never take a job where you can't get totally involved in it. Get involved in something you can give 100% of your effort to. Don't hold anything back. The mental and spiritual rewards of giving it your all and holding nothing back are enormous. The greater your effort, the greater your future.

Rule Number Five: Nothing great happens overnight. There are no shortcuts. Realizing your life's dreams and achieving your terms for being successful is a gradual process. Don't set yourself up for disappointment by expecting too much too soon. Just work hard.

All good things come to him who waits…
As long as he works like hell while he waits.
— Philine van Lidth deJune

Rule Number Six: Everything counts. There are no practice jobs. Life is not a dress rehearsal. Achievers treat every job as a precious opportunity not to be wasted. Treat every job you have as a valuable opportunity. Here's the key point: You may not be earning very much as a dishwasher right now, but you are developing work habits and a reputation that will be with you the rest of your work life.

Often, I hear young people talk about their current job or part-time job as just a "fill in job" until they can get a "real job." No matter what you are doing, <u>every job you have is a real job!</u> Every job is important, whether it's washing dishes in a restaurant, being a janitor, landscaping, or being a grunt on a construction job. It all counts. It all matters.

Rule Number Seven: Work is work. That's why they call it work! It's amazing how many people quit looking for work once they've found a job. These are the same people who make a big commotion about having to get to work but once they are there, avoid work like it was the plague. Or, they gripe and complain about how much they hate their work and then cry when they lose their jobs!

Rule Number Eight: You don't get exhausted from what you've done, you get exhausted from what you haven't done. Do whatever it takes. Get rid of the inexperience stigma by having a really great attitude and by going the extra mile. Show up early and be willing to stay late. Always volunteer for extra work. While others will try and avoid work, you go after it.

Has anybody ever told you, "Hey take it easy…don't work too hard!" Every time I hear this, I cringe—because I have waited all my life for the opportunity to work hard. I want to show the world what I can do. I want to prove how great a worker I am. I am proud of my effort. I am proud of a job well done. The only people who have the nerve to tell you not to work too hard are ignorant, broke people. Just look at where they are in life and decide if you want to be there with them. Otherwise, don't even listen to this stupid advice.

You owe it to yourself to work hard. It's the best thing you can do for your future and your family. Unfortunately, for some reason, many people believe that life owes them a living. The truth is we owe it to ourselves to earn a living. If you really want to jump-start your career, never work for money and never get yourself into the rut of thinking your company owes you a living. Work that is challenging is good for you. Being productive is good for your spirit.

A LITTLE HISTORY —
HOW "WORK" HAS CHANGED
COMPARED TO "JOBS" OF TODAY.

In the old days...

- **People did what they had to for their families to survive.** For thousands of years, everyone got up at the break of dawn and did whatever they had to do. They worked however long they had to until the job got done, just to survive!

- **They had to learn many skills to survive.** One day they might be laborers working the farm. The next day they became merchants taking their produce to the market. The day after, they became builders helping a neighbor build a home. They knew how to butcher their livestock in order to feed their families and they were craftsmen making shoes from the leather. They were survivors. They did whatever they had to do…

- **Nobody had to tell them to get to work!** They worked until they got their work done, otherwise they might not eat! The industrial revolution changed all that. This was when the seeds of the "40-hour work-week" were planted.

The era of the industrial revolution caused people to forget how to survive for themselves and made them dependent on "jobs" given to them by a company.

  How the concept of "seniority" got started. The company trained people in a specific job skill and pay raises were determined by how long they were on the job (seniority) and how proficient they were at their jobs. It wasn't based on the profitability of the company.

  Today, seniority is a dead concept. Ever hear this one? "I've been here over a year, I deserve a raise!" We don't deserve raises just because of our length of time on a job.

THIS IS AN IMPORTANT LESSON:

WISDOM KEY

> **We only get increases in pay because we have increased our value to the marketplace.** You must clearly understand your contribution to the creation of company profits, which ultimately determines your value to the marketplace. It's the marketplace that determines the number on your paycheck—not your boss!

Times have changed, and so has "employment." Just being a good employee is no longer a guarantee for employment. The new global economy, fueled by the instant transfer of information and the Internet, is creating new industries so fast that business as we once knew it is ancient history. The big long-established industries are now either dead dinosaurs or undergoing major restructuring, decentralizing, down-sizing, merging or being acquired.

Because employees lost their ability to survive on their own they became dependent on the company. They counted on the company to provide them with health insurance and retirement benefits. If the employees did their jobs adequately, they could count on being employed by the same company for a long time. The company was responsible for taking care of them. They believed the company owed them.

They viewed the company as their sole source of income rather than "their own productivity" as the basis of their value. Most employees never learned how their work effort was translated into value and how the value they created was brought to the marketplace.

What we produce today is obsolete by tomorrow. Today, we live in a world where the brightest creative minds have more resources instantly available to them than ever before. They are creating life- and world-changing innovations at a mind-boggling rate that is accelerating faster than ever.

HOW FAST OUR KNOWLEDGE MASS IS EXPANDING:

THOUSANDS OF YEARS   HUNDREDS OF YEARS   DECADES   DAILY

Just one new invention today can wipe out an entire workforce overnight! This is the world we now live in—and the world in which we're raising our children. Your world today is not the world you will know tomorrow. The thinking that got you to where you are today is not the thinking that you will need tomorrow. How adaptable are you?

Our "knowledge mass" is doubling at incredible rates of speed! Prior to the written word, everything that we knew in the world, or our "entire knowledge mass," was doubling at the rate of every few thousand years. Once we learned how to write, our entire knowledge mass started doubling every few hundred years. With the advent of computers, our knowledge mass soon started doubling every decade. Today, with the Internet, our entire knowledge mass will soon be doubling in days!

THIS RAPIDLY CHANGING WORLD IS WIPING OUT OLD OPPORTUNITIES AND CREATING NEW ONES JUST AS FAST.

Major Question:
If companies can no longer count on lifelong existence, how can employees count on lifelong employment?
The Answer is…They Can't!

Almost every week you can pick up a newspaper and read about a long-established blue chip industry or a recent start-up "has been" company that is laying off tens of thousands of workers. Sadly, when TV interviewers question laid-off workers, you see them weeping, confused and angry. They say how distraught they are because they have just lost the only job they knew how to do…

Don't let this happen to you!

Today, you must understand the difference between…
"employment" and *"employability."*

"**Employment**" is dependence on a company for a job.

"**Employability**" is dependence on you! It is <u>your</u> responsibility to become self-reliant and self-sufficient. <u>Employability</u> is really nothing more than an intense self-driven desire to survive successfully on your own.

Employment: *A concept of the past; today no one is "owed" a career.*

Employability: *The ability to survive any change in the economy –*
is now the requirement for the new worker.

So if something happened to your "employment" you would not be confused and angry, blaming your troubled company for your problem. Because now you would have confidence in your **"employability"** and your **"employability"** would allow you to immediately go find new work. Your reputation for being an exceptionally good industrious worker will always keep you in demand. If you understand this, you will never have to look for work again. It will find you!

There's a lot of truth to...
"What have you done for me lately?"

Don't rest on yesterday's accomplishments. Too many people live in the past. They always have great war stories of how they won the battle yesterday, as if that qualifies them for tomorrow's victory. Never rest on your laurels. The past is the past. You must conquer new territory every day! Don't fall into the rut of telling everyone how great you were yesterday. Focus on what incredible things you are going to accomplish tomorrow. Always be forward-looking. Tomorrow is your future. Focus on your future. Focus on where you want to be.

How to have guaranteed job security. Always do the jobs that no one else will do and you will always have job security. With that being said, there is no job security, only the last great job that you've just completed. Start preparing yourself and thinking about your next great job.

RETIREMENT IS A DEAD CONCEPT!

Today's work environment has changed so much that "RETIREMENT" is also another dead concept of the past. You can no longer count on the government to take care of you when you are old. You must develop a "survivor mentality," one that drives you to be constantly reinventing and re-educating yourself, so you can be productive every day of your life.

When you accept responsibility for your future, you hold yourself accountable for your success. When you accept the fact that you are totally responsible for your future you will readily embrace the daily discipline of self-improvement and self-learning. Never again will you be dependent on a company for your living. The security you are looking for will come from the confidence you have in your own abilities and the value you bring to the marketplace.

If a man is called to be a street sweeper, he should sweep streets even as Michelangelo painted, or Beethoven composed music, or Shakespeare wrote poetry. He should sweep streets so well that all the hosts of heaven and earth will pause to say here lived a great street sweeper, who did his job well.

— Dr. Martin Luther King, Jr.

How to Never Work Another Day in Your Life!

Discover the one thing you really love doing and make it your career.

Deep in the heart of Africa, as the hot African sun rises over the Serengeti, a gazelle wakes up running. It knows it must run faster than the fastest lion or it will get eaten. Nearby a lion wakes up and knows it must start running faster than the fastest gazelle or it will not eat. The moral of the story is that every day you must wake up running.

— African Wisdom

What's the difference between the people who are really getting somewhere, and me?

Champions of the workforce are enthusiastic about what they do for a living. All achievers in life wake up in the mornings looking forward to "getting it on!" They can't wait to get to work because it brings them fulfillment and accomplishment. No matter what's happened the day before, they start every day with a brand-new positive attitude. Every day is a fresh start on life. Every day they cultivate a new mind-set for pushing themselves to higher levels of achievement. So what they do for a living will become rewarding—both personally and financially.

> Achievers don't look for the easy jobs and they always enjoy what they do no matter what they do. It's all in their attitude!

WISDOM KEY

Work was never meant to be easy…
Work is "work" and work is hard—that's why they call it work!

IF YOU THINK THINGS ARE TOUGH AROUND HERE… IT'S BECAUSE WE ARE DOING WHAT ONLY THE TOUGH CAN DO!

There is nothing more rewarding to the soul than the exhilaration of accomplishment after a good hard day of work. Achievers never strive to go where it's easy because they know if you take the easy way you will never discover your true potential, or find out how talented you really are. They set themselves apart from the masses by looking for the difficult jobs nobody else wants to tackle. This is what makes them indispensable!

ALL WINNERS ENJOY THE SWEET SOUL-SATISFYING REWARDS OF ACCOMPLISHMENT AFTER A LONG HARD-FOUGHT STRUGGLE TO OVERCOME GREAT ADVERSITY. ALL LOSERS FOOLISHLY WONDER WHY THEIR LIVES ARE SO LOUSY AFTER THEY SEEMED TO FEEL SO GOOD WHEN THEY WERE DOING NOTHING BUT LOAFING ON THE JOB!

The harder you work as a teenager, the more fun you will have as an adult. The more fun you have as a teenager, the harder you will work as an adult.
— Wayne Gretzky's Dad

So how do you start developing a cheerful attitude about what you do for your living?

HAVE YOU EVER WATCHED A PROFESSIONAL FOOTBALL GAME? I LOVE WATCHING THE GREEN BAY PACKERS. WHAT AMAZES ME THE MOST IS THE FANS—HOW GROWN MEN CAN SIT IN BELOW-FREEZING WEATHER HALF-NAKED! NOT ONLY THAT, THEY HAVE HALF THEIR BODIES PAINTED GREEN AND THE OTHER HALF PAINTED YELLOW. TO REALLY TOP THINGS OFF, THEY WEAR BIG FOAM HATS THAT LOOK LIKE BIG SLICES OF CHEESE! FOR MORE THAN TWO HOURS, THEY JUMP UP AND DOWN AND HOLLER THEIR LUNGS OUT CHEERING. THESE FANS ARE VERY PASSIONATE AND WILDLY ENTHUSIASTIC ABOUT THE GAME OF FOOTBALL AND THEIR TEAM. WHEN WAS THE LAST TIME YOU SHARED THIS SAME TYPE OF ENTHUSIASM FOR YOUR WORK OR YOUR COMPANY?

Never trash talk about what you do for a living! It's so unfortunate we don't share the same wild enthusiasm for our work that we do for a football game, when our work is our life and our life is our work. Here's another sad thought: If you were to tell a die-hard Packer fan that you thought the Chicago Bears were a better team, the Packer fan would be willing to fight you—right now! They wouldn't let anybody trash talk their team!

But why is it that we are willing to let other people trash talk our company, which gives us our livelihood, and think nothing of it? Then there are employees who not only listen to the negative trash talk—they actually join in and help bash the very company they are working for!

When people verbally bash your company it should make you mad. You should want to stand up for the company that gives you your livelihood. You should fight for your company with the same degree of passion that you would enthusiastically cheer for your favorite sports team. The reason why most people don't stand up for their workplace is because…

Too many people "work for a living" when they should be " living for their work!"

The lesson is—*don't kill your "Golden Goose!"* Why would you want to hurt the goose that is laying the golden eggs? Rumor and gossip are very destructive to your business. If you ever hear this type of trash talk, get away from it fast! Don't let the losers in life pollute your thinking. Most people in life hate going to work and they don't like what they're doing for a living. Don't ruin your future by getting around these types of people. They are bad for you. Instead be a "Force for Good." Be a Positive Influence. Be a "Good Finder." Be a Winner. Be an Achiever. It's OK to get really excited about going to work. After all, you will be working for the rest of your life, so you might as well enjoy it.

Are You A Bricklayer or a Cathedral Builder?

**What kind of worker are you? Your attitude is everything.
"OK, I want to change. Where do I start?"**

Forget the "Job!"
Focus on the "Opportunity!"

If you're always looking for a better paying job, you're missing the point. People who are in a rut in their present jobs may think the grass is greener somewhere else. They always have only one goal in mind—to find a better paying job. If you ask them why they are unhappy, they will tell you they hate their jobs and the pay sucks. Constant "Job Seekers" are generally only concerned about what's in it for them. They want to know:

OPPORTUNITY
UNLIMITED
WEALTH

JOB
PAYCHECK

- How much is the pay?
- How does my vacation time accrue?
- Are there medical benefits? Health insurance?
- Are there cost of living increases?
- Are there advancement opportunities?
- What can you give me? Gimme, Gimme, Gimme is their cry…

It's time to stop working for today's paycheck and start working for a much greater reward – tomorrow's opportunity.

People want security without the risks. People who look for "jobs" are looking for security where there is none. There's a big difference between Job Seekers and people who create their own opportunities wherever they are. Job Seekers don't realize they have plenty of opportunity right where they are. If only they were able to follow their passions, they would have more money than they would know what to do with! Unfortunately, many people who think greater rewards are found by changing jobs have not grasped the concept that all opportunities in life begin from within.

*If only they would "positively change" themselves <u>first</u>
then all the great opportunities would come looking for them!*

WHY THE GRASS IS GREENER ON THE OTHER SIDE OF THE FENCE:

IT TAKES HARD WORK!

And by the way, the grass can always be greener where you are. Sometimes you have to be the one who makes the grass greener. When you see someone else's backyard and the lush green grass looks very promising, just remember someone had to do all the backbreaking work to cultivate, weed, and nourish this grass. You can't waltz into someone else's backyard and enjoy the fruits of their hard work. A major lesson for success in your career is to make your grass greener right where you are. Then people will seek you out to come to their "needy" yards and pay you big bucks to make more lush green grass. You will never have this opportunity if all you think you have to do is bring your lawn chair and park it on someone else's green grass.

WISDOM KEY

> Quit looking at the green grass on the other side of the fence. You must become the person responsible for making your own backyard full of the greenest grass around!
>
> • Start thinking of yourself as "fertilizer," so wherever you are, you're the one that makes the grass greener.
>
> • Start a personal program of eradicating the weeds! Start fertilizing, nurturing, and cultivating the grass God has given you. This is your opportunity.
>
> • Strive to make wherever you are, the "greenest" you can be, so others will be checking out your backyard and not the other way around!

Let's look at what a "job" really is...

A job is generally a defined set of tasks done repeatedly for a predetermined hourly pay. And this job is done within the confines of a specific location. There may be annual cost of living increases and merit increases, but only to a set amount—there is a "ceiling" to how much you can earn. As long as you do your job—and if it is not eliminated by downsizing or company bankruptcy—you may have some degree of security.

In a job, people are content to settle into "their daily grind." In a job, people go to work "just to live" and "pay their bills." They look forward to retirement and their pension. Most die broke after living a life of nonachievement. Because the real meaning of JOB is...

Just Over Broke!

The world is full of "Job Seekers"—don't be one of them! Be one of the few who are able to live their dreams. Be one of the achievers who reach their goals in life. You can do it. You are no different than anyone who has done it before.

• **Do you have a burning fire in your gut – do you want to make a difference in this world?**
• **Is your life built on values, principles and faith?**
• **Are you passionate, enthusiastic, willing to do whatever it takes, ready to roll up your shirtsleeves and go to work?**

Then maybe you are one of the rare ones
who should be creating their own opportunities!

It doesn't matter where you are in life; it's all determined by changing how you think and your willingness to go forward instead of dwelling on the past!

If you are willing to:

- Do whatever it takes
- Work hard with a positive, cheerful attitude
- Keep increasing your knowledge and job skills on a daily basis
- Take on the problems that everyone else is running from…

Then opportunity will come looking for you!

BUT! You have to be willing to do what others will not do. You must be willing to take risks, to put it all on the line.

Achievers and winners know there is no security in life. This world is filled with uncertainty. Security doesn't even exist in nature. The only security you will ever have is in your own confidence and hard work.

You have to be willing to do what others will not do today so that tomorrow you will have what others will not have.

Make this motto your own…
"I do what others will not do!"

Repeat these affirmations over and over again to yourself every day at work…

- I choose to take on the jobs no one wants.
- I choose to take on the problems everyone runs from.
- I do what others will not do!

Learn The Fundamentals
For Being An Invaluable World-Class Worker

Memorize "The Fundamentals For Being An Invaluable World-Class Worker."
Make these fundamentals your daily guide.

- There's a lot of truth to this advice—

"Whistle while you work!"

- Make up your mind that you are going to enjoy whatever it is you have to do, no matter how disgusting you may think the job is.
- Decide every day you go to work that it is going to be a great day for work.
- Be cheerful and enthusiastic about everything you do.
- While at work—BE THERE! Be fully engaged in your job. The best thing you can do for your social and home life is to take care of your job while on the job, so when you are home or with your friends, you can be fully engaged without your mind being at work.
- Dress up to go up. Always look your best. Take pride in the way you look.

You never get a second chance at first impressions.

- Shine your shoes: "You can't do deals in dirty heels!"
- Smile at everyone you meet and say something nice.
- Decide that you are going to be the best at what you do.
- Take pride in everything you do.
- Do more than you are paid to do.
- Don't be a clock-watcher. Quit counting time and make time count!
- Don't become complacent when it's slow. Push yourself to think of something productive to do. If not, you can always clean!
- Be the first to volunteer for overtime.
- Never say anything negative about what you do for a living or the company that pays you.
- Every day, better yourself by learning new job skills.
- Do your homework to improve your skills. Don't wait for the company to train you— take the initiative yourself. Self-learning is more valuable and more meaningful.
- Be a team player.
- Help others with their work whenever you can. By helping others through your service, you are developing leadership qualities.
- Managers manage things. Leaders lead people.
- Leaders serve—Managers manage.
- Managing is about doing. Leadership is about being.
- Managers help people to see themselves as they are. Leaders help people to see themselves as better than they are.
- Become very indispensable by becoming a trainer of people. People who can teach others how to do their jobs are the most valuable.
- Volunteer for special projects at work, like getting involved in the United Way or whatever projects your company has embraced. Employers like to see their employees contribute back to the community.
- **Be Thankful you have a job!**

Think About These Two Scenarios

Scenario One:
Workers who will only work as hard as they think their pay is worth.

- They can't wait until Friday to get out of work and hate when Monday morning rolls around.

- These are "clock watchers," always quick to punch in and always scamming ways to punch out later.

I'M NOT DOING ANYTHING UNTIL I KNOW WHAT'S IN IT FOR ME!

- You can quickly spot them because they are always walking around with a coffee cup in their hand.

- They make sure they get their breaks and always stretch their lunch time.

- They enjoy spreading the latest gossip about their coworkers.

- They are quick to blame management or the company for anything that goes wrong…if only they were "The Boss"—things would be done differently because they have all the answers.

- Their "what do I get?" mentality makes them more concerned about what benefits and perks they get rather than what value they are giving to their employer and the marketplace.

- They never volunteer for extra work because they don't want the company to get ahead unless they get theirs too.

- They avoid problems or point fingers when problems do arise.

- They have a sad philosophy on getting ahead in life. They think the only way to get pay raises is to quit working by going on strike.

Scenario Two:
Workers who are thankful for the opportunity to work.

- They love their jobs and can't wait for Monday mornings.
- They are cheerful and enthusiastic, no matter how tough things may be at times.
- They have an "I'll do whatever it takes" attitude and are quick to roll up their shirtsleeves and are ready to get to work.

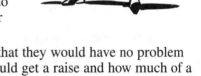

- They get to work early and are the last ones to leave. And when needed, they are the first to volunteer to work overtime and weekends.
- Many times they put longer hours in without thought of getting paid because they realize that this time is an investment in their future and they are glad to do anything they can do to protect or enhance their employment.
- They take such great pride in their work effort that they would have no problem letting their coworkers decide whether they should get a raise and how much of a raise they should get. (Are you this confident?)
- They are "Good Finders" and always have nice things to say about their associates.
- They are team players. If someone is having problems they are quick to jump in and help because they realize that they, too, may need some help.
- They understand that their effort is what makes the company a great company to work for.

**Do these scenarios seem too familiar to you?
When it comes to pay raises and promotions which worker
do you think will be at the top of the list?**

Which one are you?

Make up your mind to amaze everyone that you work for.

Unlike a job, there is no "pay ceiling" in an opportunity, and there is no "floor of security!"

You must be willing to stop working for a paycheck and start working for the greater rewards of tomorrow's opportunity.

Overheard…

One business owner to another, "Actually, I'm very generous with my employees. I encourage them to only work half-days, and I really don't care which 12 hours they work!"

**Michelangelo was a great genius.
But it wasn't his genius that created his famous sculptures.
He still had to pick up a hammer and go to work!**
— Jim Rohn

BE ALL THAT YOU CAN BE!
How do you become the "BEST" you can be?

WISDOM KEY

Study one hour a day. Improve your craft one hour every day. Practice getting better every day. If you study what really interests you for just one hour every day, at the end of the year, you will become one of the best in your office or business. In two years, you will become one of the best in your company. In three years, you will become one of the best in your chosen field. In five years, you will become a world-class talent.

Just think what you could do if you spent more than one hour!

By giving it your all, by being the best you can be, you will develop a reputation that will attract attention. Your passion will attract other people of passion. The greater your passion, the greater your influence will be and the greater the quality of people you will attract into your life. People of resources, who can help you, will want to help make you happy in the pursuit of your passion. They will open the "Doors of Opportunity" for you, and you will be able to choose where your dreams lead you.

> **Work hard on your job and you will earn a living,**
> **Work hard on yourself and you will earn a fortune!**
> — Jim Rohn

If you work hard on yourself, you will become more than you ever dreamed possible, and the financial rewards will be even greater than you can spend. The sooner you start working at it, the sooner you will find your passion.

When you find your passion or the one thing you love to do in life...

- You will look forward to going to work.
- You will become the best you can be.
- The world will recognize you for your excellence and accomplishments.

> *It's your reputation for being an excellent, industrious,*
> *enthusiastic, knowledgeable worker that matters most.*

Excellence happens when people have a burning passion to become the very best they can by doing what they love to do. They take great pride in their work, and they expect the same from others. As paying customers, we should expect only the best for our money.

Whether it is your doctor, your attorney, your stockbroker, or someone preparing your food, the question is:

Do you want someone who <u>has</u> to?
Or someone who <u>loves</u> to?

If your doctor went about his business the same way you go about yours, would you still want that doctor doing surgery on you?

If your stockbroker managed your investments the same way you manage your personal checking account, would you still want that stockbroker managing your investments?

If you were on trial for your life and your lawyer handled your case with the same "good 'nuff is OK" attitude with which you conduct your affairs—would you still want this attorney to have your life's destiny in his hands?

OR—

Would you want only their very best focused and concentrated effort?

What kind of effort are you giving to the people who have trusted you with their business? Is it your very best effort?

WISDOM KEY

If you expect only the best from someone else, you should be prepared to give the very best of yourself. How strong is your commitment to being the best that you can be? Or is good enough good enough for you? How can you expect the very best from others if you're not giving your very best? Remember, "What goes around, comes around." Don't you be the one that breaks this circle of excellence!

No amount of pay ever made a good soldier,
a good teacher, a good artist, or a good workman.
— John Ruskin

It's what you are learning and becoming... that is more important than what you are getting paid.

It's not about how long you've been on the job that matters... It's about how valuable you have become!

THE PASSION FACTOR

Don't spend a lifetime becoming good at something you don't love to do!

UNLEASH THE POWER OF YOUR DREAMS BY PURSUING THE THINGS YOU REALLY LOVE TO DO. YOUR LOVE TO HELP OTHERS WILL HELP YOU DISCOVER YOUR ONE TRUE PASSION AND YOUR HIGHER PURPOSE IN LIFE.

Winners and achievers pursue their passions with a vengeance fueled by an unquenchable burning desire to be the very best! Finding your passion will help you work the long hours you will need to establish yourself. And you will be proud of the products or services that you deliver. You will experience fulfillment and accomplishment.

Find out what you love to do. When you are just starting out in life or if you are starting over and not quite sure what you want to do, there is only one solution. Wherever you are, no matter what you are doing, great or small—give it your all! Pretty soon your reputation will precede you and the right opportunities will come looking for you. Giving it your all will help you find your true passion.

The first step to achieving personal happiness is to understand the true meaning of wealth. Most people are confused by the difference between what it means, "to accumulate possessions" and "to follow their passion." True contentment occurs when your perception of wealth follows your passion—what you hold to be important in life while you are doing what you love to do.

For example: the difference between being...

"Possession Driven" versus "Passion Driven"

<u>CATEGORY A</u> **represents "Possession Driven Values"—Perceived Happiness by the Accumulation of Material Possessions.** In this category, people who wish for only high-paying jobs are generally unhappy at work. They seek status and power to make them feel important and believe having a large home, driving the newest fancy car, wearing the latest fashions, and decorating themselves with the most expensive jewelry gives them credibility for how wealthy they would like to appear. They eat out all the time, have all the latest gadgets, and they frequently take expensive vacations. What others think of them is very important and they must be seen in all the right places, including having expensive memberships at

all the right country clubs. Self-righteous pride and huge egos drive their decisions in how they conduct themselves.

CATEGORY B represents **"Passion Driven Values"—True Happiness through the Passionate Pursuit of a Higher Quality of Life.** In this category, people seek a rewarding career doing what they are passionate about without any major thoughts of financial reward. They seek to make a positive difference in their community by unconditionally giving of themselves. By loving what they do, they are excellent in what they do—which causes them to be the best in their field. Their excellence attracts unlimited income that allows them to be debt-free and worry-free. Their contentment creates a healthy lifestyle. They are happy and contented with what they have and their thriftiness creates adequate cash resources for long-term investments that provide for a more-than-adequate retirement nest egg. Their family values and strong faith in God

I LOVE WHAT I DO! I LOVE MAKING OTHERS HAPPY!

Don't let your obsession for possessions become your passion!

This comparison of two completely different viewpoints of wealth is important because most young people consider the "luxuries of life" found under Category A as the basis for their financial goals. Category B represents a mature viewpoint of wealth and a healthier reflection of more meaningful values.

The importance of these two comparisons is that many young people who chase the material possessions like those in Category A will not achieve the values found in Category B. However, those who seek the values in Category B generally will also acquire the resources to enjoy the luxuries like those found in Category A.

---

drive their decisions as to how they conduct themselves.

Our pursuit of material things makes us do things backward. We seek high-paying jobs to get what we think we need—things that make us look good, things that make us feel good, things to give us status and make us feel important. When in fact, this pursuit leaves us worried about what we are accumulating rather than what we are becoming—leaving us empty and questioning…was it really worth it?

We spend money we don't have
To buy things we don't need
To impress people we don't like!
— Will Rogers

Money will never be an issue when you love what you do for a living. You will become so good at following your passion, that others will seek you out and gladly pay you more than you ever expected. It will be enormous, and you will be rewarded more than your wants or desires.

Instead of doing things backward, why don't we pursue our passion first and let the money follow? The ultimate goal would be to pursue our passion vigorously without thought of money or material accumulation. Finding our true passion allows us to devote time, energy, resources, and concentrated thought to what we love doing.

When greed and accumulation are the motive for achievement, then others will question the accomplishment. Likewise, people know the difference when recognition is achieved as the result of someone pursuing his or her passion; the rewards are more soul satisfying, mentally gratifying, and appreciated by all. There is no jealousy when someone pursuing the love of his or her life achieves recognition through dedicated passion and hard work.

You must love what you are doing so much...
That you are willing to do it for free!

One of the most powerful testaments about passion that I have come across is from former Harvard professor Mark Albion in his book *Making A Life, Making A Living.* He cites Srully Blotnick who completed a 20-year study of 1,500 MBA business school graduates from the years 1960 to 1980.

These 1,500 students were grouped into two categories:

POSSESSION DRIVEN: 83%, or 1,245 students, went only for the big bucks after graduation. This group, **Category A**, hoped that by finding the highest-paying jobs they eventually would have enough financial freedom to do what they really loved.

PASSION DRIVEN: 17%, or 255 students were placed in **Category B**, because they immediately sought to follow their true passion in life without regard for financial reward. Money was not an issue. Their personal satisfaction, contribution to their community, and loving what they wanted to do were their primary goals. They believed that if they pursued their true passion first the financial rewards would follow later.

The results after 20 years—there were 101 millionaires. What's astounding is the fact that **only ONE millionaire** came from Category A and **100 millionaires** came **from Category B!** What an incredible testament to following your dreams and pouring every last effort into pursuing your passion and not worrying about how much money you were going to accumulate!

The rewards of following your passion are immediate and amazing.

BECOME RICH IN YOUR NICHE!
— Mark Victor Hansen

When you follow your passion, you will be more alert to learning new things. Passion creates an almost instinctive sensitivity to things that others do not sense. You become more alert. You become more intense. Your ability to learn new things is increased. You become more creative. You find learning enjoyable. Your willingness to learn creates your expertise. Every time you reach a new level of expertise, you won't quit there. You instinctively strive to reach even higher levels because you are driven by your unquenchable passion. You work diligently to provide the best service and the best products because you are proud of what you have become.

When you are following your passion, your curiosity will be intense. You won't wait for the company to train you. You will be spending every waking hour trying to learn more about what interests you. Your mind becomes exponentially more fertile and your creativity will flourish. This creativity will stimulate your problem-solving abilities and bring you greater insight. You will discover what others cannot see.

WISDOM KEY

> **Self-learning is so much more powerful than being taught.** You will achieve greater understanding and more insightful wisdom on how to improve what you are doing through self-learning than from any outside training that you are required to take.

When you are following your passion, your "all-encompassing" alertness to the small details will be magnified. You will be especially alert to the little things that make all the difference between being excellent and being average. This attention to detail will happen only when you love what you are doing. Excellence is the natural result of loving what you do. Your excellence is an expression of your love to serve others with only the best of your ability.

This passion creates excellence; and excellence in one's chosen field ultimately provides recognition, status, and wealth for a "job well done." This recognition is more rewarding to the soul than a competitive effort to put someone else down for the "bragging rights" of a win.

The Magic of "ZONE POWER"

Passion creates "access to your zone." Intense passion lets you access a zone of peak performance that most of the world never experiences. When you are following your passion you become so good at what you love to do that you are able to "access your zone" at any time. This heightened sensitivity allows every cell of your body to execute in perfect harmony to produce an effortless performance that can't be matched outside of your zone.

Accessing your zone is a perfect example of why we need to understand the immense and awesome power that comes from "mastery of our internal resources." When we can master our internal resources we will be able to access the magical wonders of "being in a zone" any time we want! This is the magic of finding your passion. You are able to perform at peak levels of excellence "unconsciously."

All people who become excellent in their professions are able to mentally access a "zone" of almost higher conscious instinctive peak performance. People in a zone are oblivious to what is going on around them because they are so focused.

I was talking to a competitive gymnast who explained that when she is in a zone it is as if she is in a "self-contained tunnel." She is unconscious of anything that might distract her. The balance beam seems like it is two feet wide and every move she makes is in perfect form—she can't miss. When she is able to access her zone she doesn't have to consciously think about her next move. It comes instinctively without effort. Even the most difficult and challenging exercise becomes effortless. There is no worry about screwing up. She feels really great, and she feels confident. She feels like she is in her own world.

Michael Jordan often accessed this zone and when he was in it, he couldn't miss the basket even if he tried. Nobody could stop him. His mind, his vision, the ball—it was as though "they were one" and the basket rim was so huge that every shot couldn't keep from falling in. Tiger Woods experiences the same incredible phenomenon. When Tiger is in his zone, he is able to hit the golf ball with remarkable accuracy and distance. His putts are magically attracted into the cup.

All people who are following their passion can get into a zone. Although athletes are probably the most visible of people reaching incredible levels of peak performance by being in a zone, it isn't only athletes who can access their zones. Writers who are in a zone seem to have words just flow from their pen. Beautiful works of art seem to jump out of an artist's brush. Musicians who are in a zone claim that they are so inspired that beautiful music just magically seems to come together without much effort on their part.

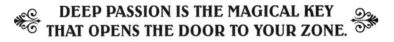

DEEP PASSION IS THE MAGICAL KEY THAT OPENS THE DOOR TO YOUR ZONE.

WISDOM KEY

When you are in your zone you are in a world of your own. Nothing else around you matters, nothing can distract you. You are in harmony with nature and everything in the universe seems to support your effort. Your thinking, your muscles, your coordination, your breathing—everything is working in harmony at peak levels of output, alertness, and achievement. Your ultimate performance will come when you are at the peak of your biorhythms while accessing your zone. It will be like everything in God's great universe is at your service!

Passion creates an inner drive that burns in your gut, that drives you to persist until you achieve, until you are the best that you can be. Ambition is your true passion being unleashed, a vision focused with laser precision, driven by nothing less than turbocharged adrenaline combined with an overwhelming determination to never give up until your dream has been successfully achieved.

— Famous Dave Anderson

When you are following your passion, you won't focus on the money. One of the side benefits is that you won't be a "clock-watcher." You will naturally want to work longer hours because you love what you do. This is a major key because working only 40 hours will just earn you a living that allows you enough to get by. Following your passion is where your fortune is made!

When you follow your passion, you won't be dependent on anyone for a job. You will be so good at what you do, people will come looking for you. They will pay you as much as they can because they will be afraid to lose you.

If you already know what your passion is—that's great! If not,
How do you find your passion?

The key is to start.

The worst thing you can do is wait until you find your passion. Whatever you are doing now, determine that you are going to get good at it. Determine that you are going to love whatever it is—even if you don't.

If something grabs you right away, it is what you should be doing. You will know it's right for you. Don't ever think you will grow to love something. You never will. Never work for what you get, work for what you can become.

The rule is:

Your opportunity to find your passion will never come to you if you are nonchalant about life. Most people say, "Hey, I'm doing my job," as if that qualifies them for continued employment. You will only earn a living—enough to get by—but nothing more. Just doing your job is not enough—you must become passionate! Only when you cultivate passion in your life will the universe reward you with the opportunities you desire.

When you find others who share your passion, the fun really starts! Love what you're doing, and you will attract others who share your passion. When you are following your passion you are creating a very powerful energy force. This energy attracts similar energy—it's called The Universal Law of Attraction.

A group of passionate people, all aiming for the same goals, taps into an even greater power of collective energy:

Collective *Passion*   Collective *Problem Solving*
Collective *Vision*   Collective *Creativity*
Collective *Wisdom*   Collective *Enthusiasm*
Collective *Learning*   Collective *Achievement*

Collective Passion Elevates the Group into Its Own Zone!

When a group of passionate people commit to a vision, it releases an awesome force. With shared passions, people are able to function as "one mind," even though they maintain their distinct individuality. People of like passions "connect" through their higher conscious thought, working in harmony with everyone's collective higher conscious thought. This mental energy is real and everyone can recognize and feel the power of their individual passions as a group.

The Power of Your "Master Mind Alliance"

Men and women of great influence understand the powerful energy of charisma created by intense passion and they thrive on it. They seek out and engage others of like passion. This is what Napoleon Hill called "creating your Master Mind Alliance." A Master Mind Alliance is a small group of people who meet weekly or at least once a month to discuss mutual interests. They fuel these meetings with their own passion, energy, and vision. You can feel these people when they walk into a room; their passion is so intense they are on fire. When this happens, communication is at its highest awareness. Thoughts can be communicated instantly and understood easily, with just a glance or a meeting of the eyes. People are able to work without sleep or food during these times. It's like everyone is on a single focused mission that doesn't have to be explained. New business start-ups and political campaigns are prime examples of this collective energy. This is also one of the reasons why you should worship collectively as part of a larger group of people all committed to the same faith. You can't access this same level of collective energy by yourself.

Be of One Mind!

Alertness, intuitiveness, and imagination created by a single, focused, burning passion stimulates a higher degree of creative problem solving. You will see this happen when several members of a group come up with the same answers at the same time or they feed off each other's ideas like a string of firecrackers exploding in rapid succession. Generally, people pass this phenomenon off as "just coincidence." It is not coincidence! The group has collectively "accessed their zone." Jazz musicians call this "being in a groove!" They are of one mind, playing unrehearsed and without music charts. They don't even have to look at each other, yet they are all in harmony. They "feel their music."

Coincidence is God's way of remaining anonymous!

The power that comes from *"being of one mind"* should be recognized and the creative energy should be allowed to percolate freely without judgment. This phenomenon must be treated with respect and faith. Any doubt or suggestion that it is coincidence will extinguish this fragile energy just like a live spark that quickly fizzles out. This synergy needs to be honored and fueled with reverence to what is taking place.

Such an intense magnitude of passion illustrates life's higher purpose. A vision that is easily shared and understood by those with the same passionate interest creates an awesome incredible force for good. Start your own Master Mind Alliance for creating a positive force in the world.

The power of this passion allows passionate people
to be capable of creating powerful changes in the world.

A group's passion can be derailed through individual greed. When the vision is solely for the accumulation of personal rewards, then the outcome will be questionable because the group takes on a "what's in it for me" agenda.

➢ Communication is difficult because everyone is suspect.
➢ Walls are put up because minds have become stubbornly fixed.
➢ Mental energy cannot flow freely and the power shifts from "mental" to "physical."
➢ Problems fester, and people become defensive and blameful.

Passion in its purest form must be free.

Unrestrained passion without hidden personal agendas allows minds to freely work together. Passionate minds working together create a very powerful "one mind" energy force that transcends time and space.

When there is "one mind" passion there will be "one mind" energy—and amazing things will happen:
1. **Answers to problems that seemed unsolvable will appear as if by magic.**
2. **Opportunities that did not exist will manifest into reality.**
3. **Doors of opportunity that were previously shut tight will spring open.**
4. **People of great resources will come into your life.**
5. **You will enter the world of enormous possibilities.**

Be of one mind!
— 2 Corinthians 13:11 (KJV)

THE POWER OF HIGHER CONSCIOUS THOUGHT TRANSFERENCE BY A GROUP IS NOT SOMETHING THAT SHOULD BE TAKEN LIGHTLY.

WISDOM KEY

Passion Boosters:
- Find your passion as soon as you can by giving everything you do your best effort.
- Get around other enthusiastic people with similar passions and energy.
- Quit hanging around people with similar problems—only similar passions!
- Associate with passionate people who can always cheer you on.

Passion creates confidence.

Confidence inspires.

Inspiration is the creative foundation for vision.

Vision gives hope and purpose.

People will eagerly commit to a vision.

The magic happens when
there is commitment to the vision.

ACTION turns vision into reality.

A clearly-defined vision creates focused energy.

This energy manifests itself in love.

Passion is loving what you do!

In the words of the great American—Will Rogers:

"If you want to be successful,
it's just this simple.
Know what you are doing.
Love what you are doing.
And believe in what you are doing.
Yes, it's just that simple."

How Much Do You Think You're Worth?
Or...
How Much Are You Actually Worth?

Ponder this awhile...

MOST PEOPLE WHO THINK THEY'RE GETTING PAID TOO LITTLE, ARE REALLY GETTING PAID TOO MUCH, BUT ARE WORTH MUCH MORE THAN THEY THINK!

Your boss does not "owe you!" You may think your boss is responsible for your paycheck. The truth is that your boss and your company have nothing to do with how much money is printed on your paycheck.

Key point...

How much is printed on your paycheck is <u>your</u> responsibility.

So how much are you really worth? (Be honest!) Most people paint a mental picture in which they are worth an incredible amount of money, even when they are getting paid peanuts. The truth is most of them are probably getting paid too much! On the other hand, they are actually worth more than they think they are—or they could be! Seems confusing, doesn't it? Think about it.

It's not about your pay. How much are you really worth? Your value has nothing to do with how much you are being paid. *Your worth is determined by how much value you are bringing to the marketplace.* That means your employer is not responsible for how much you get paid. The company that signs your paycheck is only a conduit for the value that you bring to the marketplace. It's the marketplace, the paying customer, that determines how successful you have been in creating value. Ultimately the paying customer, and not your employer, determines how much will be printed on your paycheck.

Always do more than you are paid to do. If you want to quickly stand out among your peers, do more than you are paid to do. Obviously, you can never ask for more money if you aren't already doing more. The quickest way to increase your value to the marketplace is to create substantially more profits than you are being paid for. People who give more value than what they are paid are in demand and are never ever laid off or fired.

*It is your responsibility to increase
your value to the marketplace.
It is your responsibility to learn more job skills.*

If you are not working up to your potential now, what makes you think your employer is going to pay you more with the expectation that once you are paid more you will start to put in more effort. It just doesn't make sense—does it? The only way you are guaranteed to get paid more is to always give 110% of your best effort in advance. Never hold anything back. Work <u>full-out</u> every day, then there will never be a question as to whether you deserve a raise.

Too many people are overly-concerned about what they are earning. What kind of pay do I get? What kind of benefits do I get? How long is my vacation? Be more concerned about all the things you can offer your company. Most people never achieve great things in life because they are more concerned about what they are getting than what they are giving.

**The real key to a more rewarding future
is to start asking yourself, "What am I becoming?"**

**Never work for today's paycheck.
Always work hard for tomorrow's opportunity.
Tomorrow's rewards are always greater than today's paycheck!**
— Famous Dave Anderson

**You will always be paid in direct proportion to the work you do,
how well you do it, and the difficulty of replacing you.**
— Brian Tracy

Start thinking of yourself as a "PROFIT CENTER!"

To create more than you consume should be your daily goal.

How much value are you creating? Every day you go to work, you should know how much added value or profit you are creating. How does the work you do add profit to the business you work for? Most people go to work without ever knowing how their job adds value to the marketplace. To them it's just a job.

WISDOM KEY

How do you create profits for the company you work for? Understanding the significance of this question is more important than asking, "When do I get my next raise?" It's not just about doing a job and getting a paycheck. **It's all about creating value.** People think that just because they did a job, they should get paid—the company owes them. But if you ask them what kind of value they've created, there's a good chance they don't know. All they do know is that they want to get paid. In this new economy, you better think about whatever it is you are working on right now, and then ask yourself, **"By doing this, how am I creating value? Am I a profit center for my company?"** THIS IS A VERY IMPORTANT QUESTION YOU MUST ASK YOURSELF ABOUT YOUR CAREER.

If you don't know how your work is creating value, you'd better find out! You could be replaced or your job eliminated because your bosses are probably wondering the same thing! And don't be so naïve as to think someone isn't looking at that possibility right now! The days of taking a job and then coasting, are over. Today, work is no longer just "a position." It's all about creating "profits."

The major question:

Are you an "expense" or "profit center" to your company?

You've got to be creating profits for your company—every day.

EVERY DAY YOU SHOW UP FOR WORK, YOU SHOULD BE ADDING MORE VALUE THAN WHAT YOU ARE GETTING PAID. YOU HAVE TO PRODUCE MORE THAN YOU GET PAID. **THIS IS HOW PROFITS ARE MADE.**

The more profit you create, the longer your employer will stay in business, and the more opportunity you will have to receive increased financial rewards and promotions.

WISDOM KEY

The Universe will never give you what you want, but what you can handle. And what the universe gives you is always more than what you think you can handle because that's how you grow. If you screw up what it gives you, you can be sure it will start giving you less. So if you want greater opportunities, you must become very profitable where you are right now! Don't screw up the present opportunities that have been given to you. What you do now, where you are—defines the quality of your future!

Is your work meaningful enough to be resume-building?

How valuable is the work you are doing? Is it meaningful enough to add to your resume? How valuable you are to your company can be directly answered by how often you are able to add something meaningful to your resume.

If whatever you are working on is not meaningful enough to add to your resume, why are you doing it?

Just working harder and making more money isn't always something that you can add to your resume. Make sure you have your priorities straight. Creating value by creating profits through making a difference in the world is "resume-enhancing work" with real substance. Every six months you should be adding something of value to your resume. If not, you are in a stagnant situation of your own creation.

If you're not doing valuable work, don't blame your job. The responsibility to put yourself into "opportunistic areas of advancement" rests squarely on your shoulders. But don't blame the company for where you are. Blame yourself for not being someone they can depend on.

Are you learning and growing? In the new economy, your value is no longer determined by your position, but by what you are learning and becoming. Never be satisfied with just learning your job. Try to learn one new job skill every day. If you want more financial rewards, become more than you are. Become better skilled at the job you are doing. Raise your standard of excellence. Constantly improve your job skills, so you can render a better quality of work, produce better quality products and give better quality service. You must make yourself indispensable!

MAJOR LESSON: Take opportunity over position or pay.

Many times people will give up a higher paid job for an opportunity to learn something of greater substance or value that will help them achieve their life's higher purpose.

NEXT MAJOR LESSON: Add value to those around you.

Is the kind of work you are doing able to add value to the resumes of the people who are working with you?

Be a builder of people. Are you adding value to your coworker's resumes? This is the ultimate form of achievement that contributes to life's higher purpose, giving you the satisfaction of making a positive difference in the lives of the people around you. If everyone you work with is able to add something new to their resumes every

WISDOM KEY six months, you will be part of a very successful company!

Stop focusing on what you are getting and start focusing on what you are giving.

You need to ask yourself some serious questions. Too many people today are more worried about what they are getting than what they are becoming. Ask yourself:

➤ Am I learning something new every day?
➤ Have I been considered for a promotion lately?
➤ Would my supervisor willingly give me a strong letter of recommendation?
➤ If it were up to my coworkers to determine whether I deserved a raise, how would they vote?
➤ And finally, the most important question... How many of my coworkers, would say that their career has a brighter future because of my influence?

There are two types of people in the world—the "Givers" and the "Takers."

Givers Gain, Takers Lose

Look at "Givers" and you'll see that they:

- Create value by making a positive difference in the world
- Love what they do, so they give more than what they are paid to do
- Take great pride in their work and do it excellently because they are following their passion
- Are concerned about the enjoyment, welfare and the satisfaction of other people first
- Never complain, because they enjoy what they do for a living
- Are the kind of people employers want to keep and communities embrace

Look at "Takers" and you'll see that they:

- Are only interested in what's in it for them
- Are a drain on society
- Never do more than they are paid to do because they are afraid of giving up something and not getting paid for it
- Worry a lot about being taken advantage of
- Begrudge their employer for making a profit off of them
- Are most concerned about themselves – they're very selfish
- Produce work that is always "suspect" because they aren't doing something they love to do
- Are usually the whiners and complainers
- Are only interested in protecting their own skin
- Are the workers employers are looking for ways to get rid of

Bottom line: People who are "Givers" create more value for their company.

WISDOM KEY

Always work like you are worth more. If you are getting paid $10 an hour, work like you are being paid $50 an hour and give value of $100 an hour. If you are getting paid $20 an hour, work like you are being paid $100 an hour and give value of $200 an hour. Sooner or later people will compete for you and pay you incredible amounts of money, more than you ever dreamed possible!

How many people have asked you to come work for them lately? Your true value will never be determined by how much you are getting paid but by how many people come looking for you. When is the last time someone asked you to go work for his or her company and offered to pay you substantially more money?

Here's an interesting thought...

> IF YOU HAVE TO GO LOOKING FOR A BETTER PAYING JOB, YOU'RE NOT VERY VALUABLE WHERE YOU ARE NOW!

Never scale your work by what you get paid. Your work should be to benefit the greatest number of people. The profit you create is to leave the world a better place because you were there!

> ➢ **Be a "Giver," not a "Taker."**
> ➢ **Be a value creator, not a resource drainer.**
> ➢ **Be a profit center, not an expense.**
> ➢ **Be an achiever, not a loser.**

Achievers in life will never have to worry about the economy. Consider this—the achievers in life who are at the high end of the pay scale are always looking for ways to give greater service to other people. They are genuinely interested in bettering the lives of other people. They love what they are doing and are following their passion. Because they are so focused on being builders of their community, they will tell you that money, while important, is not their highest priority. But, somehow as if by magic, money—lots of it—always flows in their direction.

If you are the best you can be; if you always give more than you are paid; if you are constantly learning new skills—you will never ever have to look for work. No matter how bad the economy may seem; employers will do everything in their power to keep their "star" employees. Isn't that great! You will never have to worry about your future!

So back to our original question...

HOW MUCH ARE YOU WORTH?

The real question is—

HOW INDISPENSABLE ARE YOU?

- If you told your employer that you were leaving, would they offer to pay you more to keep you—or would they just wish you well?

- How valuable you are is really determined by how many people are lined up at your door offering you more money if you will go work for them.

- The only way this will happen is if you become more valuable where you are right now—this is a major lesson you must learn!

The Secrets of Getting Promoted!

DO YOU THINK YOU ARE A "HARD WORKER" BUT YOU CAN'T UNDERSTAND WHY YOU NEVER GET PROMOTED?

HERE'S WHY...

The major reason workers get frustrated in their jobs, is because they haven't figured out why they always get passed over for promotions. They feel they are justified for a promotion because: they never miss a day of work; they know their job better than anyone else; they have been on their job longer than anyone else; you can always count on them to do their best; they are good honest hard workers.

So why don't these people get promoted?

Let me ask you a question. **If you owned a business and you had some people who were good hard workers, knew their jobs very well, and never missed a day of work, would you want to promote them and have them go somewhere else?**

NO!

Good, dependable, hard workers are needed right where they are! That's what makes the business run efficiently and profitably. Why would you fool with something that isn't broken? Working hard will only ensure that you have a job tomorrow, but it is not the major consideration for getting promoted.

So How Do You Get Promoted?

WISDOM KEY

Be a BUILDER OF PEOPLE. By helping others become more than they are, you become more than you are. This is the greatest secret to getting promoted. In the process of teaching, you become a better person for it. When you build people, you build profits. Great success comes from duplicating your efforts through other people.

You must be able to challenge others to higher levels of performance. When people know that you care about them, they will let you push them out of their comfort zones. The same thinking, behavior, and work performance that got them to where they are now is not the thinking, behavior, and work performance they are going to need to stretch to where your company needs to be tomorrow. They are either going to grow with you so you can promote them or you will have to find better talent outside the company.

Be a teacher. Love what you do and let it show. People who are passionate about their vocation make great teachers because their protégées are learning from a foundation of love. Your "upward mobility" is dependent on your ability to duplicate your efforts through others. This requires you to train other people to become better than they are so they can take over your job. You need to encourage, inspire, and help other people grow. In other words, you have to become more than just a hard worker. Teaching solidifies your expertise and role modeling inspires you to be at the peak of your abilities so ultimately you can be proud of the people you have influenced. When you are an effective teacher, everyone understands how to deliver maximum performance and maximum profits.

Your associates will respond correspondingly to how you think of them; always think highly of them.

"Growth" is going where you have never been before. Promotions are not easy. A lot of people want more money without the responsibility. If you have difficulty getting pushed outside of your comfort zone, you are not ready for leadership. You cannot grow if you are wishing for things to be like they used to be! Your hard work today needs to be elevated to higher levels of performance tomorrow through the development of people.

Promotions are all about more problems! Getting promoted is all about accepting the responsibility for a bigger share of problems. If you are a hard working employee, but shy away from problems, you won't be promoted. Every step up the success ladder you take, the more difficult are the problems you will face. The higher up you go—the more problems you will have and the bigger the problems will be. When you are in a leadership position you will have everyone else's problems as well. But that's OK!

Problems are growth opportunities that reveal the strength of your character and the depth of your leadership abilities. If you want to get promoted, never be a complainer when things get difficult. You are being watched!

Be a cheerleader. People who can elevate others to higher levels of performance, achievement, and profitability are always the most valuable people in any organization. You can't inspire if you are a whiner and complainer. People who enthusiastically do their jobs create a positive work environment. There are no limits to the financial rewards these people command. When you inspire, you create a work environment that promotes success and profitability.

You have to love people. You have to put your own needs and wants aside to focus on the needs and wants of other people if you are going to be able to help them reach their career goals. Go out of your way to help other people at your place of business. Don't be so wrapped up in your paycheck that you have no clue how to better the lives of your associates.

Others first. Leadership is service to others first. Once you can put the needs of your fellow associates above your own, then you will be recognized and "pegged" for the next promotion available. Your effectiveness in making those around you better will determine your success.

By the way...

If you are a frustrated hard working employee, consider this question: if you are such a hard worker why hasn't someone recruited you? My experience has been that valuable, hard workers never have to ask for raises or promotions; someone is always trying to recruit them away. If you have to ask, it's because no one thinks that highly of your work!

Also...

If you think you are a hard worker who is underpaid and you are contemplating going on strike, you will never be satisfied because you will continually think the world owes you. This is the major difference between "employment" and "employability."

Once you think someone else is controlling "your value"—you will always be a prisoner of that business. Once you understand that your destiny is always in your control, you will take steps to improve your job skills, which will bring you greater fortune than whatever you could demand by going on strike.

Going on strike is nothing more than "payment by demand." It is extortion and blackmail. Going on strike means that you are going to "hold up" for ransom the place of business that gives you your livelihood. Your extortion attempt may be successful in the short run, but no one ever wins—especially you. You have created tension and upheaval and all you get out of it will be nickels and dimes...maybe a few dollars, but certainly no fortune.

You will never get wealthy by having a "union" or "payment on demand" mentality. You will always "earn just enough to get by."

People who have an industrious work ethic will never have to fear losing their jobs. Those committed to learning new job skills every day will never be concerned with yearly "cost-of-living" pay raises. Those who can teach others how to become more than they are will always be in great demand. Their rewards will come whenever they are able to reach new heights of personal achievement regardless of whatever is happening to their business. And when their financial rewards come, they will be exponential—not just nickels and dimes.

> **One of life's greater rewards is in building people.** Job titles and payroll guidelines are meaningless to a motivated, enthusiastic, industrious worker who can inspire others to greater heights of excellence.

WISDOM KEY

The rewards you get in life are always in your control.

Character Traits that Will Keep You From Being a Builder of People:

- You cannot build people if you don't like what you do for a living.
- You cannot build people without your own strong sense of hope for the future.
- You cannot build people if you engage in gossip.
- You cannot build people if you do not have an aggressive self-improvement program.
- You cannot build people if you think your employees are there to obey your commands.
- You cannot build people if you have a "what's in it for me?" attitude.
- You cannot build people if you are cynical, a whiner, and a complainer.
- You cannot build people if you cannot accept responsibility for being held accountable.
- You cannot build people if you are challenging and argumentative.
- You cannot build people if you are judgmental and prejudiced.
- You cannot build people if you are not quick to say, "I'm sorry," or admit when you are wrong.
- You cannot build people if you want all the praise and recognition for yourself.
- You cannot build people if all you do is talk about what you've done.
- You cannot build people if all you do is talk about the "good old days."
- You cannot build people if what you are earning—disturbs you.
- You cannot build people if you think the company owes you.

Requisites for Being a Builder of People:

- You must love what you do for a living so much that others will want to have all the fun you are experiencing!
- You must strongly believe in your efforts to build a great future.
- You must be committed to building and making your company a successful one.
- You must put others ahead of yourself.
- You must be willing to unconditionally serve and support those around you.
- You must be a cheerleader, a motivator, and a coach.
- You must be "teachable," yourself, to expect the same from others.
- You must be a knowledgeable expert at your job in order to teach others.
- You must have an industrious work ethic and be a "pace setter" for others to follow.
- You must be a "problem solver" not a "problem creator."
- You must be willing to listen at all times.
- You must be willing to accept responsibility so others can count on you.
- You must have an "Attitude of Gratitude!"

A's will always hire A's.
B's will always hire C's.

Being a Builder of People is One of the Greatest Gifts You Can Give the World!

Always Go the Extra Mile With a Smile!

The Road to Success is Wide Open by Going the Extra Mile

Give first and then you will receive. Your life will be richly rewarding if you first give to your fullest extent without reservation. If you only work to the degree you have been paid, then you have been bought and paid off—nobody owes anybody anything. But that's not how the successful get their "One Up" in life. Whatever they do, they consistently give more than expected. When you give more than you are paid, you are "creating excess value," which is more commonly known as "profit." Conduct yourself, as a "Profit Center" and you will always be in demand.

- If you give, do it without expectation of something in return—this creates the magic!
- Do more than you are paid to do, to create excess value or profits.
- If you give first, know that your rewards will not be immediate, but be assured that they will be abundant—more than you could ever imagine if only you are willing to wait.
- The rewards of "delayed gratification" are always greater than "immediate self-gratification."

Go the extra mile by "Giving it everything you've got." Jump all the way in! Don't ever hold anything back, and you will live a life of achievement. Quit looking at giving more than you are getting paid as being "taken advantage of." That's a loser's way of looking at it.

Don't worry about the reward, and it will come— more than you could ever imagine.

Start looking at your extra effort as an "Investment in Your Future." <u>The extra effort is not a sacrifice</u>; it's an investment in YOU. Gladly put in the extra effort, your future deserves it!

WISDOM
KEY

Go the extra mile by "<u>Putting in your time.</u>" **The time you spend before and after your 40 hours is where your real fortune is made.** Working only 40 hours a week just gets you by. You can't experience a rich and full rewarding life working only 40 hours a week.

Go the extra mile by "<u>Being the very best you can be.</u>" **Excellence is not an option—it's the only way!** Give only the best of yourself. Start by taking more personal pride in whatever you do. You want to be proud of your work. Never settle for anything less than your absolute best.

NEVER GET USED TO BEING "GOOD ENOUGH."

Go the extra mile by "<u>Being thankful you have a job.</u>" Don't ever let your employers think they've made a mistake in hiring you. Whatever your job is, do it with a smile!

WHEN THE GOING GETS TOUGH, THE TOUGH GET GOING!

Here's the challenge!
Work longer hours and volunteer for extra work without asking to get paid for it. Make up your mind that you are going to be more productive than anyone who has ever done your job before. Decide to set the standard by which all others will be judged. Decide that whoever comes after you will have to work hard to fill your shoes. Make yourself indispensable. Make sure you're the one everyone can count on to get the job done right. If you do these simple things...
You'll be amazed by the results.

WISDOM
KEY

Work more enthusiastically, with the biggest smile you've got, and you'll be amazed at what will happen. You'll either:

- **Get a raise because your employer will be afraid to lose you, or …**
- **Somebody down the street, who can pay you more, will come looking for you!**

Only you can go the extra mile. Going the extra mile is a personal commitment. It isn't something your employer can ask you to do. If you want to work to higher levels of achievement, only you can make it happen. No matter what your background is—no matter where you are presently—you have the potential power to be whatever you want to be!

 MY GOAL IN MY WORK LIFE HAS ALWAYS BEEN TO GET PEOPLE TO SAY, "NOW THERE GOES THE MOST DEDICATED, HARDEST WORKING PERSON I HAVE EVER MET!" WHAT DO PEOPLE SAY ABOUT YOU?

To become more than you are, fix your mind on your dream. The more you dream about becoming something greater than you are, the more your mind will fix on that dream. Then something amazing happens. Your mind starts turning your dreams into a burning desire to achieve your goals.

> **If you keep nourishing this burning desire with daily feedings of learning and accomplishments…**
> **If you keep giving yourself daily doses of positive affirmations, and repeat them over and over again to yourself every minute of the day, and**
> **If you keep going the extra mile, then sooner or later…**
> **Your passion will turn into an unstoppable "determination to persist" until your dreams start coming true.**

Leave the masses behind by going the extra mile. This is the quickest way to stand out in a crowd. Determine that, whatever you do, you are absolutely going to give it 100%…110%…120% of your effort. You will dig deeper and give even more!

When you go the extra mile after everyone else has quit, you will never find any traffic jams, road rage, tolls, speed bumps, or construction going on. The road to success is wide open, yours to travel freely. *This is where your fortune is made.*

Discouraged about your work? It's time to change your attitude... or your job.

Sometimes, if you are having a hard time improving your attitude, it's best to find a new job. However, don't ever quit because your feelings are hurt.

IT'S EASIER TO GET A BETTER JOB WHILE EMPLOYED THAN IT IS IF YOU ARE UNEMPLOYED!

<u>**You will never get a better job by being disgruntled.**</u> **The universe does not owe you a career.** It is your responsibility to always be the very best worker you can be no matter how lousy you think your job is. No matter what you get paid, always be thankful you have the opportunity to work. If you find yourself in a job where you're thinking, "There's just no way I will ever like doing this," then you need to make changes within you! Your job has nothing to do with your attitude. It's all in your mind.

If you are bored...it's because you're boring!

Whether you find your job rewarding is really up to you! What kind of effort have you put into your job to make it more interesting? Have you gone all-out and not held anything back? What new job skills have you learned? You will create an incredible future with no limits by looking for the good in everything you do. Say only positive things while at work. Never gripe or complain. You'll be amazed at how wonderful your work will become!

Always remember that your reputation is your most important possession. Even if you don't like your present job, don't become a whiner and complainer. Everyone around you will think that you are sour grapes because most people appreciate their opportunity to work and they love what they are doing. So don't stick out like a sore thumb. Be thankful you have a job. Don't get a reputation for being ungrateful.

If you don't love what you're doing—QUIT! Many people go to work every day of their lives and hate what they are doing. When you are engaged every day of your life doing something you don't like, your life will soon become miserable and unfulfilled.

WHAT'S REALLY AMAZING IS HOW PEOPLE WILL GRUMBLE AND COMPLAIN ABOUT THEIR JOBS AND THEN CRY AND THINK THEIR WORLDS HAVE JUST CAVED IN WHEN THEY GET FIRED! YOU WOULD BE SURPRISED AT HOW MANY PEOPLE ACTUALLY DO LOVE THEIR JOBS ONCE THEY'VE BEEN FIRED!

People who consider their jobs a "daily grind" hate what they're doing. Almost 75% of the people in America would rather be doing something else. They generally have the attitude that the company owes them and if the company paid them more money, they just might like their jobs! Unfortunately, it's not going to happen.

Finally, if things aren't going to change and there's no way that you are ever going to like what you are doing—then you need to change! Quit blaming your job. It is what it is. Quit blaming your company for your own lack of interest! Do yourself a favor, do your family a favor and do your employer a favor—QUIT! Sometimes just being able to move on is refreshing and wipes the slate clean. Don't stagnate—get a fresh start!

WISDOM KEY

Go find something you really like to do and start being happy about what you do for a living. Life's too short for you to be unhappy doing something you don't love doing. But when you leave...leave on a good note.

MOST IMPORTANTLY!
1. Don't burn any bridges.
2. Thank your employer for the opportunity to work.
3. Always be grateful for your paycheck.

Don't Bite The Hand That Feeds You!

Introducing the concept of...

YOU Inc.

The most important career lesson you can ever learn is this...

YOU are always "self-employed" no matter who signs your paycheck.

If you want to achieve a rewarding career, work as if you owned the business!

People who own businesses are passionate about what they do for a living. This passion attracts customers, employees, suppliers, and investors, who are willing to support their business. If you haven't found your passion yet and are working for someone else, work as if you owned that business. It will change your perspective as to how you view your job. Your ability to think as a business owner will inspire you to become a more passionate person every day you go to work.

Stop thinking of yourself just as an employee. The most important "thinking change" you must adopt for your career is to shift from being an employee to being in business for yourself. You need to change from the mentality of being "an employee of a company" to being the "President of your own enterprise." You alone are responsible for your future!

YOU Inc. is providing products and services to the marketplace and it is the marketplace that ultimately pays you. The company that signs your paycheck is only the conduit through which you bring your product and services to the marketplace. So...

The company that signs your paycheck is your biggest client!

This puts the responsibility for your success squarely on your shoulders. Job security is gone! You are now the captain of your own ship. No more excuses. Your destiny is in your hands. You are responsible for the quality of the product and services you bring to the marketplace. How excellent is your product? Is the service you provide the best that you can provide?

If the company that signs your paycheck is the only big client you have, how dedicated are you to your single most important customer?

Thinking you are the president of your own company will be hard work. Working "as if" you actually owned the company will be even harder!

This is "as if" thinking:

How you view the company that signs your paycheck should be as important "as if" it were your own business. The way you treat the company's assets should show the same respect "as if" you had invested every dollar you worked for into it—including the last hard-earned dollars you borrowed from your parents' retirement fund. It's "as if" you screw this up, everything your parents worked for all of their lives would be lost. Would you want this on your conscious? Your present work is no different!

The question is this: Do you treat the place where you work "as if" you owned the business? Are you working as hard "as if" you owned this business? Is the quality of your work the best that you can give, "as if" you owned this business?

**I challenge you to thoroughly understand this concept of YOU Inc.–
If you do, you will have a very rewarding career and all the opportunities you could ever dream of will come looking for you!**

These are the philosophies of...

YOU Inc.

Wherever you work,
it is always <u>your</u> business.

Your personal business of becoming the best that you can be! As the sole owner of your company, you must constantly critique your personal performance. You must accept responsibility for your own development and growth.

The business community is always looking for individuals who are constantly self-improving, who are self-driven, who are motivated to learn new job skills—individuals who are committed every day to raising their own "Standards of Excellence."

The strength of any company today, will come from employees who have accepted "the responsibility" for their own destiny.

This new philosophy of self-reliance is becoming known as: YOU Inc. You must now see yourself as being the "President" of a company of "ONE." You are now an entrepreneur who is investing in himself or herself. The goal is to deliver the best possible products and services you can produce, to whomever you are working for. It is your responsibility to stay competitive in today's fast-changing marketplace. Only by taking on this responsibility, yourself, will you help to keep your company competitive.

"Good, Better, Best…Never Let It Rest!"

YOU Inc. changes the way you look at everything! No longer will you have to wait for the company to train you. As president of your own company, it's your responsibility to stay on top of your game by constantly renewing yourself.

1. **How much have you invested in your company lately?**
2. **How big is your Research and Development budget for YOU Inc.**
3. **How much are you investing in your Training Department?**

If outside investors were looking at your YOU Inc. Prospectus, would they be impressed with your commitment to Research, Development, and Training?

How much you are investing in yourself will mirror the value you place on yourself! How much are you spending weekly, monthly, or yearly to keep YOU Inc. up-to-date? Is $20 a week too much? That's only $1,040 a year invested in YOU Inc. Do you think $5,000 or maybe $10,000 a year is enough to keep You Inc. fully up-to-date?

Then ask yourself, are you even spending the $20 a week? When is the last time you invested in a $20 book to become better at your job? When is the last time you attended any training seminars to become better at your job?

How much should you be investing in training for your own company? Hopefully, your answer is, "As much as I can!"

You may be wondering…

How do I stay competitive with all the millions of other YOU Inc.'s out there?

You have to wake up every morning with a fierce passion to go out and compete. Every day you must keep your business up-to-date. Otherwise, some other new, bright, and passionate YOU Inc. will steal your opportunity.

In order to be competitive, you must crash through self-induced comfort zones. Saying that you have five years' experience, 10 years' experience, even 20 years' experience doesn't mean anything anymore. Nobody's going to pay you for your old products that may be out of date, or your tired worn-out service!

YOU CAN'T BE SO ARROGANT AS TO THINK THE KNOWLEDGE YOU GAINED YESTERDAY IS RELEVANT FOR TODAY. ARE YOU NAÏVE ENOUGH TO THINK YOUR CUSTOMERS DON'T WANT THE LATEST AND THE BEST? THE THINKING AND BEHAVIOR THAT GOT YOU TO WHERE YOU ARE TODAY IS NOT THE THINKING AND BEHAVIOR THAT YOU WILL NEED TO STRETCH TO WHERE YOUR BUSINESS NEEDS TO BE TOMORROW!

Saying you have 10 years' experience may be a liability in today's new economy of accelerated change!

You must do everything differently than you are doing now. You must reinvent yourself. Your present job skills, work experience and education are rapidly becoming yesterday's old news. Daily improvement is the only way to be competitive in today's new marketplace. The profits you create daily will keep you in demand.

WISDOM KEY

Every day you must conduct yourself as if you were just starting in business again. When a new business starts up, it is hungry for customers and eager to please, satisfy, delight, and "wow" each customer.
Every day you must rededicate yourself to being a "new" business.

You must accept responsibility for whatever problems come your way. In the old "employee mentality," it was always easy to say it wasn't your problem. In the old employee way of thinking, it was always easy to place the blame on your supervisors or to blame "the company" when things didn't go right.

As an owner, you understand that problems can no longer be swept under the rug. You can't just hope they'll disappear. You know that you must meet your challenges head-on and with a sense of urgency.

As an owner of your own company—you understand "The Buck Stops Here!"

From now on...

- **You will be "solution conscious" not "problem conscious."**
- **Your focus will be how to get the job done right, no matter what it takes.**

As an owner, it is your responsibility to find and implement the solutions.

As an owner, you will never talk badly about your company. One of the most devastating behaviors in any business is gossip and spreading of rumors. Presidents are proud of their companies. They "talk their business up" to everyone they meet.

As an owner, you will treat company assets with the same respect as if you really did own the business. With the old "employee mentality," it was easy to treat even small assets, like office supplies, with a sense that "the company will never miss it." Padding the expense account is no longer acceptable because the money you take is money that is no longer available for you to reinvest and grow your company. As owner, you now realize that all assets, no matter how small, are important.

...even pennies add up to profits, and that's your future.

When making a decision to spend money, you will treat every investment like it was your own money. You will conduct yourself as a "PROFIT CENTER."

As the president of your own company, it is your responsibility to keep expanding your earning ability.

If you want YOU Inc. to make more money, you will look at yourself in the mirror and ask yourself:

"How can I improve the profitability of my company?"
"How can I bring more value to the marketplace?"

That means—

- **You must learn to do things that you cannot do today.**

- **You must go where you have never gone before.**

- **You must give of yourself more than you ever thought possible.**

- **You must believe in yourself more than ever before.**

IN OTHER WORDS: GIVING UP IS NO LONGER AN OPTION!

You must strive to be excellent and up-to-date in the products and services you provide. You can no longer be satisfied with doing just a "good enough job" and being an average worker. As an owner, you will constantly be pushing yourself to learn new job skills, so you can provide increased value to the marketplace every day. You want to be proud of your business.

Ask yourself:

- Do I have eager customers lined up for my product and services?
- How much will the marketplace pay me for my product and services?

YOUR ANSWER WILL BE VERY TELLING ABOUT HOW EFFECTIVE YOU ARE AS AN EMPLOYEE!

Under the new philosophy of being President of your own company—YOU Inc.— you will be judged by the quality of the product and services you bring to the marketplace. What you have to sell will be judged by the highest standards of excellence, so if your product or services are outstanding—

The best qualified buyers will search you out and pay you more than your expectations. You will be in demand.

As President of YOU Inc., you will conduct all your business with a deep sense of integrity, loyalty and honesty. You will be a role model for the highest work ethics. How strong are you as a leader? What kind of a reputation have you created for yourself so far?

Your fellow associates:

- Do they believe in you?
- Would they want to be your partner?
- Would they believe in you so much that they would follow you if you moved your business to another city?

Here are a few sobering questions:

- How much would investors be willing to invest in your YOU Inc.?
- Would they invest $1,000,000?...$100,000?...$10,000?...$1,000?
- You're really in trouble if you can't find enough investors to give you $100!

How does your prospectus for YOU Inc. look?

Could you take your YOU Inc. public?

Would the public invest in "YOU" as a company?

Here's an equally important question regarding how successful you have been so far:

"How much could you invest in somebody else's YOU Inc.?"

Even though you don't own your own business right now, how you have been conducting yourself as an employee should be with the same integrity and industriousness as if you owned the business where you work. Your reputation as an employee should attract people wanting to invest in you. And your reputation should allow you to raise capital to invest in other YOU Inc. opportunities. Today, I can raise tens of millions of dollars for a new enterprise because people believe in me; they trust me, and more importantly—I DELIVER BEYOND THEIR EXPECTATIONS!

How you answer these questions should challenge you to upgrade your personal mission statement and goals.

There's no faster way to succeed than understanding the concept of YOU Inc.

Generally, the "employed" are coasting along going nowhere. They just don't "get it!" Quit being one of the masses. Instead, work as if you owned the business. There is no faster way of bringing attention to yourself from the people most important to your career than by implementing the philosophies of YOU Inc. The self-employed are DYNAMOS! They are not satisfied just coasting through life.

As President of YOU Inc., you will become a dynamo. You will be a walking billboard for your company. You will be living life to its fullest. You will be more productive, and your thirst to learn more and do more will allow you to feast on all the goodness life has to offer.

**WISDOM
KEY**

This change in thinking—going from just being an employee to taking ownership of your destiny and becoming the president of YOU Inc.—is probably one of the most important changes you will ever make for your career.

REMEMBER, NO MATTER WHO SIGNS YOUR PAYCHECK, ULTIMATELY...YOUR SUCCESS IS ALL UP TO YOU!

Building your $1,000,000 Network!
It's Not What You Know,
It's Who You Know!

There's a whole lot of truth to the above statement. Sometimes, it is really about WHO you know, not just WHAT you know! You must become masterful in building your network. Building a comprehensive address file of the people you meet is one of the success skills learned early by all achievers. Those who are most successful in their careers have mastered the art of "building a network." Throughout your lifetime, you will meet incredible and interesting people— potential resources who can help you in building your career or your business.

Why Networking?

1. A great network gives you access to others with brilliant ideas and an unlimited treasure-trove of resources you may not have yet.
2. A great network gives you access to the invaluable life experiences of others. Why spend a lifetime figuring out things the hard way when you can tap into the experiences of someone who has already gone through the trial and error to find out the right way of getting things done?
3. Why go it alone? Success is all about helping others achieve their dreams. Your network will abundantly help you as you unselfishly help them.

WISDOM KEY

Your ability to achieve the greatest of your dreams is directly mirrored by the extent and quality of your network. The people who know how to get things done also have the most developed networks. The Million-Dollar Question, "How big is your network?"

The potential power of your network is tremendous. Your network isn't just made up of *your* contacts but is exponentially multiplied by the infinite contacts of everyone in your network. Imagine the brilliant brainpower, creative talent, problem-solving experiences, and financial resources—just waiting to be tapped!

Getting Started

➢ Every day meet and greet someone who will be a resource to you
➢ Keep a computerized phone and address list of personal and business associates
➢ Ask for everyone's business card
➢ Give everyone your business card
➢ Ask for everyone's e-mail address

Build your network by getting involved. Get active in your church, volunteer to help out with the church picnic. Attend community meetings, the local chamber of commerce, the Rotary, or the Lions Club. Get active in your industry; attend lectures and seminars or association meetings. And when these events are over, don't just rush out and go home. Linger around, meet and greet people. Make a point of handing out your business card to everyone in the room wherever you go!

You've got to pollinate! I'll never forget one awards banquet I attended and I had just greeted a very successful man and his wife. After a few minutes, he excused himself because he explained he had to "continue making his rounds." Another in our party exclaimed to the wife, "Your husband is the ultimate host, he seems to know everyone in town!" We all knew that by the end of the evening, he would have greeted everyone in the room. The wife replied, "Oh, he's just like a honeybee, the children refer to what their father does as pollinating!"

Building a great network or a $1,000,000 address book is like gardening. You have to work at maintaining your garden (keep your list up-to-date). You have to nurture your garden (you have to stay in touch). You have to cross-pollinate! Learn how to use the resources that can be found in other people's networks by simply asking, "Do you know someone who specializes in_ _ _ that can help me?"

Become a prolific note writer! Today, the Internet has made it easy for people to keep in touch, but the value of writing "a good old-fashioned" handwritten note cannot be overlooked. When you meet people, and they give you a business card, don't just throw this card in a drawer and forget about it. Make notes about your meeting and highlight anything you found interesting about your new acquaintance. If he or she has mentioned a spouse's name, children, pets, hobbies, or special interest, WRITE IT DOWN. Next, immediately mail a short note saying how much you enjoyed meeting this person and that you look forward to the next time you will have the opportunity to visit again.

If you know what interests them or what they do for a living and somewhere in the coming years, you come across an article in your newspaper or a magazine and you know this article will interest them—send it to them. They will be impressed that you remembered them. Small gestures like this today will pay great dividends in your future!

Remember...

It's Not What You Know,
It's WHAT YOU KNOW About Who You Know!
—Harvey Mackay

The Secret to building a $1,000,000 Network. STAY IN TOUCH! The key is to stay on, the giving end not the receiving end! Learn how to prime the pump by always giving something first. The next time you need a favor, you will find doors of opportunity swinging open for you and resources in abundance.

Reasons To Stay In Touch

- You hear of happenings in the lives of network contacts
- Promotions
- Birthdays
- Graduations
- Anniversaries
- Bereavements
- Holidays
- Something interesting has happened in your life
- Any other good reason you can think of!

Building Your Network

1. **Close Associates:** Friends, family, people at work.
2. **Community Organizations:** The local chamber of commerce, PTA, school sports, church or religious organizations, Rotary, Lions, Toastmasters, AA, etc.
3. **Industry Associations:** Trade shows, conventions, lectures, and seminars.
4. **Community Officials:** Law enforcement, firefighters, trash pickup, librarians, and postal employees. Remember them at Christmas or take cookies to the station. If you ever need help—they'll be there to help you in a flash!
5. **Service Providers:** Banker, travel agent, insurance agent, doctor, lawyers, accountants, real estate agent, restaurant owner, host, and waitstaff—make sure they all know your name by leaving generous tips. Make sure you have the names of a GOOD electrician, plumber, carpenter, handymen, and yard-workers. These are all people you need to establish a relationship with. Make sure you find the best because one thing that I have found is that your best professionals always associate with the best of their peers and will always recommend the best when asked.
6. **Public Relations Specialists:** You don't need to be a celebrity to have one! Check with your local newspaper to see who they would recommend. A good PR agent will be well-known to the media. When you are just starting out, an investment in a good public relations campaign will help jump-start your career or business. The free publicity you'll receive will pay off in huge dividends. Even if you and your PR agent part ways, continue to send updates of anything interesting to them. You'll never know when they may be looking to fill a certain spot and your updates may be just what they are looking for.
7. **Local Media:** Community Newspapers, Local Radio Talk-Shows, Local Cable TV, Local Life Style Magazines, and Alternative Newspapers (like the Reader or City Pages). These community outlets are always looking to interview interesting people in their communities. Become the expert by writing a column, or be a guest on a local talk show. Once you have made a contact with a media person, include them in your updates and holiday mailings. Hint: Don't be afraid of them…they are people just like you and me and they thrive on your recognition. It's easier to meet these people than you think. You can find celebrity media people at celebrity golf fund-raisers, community fund-raisers, and award banquets.

Become the master of "keeping in touch." You never know when a past contact may be worth a million dollars to you…or when you may become worth a million dollars to a past contact! Think about it. Then, put it into action. By reading "Famous Dave's LifeSkills for Success," you're already miles ahead of the pack!

The Networking Pro

LET'S SUM THINGS UP!

What does this mean to me?

1. **Experience the greatest happiness in your career by finding your one true passion.** When you have found your passion you won't have to worry about working for money. Never work for today's paycheck, always work for tomorrow's opportunity, because the rewards are greater.

2. **Your "can do" attitude will create unlimited opportunities.** An enthusiastic "can do" attitude is the key to creating your own opportunities. Always set the standards for everyone else to follow.

3. **Every job is an important job.** You should never be so arrogant as to think that any job is beneath you. There are no "dress rehearsals" in life. Make everything you do count. Always be grateful for the opportunity to work.

4. **Profits are created by creating more than you consume.** Your value to the marketplace will be determined by how effective you are in creating profits. Become a "Profit Center" instead of an "Expense" and the world will beat a path to your door!

5. **Always go the extra mile with a smile!** You must always give more than you are being paid and you will never have to look for another job. Opportunities will come looking for you!

6. **You are the President of YOU Inc.** Treat every job as if you were in business for yourself. Every day rededicate yourself to being a "new" business; hungry for customers and eager to please!

7. **Building your $1,000,000 Network!** It's not what you know; it's who you know. Throughout your lifetime, you will meet incredible and interesting people—resources who can help you in buidling your career or your business. Become the master of "keeping in touch." You never know when a past contact may be worth a million dollars to you!

CALL TO ACTION:

1. Follow your dreams by finding your passion. Find out what you really love doing and you will never work another day in your life again!

2. Develop a reputation for being a really great worker who is in demand by the marketplace.

3. Learn how to become a profit center by always creating more than you consume.

WHAT YOU CAN ACCOMPLISH:

You will enjoy a richly rewarding career doing what you love to do by following your dreams. You will love going to work and your passion will cause you to be recognized as "tops" in your industry. You will never have to fear losing your job because employers or business opportunities will be waiting in line for you. An industrious work ethic, cheerful attitude, and a willingness to go the extra mile to take on the jobs or problems that nobody else wants will create unlimited opportunities for you, regardless of what condition the economy is in.

Sources & Inspiration

The information in these books is powerful. I urge you to buy these books and read them over and over again until they become part of your daily life.

Dennis Waitley, *Empires of the Mind,* (William Morrow and Company, Inc., New York, N.Y. 1995)

Les Brown, *Live Your Dreams,* (Avon Books, New York, N.Y. 1990)

Daniel Goldman, *Emotional Intelligence,* (Bantam Books, New York, N.Y. 1995)

Mark Albion, *Making A Life, Making A Living,* (Warner Books, New York, N.Y. 2000)

Roger Dawson, *13 Secrets of Power Performance,* (Prentice Hall, Paramus, N.J. 1994)

Dr. Robert Anthony, *Doing What You Love, Loving What You Do,* (Berkley Books, New York, N.Y. 1991)

Stephen C. Lundin, Ph.D., Harry Paul, John Christensen, *Fish!,* (Hyperion, New York, N.Y. 2000)

Spencer Johnson, M.D., *Who Moved My Cheese?,* (G. P. Putnam's Sons, New York, N.Y. 1998)

Zig Ziglar, *Over The Top,* (Thomas Nelson Publishers, Nashville, Tenn. 1997)

Joseph H. Boyett and Henry P. Conn, *Workplace 2000,* (Plume Books, Penguin, New York, N.Y. 1991)

Brian Tracy, *Create Your Own Future,* (John Wiley & Sons, Inc., Hoboken, N.J. 2002)
I highly recommend this book!

Harvey Mackay, *Dig Your Before You're Thirsty,* (A Currency Book, Bantam Doubleday Dell Publishing Group, Inc., New York, N.Y. 1997)
I highly recommend this book!

Lesson Seven: Wealth

Lesson Seven: Total Wealth

Have you ever wondered what it would be like to have a million dollars, and be free to go where you want, do what you want, and follow your dreams? Have you ever wished that you would win the lottery or that some rich aunt you didn't know would die and leave you a fortune? Quit wishing and take control of your financial destiny!

The fact is: Wealth does not come from what you earn. You cannot work yourself rich. Wealth only comes from the size of your investment portfolio. We have spent our youth learning how to earn a living when we should have been learning how to build our financial empire. However, IT'S NOT ABOUT THE MONEY! You should aspire to become a millionaire not for the money, but for what you become in the process. <u>What you become</u> is the major secret to unlimited wealth and success.

PURPOSE:

Don't spend a lifetime just getting by. Quit working just to earn a living and start building your fortune. No matter how old you are or what your job pays, the key is to start saving and investing right now. There is no reason why you can't live debt free in the affluent lifestyle you have always dreamed about.

If you have never studied wealth, how do you expect to become wealthy? **The Lesson on Total Wealth** provides a step-by-step method for turning any income into the "seeds" of your financial empire. The key lesson is that it's not what you earn but what you save and invest that really counts. Anybody can achieve great wealth by following these time-tested "Secrets of the Rich."

FOR RICHER, FOR POORER

THE STORY OF THE
Havemores and the Havenots

The Players:

Joe "Beer Belly" Havenot

- Just barely an average student
- Doesn't really enjoy going to school
- Active in sports
- Spends most of his free time hangin' out with the boys
- Enjoys being the life of the party and wouldn't think of missing one
- Mom usually cleans his room
- Always broke and secretly raids the family piggy bank
- Spends all of his money as soon as he gets it
- Started drinking at high school parties
- Loves watching TV
- You can't tell him anything because he knows it all
- Doesn't have a clue about his future

Party Mary

- Always concerned about what others think of her
- Has to have the latest fashions
- Envious of what all the other girls have
- Loves gossiping about her friends
- Enjoys going to the mall with her friends and just hangin' out
- Just barely an average student
- Likes to watch soap operas
- Enjoys being the life of the party and wouldn't think of missing one
- Always broke, but Dad spoils her
- Hates helping Mom with the housework
- Would rather eat fast food or microwave something
- Loves watching TV
- Doesn't have a clue about her future

Harry Havemore

- Fairly good student
- Active in school functions
- Active in his local church
- Had a lemonade stand and a newspaper route when he was a kid
- Helped Dad wash the family car, do yard work, and home repair
- Active in the Boy Scouts and loves camping outdoors
- Earns extra money mowing neighbors' lawns
- Has a fairly sizable savings account
- Has small investments in Nike, Coke, Apple and Microsoft
- Loves baseball and played high school football
- Plans on going to college or Vocational Technical College

Thrifty Annie

- Fairly good student
- Active in school functions
- Active in her local church
- Takes pride in how clean and organized her room is at all times
- Earns extra money baby-sitting
- Learned from Mother the value of saving by helping her clip coupons
- Has a fairly sizable savings account
- Learned how to cook homemade meals
- Eagerly helps family with household chores
- Loves to dance
- Plans on joining the Peace Corps after high school
- Plans on going to college

Before we get into the "meat" of wealth building...

Let me first describe the stories of two American families. My goal is to get you thinking about whether you are on the right track in your financial life. As you read these stories, I think you will realize that your philosophies determine much of your financial success. You can't operate at peak performance in some areas and coast through others without seeing a negative effect in your overall progress.

The Stories:

The Havenots

Joe "Beer Belly" Havenot, just graduating from high school, has saved up $1,000 from his summer job. He borrows another $1,000 from his parents and buys his first car—a $26,000 flashy 2-seater sports car. He puts down $2,000 and finances the rest at 10% interest. He will make $300 monthly payments for six years. His new car loses 33% of its value in the first year and 20% of its value in each of the next two years. He installs an $800 stereo system in his car—which he also finances at a high rate—to impress his friends. In addition, Joe's sports car eats a lot of gasoline, which strains his monthly budget—if he even has a budget.

When he pays off his car in six years, it will be worth a few thousand dollars. Plus, because it's a sports car, he'll need to sell it and move up to a bigger model when he starts raising a family.

But Joe Beer Belly enjoys having his sports car and loves showing it off. He meets Party Mary at a local watering hole. They love partying together and end up engaged. They agree to get married in six months because they find out that Party Mary is pregnant. They have a big wedding and all their friends are invited—everyone gets drunk and has a good time, although later no one can remember a thing.

The new couple, Joe and Mary Havenot, have to scrap their plans for college because Joe will now have to work to support Mary, who needs to take care of the baby. Because they had such a big wedding and because neither of them had any savings, they don't have enough money for a down payment on a house, so they have to live in an apartment. Their rent is $1,200 a month, which makes it hard to save up for a down payment. And paying rent does not build equity.

Mary eventually goes to work but as the family income rises, so does spending. They buy jet skis, snowmobiles and Joe buys himself a motorcycle. Their kids are spoiled and get every toy they want. The Havenots enjoy entertaining their friends and they eat out all the time. They love taking vacations, which they pay for with their credit cards.

Despite all outward appearances, things are not well at home. They are starting to argue all the time because there never seems to be enough money. The Havenots don't have a family budget because they can never sit down long enough together to talk about their family finances without getting mad and blaming each other.

Joe blames Mary for getting pregnant and Mary blames Joe for not earning enough money and for spending the little he does make on booze. Joe has started hanging out with the boys at the local tavern—he feels he needs his "relaxation and space." He feels he deserves his night out, but once he starts drinking, he loses all concern for the family finances and it's very easy for him to spend $50-$100 a night drinking, including buying drinks for his buddies.

The Havenots have overextended their credit cards. They owe over $8,000 on their credit cards and they can only make the minimum payment of 3% or $240. The finance charge is 17%, so at this rate, they will never pay off the debt. In addition, they have bought all their apartment furniture with no money down and no payments for a whole year. That debt is coming due.

They can't borrow any money to pay off the high interest debts because they have no collateral and no savings. Joe's fancy sports car is worth nothing because it is depreciating faster than he can pay it off. Plus he is having a tough time keeping a job because of his drinking.

Both Joe Beer Belly and Party Mary are smokers. They each smoke a pack and a half every day on average, which is almost 10 bucks a day or 70 bucks a week just for cigarettes! Their children breathe this secondhand smoke and it is almost certain that they will be smokers too. Everyone in the household seems to be fighting off colds and illness most of the time and their kids' clothing smells like ashtrays. But wait! Here's the more startling fact: if they were to quit smoking and started to invest this $70 a week at 10% interest, over a 45 year time period, they would net over $2,800,000!

Mary never cooks because it is easier to stop off at fast food restaurants and buy burgers, fries, and pop for the kids. The family never sits around the family table to eat and talk about things as a family, but instead they watch TV while they eat their fast food.

Mary is starting to get angry with Joe because he has fallen into a rut. He gets home from work, grabs a beer and sits down in front of the TV until it's time for bed. She is mad because they can't save for a down payment and the apartment is getting too small for their growing family. Mary starts to drink at home to take her mind off the problems.

The Havenots' future is pretty grim. It's a good bet that they will probably file for bankruptcy, and unless they can pull things together, they will probably file for a divorce too and the kids will grow up in single parent homes.

The Havenots are an American tragedy that unfortunately is too common.

The Havemores

Harry Havemore, after graduating from high school, bought his first car—a used medium-sized car that gets good gas mileage. He pays $2,000 cash for it. Unlike Joe, who has to make $300 monthly car payments, Harry invests $300 a month in a stock mutual fund that averages 10% a year (the historical average of the S&P 500 since its inception has stood steady between 10% and 12.5%.)

Ever since Thrifty Mary was old enough, she was able to save about $50 a month by babysitting and cleaning houses for neighbors. During the summer she earned even more, working as a waitress. By the time she marries Harry, she has saved almost $10,000, which contributes to their down payment on a first home.

Harry meets Thrifty Annie at a church retreat. They decide to get married after they both finish college. They have a nice wedding but with careful budgeting and planning it costs less than they had anticipated.

The Havemores search garage sales and ask relatives for old furniture so they can furnish their home, acquiring what they need as they have the cash. They both understand that new cars are the worst investment anyone could make so they keep Harry's beater and plan to keep it as long as it is running good. In the meantime, they start saving for a newer used car (used with low mileage) for when their family grows.

Almost immediately after they are married, the Havemores sit down and plan their financial future. With the help of an accountant and a financial planner, they determine that they will immediately save 10% of their earnings for long-term investments and 10% for short-term savings for planned budgeted expenses. Another 10% goes to charity, and they will live on the remaining 70%.

The first savings account they establish is an emergency fund, with the goal of accumulating an amount equal to one spouse's yearly salary. Twice a year they meet with their financial advisors to update their financial planning and to discuss any investment choices. Both maximize their tax free 401(k) investment programs at work and contribute to a Roth IRA account.

They don't make a big deal out of it, but they spend a few minutes each week going over their weekly budget and making sure their checking account is balanced. They make it a point to talk to each other about their finances. Once they start a family, they teach their children to respect money, giving allowances for completed chores. The kids are responsible for managing the money in their piggy banks. In addition, they help their mom and dad balance the checkbook and help cut out coupons.

In order to meet their financial goals, the Havemores stick to their budget and have agreed that no partner may spend more than $50 without advising the other. They vow never to use their credit cards except in emergencies and they keep them frozen in ice in their freezer. Both agree that if they can't pay for something in cash—then they don't need it.

They plan all their family meals at home and all lunches are "brown bagged" and taken to work. They religiously clip coupons and buy nothing unless it is on sale. They make eating out a special occasion. All entertainment is planned and paid for in cash. Instead of watching TV, they take long walks together in the evening. Both Harry and Annie love to read and make it a practice to visit the local library with their children. For entertainment, they play board games involving the whole family.

The Havemores are going to enjoy a rewarding future. They will have the money set aside for their children's education, they will be able to pay off their home mortgage and they will be able to retire with a fairly substantial retirement nest egg. They especially feel blessed because through their tithing and generosity they have helped many less fortunate people over the years.

The Havemores are an American success story.

$ECRETS OF THE WEALTHY

➤ Do you live from paycheck to paycheck?

➤ Do you think a better-paying job is your only answer to stress caused by overwhelming debt?

➤ Is winning the lottery your only hope of ever getting rich?

➤ Are you working harder to achieve a richer, more fulfilling lifestyle, but despite all your efforts, you seem to be getting further and further into debt?

The real question is:
"Have you ever seriously studied how to become rich?"

If the answer is NO—
...then the reason for your lack of success is obvious.

But there is good news—
The American Dream doesn't have to be...just a dream!

The first thing to remember:

No matter what your income, if you learn these simple rules for saving and investing your hard-earned money, soon you too will have financial prosperity beyond your wildest dreams!

Nothing remains the same. One of the most fundamental laws of your financial life is the law of change. You are either growing or you are dying. You are either renewing or you are fading into obsolescence. You are either going forward or you are going backward.

You are either getting richer or you are getting poorer.

Money, to many people, is a sore subject. We have been brought up to believe it is in poor taste to talk about money and that our financial affairs are very private matters. With all this secrecy, is it any wonder why people in financial distress don't know how to solve their money problems?

People are quick to say that making money is not their measurement of success and that other things in life, like family, are more important to them. That's OK and I understand this. However, the truth is, all people are concerned about money, whether they are willing to admit it or not.

In fact, people who will lie about their money— generally will lie about other things as well!

You cannot have the best family relationships if you are always stressed-out over money. The number one cause of arguments between young couples is deciding how to spend their money and wondering where it all went.

Learning how to manage one's financial affairs is important today because the whole world is changing so fast that what you expect out of life is going to be financially very complex. With the rise and fall of the stock market, whole industries are given life through initial public offerings and squashed just as fast. *This new financial environment demands that we learn the difference between:*

- **Employment and Employability**
- **Disposable Income and Discretionary Income**
- **Saving and Investing**

The difference between employment and employability is that "employment" means the job owns you and "employability" means you can go anywhere and get a job immediately. "Disposable income" means that you mistakenly believe that money is only for spending and "discretionary income" means you understand that you have choices to preserving and building your wealth. "Saving" is only half of the wealth-building equation but gets you nowhere if that's all you do with your money; "investing" is really the magical ingredient that builds wealth over time.

We need to learn how to spend money the right way—wisely! We need to be taught how to earn, budget, save, and invest. Few of us have had proper instruction about money from our parents or teachers. Families aren't as close as they used to be, and this makes it hard to learn money strategies at home. Plus the fact that many parents are poor financial role models for their children.

In the old days, it was so so simple—you would go to school, learn a trade or a profession, work hard, stay with the same company until retirement, and then live happily ever after on your pension. Today, most people are finding themselves disillusioned and broke by the time they are ready to retire. Pensions are no longer guaranteed and lifetime investments are wiped out overnight. Where did the money go? I doubt that many of us would really know where our money disappears to every day. The only thing we are sure of is that we don't have enough!

In the old days, delayed gratification was a commonly understood virtue.
If you couldn't afford to buy something with cash—you didn't need it.
It was just that simple.

Today, life is more complex. Products are obsolete within hours of production. We can communicate anywhere in the world in seconds. Instead of a nation with "local economies," we are now part of a "global economy." Millionaires are more common than ever before and billionaires are being made overnight. At the same time, business and personal bankruptcies are increasing at an alarming rate. And forget about a single-track career—you can now expect to change jobs many times.

Change is happening so fast that we want whatever satisfies our personal appetites—right now. We can't wait. This impatience has given rise to overspending on credit cards.

We have not learned how to control our impulses.
Delayed gratification is now a forgotten virtue.

Our "I want it now" attitude and impulsive spending habits keep us forever and deeper in debt and we can't get off the never-ending merry-go-round of financial crisis. The typical American household has racked up enormous debt through overextending limits on high-interest credit cards, car loans that exceed the value of the car, "buy now/pay later" shopping sprees, and the biggest culprit of them all—losing track of our pocket change.

We live in a country that loves to spend money. Nowhere in the world is spending so rampant and saving habits so pitiful than here in the United States.

Most people find they have too much
"month" left at the end of the money!

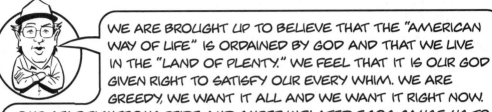

WE ARE BROUGHT UP TO BELIEVE THAT THE "AMERICAN WAY OF LIFE" IS ORDAINED BY GOD AND THAT WE LIVE IN THE "LAND OF PLENTY." WE FEEL THAT IT IS OUR GOD GIVEN RIGHT TO SATISFY OUR EVERY WHIM. WE ARE GREEDY, WE WANT IT ALL AND WE WANT IT RIGHT NOW. OUR SELF-RIGHTEOUS PRIDE AND SUPER-INFLATED EGOS CAUSE US TO BE OVERLY CONCERNED WITH WHAT OTHER PEOPLE THINK OF US.

Most Americans have the wrong mental picture of wealth. They think having money is playing the part of the "Big Spender"—parties with all the right people, fancy cars, big mansions with servants, yachts, the latest trendy clothes, and expensive jewelry. Actually, many people who live like this only look and act rich. Truth be known, they are overdrawn on their credit cards and stressed-out over where the money is going to come from to pay their bills.

Money spent on outward appearances and immediate pleasures is generally money that is soon gone.

WISDOM KEY

There are four lessons to be learned here:
- Don't be concerned with what others think of you.
- Don't buy material possessions for sole purpose of satisfying your ego.
- Don't judge other people's wealth by their possessions—they really may be broke!
- Get your priorities straight and build them on a foundation of character, principles, and values.

KEY LESSON: All it takes is a little money to become wealthy!

There is hope for everyone. It isn't always the rich and famous who enjoy the rewards of financial prosperity. Today, common people who have diligently saved something every paycheck, retain the majority of their wealth by living on less than what they earn. They have come to understand one of the true secrets of long lasting wealth:

Even small amounts of money, invested over long periods of time, will grow into incredible fortunes.

Financial happiness and prosperity begins with learning how to appreciate and nurture the money you have. If you worry about what you don't have, you will never think positively about growing the money you've got right now. Simply being happy with what you've got will ultimately give you the right attitude for acquiring great wealth!

Taking the time to study wealth, budgeting your income, spending your money wisely, saving and investing—these are the fundamentals. Delayed gratification, discipline, and patience will be your keys to living a life of self-respect and financial stability.

In addition, there are other intangible rewards for good money management. You'll feel good about your financial future and gain a sense of achievement in your ability to save and invest. The real payoff comes when you see your net worth rising, your credit rating strengthening, and your financial dreams becoming reality.

Begin with trust.
All financial success starts with Integrity and Honesty.

Your financial future is going to be built on the depth of your integrity. People have to trust you. Are you somebody people can trust to handle their money? Are you associating with other people whose integrity is so impeccable that you can trust them with your hard-earned money?

How much money could you trust your present friends with? If your answer is, "not much," then you are hanging around the wrong people!

Here's a sobering question. How much money do you think someone could trust you with? Would they trust you with $1,000,000? Would they only trust you with $100,000? $10,000? Or maybe not even $1,000? How about just a measly 100 bucks? If you were to call your friends or business associates, how much money could you raise right now? Your answer will determine how quickly you will become financially successful.

The greater the amount, the greater the trust. The lesser the amount, the longer it will take you to build their trust in you to manage large amounts of their valuable financial resources.

How much responsibility or money people can invest in you, or with you, will ultimately determine how successful you are in life.

Here's another sobering question. Are there aspects of your life that would cause people not to trust you, if they knew about these things? How completely honest are you with your spouse or family? How honest are you with the people you work with? Do you deliberately try to get out of paying for things that you rightfully owe money for? At work, do you think nothing of taking things that don't belong to you? Do you cheat on your expense reports? Do you cheat on your taxes?

Finally, here's the real question: If the people with whom you have entrusted your money were to conduct their financial affairs the same way you conduct yours—would you still trust them?

> There is a fundamental rule about money—in order for you to have financial success—people have to trust you.

WISDOM KEY

Remember, money needs to flow if it is to grow. In order for money to flow—it needs trustworthy people to handle it and to move it around. Money, when it is being "moved around," has to be accounted for.

"Successful money" is well documented, and "wasted money" has no track record.

Successful managers of money have solid reputations for honesty and integrity.

In this world of uncertainty, Honesty and Integrity are " *magnets*" for money.

Money Problems

Don't Pass Up This Section! Study this section carefully because, even if it doesn't seem like it right now, and even if you are not broke, you may be headed for financial disaster. Before we can begin to discuss strategies of wealth building, you first need to take an inventory of your present financial position.

Facing up to the realities of money problems is one area where you have to be completely honest with yourself. Unless you are in the top 5% of Americans who have achieved financial independence, you are probably in the 95% who have difficulties in managing their money.

Out-Of-Control Money Behavior Can Cause Addictive-Like Symptoms

Money has the same addictive qualities of other substances that we can't get enough of to satisfy our impulses, urges, cravings, and wants. Like other substance abuse, we find ourselves in complete denial. We lie that money is not important to us. We lie about how much money we make. We lie about how much money we've spent.

Like other addictions, there are also side effects associated with a money addiction. We can suffer from having cravings for money and we can suffer withdrawal symptoms from not having enough money. Money can make us irrational and impulsive. It can cause mood swings from moments of euphoria to long-term depression and if not treated, it can even cause suicidal tendencies. Like other addictions, money can become an obsession in which we spend every waking hour thinking about money, worrying over money, scheming how we are going to get more money to satisfy our cravings. Like all addictions, you feel entitled to spend money you don't have on your pleasures because it keeps you sane. You justify spending money that should be going to pay bills because of your need to feel good. And feeling good is necessary if you are going earn more money. "How does anybody expect you to pay them off, if you are feeling miserable and can't work?"

With our money addictions, we crave instant gratification. And we are quick to justify our compulsive spending habits, as if it doesn't really mean anything to anyone else. It isn't their problem. Our spending isn't harming anyone, so why should they care? Going shopping with the girls—what's wrong with that? Gambling ourselves into debt— it's just socializing with our friends…we're not hurting anyone, right? Out of control spending can ruin our health by causing worry, stress, fatigue, and insomnia, which eventually can cause serious health problems. Bankruptcy or financial failure has had the same stigma as being "pegged" as an alcoholic. This stigma has kept many people and married couples from dealing with their financial problems openly and honestly. And denial has kept them from getting professional help for fear of being seen as "out of control" or being a failure. People don't want to feel like they can't handle their own money problems.

Telltale Signs That You Have Money Problems

- You buy things you can't afford.
- You never have enough money no matter how much you earn.
- You are living paycheck to paycheck.
- "Saving up" to buy something is a foreign concept to you.
- You do not budget your household finances.
- You are embarrassed to say, "I can't afford that right now."
- You constantly borrow from friends, family, and coworkers.
- You often tell lies about how much money you earn.
- You're always first to buy dinner or drinks so you'll be liked.
- You are afraid to discuss your money problems with your spouse or your business associates.
- You cheat on your taxes.
- You claim higher deductions on your paycheck so you can get a big refund check because it's the only way that you can save money.
- You are afraid to answer the phone because of bill collectors or attorneys.
- You get frequent bank warnings about overdraft notices.
- Stores are denying credit card purchases because you are overextended.
- Utility companies threaten you with disconnection.
- You never balance your checkbook.
- You never understood how to balance your checkbook.
- You have more than one checking account and you often "rob Peter to pay Paul."
- You lose your temper then get depressed when forced to discuss money problems.
- You avoid talking to or facing creditors and people you owe money to.
- You have considered filing for bankruptcy.
- You blame your job, your boss, the economy, your spouse, and family for your money problems.
- You have forgotten about debts you owe to family and friends.
- You are hanging onto false hopes of hitting it big, winning the lottery, and getting an inheritance from a rich uncle.
- You are chronically late in paying bills or debts.
- Your credit cards are overextended and you are only paying the minimum monthly payment.
- You think you are not being paid enough and your employers are taking advantage of you.
- When you are depressed or nervous, you have to go shopping.
- You love to gamble and consider it "only entertainment."
- You have to have the latest car, fashion, toy or gadget even though you can't afford them.
- You resent the rich.
- You have negative thoughts about money because your parents argued over the family finances.
- You have a "what's in it for me" and an "I want it now" attitude.

If any of the above seems too familiar... You may be a financial disaster waiting to happen!

**WISDOM
KEY**

GETTING OUT OF DEBT

- **You must take immediate action to change how you have been conducting your financial affairs.**
- **You must change your attitude from one of pessimism to one of optimism.**
- **You must change your behavior from one of impulse to one of discipline.**
- **You must start thinking that money is for saving, not spending.**

**There is no dignity quite so impressive and no independence
quite so important as living within your means.**

— Calvin Coolidge

The first step in getting yourself out of debt is...

Change Your Attitude!

Quit feeling sorry for yourself. Get out of your "pity party." You must not spend your valuable time and precious energy feeling sorry for yourself over the money you have lost and the opportunities that never materialized.

Don't live in the past! You can never move forward if you are letting your past ruin your outlook for the future. You must forget everything that happened to you in the past. You have to let go and let the past be the past.

Forgive and Forget. You must not blame anyone for where you are today. You must forgive people who owe you money and you must make restitution to the people you owe money to. Forgiveness starts the healing process and frees your mind, so you can look forward to the future. It's the only way that you can start out fresh all over again with a clean slate.

Your attitude has to change from one of pessimism to one of hope. If you think everything is hopeless, it probably will be. You must completely wash your entire system clean of all doubt. Here's something that you must understand if your life is going to change for the better. This next sentence is so important, make sure you fully comprehend its significance—

...your internal pessimism will always manifest itself externally into your real world.

This means your lack of hope will become self-fulfilling. If you are pessimistic, you will attract unfortunate circumstances into your life. That's why you have to change yourself from within. You must remove the pessimism and fill yourself with outrageous, unfettered, enthusiastic optimism.

From now on, let only your internal optimism manifest itself externally into your real world.

WISDOM KEY

> **The road to great wealth starts with great faith. Believe that you can be debt free!** You must believe with your heart, soul, mind, and every cell of your body that you will overcome your debts and become financially free. No matter how far down in the hole you think you are, you can turn things around and dig yourself out. But it will never happen until you believe fully that you can do it and you are willing to take immediate action. Start seeing yourself as being debt free. Believe that you can be debt free. Then take immediate action to become debt free. The strength of your faith will move you forward.

Get Honest. Make honesty and integrity your highest priorities. Many marriages and careers have been destroyed because of a lack of honesty in dealing with money problems at home. The only way to start turning your financial affairs around is by dealing with money problems openly and honestly.

Start by being Honest with yourself. You must be willing to acknowledge how much trouble you have gotten yourself into. Don't ignore your problems and hope they will go away. If you are not honest with yourself, you can never be honest with anyone else. If you lose your integrity and are no longer considered an honest person, you will never get to enjoy the rewards of financial success.

No More Excuses! Your mind must be free from all excuses and all negative experiences. Cleanse your mind, body, and soul of negative baggage. You must be ready to start from scratch and live a life free from excuses!

You must accept responsibility for your actions. No one ever achieves great success in life without accepting full responsibility for where they are in life. While success is easy to accept, failure must be accepted with the same degree of accountability. Many people want responsibility but few are willing to be held accountable. <u>Responsibility without accountability is meaningless.</u>

You must take action. Once you have cleansed your spirit and your mind is free from the past—you must take action. You must start conditioning your mind to accept the fact that you will do whatever it takes to get yourself out of debt. You must begin now to make positive changes in your life. ACTION must replace your fears!

You will have to sacrifice. You will have to work harder than ever, and get used to doing things that you have never done. You must accept the fact that you can't live your life in the same manner that has gotten you into financial trouble. No more spending money you don't have!

Become wealthy by acting your wage!

Quit pretending to be someone you're not! There is no honor in pretending to be wealthier than you are. Generally, people can see right through this farce and quickly assess who you really are. There is more honor in being truthful. People of substance appreciate the honesty of someone just starting out because more than likely they have been there themselves. Your enthusiasm, willingness to learn, and an industrious work ethic is far more important than an expensive pen in your pocket!

Get good advice. You must swallow your pride and ego and get advice. You must seek out competent help from someone who is financially successful. If you really knew what you were doing, you wouldn't be broke in the first place. Quit seeking advice from friends and relatives who are just as financially troubled as you are.

Getting out of debt will take time. But that's OK, because in the end, the rewards of having all your debts paid off are sweet and spiritually refreshing. Your financial shackles are released, and the weight of the world is lifted from your shoulders.

WHERE TO START

Take a financial inventory of yourself. Make a list of your assets and resources. Next, you will need to make a list of all your debts and income to create a budget to live on. This inventory will give you a starting point so you can create measurable financial goals.

Budget your income. Start by listing priorities. This is a no-frills, bare-bones budget of only your absolute necessities: housing, food, utilities, and work-related expenses. What's left will be allocated to paying off debt.

Keep track of your spending. Keep a 3x5 card in your pocket and itemize all expenditures. Tally it up weekly and then monthly, itemizing each expenditure according to your budget categories.

Keep your checkbook balanced. Get in the habit of regularly balancing your checkbook. If you're married, make this a "togetherness" thing. This keeps everything on the up and up—no secrets.

GO FROM JUGGLING YOUR CHECKBOOK TO BALANCING YOUR CHECKBOOK!

It's not what you earn that's important—
it's what you keep that's important!

WISDOM KEY

> **Quit thinking that you're not being paid enough where you are.** The greatest secret to wealth is to remember…It's not how much you earn that's important—<u>it's what you keep</u> that's important. ***What you keep is your responsibility!***

Start saving by setting goals. Set a weekly goal of an exact amount of money that you will save to be allocated to paying off some of your debt. Paying down your debts is your first goal.

Sacrifice. Get comfortable with the fact that you will have to sacrifice. The most important words in your life will be…

No! I can't afford it right now.

WISDOM KEY

> **Change your spending habits.** Learn to conquer the bad "impulsive spending" habit by conditioning yourself to **"walk away."** When you find yourself "feverish" to buy something you can't afford and probably don't need, walk away immediately.

Make a list of all your debts by creditor. List all high interest debts first. List highest amounts owed next. You will want to pay off all high interest loans first. Next you will want to pay off all loans where the interest is not tax deductible.

Talk to the people you owe money to. Don't ignore creditor phone calls or letters. Put your ego aside and call your creditors. They will be more willing to work with you if you don't ignore them. Be up front with them about your financial condition and work out a repayment plan.

Reduce payments. Call all your creditors and negotiate lower monthly payments. Lower your monthly payment by reducing interest on debt and ask to have "delay of payment fees" dropped.

Lower your home mortgage payments. If you own your own home, check to see if the current lending rates have dropped. You might be able to reduce your monthly mortgage payments by refinancing at a lower interest rate.

Debt consolidation should only be considered as your last resort. It will increase your debt over a longer period of time and you will be tempted to spend your newfound credit. Better to bite the bullet and force yourself to pay off your debts faster. Only consider debt consolidation if the new interest rate is substantially lower. The most important thing is to keep your resolve to pay off your debts ASAP!

Destroy all but one credit card. Take this one credit card, place it in a plastic bag, and freeze it in ice. Use it only in emergencies or for business travel.

No more new debt. Learn how to pay for everything in cash. Learn how to be content with what you have. Don't buy anything unless you have budgeted for it and you have the cash in hand!

Increase your income. Figure out ways to increase your weekly income by volunteering for overtime and by getting a second job. Any additional money—no matter how small the amount—should be immediately used to pay down debt.

Get rid of the "I deserve it" mentality. Remember that you are in a time of sacrifice. Don't be tempted to think that since you've been through so much adversity you owe it to yourself to splurge.

Simplify your life by getting rid of the clutter. Clean out your house and hold garage sales. Sell off the "toys" that you really don't need but cost you money to maintain: snowmobiles, jet skis, motorcycles, boats, etc.

Quit Accumulating! It is human nature to accumulate. Our "feast or famine" genetic history creates a "fear of loss" mentality, causing us to worry that we will never have enough. However, you will never be happy accumulating more stuff. You will always want more.

Get used to having money problems. People often think that if they had more money they wouldn't have problems. The fact is, no matter what you earn or how successful you become, you will always have money problems. High-income people go broke as easily as low-income people do. Remember, it's not what you earn that makes you wealthy; it's what you keep, save, and invest. This is something most people never get! You will be hounded by friends and family who want something for nothing, as if you "owe" them. They will want to borrow money and give no thought to paying it back. Friends, neighbors, relatives, and people you don't even know will want to sell you all sorts of things you don't need. Then there is every size, shape, and color of charity organizations that will want you to do your civic duty and donate to their causes. So whether you have little money or lots of money—you will always have some sort of money problem. Get used to it!

"Don't count your chickens before they hatch!" Or as a Sales Manager once advised me, "It's not a sale until you can dance on the check!" Planning how to spend money you haven't received yet or spending money you don't have is the financial downfall of many young people. *Don't make plans for money that is not yet in your possession!*

"There's a sucker born every minute." If it's too good to be true, it probably is. Run from those who tell you they are going to make you a "ton of money." They've probably never done it before and probably have no clue. Don't let them practice on you! Don't be a sucker.

Be grateful to God for what you DO have. The key is to be happy with what God has already given us. If we are jealous or envious of other people's material possessions, we lose appreciation for what God has abundantly given us. It is difficult to have an attitude of gratitude when you are envious of someone else's stuff. Make a list of all the things you have to be thankful for and focus on these things—forget about what you don't have.

"Broke" Jokes Aren't Always Funny!

I used to be so broke that whenever I walked by a bank, the alarm went off!

I used to be so broke, I would go down to Kentucky Fried Chicken and lick other people's fingers!

CREDIT CARDS:
THE WORST FORM
OF CREDIT.

*They should only be
used in emergencies
and paid off immediately!*

Credit Cards can lead you to bankruptcy! One of the
single biggest causes of financial trouble is the use of high-interest credit
cards to buy things you can't afford. According to *USA Today*, January 5, 2001,
"Managing Your Money," the average American has credit card debts of about $8,000 in
2000 compared to only $3,000 in 1990. If they had more than one credit card or higher
credit limits—their debt was even higher!

Young people often feel "on top of the world" because they have many credit cards.
They are fooled by their borrowing power. This is dangerous. Credit cards should not be
viewed as "status symbols" but should be held in contempt. It is better to have a pocketful
of cash than a pocketful of credit cards!

❧ YOU SPEND LESS WHEN YOU PAY FOR EVERYTHING IN CASH. ❧

Credit Card "Foolishness."

- You pay only the monthly minimum.
- You have no idea what the true annual interest rate is on your cards.
- You increase the credit limit on your cards without paying them off first.
- You have no idea of your total charges until you get your monthly bill.
- You are embarrassed when a merchant tells you that you have exceeded your credit limit.
- You buy things on credit you don't need, like entertainment, vacations, dinners out, and luxury toys.

How To Prevent The "Credit Card Trap"

- Cut up all credit cards, except one to be used for emergencies. Place it in a plastic bag and keep it frozen in a block of ice in your freezer.
- Apply only for credit cards with the lowest interest.

- Always keep track of your credit card purchases the same way you keep track of your cash or check purchases.
- Always pay off your balance at the end of each month.
- Your lifestyle should not be bought on credit—pay cash.
- Never entertain yourself on credit.
- Never buy household purchases on credit. These should be planned for and bought with cash.
- Never use credit cards with high interest rates to buy depreciating assets like cars.
- Never pay just the minimum balances on credit cards or you will be paying double to triple what the item costs and you will never be able to recover investment costs of your purchase.
- Never run up debt higher in interest percentage points than the percentage of your investment gains. If you are running up credit card debts that have repayment interest rates of 18% and you are only earning 3% on your bank savings account—you are soon headed for trouble!
- Instead of credit cards, get yourself a Visa or MasterCard Debit card. They have the same advantages of regular credit cards for renting cars or for registering into hotels, but their use debits your cash balance immediately. So it's like spending cash, without the high interest rates.

Credit cards will fool you ...'till they DOOM you!

PROSPERITY CONSCIOUSNESS

WEALTH IS ATTITUDE!

**Now that we've gotten all the negative stuff out
of the way, let's start working on developing
the right attitude for creating wealth!**

**All winners in life...
All successful people who have attained wealth...
All achievers who have overcome great adversities to become rich...
Have one thing in common—**

*...An optimistic Positive Attitude that burns
through every cell of their bodies.*

- Winners are determined to never, ever, ever quit.
- When challenged with a problem, winners don't waste energy making excuses. They energize themselves to find solutions.
- Winners believe that all problems were sent by God to make them better people.
- Winners have an uncommon faith in God that gives them uncommon strength to do what others will not or cannot do. Winners pray uncommonly powerful prayers for uncommon results.
- Winners always look for the positive in every situation.
- Winners never look down on anyone, but always find the good in everyone they meet.
- Winners believe with their mind, body, and spirit that they will succeed.

**WINNERS ARE THANKFUL TO GOD
FOR ALL HIS BLESSINGS.**

ALL WINNERS GIVE GOD THE CREDIT FOR THEIR SUCCESS.

**IF YOU ARE GOING TO GIVE GOD THE CREDIT,
YOUR EFFORT BETTER BE WORTHY OF GOD!**

*People who have achieved financial success believe
beyond any doubt they were destined for prosperity.*

WHEN YOU HAVE THE RIGHT ATTITUDE, YOUR VALUES WILL BE PRIORITIZED TO DOING THE RIGHT THINGS AT ALL TIMES. IF YOU HAVE HONESTY THAT CANNOT BE QUESTIONED, INTEGRITY THAT NEVER WAIVERS, AND YOU HAVE AN INDUSTRIOUS WORK ETHIC — YOU WILL ATTRACT ALL THE WEALTH THAT YOU COULD EVER DREAM OF.

Your present financial condition is a direct reflection of your values.

If you have a positive attitude,
If you are goal-oriented,
If you have well-thought-out life plans,
If you are industrious with a strong work ethic,
If you are disciplined in controlling your impulses,
If you are have a complete grasp of delayed gratification,
If you are consistent in saving and investing,
If you have a quick generosity in helping the less fortunate,

...then YOU WILL attract great wealth.

If you have a "what's in for me," attitude,
If you believe your company is taking advantage of you by not paying you enough,
If you are cynical and have an "I'll believe it when I see it happen," attitude,
If you are impulsive in your spending habits,
If you do not have a written plan for your life,
If you do not have financial goals and you do not follow a budget,
If you care too much about what others think of you,
If you have bought expensive toys and luxuries you can't afford,
If you don't help the less fortunate,

...then you will NEVER attract any kind of wealth.

In fact, you probably are working for money that is already spent!

**WISDOM
KEY**

> ## Here's a fundamental rule about money—
> ## *Money flees from people with negative attitudes!*

Feeling sorry for yourself will not attract money or opportunity. No matter what has happened to you in the past—whether it is failure, being laid off, bankruptcy, bad credit, unpaid loans, or lost opportunities—you must not let this keep you from having a positive attitude about your financial future. Put these things behind you and invest your valuable time and energy in what's before you.

DEVELOP THE RIGHT ATTITUDES ABOUT MONEY

Acquiring money and great wealth is a good thing. It is not evil like many people think. In fact, the greater the love in your heart, the greater your foundation for building great wealth! Actually, money is neither good nor bad. It's just a transfer of energy! However, the lack of money generally creates opportunities for poor judgment, greed (wanting things you don't have), scheming, lying and thievery.

1 Timothy 6:10 says, "The love of money is the root of all evil," *it does not say* money is the root of all evil. There is a big difference in these two statements. There is nothing spiritual about being poor.

NO MATTER WHAT YOUR BACKGROUND, NO MATTER WHAT YOU'VE BEEN THROUGH, OR YOUR PRESENT FINANCIAL CONDITION—YOU WERE MEANT TO LIVE A LIFE OF PROSPERITY.

Change how you think and talk. If you hate being broke but can't see yourself as living the life of a successful person, you will never attract wealth and good things into your life. If you speak the language of poverty, that is exactly what you will attract. How you think determines how you will speak. How you speak determines what you will attract. If you whine, complain, spread rumors, and gossip, then you will attract only the negative. If you talk positively, speak of hope, and say only good things, then you will attract abundance and wealth. Your future obeys your words. How have you been thinking and talking? Just look around you and see!

You deserve to live a life free from stress and debt.

You must believe this and you must believe this strongly. There can be no doubt in your mind that you don't deserve the very best of all that life has to offer. You are no different from anyone else who has achieved financial prosperity. You must look to the future with hope and faith and believe every day that new opportunities will come your way.

We spent most of our youth "learning how to make a living" when we should have spent this valuable time "learning how to make a fortune!"

Start Every Day With A Positive Attitude!

Successful people start out every day with a positive attitude. No matter what has happened the day before, today must be treasured as a new opportunity.

Remember…"Today is the first day of the rest of your life."

Yesterday is history, and Tomorrow is a mystery.
Today is the present. That's why Today is a gift!

Every morning when you get up, start the day fresh with *
thank God for giving you a brand-new opportunity. Pray a
your day off right. Here's one I recommend:

Every Day Is A Beautiful Day To Be ...

What a great day it is! It's a fantastic day! It's a beautiful day to be alive. Dear God, you have given me this day to be the best that I can be. Thank you for giving me strength and wisdom to meet life's challenges head-on and I ask you for your guidance in all decisions I make today and that these decisions will be the right ones that will give Glory and Honor to your name.

You have blessed me abundantly and I want to thank you dear God for everything you have given me. Watch over me and my family throughout the day. Protect us and make sure no harm comes our way. I thank you Lord for the opportunity to work and I thank you for this great country that we live in.

And dear heavenly father, when problems come my way and life's adversities challenge me, help me not to be afraid of them but let me see them as opportunities that you have given me so that I can become more than I am. So I pray, not for you to take these problems from me, but for you to give me the wisdom and the strength to overcome these problems. Overcoming life's challenges will allow me to become a greater person, able to serve you more than I can right now.

Today I will be kind and caring to everyone I meet. I will be enthusiastic, energetic, and a breath of fresh air wherever I go. I will do all my work cheerfully and to the very best of my ability. I believe that I was born for achievement. I believe your word that I was destined for financial prosperity, so bless me with all your gifts and overflowing abundance. Oh thank you God for letting me be alive today! Thank You, Thank You, Thank You...It's a beautiful day to be alive!

Amen

force Your "Po$itive Money Attitude" All Day Long!

hroughout the day, remind yourself to keep a positive mental attitude through epetitive affirmations. Positive affirmations help to keep you focused on your long-range goals so you aren't easily tempted by peer pressure, personal desires, mass media advertising that causes you to spend money carelessly, or developing nonproductive negative thinking.

Repeat these positive affirmations to yourself daily:

- I am positive, energetic, and enthusiastic.
- Money is energy and it is attracted to me.
- I am doing what I love to do.
- Every day in every way, I get better every day.
- Good, better, best, never let it rest!
- Mediocrity is not acceptable to me—I will give only my very best.
- I am proud of everything that I do.
- Every day I am a profit center. I create more than I deplete.
- My goal is to make more than I use.
- I vow never to be considered an expense to anyone!
- I vow always to be considered an asset.
- I am in demand wherever I go because I do what others will not do.
- I respect my money.
- I don't owe money, I own money.
- Money is attracted to me because I make it grow!
- I am an investor, not a spender.
- I am Responsible, I am Accountable, I am Profitable!
- I am Happy, I am Healthy, I am Wealthy!
- I am industrious at earning money.
- I am in control of my impulses and I am good at saving money.
- I am proud of my money management abilities.
- I am very good at keeping track of my money.
- I am very good at staying within my budget.
- I invest in appreciating assets not depreciating luxuries.
- Thriftiness is a virtue!
- I am patient as I watch my money grow.
- I am a Giver not a Taker.
- God has blessed me and I am thankful.
- God is blessing me greatly so that I can help others.
- I am quick to give to the less fortunate.
- As I become wealthy I am able to enrich the lives of others.

Read this Carefully:

Once you have cleansed your mind of all negatives...
Once you have adopted a positive philosophy of thinking...
Once you have written out your goals...
Once you have visualized yourself achieving your financial goals...

THEN

You must avoid all influences that go against the positive direction you have set for yourself...
You must avoid all influences that will weaken your resolve for achievement...
Finally, you must let nothing destroy the strength of your convictions.

IMPORTANT!

Surround yourself only with what belongs in your future. Put in front of you only that which belongs in you! What's around you will influence you. What's around you will determine your destiny. Believe this—it's a fact!

Repeat this affirmation over and over again to yourself...

I am destined for great financial success!

**Don't judge each day by the harvest you reap,
But by the seeds you plant.**
— Robert Louis Stevenson

THE REAL VALUE OF MONEY

Money gives you:

- Access to education and the ability to gain knowledge
- Access to resources and the ability to network with other resourceful people
- The ability to pay bills without stress
- The ability to travel and experience the great wonders of the world
- The opportunity to attend significant events
- The opportunity to help the less fortunate
- The ability to contribute to your community
- Access to great people of influence
- The capacity to follow your passion
- The ability to take care of your health
- The ability to provide for your family
- The ability to do great things with your family
- The ability to generously support your faith

A wise man once said...

Measure your wealth not by the things you have
but by the things for which you would not take money.

Success and wealth require teamwork on the part of many people. There is no such thing as a "self-made millionaire." People who have achieved great financial success and independence are quick to point out that they couldn't have achieved their wealth without the hard work, dedication, and loyalty of many other people.

Self-righteous pride will keep you from achieving true long-lasting wealth. Ego, arrogance and conceit will sour your financial relationships. Success is not one-sided—it has to be a win/win situation for everyone involved. Those who have succeeded in life understand that God has blessed them and they are no better than anyone else.

Becoming wealthy is a good thing! Millionaires are confident, friendly, trustworthy, respectful and open to helping others. Having money requires discipline and responsibility and elevates you to being a role model for others. Wealth allows you to give back to the community. How can you be generous if you have nothing to give? The best way to help the poor is to not be poor yourself! Remember...poor people cannot help poor people.

THE POOR DO NOT NEED CHARITY. THEY NEED INSPIRATION AND EXPOSURE TO A NEW WAY OF THINKING. LONG-TERM HANDOUTS ONLY PROMOTE LONG-TERM POVERTY.

Challenge yourself to become a millionaire, not so much for the money, but for what you become in the process. In the end, it's the process of becoming a millionaire that is so much more valuable than the money. It's what you learn and accomplish that makes you valuable.

GET YOUR MBA!

Everyone should strive to get their MBA and I'm not just not talking about a Masters in Business Administration. The MBA I'm talking about is a MASSIVE BANK ACCOUNT! It's unfortunate that we spend our formative years in school learning how to "earn a living" when we should have been learning how to "create our financial empire!"

THE PHILOSOPHY OF WEALTH

Along with having a great attitude, it's also important to have the right philosophies about having money and achieving wealth.

Achieving wealth builds character. Money is attracted to positive, energetic people with great ideas and unstoppable persistence. Your development as a total person will affect your ability to have more. As you become more, you will earn more. The quality of person you become will directly influence the quality of life you will live. Achieving great success in life helps build great character.

Unquestionable character, not money, is the ultimate treasure that unlocks all other wealth.

BEING RICH HAS NOTHING TO DO WITH BEING LUCKY, BEING BORN ON THE RIGHT SIDE OF THE TRACKS, EDUCATION, OR HAVING THE RIGHT PARENTS. THE SAME WAY BEING POOR HAS NOTHING TO DO WITH HAVING BAD LUCK, LACK OF OPPORTUNITY, WRONG SKIN COLOR, POOR EDUCATION, OR BEING UGLY. WEALTH IS THE RESULT OF FAITH, DREAMS, GOALS, PASSION, HARD WORK, A WILLINGNESS TO LEARN, DISCIPLINE, AND COMMITMENT TO ACTION. WEALTH COMES FROM NEVER GIVING UP WHEN OTHERS HAVE QUIT. BEING WEALTHY IS STRICTLY A CHOICE.

WISDOM KEY

The most important aspect of wealth is not the ability to accumulate money, gain status, or wield power. Wealth gives us the ability to become greater than we are for the purposes of making a positive difference in our community and the world that we live in. This is our higher purpose in life.

The greatest good you can do for another is not just to share your riches but to reveal to him his own.
— Benjamin Disraeli

Becoming Rich Requires a Better Understanding of Wealth.

Wealth is not measured by:

- How fancy your car is
- How big your house is
- Where your house is
- If you are a member of a country club
- Wearing only the latest fashions
- Eating in expensive restaurants
- Eating out all the time
- Going on expensive vacations
- Wearing expensive jewelry

Real wealth is measured by what you can give away!

The Best Things In Life Are Free!

Money can buy:
things, services, experiences, education, and independence.

Money cannot buy:
happiness, love, wisdom, values, reputation, and spirituality.

The man is richest whose pleasures are the cheapest!
— Henry David Thoreau

Money will buy–
A bed, but not rest.
A book, but not wisdom.
Food, but not good taste.
Medicine, but not health.
Luxuries, but not well-being.
Amusement, but not happiness.
— Adapted, Author Unknown

You will never achieve great wealth if you manage your financial affairs like a poor person!

A wealthy person respects money. Start seeing your money—however much or little you have right now—as "the seeds" to your fortune. Wealthy people do not play fast and loose with the seeds to their financial future. Start managing your financial affairs like a person of great wealth.

WISDOM KEY

> **The most important lesson you can learn is that you don't have to be rich to become wealthy.** All you need to do is learn the habits of wealthy people. Learn the difference between how the poor and the wealthy think and behave, and then do what wealthy people do. Becoming wealthy is only a matter of changing your attitude, learning new habits, and acquiring industrious behaviors.

Most wealthy people have been broke at some point in their lives. Almost all of them started out where you are right now or worse. The difference is they changed how they were thinking and how they behaved and disciplined themselves into a completely different way of living. At no time did they ever believe that they were poor or behave the way that poor people behave! Wealthy people are winners. Winners never quit doing what made them successful in the first place.

Being "poor" is a way of thinking and an unfortunate "mind-set." Being "poor" is a way of living because you don't have any hope of ever getting better. Being "broke" is only the present condition of your bank account. Being broke just means that you have a whole lot of stuff that you can't afford. If you are broke but have a winning attitude and a wealthy philosophy—you won't be broke for long. If you have an "I'm poor" philosophy—you will always be poor.

Being poor is just a negative attitude combined with bad habits! If individuals with a "poor attitude" win the lottery, they will eventually become poor again. Their lifestyle will cause them to get into trouble. They won't know how to invest their money. They will go on a spending spree, buying luxuries that soon depreciate or go out of style. They gamble their money away playing the role of the "big spender." People with poor attitudes do what poor people do...they squander away their time and their money.

Wealth is Strictly a Choice!

The choice between being rich or poor—is only attitude.

Being rich is an attitude! If rich people have strokes of bad luck and go broke—they will eventually become rich again because they have a positive attitude with a "wealth" mentality and they still have the good habits that got them wealthy in the first place. They have an industrious work ethic and are easily employable. Their lifestyles are filled with good habits, and because of their prior successes, they have cultivated many contacts and relationships. They are disciplined and soon their savings and investment habits will be creating new fortunes.

Perhaps you've heard the saying, "The poor get poorer and the rich get richer?" There is a lot of truth to this statement but not in the reason you may think! Often when we hear this statement, the first thing that comes to mind is that somehow the rich are taking advantage of the poor. Or, that only the rich have all the good luck.

The real meaning behind this statement is that…
Poor people will always do what poor people do. And the rich will always do what rich people do. It's all about the choices people make when it comes to habits and attitude.

IN OTHER WORDS... HAVE YOU EVER HEARD MILLIONAIRES EXCLAIM THAT IF THEY LOST EVERYTHING TODAY — IN A SHORT TIME, THEY WOULD BECOME MILLIONAIRES AGAIN?
…It's because of their attitude!

WISDOM KEY

Here's the secret: The millionaires' confidence doesn't come from what they accumulate—it comes from the experience, knowledge, and wisdom that they gained in the process of becoming wealthy. This experience and knowledge is their "true wealth" and gives them the confidence to do it all over again. Experience along with massive ACTION is powerful!

All Wealth Starts From Within

True wealth does not come from coveting or trying to acquire other people's wealth. True wealth comes from learning how to use your own creative powers to create your own wealth. If you covet someone else's wealth, you will find yourself competing for someone else's creativity. No good ever comes from this type of greed. Accumulating someone else's wealth is short-lived—it is yours today and someone else's tomorrow.

Wealth that is generated through your own creativity is long-lasting. It can never be "competed for" or "transferred" unless you give your permission. True wealth is determined by your ability to acquire anything you want without violating the rights of others or taking away from what should be available to others. True wealth is a win/win situation for everyone.

Great wealth does not come from hard work alone. Great wealth comes from creating new opportunities and the transference of knowledge to support or enhance the lifestyles of the greatest number of people. Become a slave to the masses, and the masses will make you wealthy!

Wealth needs to be appreciated. The more grateful you are, the greater your access to wealth. So adopt an "attitude of gratitude!" If you have an attitude that the world owes you, then wealth will flee from you. If you freely want to give back to the world, then unlimited wealth will be made available to you.

**The bird of paradise alights only
upon the hand that does not grasp!**
— John Berry

We are limited only by our own ignorance and laziness.

If you spend all your time thinking about how poor you are, you are actually attracting poverty. If you have ever thought, "What's the use—opportunity has already passed me by," just remember this...

No one has ever been kept in poverty because of a short supply of opportunity or wealth.
No person is poor because there is not enough to go around.
No person is poor because of the economy.

WISDOM KEY

There is no end to the wealth created from your own originality and hard work! If you spend your time being thankful for how richly blessed you are, eventually you will attract great wealth even if you don't have much money right now.

Understanding the Differences Between How Poor People Think and How the Wealthy Think

If you fail to plan your life...
You will fall prey to the plans of the people around you!

Who do you spend your time with? What kind of plans do they have for their lives? The answers could be very telling as to what is happening in your own life! That is why it is critical to understand the following thought processes which show the differences between how people with poor attitudes think and how people with wealthy attitudes think.

The following statements are not meant to bash the average American who is currently experiencing financial difficulties. I will warn you, however, that the following comparisons were not meant to inspire you but to jar you out of your comfort zone so you don't end up poor. If you feel in any way uncomfortable, then perhaps you need to rethink your philosophies on wealth. This in no way should be interpreted as implying that the average American with debt is a poor person. But it does point out very vividly that poor people are most often the victims of their own negative thinking and if you don't want to end up being permanently poor then you better learn quickly how to improve your attitude about wealth. Being wealthy is strictly a choice, the same way being poor is a choice. Being broke is a temporary predicament, while being poor is the long-term result of a stubborn mind-set or an unwillingness to discipline one's self to get more knowledge to become wealthy. With 97% of the people in America experiencing financial difficulties, the following comparisons are important for you to understand if you don't want to wake up one day and wonder why the world has passed you by!

Poor people <u>owe</u> money.
Wealthy people <u>own</u> money.

Poor people <u>try</u> to save money.
Wealthy people <u>invest</u> money without fail.

Poor people have "good" excuses about why they can't save.
Wealthy people put money away to invest religiously without excuses.

Poor people do not budget or have a financial plan for their lives.
Wealthy people have carefully thought out financial plans and they follow their budgets.
They do not cheat on their plans.

Poor people work for their money.
Wealthy people have their money work for them.

Poor people believe that money is for spending.
Wealthy people believe that money is for saving, so that they will be able to invest when
the opportunity arises.

Poor people impulsively spend their money.
Wealthy people spend only what they have budgeted for.

Poor people spend their money and invest what is left.
Wealthy people invest their money and spend what is left.

Poor people spend money they don't have.
Wealthy people sacrifice and save up to buy what they need. They never spend the
"seeds" of their investments.

Poor people keep spending more as their incomes increase.
Wealthy people keep a lid on spending even though their incomes may rise.

Poor people impulsively spend their money, swayed by advertisers and peer pressure.
Wealthy people spend only according to their values and goals in life.

Poor people spend their "bill paying money" on their pleasures, they consider their
pleasures more important than their creditors.
Wealthy people protect their reputations and integrity by always paying their bills on time.

Poor people entertain themselves on their credit cards.
Wealthy people never entertain themselves on credit—they pay cash for all entertainment,
pleasure, toys, and vacations.

Poor people work to fulfill only their desires.
Wealthy people understand their first goal is to fulfill the desires of other people first.

Poor people think that getting wealthy is somehow wrong.
Wealthy people understand that creating happy customers and giving great service
creates great wealth, which is commendable.

Poor people seek to "get rich quick."
Wealthy people understand the value of compound interest and saving small amounts of money, without fail, over long periods of time.

Poor people have an "I want it now" attitude.
Wealthy people understand that delayed gratification yields greater long-term rewards.

Poor people are only interested in "what's in it for me?"
Wealthy people are giving and interested in making a difference in their communities.

Poor people think the government owes them and they have an "entitlement mentality."
Wealthy people understand that nothing is going to be handed to them and they alone are responsible for earning a living.

Poor people are depressed because they want things that they have not earned.
The wealthy enjoy the fruits of what they have worked for.

Poor people want to make up their own rules.
Wealthy people understand that rules are good and keep the world from operating in chaos.

Poor people are blameful and do not accept responsibility for their actions.
Wealthy people accept full responsibility for their actions.

Poor people are problem conscious.
Wealthy people are solution conscious.

Poor people watch TV.
The wealthy do not watch TV.

Poor people resist learning and reading.
Wealthy people are engaged in lifelong learning and are voracious readers.

Poor people resist change like it was "The Plague."
Wealthy people seek change constantly to continually better themselves.

Poor people listen to their "poor" friends for advice and resent advice from the successful.
Wealthy people seek professional advice only from winners—and they listen.

Poor people hang around losers who whine and complain.
Wealthy people hang with winners who have big dreams, big ideas, and big ambitions.

Poor people think money will buy them happiness.
Wealthy people understand that money only creates freedom and that true happiness has nothing to do with money.

THIS WAS NOT MEANT TO BE AN INDICTMENT THAT ALL POOR PEOPLE ARE BAD PEOPLE. IT IS A DECLARATION TO SAY, "IT IS A SIN TO THINK LIKE A POOR PERSON AND BELIEVE THAT YOU WERE MEANT TO BE POOR." JESUS SAID, "I HAVE COME THAT THEY MIGHT HAVE LIFE AND THAT THEY MIGHT HAVE IT MORE ABUNDANTLY." JESUS <u>DID NOT</u> SAY, "I HAVE COME THAT YOU MIGHT LIVE YOUR LIFE IN POVERTY!" POOR PEOPLE MUST CHANGE HOW THEY ARE THINKING IF THEY ARE EVER GOING TO EXPERIENCE THE REWARDS OF THE LIFE THEY DESERVE, LIKE ANYONE ELSE.

Only you can quit polluting your mind with all the "negative thinking" of a poor person.

Start thinking like the wealthy and eventually–

All the rewards of God's great universe will be yours forever!

You Deserve it!

The LifeSkills Financial Declaration
24 Golden Rules for Personal Financial Empowerment

From this day forward, I have made my choice. I declare my vigilant and lifelong commitment to financial empowerment. I pledge the following:

1. I will conduct all my financial affairs with complete honesty and integrity.

2. I will faithfully put money aside every paycheck for investing in my future.
   - I will tithe my first 10% to support my faith.
   - I will save 10% for the long-term and under no circumstances will I touch this savings account unless it is for a life-or-death situation.
   - I will save 10% for short-term needs.
   - I will live on the remaining 70%.

3. I will create a budget and live within my means.

4. I will measure my personal wealth by net worth, not income.

5. I will be a disciplined and knowledgeable consumer. I will plan my spending to take advantage of all sales and discounts.

6. I will do without until I can save up and pay cash for all my everyday needs—borrowing only for education, home mortgage, or emergency medical needs. This means I will buy only used cars until I can buy a new one with cash!

7. I will pay all my bills on time without fail! No monthly carry-over credit card debt.

8. I will study to become a proactive and informed investor.

9. My first priority will be to buy my first house.

10. I will seek, find, and build a relationship with a successful investment advisor with a proven track record.

11. I will start building a balanced investment portfolio.

12. I will learn how to properly write checks and regularly, without fail, keep my checkbook balanced!

13. I will organize my important paperwork and I will learn how to use file folders and a personalized computer accounting system.

14. I will learn how to periodically check my credit report.

15. **I will develop a relationship with a local bank and a personal banker.**

16. **I will start building a "Line of Credit" for borrowing purposes.**

17. **I will learn how to buy the right insurances.**

18. **I will seek, find, and build a relationship with a successful certified public accountant, who will help guide me to properly pay only the appropriate taxes!**

19. **I will keep a well-documented paper trail for income tax planning.**

20. **I will give generously to those in need and I will use a portion of my personal wealth to strengthen my community.**

21. **I will maximize my earning power through a commitment to lifelong learning career development, technological literacy and professional excellence.**

22. **I will teach tithing, business and financial principles to my children.**

23. **I will ensure that my wealth is protected, invested, and passed on to future generations.**

24. **I will always be grateful, no matter what I may or may not possess, giving thanks for all that God has so richly blessed me with.**

This financial declaration was inspired by the 10 Declarations of Financial Empowerment developed by Black Enterprise Magazine. They were further expanded and developed into the 24 Golden Rules for Personal Financial Empowerment by Famous Dave Anderson. (I highly recommend reading Black Enterprise Magazine for people of all colors!)

How To Become Financially Successful

Becoming wealthy is like anything else in life— it requires you to become better than you are.

Healthy people do what healthy people do. If you want to become healthy you have to eat fruits and vegetables, not cheeseburgers and french fries. And you have to force yourself to exercise. You have to do the same thing over and over again every day until you become healthy. You have to stay the course even when it seems boring. After a while you will enjoy the benefits of sacrificing the apple pie à la-mode. You'll be healthy and feeling the best you've ever felt!

Educated people do what educated people do. If you want to be a smarter person, educated and knowledgeable, you have to force yourself to read, go to school, attend seminars and lectures—even though it would be easier to watch TV. Buying a TV costs little, but watching it can be expensive. It can rob you of opportunities and steal valuable, productive time that could be spent pursuing your dreams.

It takes discipline to pick up a book and read when it would be easier to go to the movies. Once you have committed yourself to lifelong learning, do the same thing over and over again every day until learning becomes easy for you. The rewards of having wisdom and knowledge are priceless, and you will be glad you sacrificed watching TV to pick up a book and read.

The same holds true for becoming wealthy. *Here's the lesson...*

Wealthy people do what wealthy people do. You have to change how you have been conducting your financial affairs. If you expect to be wealthy, you must think and live like the wealthy—now! You have to force yourself to stick to following your budget like a wealthy person. You can't have everything you want—you will have to spend less than you earn. You have to sacrifice, save and invest your money. Your goal is to start thinking and behaving like the wealthy.

A poor man refuses to take the time to sit down and plan for his future. A foolish poor man stubbornly resists setting spending limits for himself. The wealthy man plans his financial future. He religiously commits himself to the fundamentals and doesn't get bored with the details of repeating the same wealthy habits over and over again—every day without fail.

If there were only four laws of gaining great wealth they would simply be: **1. Spend less than you earn.** **2. Be happy with what you've got.** **3. You must do more than just save—you must invest.** **4. Learn the value of Time and Compound Interest.**

WISDOM KEY

KEY LESSON: WEALTH IS NOT INCOME!

Wealth does not come from your paycheck. Wealth is created from the money you save and invest. The key word is INVEST. Working harder and longer hours only creates a bigger paycheck but still does not create wealth. *You cannot work yourself "rich!"* However, a bigger paycheck will give you more "seeds" for investing.

GREAT WEALTH IS CREATED <u>ONLY</u> FROM THE SEEDS OF YOUR INVESTMENTS. SO IF YOU ARE GOING TO BECOME WEALTHY—YOU BETTER LEARN HOW TO INVEST, AND QUIT SPENDING THE SEEDS OF YOUR FUTURE WEALTH!

Understanding the Formula for Wealth

Saving money is a discipline. But it has a simple formula. Saved money comes from spending less than you earn. So the simplest formula would be:

$$\textbf{Earnings} - \textbf{Expenses} = \textbf{Savings}$$

Wealth is created when savings are turned into investments. So the prior formula progresses to:

$$\textbf{Earnings} - \textbf{Expenses} = \textbf{Savings} \times \textbf{Investing} = \textbf{Wealth}$$

Time can grow even the smallest amount of money into a huge fortune. Long lasting wealth is created when your investments are allowed to grow over time. Money can always be replaced but time, once gone, is lost forever.

Great wealth is created when earnings are multiplied by the intensity and depth of your passion. <u>So the best money formula would be:</u>

$$\textbf{(Great Passion creates Great Earnings)} - \textbf{Expenses}$$
$$= \textbf{Savings} \times \textbf{(Investing} \times \textbf{Time)} = \textbf{Great Wealth}$$

**If Savings is the mother of wealth,
then Time is the father,
and Great Fortune is the child.**
— Famous Dave Anderson

Time and Compound Interest are magical ingredients. When added to money—they create wealth that grows exponentially.

LEARNING ABOUT WEALTH

Here are two interesting questions:

How come they never teach "Investing 101" in Business School?

If you haven't studied wealth, how do you expect to be wealthy?

   All financial success begins at home. Financial success starts with being completely honest in all your financial affairs. Most people spend considerable effort wanting everyone to think they are rolling in money or financially well-off. Just remember, things aren't always as they appear! Most people would be horrified if their personal financial statements were made public! Be honest in paying your taxes and start paying all debts that you owe on time. Never cheat anyone out of something that is rightfully his or hers.

   Financial success requires complete accountability. You must start keeping track of your money. To become wealthy requires accountability. There is great responsibility to having money. You will never be successful in your professional life if you are not serious about something as simple as keeping a balance in your checkbook.

   Staying out of debt is really simple. You must constantly be improving yourself and your job skills so you can earn more money and <u>you must always spend less than you earn.</u>

How to find better money-making opportunities.

FIRST, START WHERE YOU ARE AND DO IT RIGHT NOW. QUIT THINKING THAT THE GRASS IS GREENER SOMEPLACE ELSE. YOU CAN FIND GREENER GRASS RIGHT WHERE YOU ARE. JUST MAKE UP YOUR MIND THAT YOU ARE THE "FERTILIZER!"

The following paraphrased story is a powerful illustration of being able to find opportunity right in your own backyard. *"Acres Of Diamonds"* is a true story written in the late 1800s by the founder of Temple University—Russell H. Conwell.

This story takes place many years ago deep in the heart of Africa. There was this hard working African farmer who day after day kept hearing some pretty amazing stories of other farmers giving up the hard life of farming after making huge fortunes discovering diamond mines in the rich African soil. These incredible stories of overnight wealth were too much for this simple farmer. Millions of dollars and great wealth were being made every day and he was being left out. He could hardly stand himself—he was so envious, he couldn't wait to sell his farm and go prospecting for the precious diamonds. His greed was so strong it made him act impulsively and without thinking. After selling his farm, he spent the rest of his life searching the vast African continent. But luck wasn't on his side. Unsuccessfully, day after day, he searched for the precious African diamonds that were so highly sought after by the world's gem merchants. Finally—mentally, physically and financially broken—he threw himself into a raging African river and drowned.

As the legend goes, the man who had bought the farm crossed a small river on the property one day and saw a brilliant sparkle flashing from the river's bottom. He reached down and picked up this gleaming rock. He brought the pretty rock home and placed it on his fireplace mantel. Sometime later, a visitor noticed the glistening rock and picked it up. It sparkled and glistened as he turned it over in his hands, and then he nearly fainted. He asked the farmer if he knew what he had found? The farmer said he thought the rock was interesting and might be quartz crystal. Then the visitor, still shaking and trembling, informed the farmer that this gleaming rock could be one of the largest diamonds ever discovered!

This simple farmer couldn't believe it was possible. But if it was, he told the visitor, there was a riverbed full of them in his own backyard! Quickly, they ran out to the little river and sure enough, the old river bottom shimmered with the sparkling rocks. How tragic. This farm—which the first farmer sold so he could search for diamonds—turned out to be the richest and most productive diamond mine ever found on the African continent. The farmer had owned free and clear "Acres of Diamonds." But in his blind ambition to make a fast buck, he sold his farm for practically nothing so he could find his fame and fortune elsewhere. He thought the grass was greener somewhere else.

THE MORAL OF THIS STORY IS SIGNIFICANT...
IF THE FIRST FARMER HAD TAKEN TIME TO STUDY AND
PREPARE HIMSELF FOR DIAMOND PROSPECTING, HE WOULD
HAVE LEARNED WHAT DIAMONDS LOOKED LIKE IN THEIR
NATURAL ROUGH FORM. HE NEEDED TO DISCOVER WHAT
HE ALREADY POSSESSED. WE ALL START OUT IN OUR
OWN NATURAL ROUGH FORM. WE NEED TO DISCOVER THE TREASURES
THAT ARE ALREADY AROUND US AND WITHIN US.

This farmer should have realized that if he had explored his own backyard he would have been rich beyond his wildest dreams. Too often we miss the opportunities God has given us when they are staring us right in the face. We must patiently work on ourselves and we must work with greater enthusiasm in our own jobs to find the wealth that is there. In order to become wealthy, we must take the time to diligently study wealth building. We must become proficient at investing or we will spend a lifetime being envious of someone else's "acres of diamonds."

People who are always envious of the opportunities found elsewhere, spend their entire lives chasing rainbows they can't catch.

ONE OF LIFE'S GREATEST LESSONS IS
THAT WE MAKE OUR OWN OPPORTUNITIES
RIGHT WHERE WE ARE!

TAKE CHARGE OF YOUR FINANCIAL DESTINY

It's entirely up to you to discover your own hidden treasures.

Starting right now, look at your present job differently. Have you sharpened your skills to "mine" the opportunities that are already in front of you? When we see "sparkling" opportunities in someone else's backyard, it's only because the other guy has worked incredibly hard to create his own diamond mine.

Too often we think the grass is greener on the other side of the fence. But have we ever stopped to think that the reason why the grass is greener than ours is because someone has planted good seeds, pulled out weeds, cultivated the soil, and carefully nurtured, over time, their own little piece of God's good earth? You see, we are all given the same piece of land and it's up to us to make something out of it. Start being successful where you are now—it's all up to you!

WISDOM KEY

> **Be happy where you are.** Be grateful you have a job. If you hate your job, it will show and people who can give you better-paying jobs will never consider you, because you look and behave like such a lousy worker. So if you hate your job, change your attitude. If you start liking your job, you will find something interesting starts to happen—opportunities will start coming your way and you will begin earning more money than you ever thought possible. Then the most amazing thing will happen—you will start loving your job!

Work harder than you have ever worked before. That's the secret—acquiring a better attitude and then focusing all your energies toward your present job. Give it your all, like you have never done before.

While you are at work, commit to learning new job skills every day. Don't wait until someone offers to train you—take it upon yourself to ask or be observant in learning new skills.

When you are at home, continue your quest for self-improvement by religiously studying at least one hour every night to become the best you can be. Every day, rededicate yourself to improving your standards of excellence.

If you do this—

You will outwork 80% of your coworkers and outsmart 15% of the rest. Your commitment to self-improvement by studying one hour every night over five years will put you in the top 5% of the wealthiest people in America!

You will become successful wherever you are by creating large profits for whoever pays you. You will be so valuable that your employer will pay you an above-average salary just to keep you. In addition, you will get bonuses, rewards and recognition for your outstanding effort. They will do whatever it takes to keep you happy.

Once you have created a reputation for being an industrious worker who takes great pride in a job well done, your income will rise progressively. And, you will be in demand by only the best employers in the marketplace who can afford to pay you whatever you ask.

Excellence is not an option! Excellence is your ONLY option. From now on, never be satisfied with anything less than the best that you can be. You must be proud of what you do. Pride and Excellence will help you stand out in a crowd of people who are only doing just enough to get by.

Don't make your money your obsession. Instead, make your passion your obsession. When money is your obsession, you will never be satisfied and frustration will rule your life. When you follow your passion, your spirit will be satisfied and the depth of your passion will positively affect those around you. The money will follow.

**Creating a spirit of positive difference will be sweet
to the soul and great financial success will be the end reward.**

Stop wasting your time daydreaming about "getting rich quick." True wealth never happens overnight. Quit chasing "get-rich-quick" schemes, no matter how fantastic they may seem. When something sounds too good to be true, usually it is!

One of the keys to building wealth is "TIME." Longevity is more important to growing money than earning more money. While earning more money is always important, the real key is saving from what you are already earning no matter how little money you may think it is and investing it over long periods of time untouched. In order for time to be effective it has two companions: "sacrifice" and "patience."

Don't increase your spending just because you are earning more! This increased income must not automatically change your spending habits. Increased earning power should not trigger spending sprees. Don't abandon the frugality and thriftiness that was part of your wealth-building discipline. Your responsibility in becoming wealthy is to understand the difference between "luxury indulgences" and buying the "best quality" you can afford.

Quit pretending that you have more money than you are earning. The only way to be happy is to never be concerned about what others think of you and never be envious of what your neighbors have—more than likely they can't afford it either. When you are happy with what you have, you won't be tempted to buy on impulse things you don't need. Never buy something or spend money just to impress someone. All successful people control their impulses. Don't be the big spender by always offering to pick up the entire lunch or dinner check. Don't feel like you have to overspend when buying presents for friends or family.

True wealth is not measured by what you accumulate. There are two kinds of accumulation—"depreciating pleasures" and "appreciating assets." This distinction is important because poor people and middle class people often work hard to accumulate "stuff" in an effort to make their lifestyle better. But their "debt-to-earning ratio" has never changed, even though they are making more money. In other words, their toys not only are depreciating, they are costing money just to maintain.

**You can keep earning more money but if your spending habits
are out of whack, you will never become wealthy.**

The wealthy buy appreciating assets that are not a drain on their liquidity. Their assets MAKE them money, they don't COST them money. Their assets generally return a profit and it is from these profits that the wealthy entertain themselves, unlike the middle class and the poor who borrow for their enjoyment.

One of the rules of the wealthy is to never spend the principal. The principal, or savings, are the seeds for your investing. Budget your spending to only live off the interest.

Start thinking "thriftiness." Start living on less than you earn. Thriftiness doesn't mean that you have to be a "cheapskate"—there's a big difference. We must learn that it's all right to live cheaply. Thriftiness is a virtue and frugality doesn't necessarily mean that you're a "tightwad." Thrifty living means that you are living within your means and that you control your spending. The key to spending less is being happy with what you've got.

Start keeping track of your money. In order to budget your money, you need to first know where it is going. You would be surprised at where all that "pocket change" goes. Start by taking a 3x5 card, and for several months keep a daily record of everything you are spending money on. Carry only the minimum amount of cash that you will need during the day.

Keeping track of how you are spending your money will open your eyes about your personal spending habits— both good and bad!

Get in the habit of always asking for a receipt. Every week, tally up what you spent and categorize it. This will help you define your personal budget and financial planning. Remember, it's not so much the big-ticket items that we buy, but our daily spending habits that keep us from building our fortune. Keeping your receipts will come in handy for determining where your money goes, as well as being documentation for the IRS.

WISDOM KEY

Every penny counts! It's not our major financial decisions that break us and drive us into the poor house, but our everyday impulsive and nonchalant spending habits. It's the wasted nickels, dimes, quarters, and dollars spent carelessly and casually throughout the day that slowly drain us of our "could-have-been" fortunes. The fact is that every penny does count. There's a lot of truth to the old adage...

"A penny saved is a penny earned."

Here's how important your "loose change" could be to your becoming wealthy.

Quick!—Look in your pockets—there's a fortune there! If you were to save all your loose change every day including a few loose one-dollar bills—do you think you could find a lousy two dollars? I bet everyone could with ease. Two dollars is nothing more than a couple cans of pop, newspapers, gossip magazines, gourmet coffee, snacks, or candy bars. All people could find two dollars if they really understood that investing two dollars a day could turn into a real fortune!

Two dollars multiplied by 30 days in a month equals $60 dollars or $720 a year. In 20 years, you will have saved $14,400—doesn't sound like a lot of money but this is where it gets interesting. If you were to keep saving your pocket change and invested it in a stock mutual fund for 20 years that averaged an annual rate of 10%—at the end of 20 years you would end up with **$45,941.81.** On an investment of only $14,400!

➤ How many of your friends have a $45,000 sitting in the bank right now?

➤ The incredible thing to remember is that…it's just "pocket change!"

➤ How much more could you invest if you made up your mind to really save?

WISDOM KEY

The average American could find an extra 10-20% extra cash every year just by getting a handle on their daily spending habits. Getting control of your money is a discipline you must acquire if you are ever going to experience the rewards of wealth. This control lets you master your money rather than becoming a slave to your debts.

Wealth Begins by Learning How to Budget

A wise man once said...

**The difference between a poor person and a wealthy person
is only 2 cents! The poor person earns $1.00 and spends $1.01.
A wealthy person earns a $1.00 and spends 99 cents!**

You must change how you think about money. All Americans call the money in their pockets—"spending money." As a nation we call our income—our "disposable income." We need to get it out of our heads that "money is for spending."

We must adopt a new philosophy that money is for saving and saved money is for investing.

The only way we will have money for saving is to budget.

Having money demands responsibility. Most people never understand this. Carefully budget your money. Determine how much money you are going to spend, how much you are going to save and how you are going to invest what you save. You also have to have a plan for how you are going to respond to friends and family when it comes to lending money and spending money on your daily activities.

Don't take this process lightly. Budgeting requires planning. Have you ever heard the saying, "If you fail to plan, you are planning to fail?" This statement speaks the truth when it comes to your financial condition. Most people find themselves in financial trouble, at some point in their life, because they failed to plan, budget and save.

➢ **The first step in determining how to budget your income...
is creating a financial plan for your life and putting it on paper.**

➢ **Unfortunately for most Americans, managing their financial affairs is nothing more than... "I have it all figured out in my mind."**

➢ **When it's not written down on paper and right in front of your face...
it's really "out of sight and out of mind!"**

Your "plan" is really your philosophy on how you are going to spend your money. The key questions are: What do you want your current lifestyle to be like? How do you want your lifestyle to be when you retire? How thankful are you for what has already been given to you? (This will be expressed in how generous you are to people in need.) This planning process requires your time and careful thought.

Your budget is created by dividing up your income according to your financial plan for your life. This is where most people fail in their budgeting process.

Typically, people pay everyone else first. And then, if there is any money left and if they don't blow it on their impulsive pleasures, they just might have something to save.

YOU NEED TO START PAYING YOURSELF FIRST! "Wow," you're thinking to yourself, "I thought I was already getting paid." When I say you need to start paying yourself first, I am talking about setting aside at least 10% of your money in an investment account for your future before you allocate any money to live on. Otherwise, you are like all the rest of the financially destitute people—they work, spend their money and then whatever is left, they save. Your new goal is to <u>save for your future first</u>, then whatever is left you budget to live on.

Successful budgeting that leads to a rewarding lifestyle starts with being thankful. The Bible says to give of your first fruits. Then you pay yourself next. What's left is what you live on. I call this the **10-10-10-70 Financial Plan for Success.**

The 10-10-10-70 Financial Plan for Success or Asset Allocation

Wealth begins by giving first. In this financial plan, I recommend that the first 10% of your income be given to your faith as an expression of your gratitude for the blessings that you have and the blessings that you will receive.

The next 10% is money you will invest long-term—this is money you absolutely cannot touch under any circumstances except in extreme life or death matters. The next

10% is money you save and invest for the short-term—for emergencies, vacations, new cars, major household expenditures, etc. The remaining 70% is the money you budget to live on. More will be detailed on Asset Allocation in the Investing section of this chapter.

It takes discipline and character to budget, save, and invest money. When it comes to financial matters, don't let your impulses ruin your life. You will have to sacrifice. You will have to learn how to be content and happy with what you have.

Don't let what you think are emergencies make you spend your savings unless it is an extreme life or death matter.

The wise person saves for the future.
But the foolish person spends all that he gets.
— Proverbs 21:20 (paraphrased)

WISDOM KEY

Your ability to allocate your assets is the most important process you will ever undertake in building your wealth. Asset Allocation is nothing more than determining what to do with your money. In the chapter on budgeting we introduced the 10-10-10-70 Plan. The first 10% is always set aside for tithing or giving. The next 10% is set aside for long-term investing. The third 10% is set aside for short-term investing and the final 70% is what you live on.

Imagine your money being divided up into four piggy banks:

Piggy Bank #1 is your "Charity Piggy Bank." The first 10% of your money is for giving and tithing. Tithing is so important that I have devoted a whole section to this topic (see page 439).

Piggy Bank #2 is your "Security Piggy Bank." This 10% of your money is invested for the long-term. This is money that you can never touch under any circumstances except in "life or death" emergencies.

Your "Security Piggy Bank" includes:
- Accessible cash equal to six months of your salary
- 401K or IRA investments
- Insurance
- T-bills or Treasury Bills, Municipal Bonds, Money Market Funds

Piggy Bank #3 is your "Growth Piggy Bank." This 10% of your money is invested for greater growth and involves more risk. Money should never be put into this piggy bank unless you have filled first Piggy Banks #1 and #2. This is also your "profit" piggy bank. When profits are taken from selling your investments, equal amounts of your capital gains should be divided back into your four piggy banks.

Your "Growth Piggy Bank" is divided into two parts:

Buy and Hold Investments
- Long-term mutual funds
- Blue Chip dividend-paying stocks
- Real Estate

Momentum Investments
- IPO investments
- Individual stocks in emerging markets or new technology
- Options
- Business Ownership Investing

Piggy Bank #4 is your "Livin' High on the Hog Piggy Bank." This money is your recreation and dream bank. You use this money for buying cars, entertainment, vacations, and anything else that depreciates or luxury items that are nice to have but not really necessary. "Wait a second," you say, "If the money for the first three piggy banks has already been used, where is the money coming from for this bank?" This money is "creative money"—money that you have creatively squeezed out of the 70% used for daily living expenses. In other words, it's sacrifice money—money you have saved by "doing without." Nothing gets put into this piggy bank until you have made significant advances on filling up piggy banks #1 through #3.

Warning! There is no stopper in this piggy bank. Whatever money you put into this piggy bank disappears. However, you do need to put something into this piggy bank because everyone needs to celebrate life. Unfortunately, most people start filling this piggy bank first before they ever make a contribution to piggy banks #1 through #3. Then they wonder where their money went when they wake up—too late to realize they have nothing left for their future!

Where is your money going?

Do your budgets fail because you have no idea where your money is going? Are you spending money on things that you have not placed in your budget? You need to run your home just like a business. All businesses must keep track of how they spend their money. All businesses have budgets. They know where and when they are going to spend money and they know how much they need to set aside for investing to ensure they are going to have a future. You are no different! Remember, you are a business: YOU, Inc. com—budget your money accordingly!

How To Start The Budget Process

Know where your money is going. Keep track of all your spending on a 3x5 card and categorize according to your budget. Every week, take your 3x5 cards and all receipts and tally them up according to your budget categories.

Prioritize your spending. When keeping track of your money, identify your expenditure by prioritizing it by level of importance. "A" being the highest priority and "D" being the lowest priority.

A — Can't live without it: food, rent, etc.
B — Important to my well-being: books, clothes, haircuts, etc.
C — Makes me feel good but I don't really need it: exotic vacations, beauty spa, snowmobiles, jet skis, motorcycles, etc. (clothes may belong here if they are bought impulsively!)
D — Impulsive Trivial Expenditures: candy bars, gourmet coffee, pop, etc.

IMPORTANT: Don't spend any money on your **B's, C's,** and **D's** before you have your **A's,** all paid for!

Keep your budget up-to-date. At least once a month, or when you pay your bills, balance your checkbook and update your budget according to what you actually spent versus what you originally budgeted for.

KEEPING UP WITH YOUR NEIGHBORS IS ONE OF THE BIGGEST THREATS TO BUDGETING.

Stick to your budget. Once you have set a budget, you need to agree with your partner that you will not spend anything over $50 without advising each other. All changes to the family budget should be discussed. Once you make a change, you must rework your budget.

In developing your budget, be accurate. Don't overestimate to give yourself "wiggle" room. Your budget should be exact numbers. If you've padded your budget, you can't realize the true rewards of beating your budget. If you have a habit of only using "ballpark" figures, you are cultivating bad habits of casualness when it comes to your finances.

DON'T TRY AND <u>MEET</u> YOUR BUDGET — FORCE YOURSELF TO <u>BEAT</u> YOUR BUDGET.

Money has to be counted in EXACT figures!

The following is a list of Household Expenses
for consideration in developing your budget.

INCOME
  Annual Income
  Additional Income
  Total Income
  Minus 30% Taxes
  Income After Taxes (100%)

SAVINGS
  Retirement investments (10%)

CHARITY AND TITHING (10%)

HOUSING
  Mortgage or Rent (25%)
  Repairs or maintenance
  Homeowners or renters insurance
  Real Estate Taxes
  Personal Property Taxes
  Lawn and Garden

UTILITIES
  Gas
  Water
  Electricity
  Sanitation

DAILY LIVING EXPENSES
  Groceries
  Telephone
  Cell Phone
  Internet
  Pager

TRANSPORTATION (10%)
  Car Payments
  Repairs or maintenance
  Gas
  Insurance
  Parking
  License Plates and Fees
  Bus Fare

MEDICAL
  Doctor Bills
  Dental Bills
  Co-Pay Prescriptions

CLOTHING
  Dry-cleaning

EDUCATION
  Tuition
  Continued Education
  Seminars/lectures
  Books

ENTERTAINMENT AND WELL-BEING
  Eating Out
  Entertainment/Movies/Sports/Plays
  Cable TV/Satellite TV
  Movie Rentals
  Vacation
  Health Club/Fitness Center/Spa

INSURANCE
  Life
  Health
  Disability (If you're young, this could be more
  important than life insurance)
  Dental

MISCELLANEOUS LIVING EXPENSES
  Child Care
  Children's Allowances
  Newspaper and Magazine subscriptions
  Personal grooming
  Organization Dues (Rotary, Lions Club, etc.)
  Gifts (birthdays, weddings, holidays)
  Holiday decorations
  Legal Fees
  Accounting Fees
  Child support
  Alimony

ADDITIONAL SAVING REQUIREMENTS (10%)
  Emergency Savings
    (six-month salary minimum)
  Major Household
    (new furniture, new computer, etc.)
  New Car
  Major Projects (remodeling)
  Major Vacation

The Envelope Method of Household Budgeting

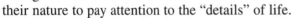

If you can't balance your checkbook—get rid of it! Let's face it, for some people, balancing a checkbook and maintaining a household budget is simply asking too much. It isn't in their nature to pay attention to the "details" of life.

Don't ruin your credit rating because you can't balance your checkbook and run the risk of bouncing checks. It doesn't do you any good to have a checkbook if you're going to continually bounce checks because you can't keep a balance. Or if you are just starting out in life or starting over, you may need a simple method of keeping track of paying your bills on time so you can get in the habit of managing your money.

The simplest and easiest way to stick to a household budget is the tried-and-true old-fashioned "Envelope Method" of household budgeting.

I remember my parents using envelopes and they never were late in paying their bills. Every payday their checks were cashed and the money was divided up into envelopes that were all marked in big black Magic Marker letters: rent, car payment, groceries, electric bill, gas bill, tithing, emergency money, and vacation. On every envelope was written how much was in each envelope and the due date.

When it came time to pay their bills, my parents had their envelope money turned into money orders, which were sent in to pay their bills. The carbon copy of the money order served as their record of payment. They were never late in paying their bills and they had an excellent credit record.

Just being able to budget is not enough. While it is very important to plan how you will spend your money, you must also be able to spend your money wisely. Most people will still have to learn how to spend their money correctly!

Learn How to Spend Money!

Many people may think the last thing you need to learn is how to spend money—after all, aren't you broke because you've been too good at spending money?

THE FACT IS, IF YOU ARE BROKE, YOU ARE NOT GOOD AT SPENDING MONEY, YOU ARE GOOD AT WASTING MONEY!

If you are going to spend money, try to get the most value out of your money by learning how to maximize the value of your dollar.

How to Become a Smart Shopper and Spend Your Hard-Earned Money the Right Way!

- **Do your homework!** It takes work to find the best prices and the best quality for your hard-earned money.
- **Don't shop with the "I deserve it" mentality.**
- **Budget.** All major expenditures should be budgeted for and money set aside. Never buy something on sale if you haven't set aside the money for it.
- **NEVER BUY "RETAIL."** Always try to buy when things are on sale.
- **Shop for the lowest price.** Join a wholesale club and buy in quantity when it makes sense.
- **Shop around.** Check at least three sources for the best price and service. Look for a company that has a track record and has been around for awhile.
- **Try to get quotes by FAX.**
- **Negotiate every purchase.** Paying cash will give you leverage to ask for a lower price. Don't fall in love with your purchase until you own it.
- **Don't get into a buying fever.** You will never be able to negotiate price.
- **After asking for a lower price—SHUT UP!** The first person who speaks loses. You can never talk the price down, but the other person, for fear of losing the sale, will offer to lower the price when he starts getting uncomfortable because you haven't said anything.
- **Never agree to the first price they quote you.** Tell them it's too much…then shut up

again. Be prepared to walk away and mean it. If the price is not in your budget, don't get pressured into spending more than you can afford.

- **Everyone wins.** Finally, successful negotiation must be a win/win situation for both parties. If the seller thinks what you are offering is too low then you must be prepared to give and take. For example, you may counter…"OK, I'll agree to the $2,000 price but you have to throw in the tax and free delivery."

- **Shop the last Sunday of the month.** Store owners are always trying to meet sales figures for the month. You can negotiate lower prices with sales-starved store owners or managers. Make sure you talk to the owner or manager because the "sales help" doesn't care or is not authorized to give discounts.

- **Shop holidays.** I am not just referring to Christmas. I am talking about holidays like Memorial Day weekend and Labor Day. Typically people travel out of town on these weekends and retailers hold big sales (as much as 50% off) to stimulate in-store traffic.

- **Always get help.** If you don't know enough about what you are buying, find a friend who is more knowledgeable than you and get his or her advice.

- **Don't rush into a decision because the salesperson says you have to!** Any major financial decision should be thought out carefully. Never rush. Take your time and get more advice or more information. Never be pressured into making a decision or signing any contracts until you are completely satisfied that you know exactly what you are committing yourself to.

- **If you have any concerns, the best advice is to sleep on it.** Wait several days. If the other party has problems with this, you should be suspicious. Above all, you—not the other person trying to sell you something—need to be in control of your money and your decisions.

- **Never buy under pressure.** If you are uncomfortable about the circumstances, don't buy. Never buy something because you're afraid you'll "miss out" on a good deal. You will find that there are never any real lost opportunities because other "good deals" will always come around if they were "meant to be."

- **Postpone all major purchases for 30 days.** You will make a better buying decision after the "heat of the moment" has passed. Waiting will also help you determine whether you really need it.

- **Plan to buy the best quality you can afford.** Always buy quality; never buy things that are cheaply made. There's much truth to the saying: "The bitterness of poor quality lingers on long after the sweetness of price." Invest in things that will last and serve you well.

WISDOM KEY

> When it comes to your profession or your education—always buy the best quality tools or knowledge you can afford. Excellence can only come from a quality beginning.

- **Buy only what you need.** Buying the best quality doesn't mean spending more money to buy the deluxe model or the latest model with all the newest and trendiest gadgets.

- **Make everything you own last a little bit longer.** Wear everything out. Use everything up. The amount of money that you will save over time will be incredible just by making things last 25% longer. Keep your car one year longer.
- **Buy used whenever it is appropriate and possible.** Buy items that are display models, slightly used or cosmetically damaged.
- **Check return policies.** On major purchases, find out state laws on return policies. Always keep your receipts.
- **Go to garage sales, flea markets and factory outlet stores.** Check out values found at thrift stores and consignment shops. Buy last year's models on running shoes.
- **Shop "off-season sales."** For example, Christmas wrapping paper and ornaments are often as much as 50% off right after Christmas.
- **Something old, something borrowed.** If you are buying furnishings for your first home or your first apartment, shop yard sales and garage sales. Do not be above asking relatives for things they may not need anymore. Do not try and outfit your home all at once. Take your time and buy everything on sale.
- **Eat at home more often and take your lunch to work.** Make eating out a special occasion. Planning your lunches and family meals at home will help you with your weekly budgeting.
- **Save on your food bills.** Clip grocery coupons for <u>items you regularly buy</u>. Visit the bakery outlet store for day-old items and other bargains. Never shop without a list and follow the set amount that you have budgeted and get your children involved, so they learn about "value shopping."
- **Buy in bulk.** Try to buy things you frequently need in bulk—it's cheaper.
- **Do not borrow for everyday living expenses.** Do not charge groceries or clothing. You should never use your credit card to buy or rent anything you can't pay back at the end of the month. Never keep a balance on your credit cards. Credit cards should only be used for renting cars and hotel rooms.
- **Pleasures should not be bought on credit. Do not buy entertainment, vacations, dining out, or any other pleasures on credit. All entertainment and pleasure toys should be planned for, saved for, and paid for with cash.**
- **Practice "NO MONEY FUN!" Make finding cheap entertainment an adventure. If you don't have the money for entertainment, do something free—like going to the zoo, having a backyard picnic, going for a bike ride, walking, or playing board games with your family. Whatever you do—don't watch TV!**
- **Rent home movies.** Don't spend big money on all the latest movies at the theater and especially don't get gouged by huge prices they charge for popcorn and pop. Rent the latest releases and pop your own popcorn (not the microwave kind—it's expensive and unhealthy—use an air popper and buy the popcorn in bulk.)

Fundamental to learning how to spend your money wisely is knowing the difference between a "luxury indulgence" and a "quality investment" you can afford. Buying something trendy is not always a wise decision. Often, you are buying "name" products at inflated prices because it's fashionable and trendy at the moment. The best advice is to buy the best quality you can afford and plan to keep that item for as long as possible.

FOR PARTNERS: Spend time with your spouse or partner on a weekly basis talking about your finances. Together, keep track of your spending.

WISDOM KEY

PARTNERS WHO HAVE A HARD TIME TALKING ABOUT THEIR FINANCES WILL HAVE A HARD TIME WITH THEIR FINANCES!

Some families <u>carefully go over</u> their budgets each month.

Some families <u>just go over</u> their budgets each month!

You should never enter into any relationship until you can first manage your money.

WISDOM KEY

CASH *is* King!

There is truth in calling it the "Almighty Dollar!"

Start paying cash for all your purchases. Do not get into the habit of buying things on credit. Paying cash for all your purchases will go a long way in keeping you out of debt. Paying cash will force you to save in order to buy something and will cause you to think about whether you really need it. You will spend less when you buy with cash. Remember to keep track of all cash that is spent.

Unplanned purchases have the same effect as an unexpected emergency! It's too easy to lose track of your spending when you are ringing up unplanned purchases on a credit card. Never make an unplanned purchase because something is on sale and you think you are saving money. If you bought an unplanned set of furniture that was listed for $5,000 and it was on sale for $2,500 but you had to drain your savings account to buy it…did you save money? The answer is NO!

This is where people get caught up in the "buy now and save later" syndrome. If this purchase was unplanned, you just threw your budget out of whack forever. You will be forced to make adjustments to your budget and you will be forced to spend money that you really don't have. All major purchases should be planned for and saved for.

Never buy something until you have the money saved up to buy what you need and pay for it in cash—especially when it's on sale!

I OWE, I OWE, I OWE...SO IT'S OFF TO WORK I GO!
MOST PEOPLE WORK FOR MONEY THAT IS ALREADY SPENT.

**That means they are living beyond their means. This has to change.
Start living on less than you earn.**

Saving for emergencies and surprises. Before you invest any money, you need to save at least six months' worth of your salary to be reserved for emergencies and life's little surprises. Typical emergencies include: being laid off, car repairs, car accidents, deaths in the family, sickness, unplanned pregnancies, larger-than-expected tax bills, and unplanned home repairs. Don't just have this money sitting around—invest it. But make sure you can get to it in case of emergencies.

> **Your emergency money should be used only for minor emergencies. All major emergencies should be covered by insurance.**

**WISDOM
KEY**

GET ADVICE!

If you are not wealthy now, it's obvious that you don't know how it's done! Or, you have been listening to the wrong people. Whatever you do, don't get advice from well-meaning friends or relatives who don't have a clue themselves. Without being too rude…

IF YOUR PARENTS HAVE NEVER BEEN FINANCIALLY SUCCESSFUL THEMSELVES...BE CAREFUL ABOUT TAKING FINANCIAL ADVICE FROM THEM!

The best idea is to get advice from competent professionals who have successful track records. There are many financial professionals you will need in your life. These professionals will become your mastermind group that will help guide you in your quest for wealth. You will need:

1. A **Banker** who believes in you.
2. A **Certified Public Accountant** to help you in financial decisions and in filing your state and federal taxes.
3. An **Insurance Professional** to help protect your family, your assets, and your future.
4. A **Stock Broker,** since most of your savings will be invested in stocks or stock mutual funds.
5. A **Financial Planner** who will assist you in developing a financial plan for your life as well as working with your accountant to plan for your taxes. Always retain your financial advisor on a fee-for-service basis only.
6. An **Estate Planning Lawyer** who will help you obtain the right legal documents to protect your family. It's important that you have a will, in case of your untimely death.

Make your mastermind group your "Dream Team!"

How to Pick Your Financial Advisors

The easiest way to start is to ask someone wealthy for a referral. If you are just starting out in life and have no wealthy friends, then you will have to do your homework. The best advice is to be active in your community. Join the local chamber of commerce, church, Rotary or Lions Club. Generally, involvement in these groups will give you exposure to the "movers and shakers" in any community.

- **Find someone you can talk to in confidence.**
- **Be prepared to ask questions both personally and about the company.**
- **Find out how long they have been in business.**
- **Ask for a list of references.**
- **Find out the person's credentials.**
- **Find out their track record.**
- **Find out what kind of investments they recommend.**

Find out how they usually work with clients. How often do they like to meet with their clients—monthly, quarterly, yearly? Whatever their answer is—make sure that you meet with them to discuss your financial condition no less than once every six months.

**WISDOM
KEY**

The best professional advice is going to cost you more than you think you can afford, but look at it as an investment in your financial future. Cheap advice is really expensive and could ruin you. You really do get what you pay for!

Besides helping you plan your future...

One of the most compelling reasons to have a good financial planner and a good accountant is to plan how you are going to handle your taxes. This is discussed next!

TAXES, TAXES, TAXES AND MORE TAXES!

According to the Tax Reduction Institute...

- *The average American family must now work two or more jobs just to keep their heads above water.*
- *Taxes are the largest expense for most people. Taxes exceed what people pay for food, housing, and transportation combined!*
- *According to the American Taxpayer Union, in 1958 the average American paid 18% of gross income in Federal, State, and Social Security taxes. In 2000, the average American spent over 41% of gross income on taxes!*

Learn how to properly pay taxes. Learn the difference between "Tax Evasion" and "Tax Avoidance."

Tax <u>Evasion</u> is illegal but Tax <u>Avoidance</u> is legally encouraged.

There should be no April 15th surprises! Practice tax saving techniques throughout the year. Preparing for April 15th begins in May of the preceding year. Don't complain on April 15th if you haven't done any tax planning all year.

Your goal, when it comes to paying taxes, is to never owe taxes at the end of the year. Nor should you expect a refund. Many Americans look forward to getting a huge tax refund at the end of the year. This is bad financial planning because if you get a refund, then you gave the government free use of your money when you could have been investing it!

We overpay because we don't have a clue! According to *USA Today*, "Managing Your Money," almost 90 million Americans make interest-free loans to the federal government by overpaying on their income taxes! The problem is not really about taxation. We have a responsibility to pay taxes. It's important for us to be good taxpaying citizens, especially if we want to enjoy the American lifestyle as we know it. The problem comes when we are negligent in our responsibility to understand exactly what we legally owe and what we legally don't have to pay. And, unfortunately tax books do not make the *New York Times* "Best Sellers List," so we kind of bumble our way through life, grumbling about paying taxes, without taking the time to completely understand what is actually required of us.

If the government is going to take one-third or more of your income every year—don't you think you should find out more about your tax responsibility?

You are guilty until proven innocent!

Take control of your taxes. The IRS assumes you are guilty until proven innocent. It is your responsibility to keep good records. It is your responsibility to understand your tax liabilities. One of the greatest myths that people blindly tell themselves is, "My accountant handles all my taxes." That's about as silly as saying "My doctor is responsible for my health," or "My banker is responsible for my wealth."

From now on:

- **You must be able to document:** your income, your spending, allowable deductions, and your charitable contributions.
- **You need a good paper trail.** You need a good filing system and you must be able to record good details daily, in a permanent journal.
- **You must save all your receipts.** <u>You must get into the habit of asking for receipts for everything you buy.</u>

You get in control of your taxes by becoming good at managing the records created by your income and your spending. <u>The better your records, the more aggressive your accountant can be in your tax deductions.</u>

For more information contact:

The Tax Reduction Institute, Inc.
13200 Executive Park Terrace   Germantown, Maryland 20874
(301) 972-3600   trisem@aol.com   www.taxreductioninstitute.com

**WISDOM
KEY**

Don't pay taxes until you get the full value of your money.
Maximize your money by stashing all you can in your IRA, a 401(k) plan or other tax-deductible individual retirement plan. You will postpone your income tax bill and you will be investing 100% of your money tax free! Sure you will have to pay taxes when you take your money out but you will be getting the benefits of investing it at 100% of its full value up front.

For example, if you earned $1,000, you would pay approximately $333 in state and federal taxes leaving you only $777 to use and you would probably pay another 5% to 8% on sales taxes. You keep losing the value of your money! Wouldn't you rather invest $1,000 rather than $777?

J. Paul Getty had very good advice when he said...

"One of the keys to building wealth is not to pay taxes on money until you use it."

By investing your $1,000 in a tax-deferred retirement account, you get the full power of your money to invest and multiply. When the day comes for you to withdraw your money, your tax deferred growth will more than make up for the eventual taxes that you will have to pay.

When it comes to taxes and the IRS, my recommendations should only be taken as ideas that should be further discussed with your tax advisor or accountant. Make sure you get good advice from a seasoned professional.

Summary

- Get good tax advice from a seasoned professional.
- You have a responsibility to learn how to manage your financial affairs to minimize your tax liability.
- Plan for next year's taxes <u>immediately</u> after you pay this year's taxes.
- Keep good detailed records and ask for receipts for everything you buy.
- Your goal should be to only pay the required amount of tax—avoid payments and refunds on tax day.
- Maximize your tax-free retirement investments.
- Start your own business and get the tax advantages of the wealthy!
- Attend seminars conducted by tax professionals.

Start Your Own Business

The American Dream Doesn't Have to be Just a Dream!

The United States of America is the land of opportunity. There is no greater place in the world to follow your dreams and start your own business than right here. Anyone who is going to be aggressive in wealth building will probably get involved in some sort of business enterprise. This is a great country for entrepreneurial endeavors. My hope is that this book will inspire you to become so great at what you passionately do for living that you could start your own business selling your product or service directly to the marketplace that is ultimately buying your services anyway. Unfortunately, most Americans do not recognize the incredible opportunities that are right in front of them. Do you realize that immigrants who dream their whole life of coming to America just for the opportunity to work have four times the rate of becoming millionaires than the people who already live here! Go ahead and start your own business. If you are organized, a self-starter, willing to work hard, and an expert in your field—there is a very good chance that you will be very successful in running your own business.

It's easier than you think to start your own business. You don't need to be a Donald Trump or a Bill Gates to start your own business. Anyone can start a simple home-based business. You don't need a lot of money or a complicated money-intensive enterprise to get started in business. You could be a schoolteacher who offers at-home seminars on how to "Jump-start your child's education at home" or a homemaker offering home-organizing or babysitting services. Even though you may be just starting out in your career, you may have excellent computer skills—so you could offer technology advice or consulting on a part-time basis.

There are many tax advantages to starting your own business. Starting your own business and working out of your home allows you to write off certain car expenses, telephone expenses, some entertainment expenses, business meals, and home office expenses. In addition, you could hire your children or spouse and get reimbursed for health and medical expenses! For more information on how to start your own business, check the yellow pages for your local Small Business Administration.

**It's Up To You To Break The Cycle of Poverty and Mediocrity
by Teaching Your Children Wealth Building!**

   One of the most important lessons you can teach your children is to be financially independent. Parents need to be talking to their children about money. Start teaching your children about money by showing them how you balance your checkbook. And older children need to be talking to their parents about money, because "How to Manage Money" and "How to Be Fiscally Responsible" are important courses that unfortunately are not taught in school.

   Children today have a hard time grasping the value of money. For the most part, they see their parents paying for goods and services with checks and credit cards and the only real money they ever see comes out of an ATM! If parents fail to teach their children about money—then who will?

Unfortunately, most parents are poor role models for their children when it comes to personal finance.

   Training your children to be financially responsible when they are adults begins at home with their weekly allowances. Allowances should never be considered free money. Work responsibilities or daily chores should be part of the requirements for receiving an allowance. It's best to treat your child's money as wages. It's important that they never get the idea that money is owed to them without something being given in return.

   How allowance money should be handled. Start by teaching the concept of generosity and tithing. The giving concept helps instill values and shows children there is more to life than just working to accumulate things. Have them set aside 10% or "the first fruits" for tithing to your faith right away. The remaining 90% should be divided into thirds.

One-third goes to long-term savings. This money should be put into individual stocks that the child is familiar with like Coca-Cola, Nike, AOL, Microsoft, or Apple. These investments teach your child how money grows in value over time and also about the concept of "risk" in investing. No matter how good a company may be, sometimes the stock will decline in value. But over a long time, the gains should outweigh the declines, if the company is a good company.

One-third should go into a short-term savings account. This savings account is for things your child wants to buy, but must save for. The most important lesson to be learned here is that patience is required if they don't have enough money to buy something today.

The remaining one-third of the child's allowance should be for "spending as you wish."

Buy your child an IRA for his or her retirement. Here's a wonderful gift that you can give your children if you can afford it. Each parent can give up to $10,000 per year tax-free for a total of $20,000. Buying each of your children a long-term investment will teach them the power of compounding interest but also the importance of saving for their retirement, even at a young age.

Even kids can get started on becoming financially independent. Kids can make profits long before they can legitimately earn wages.

— Jim Rohn

How to Borrow Money, How to Lend Money, Or... Throwing Your Money Away!

> IF YOU'RE EVER RUNNING SHORT OF ENEMIES JUST GIVE SOME MONEY TO ONE OF YOUR FRIENDS!

This section could also be titled "How To Keep Your Sanity!" One of the most difficult things in life is to lend money to friends when you know darn well that they're not going to pay you back. The following thoughts will help you determine when you should borrow money and when you should lend money.

Shakespeare said...

Neither a borrower, nor a lender be.

At one time, it was illegal to be in debt. People who could not pay their bills were sent to "Debtor's Prison." Today, we are living in a society that not only encourages debt, but what's even more baffling is the fact that people are actually penalized for prepaying their debt!

There are only three things that you should borrow money for:
1. Your education
2. Your home
3. Home repairs or home improvements

Everything else you either need to save up for or only buy if you have the cash.

> YOU ARE IN BIG TROUBLE IF ALL THE INCOME THAT YOU WORK FOR — ONLY GOES TO PAY OFF YOUR DEBTS!

In order to stay out of debt, you must know the difference between "smart borrowing" and "runaway debt" that's out of control.

"Smart borrowing"—to acquire revenue-generating, appreciating assets that guarantee your ability to repay—is a powerful strategy for amassing great wealth. "Runaway debt"—created by acquiring depreciating pleasures multiplied by your lack of discipline—is quickly turned into a powerful destructive force that will ruin you.

Borrowing power is the ability to borrow against "something of value"— this is called "collateral." Your borrowing power will be equal to the value of your collateral. Smart financial planning, good credit, honesty, trust, and borrowing to buy appreciating assets that generate positive cash flow creates a track record of strong borrowing power.

Debt is created when you borrow money to pay for something that quickly loses value and you are still making payments on something that is no longer equal to the money you owe.

It doesn't take much to buy your way into runaway debt. One of the worst things you can do is buy a new car because it will lose the majority of its value the second you drive it off the showroom floor. This type of debt is the most dangerous because interest rates often far exceed your ability to repay, and the things that you buy are quickly worth less than the debt that you owe on them.

This is the major difference between the "Havemores" who spend $30,000 as a down payment on an apartment building that generates positive cash flow and the "Havenots" who spend $30,000 on a sports car that quickly depreciates and requires fuel and expensive upkeep for repairs. Continually pouring good money into something that is losing value daily creates negative cash flow.

Runaway debt can really destroy people's lives.
It crushes any hope for tomorrow and
kills dreams of getting ahead in life.

Freedom from debt is refreshing to the spirit and is far more satisfying than any material possessions you can accumulate by spending what you don't have.

It's best not to make financial commitments for money you haven't earned. But, if you *must* borrow:

1. You should only borrow to buy appreciating assets.
2. It's a plus if what you are buying also creates positive cash flow.
3. Your collateral should exceed the value that you are borrowing; so if you ever have to sell—the sale price will pay off your debt and you get back your original investment.

4. Your monthly payment should not strain your household budget. You should comfortably be able to pay all your bills.
5. If you are uncomfortable in knowing even the slightest financial emergency will upset your financial stability, then you should not even think of borrowing.
6. Never borrow money on contracts that contain a prepayment penalty.

A few thoughts on lending money...

As you start to get ahead in life, you will find that your friends, neighbors, and relatives will want to borrow money from you. First of all, you need to get several things clear in your head....

NUMBER ONE: You are not a bank.

NUMBER TWO: You don't owe it to anyone to have to lend them money.

The fact is, despite what they tell you and despite how much they swear on their mother's grave—it's almost guaranteed that they will never pay you back.

Do not co-sign loans. Every once in awhile, someone will ask you to co-sign a car loan or bank loan for them. Helping people to create more debt only gets them into further trouble. The main reason some people need a cosigner is very fundamental—the bank thinks they are a bad risk! That ought to tell you something!

Bank lending officers are highly trained to analyze people's ability to repay debt. If they think someone is unable to repay a loan because of a bad repayment track record, what makes you the expert to believe that your co-signing a loan is going to change your friend's history of being a bad credit risk?

If you must lend a friend money, here's how to handle it.

Now that I've advised you not to co-sign any loans, there is one exception—if you are going to lend a friend money, only do it by co-signing a bank loan. If you absolutely have to help someone out during a time of extreme emergency, it is better that he or she be required to make payments to a bank instead of making payments to you.

When people have to pay a bank, they somehow feel more obligated to pay the bank back instead of thinking that just because you're a friend, you will understand and cut them some slack. This will keep the friendship intact, and you won't have to become a jerk in their eyes by making your friends pay up their bad debts.

When it comes to lending money, always have full agreement with your spouse or partner. Remember, you are playing fast and loose with your family's financial future when you bail others out because they aren't disciplined enough to plan for their own emergencies.

If you find yourself in a position where you really want to help a friend or loved one during a difficult time, get it clear in your head that you are making a gift to them. Don't expect to see that money ever again. If you really believe that you are making a loan to them, nine times out of ten, you will never get repaid. Nonpayment of loans has destroyed many close friendships. By not expecting repayment, you won't be setting yourself up for disappointment later on. It's the only way you will have peace of mind.

You cannot fully enjoy spending what does not belong to you!
You can never go broke when you have no debt!

Protect your credit rating at all costs!

Protect your credit as closely as you would protect your reputation. A bad credit report may keep you from getting credit to buy a car or keep you from buying your first home. A bad credit report may even keep you from getting a better job! Many employers sometimes pull up a credit report as an employment consideration.

INTEGRITY, TRUSTWORTHINESS, HONESTY, DEPENDABILITY, FISCAL RESPONSIBILITY, FIDUCIARY WORTHINESS, AND FINANCIAL STEWARDSHIP CAN ALL BE INTERPRETED BY YOUR CREDIT REPORT.

Pay all your bills on time. You must pay all the debts that you owe before the due date. Your credit report is as important as your integrity and reputation. If you are a "delinquent" bill payer, your credit report will show it. An ongoing balance on your credit cards that never gets paid off will show up on your credit report. Bounced checks will show up on your credit report. If you get turned down for a credit card application, that will turn up on your credit report as well.

I'll say it again, "Protect your credit rating at all costs."

HOW TO CHECK YOUR CREDIT:

EQUIFAX	1-800-685-1111	www.equifax.com
EXPERIAN	1-888-397-3742	www.experian.com
TRANSUNION	1-800-916-8800	www.tuc.com

GIVE IT—TO KEEP IT!

"Only by giving can you keep it."

Turbocharge Your Wealth Building By Learning How To Give Your Money Away!

**You make a living by what you get.
You make a life by what you give.**
— Sir Winston Churchill

Now that I've talked you into keeping all your money, I'm going to turn the tables on you. You must give your money away! Money loves generous people. Money is attracted to generous people. You'll never become really wealthy by being a tightwad!

Motivational speaker Zig Ziglar says...

**You can get whatever you want out of life by
giving enough to other people first!**

**WISDOM
KEY**

Wealth is not measured by what you accumulate, but by what you are able to give away. It's not what you acquire in life that's important but what you become that determines your value here on earth.

WHAT YOU ARE ABLE TO GIVE AWAY, BOTH OF YOURSELF AND YOUR RESOURCES, DIRECTLY MIRRORS HOW BIG YOU HAVE BECOME AS A PERSON.

Give your first fruits to God. Your giving also reflects how thankful you are for what God has so graciously given to you. God loves a cheerful giver. The most important lesson that you could learn about giving…

Giving does not weaken you—it strengthens you.

One of the major keys to success is having an unshakable faith that good things are going to happen to you without question. Giving your first fruits to God demonstrates your gratitude and your expectation that more is on the way.

If you waver and think to yourself—giving to God "first" is out of the question because there are more important and urgent things that you want to do with your money—then you are of weak faith and you will have a hard time being successful. All successful people demonstrate the strength of their faith by being generous.

WISDOM KEY

Great faith attracts unlimited resources from a great God. Without faith, you can only do what's humanly possible. If you are going to experience great wealth, you need to accomplish great things. Accomplishing great things requires great faith. Be a person of great faith!

Remember…with God, all things are possible. By yourself, you can only do what's humanly possible. Giving makes you bigger than you really are! Those who cannot give cannot fulfill their responsibility as a citizen, as a parent, and as a child of God.

Honor God with the first fruits of all you earn.
— Proverbs 3:9

"Bring all the tithes (10%) to the Temple, so that there will be enough food there. If you do," says the Lord Almighty, "I will open the windows of heaven for you. I will pour out a blessing so great you won't have enough room to take it in! Try it! Let me prove it to you!

Your crops will be abundant, for I will guard them from insects and disease. Your grapes will not shrivel before they are ripe," says the Lord Almighty. "Then all nations will call you blessed, for your land will be such a delight," says the Lord Almighty.

— Malachi 3:10-12 (Paraphrased)

Giving back to God is thanking God for the opportunity to work. In fact, the Bible clearly states that God expects the first fruits of your labor. God has given you His very best. Give God your very best.

The Bible doesn't say…

Spend all you can so you can enjoy yourself, and then give what's left to God!

But unfortunately that's the attitude of most people—then they wonder why nothing good ever comes their way. The Bible clearly states your responsibility in tithing. Even the widow, who gave her last mite at the temple, recognized how important it was to give back to God. When Jesus saw her give her last mite, he didn't go and give it back to her because she was poor…he knew how important it was for her to give what she could. And because of her obedience and faith, he blessed her.

TWO MAJOR LESSONS IN GIVING:

1. **Give UP for Abundance (giving to God first).** Proverbs 3:9-10 "Honor the Lord with thy substance, and with the first fruits of all thine increase: So shall thy barns be filled with plenty, and thy presses shall burst out with new wine."

2. **Give DOWN for Blessings (giving to the needy).** Psalms 41:1-2 "Blessed is he that considereth the poor: the Lord will deliver him in time of trouble. The Lord will preserve him, and keep him alive; and he shall be blessed on the earth: and thou wilt not deliver him unto the will of his enemies."

When you honor God with your first fruits—God will honor you back—guaranteed. God will bless you in your financial affairs, open doors that were previously closed to you, and give you wisdom in making the right decisions. This is a guaranteed promise that God makes to you.

Money must be moving for it to create wealth. Remember, money is transfer of energy. If you are stingy with your money and keep it locked away only for yourself, it is useless. When you are generous with your money, you are unlocking the floodgates of God's great universe. If you don't give, you are clogging up the pipes and money can't move.

When is the last time you gave anything back to God? What have you given to help the poor and the less fortunate? There's a saying that goes, "The bigger the window that you give out of—the more that can be shoved back your way!"

The best time to start giving is right now. Sometimes people don't give because they think that their little amount of money doesn't really make any difference—but it does. The real benefit is to you. Remember the widow's mite? You are developing "generosity habits" that will be with you forever.

Besides, it's easier to give 10% of $10, or even 10% of $100, than to give 10% of $100,000. If you are used to giving, when you are able to give 10% of $1 million or more someday— you won't think twice. Experience will show you that whatever you give, returns to you many times over.

When you give—give without reservation. Give freely from your heart. The Bible says, "God loves a cheerful giver."

Give anonymously. Don't give looking for attention. Don't give as a "tactic," expecting to get more—that's trying to manipulate God for selfish reasons. Give without expecting anything back. When you give from your heart because you truly are thankful and you want to help others, God will bless you unconditionally and with great abundance.

Be generous—it's the best way to guarantee that money will be attracted to you. Don't take this issue lightly. Giving and generosity are the most important fundamentals to building your financial future. Money is attracted to people that are generous from the heart. Having money lets you make a difference in the world.

Wealth requires responsibility to others. "To whom much is given, much is expected." Your wealth is not just for yourself. Successful use of your wealth creates job opportunities and a better way of life for many others.

If you don't give—don't expect God's help. It's that simple.

Each of us will one day be judged
by our standard of life,
not by our standard of living;
by our measure of giving,
not by our measure of wealth;
by our simple goodness,
not by our seeming greatness.

— William Arthur Ward

Money is like manure, you have to
spread it around or it smells!
— J. Paul Getty

THE $ECRET$ OF INVE$TING!

Just don't save your money
because you'll lose it...
(I don't mean you will really lose it, but just saving money never beats the rate of inflation.)

Great wealth is created only from Investing!
Investing isn't just for the wealthy, it's the
only way to become wealthy.

This is not the American Dream! Insurance actuarial tables show us that if you take 100 people, who all start out at the same place in life, and follow them until they are age 65, you would find:

Only 1% will become very wealthy.

4% will be financially independent.

15% will still be working until they die, because they have to.

80% will be flat broke and taken care of by the government. And half of that 80% will live out their lives in nursing homes, unable to care for or feed themselves.

There is absolutely no reason why you have to end up being taken care of by the government. Start planning for your future now by learning about wealth creation. Knowledge and a commitment to saving and investing your earnings will free you to adapt a lifestyle that will put you in the top 5% of the world's wealthiest people! Everyone can do this—you don't have to be privileged. It takes responsibility to have money. Unfortunately, most people do not understand this. People daydream about spending their next paycheck before they have even earned it. They believe that money is for spending and that's why they call the money left over from paying their bills— "spending money!"

> **You will never experience great wealth or have access to financial resources until you understand this fundamental rule of money: money, being energy, needs to grow and multiply.** If you cannot discipline yourself to learn how to save, invest and grow your money—you will lose it!

Financial security comes only from learning how to invest your savings. Taking responsibility for an investment strategy is not a new concept. It's been a fundamental part of wealth-building as long as there has been money.

Even in the Bible, the parable of the talents (a talent is a Biblical measure of money) states very clearly that you must be responsible for investing your talents or you will lose them. Read the following aloud to yourself…

Matthew 25:14-30 (KJV)

The Parable of the Talents

For the kingdom of heaven is as a rich man traveling into a far country, who called his own servants and delivered unto them his goods. And unto one he gave five talents, another he gave two talents, and one talent to another; and immediately he went on his journey.

Then he that had received the five talents went and traded them and made another five talents. And likewise he who had received the two talents, he gained two more also. But he who had received the one talent went and dug in the ground and hid his lord's money.

After a long time the lord of those servants came and settled his accounts with them. And so he that had received the five talents, he came and brought the other five talents, saying, "Lord, thou delivered to me five talents: look, I have gained five more talents besides your original five." His lord said unto him, "Well done thou good and faithful servant; you were faithful over a few things, I will make you ruler over many things. Enter into the joy of your lord."

He also who had received two talents came and said, "Lord, thou delivered to me two talents; look, I have gained two more talents besides your original two." His lord said unto him, "Well done thou good and faithful servant; you were faithful over a few things, I will make you ruler over many things. Enter into the joy of your lord."

Then he who had received the one talent came and said, "Lord, I knew you to be a hard man, reaping where you have not sown, and gathering where you have not scattered seed. And I was afraid, and went and hid your one talent in the ground. Look, there you have what is yours."

But his lord answered and said to him, "You wicked and lazy servant, you knew that I reap where I have not sown, and gather were I have not scattered seed. So you ought to have deposited my money with the bankers, and at my coming I would have received back my one talent with interest. Therefore take the one talent from him and give it to him that has ten talents.

For to everyone who has, more will be given, and he will have abundance; but from him who does not have, even what he has will be taken away. And cast the unprofitable servant into the outer darkness; where there shall be weeping and gnashing of teeth."

HERE'S THE LESSON: From this old Biblical parable it's very clear that we all are responsible for investing our money and if we don't, what we do have will be taken away from us and given to the person who has the most.

This old parable, which is many thousands of years old, pretty much states, "The rich get richer and the poor get poorer!" It's also very clear that those people who are lazy and don't do anything with their money or they are going to have a tough time—they are going to be weeping and gnashing their teeth.

Money is smart. It doesn't hang around lazy fools!

START INVESTING NOW!

Money will always flow to the person who knows how to invest it and make it grow.
Money needs to be appreciated, put to work, and invested.

Investing is wealth-building. There has never been a better time to start building your wealth. Whether the market is rising or falling, now is always the right time to start investing. However, saving your money in a bank account is similar to the lazy man in the parable who just buried his money. Investment knowledge that creates wealth-building is available to everyone.

The single greatest tragedy experienced by the average family is not knowing what to do with their money once they've earned it! We've spent our whole lifetime learning how to earn money, but we've never learned the correct way to invest our money.

THE REASON WE CALL IT "TAKE-HOME PAY".
IS BECAUSE YOU CAN'T AFFORD TO TAKE IT
ANYWHERE ELSE!

Start with what you have. Many people starting out find it hard to save because they don't think that they are earning enough. Only when they get a "real paying job" will they start saving for the future. Unfortunately, by the time they get a real job that pays them well, they have not developed good financial habits of saving and investing. They think you need to have a great job and a high salary to get wealthy; nothing could be further from the truth.

The fact is that all you need is a little bit of money on an ongoing basis, patience, and a whole lot of time. Wealth is the child of passion and discipline. The more passionate you are, the greater your opportunity for wealth. The more disciplined you are—the more money you will have to invest.

You must do your homework! If you don't have a clue about investing your money, you will have to design a personal long-term goal for becoming proficient at investing if you expect to get wealthy. There is no other way! You must read investment books and magazines to gain personal knowledge. You must attend lectures and seminars on investing your money. After all, it is your money. It is your responsibility to learn how to invest it. Nobody will ever be more concerned about your money than you.

**WISDOM
KEY**

The major secret to wealth is not to try to get a lot of money quickly in the shortest amount of time (although it would be nice) but to invest a little money consistently without fail, over a long period of time.

How to Have One Million Dollars by Age 65

Bank Savings Plan
Assumed Rate of Return: 3%

Age	Monthly Investment	Years	Result
20	$876.92	45	$ 1,000,000
25	$1,079.84	40	$ 1,000,000
30	$1,348.50	35	$ 1,000,000
35	$1,716.04	30	$ 1,000,000
40	$2,242.11	25	$ 1,000,000
45	$3,045.98	20	$ 1,000,000
50	$4,405.82	15	$ 1,000,000
55	$7,156.07	10	$ 1,000,000
60	$15,468.69	5	$ 1,000,000

Investing in the S&P 500
Assumed Rate of Return: 10%

Age	Monthly Investment	Years	Result
20	$95.40	45	$ 1,000,000
25	$158.13	40	$ 1,000,000
30	$263.39	35	$ 1,000,000
35	$442.38	30	$ 1,000,000
40	$753.67	25	$ 1,000,000
45	$1,316.88	20	$ 1,000,000
50	$2,412.72	15	$ 1,000,000
55	$4,881.74	10	$ 1,000,000
60	$12,913.71	5	$ 1,000,000

Conservative Investing
Assumed Rate of Return: 12.5%

Age	Monthly Investment	Years	Result
20	$38.82	45	$ 1,000,000
25	$72.53	40	$ 1,000,000
30	$135.88	35	$ 1,000,000
35	$255.91	30	$ 1,000,000
40	$486.87	25	$ 1,000,000
45	$944.74	20	$ 1,000,000
50	$1,908.55	15	$ 1,000,000
55	$4,220.95	10	$ 1,000,000
60	$12,081.27	5	$ 1,000,000

Aggressive Portfolio
Assumed Rate of Return: 15%

Age	Monthly Investment	Years	Result
20	$15.28	45	$ 1,000,000
25	$32.24	40	$ 1,000,000
30	$68.13	35	$ 1,000,000
35	$144.44	30	$ 1,000,000
40	$308.31	25	$ 1,000,000
45	$667.90	20	$ 1,000,000
50	$1,495.87	15	$ 1,000,000
55	$3,633.50	10	$ 1,000,000
60	$11,289.93	5	$ 1,000,000

There are three important lessons to be learned by this chart:

1. Bank savings accounts are <u>not</u> the best places to grow your money.

2. It only takes a small amount of money saved consistently over time to become a millionaire.

3. The sooner you start, the easier it is to become wealthy.

The incredible magic of turning small savings into small fortunes!

The Magic Penny

Question:

If you were walking on the beach one day and found a magical genie bottle, when the genie popped out and offered you a choice between getting one million dollars in cold hard cash right now or a "magic penny" that doubled every day just for one month only, *which would you take?*

If you answered the magic penny—you are a financial genius!

Here's what happens to a penny if it doubles every day for 30 days.

Day 1	.01	Day 11	10.24	Day 21	10,485.76
Day 2	.02	Day 12	20.48	Day 22	20,971.52
Day 3	.04	Day 13	40.96	Day 23	41,943.04
Day 4	.08	Day 14	81.92	Day 24	83,886.08
Day 5	.16	Day 15	163.84	Day 25	167,772.16
Day 6	.32	Day 16	327.68	Day 26	335,544.32
Day 7	.64	Day 17	655.36	Day 27	671,088.64
Day 8	1.28	Day 18	1,310.72	Day 28	1,342,177.28
Day 9	2.56	Day 19	2,621.44	Day 29	2,684,354.56
Day 10	5.12	Day 20	5,242.88	Day 30	5,368,708.12

In 30 days, your magic penny would have doubled to $5,368,708.12!

This simple illustration demonstrates how small savings can be turned into fortunes.

Here's my challenge to you…

HOW CAN YOU DOUBLE YOUR VALUE TO THE MARKETPLACE EVERY DAY?

The Power of Compound Interest

𝕭aron 𝖛on 𝕽othchild once said...

I don't know what the 7 wonders of the world are, but I do know that the 8th wonder of the world is... COMPOUND INTEREST!

Compound Interest is an incredible financial concept. Time and compound interest are magical ingredients—when added to money, they create exponential wealth. One without the other will not work.

Understanding "The Power of Compound Interest" is very important because it can either create phenomenal wealth or it can financially ruin you. Most Americans run into financial problems because they buy a few things on credit cards with high interest rates and think nothing of it. It seems that they are only making a few small purchases here and there—but over time it all adds up.

The real problem comes when they only make minimum payments of 3% on their balance and their credit card interest rates are high—14% to 18%. You don't have to be a genius to quickly realize that the interest rates are going to keep compounding or multiplying their debt until they have fallen so deep into financial quicksand that they can't get out.

 **WARNING!** *Don't start out in life by having compound interest as your enemy.*

WISDOM KEY

Make compound interest your friend. Start your investing at an early age, or as soon as you can, and let compound interest start working for you. Compound Interest is a powerful concept. It can either work diligently for you or it can be just as powerful working against you. It can either build your investment portfolio exponentially or it can build your debt exponentially, it all depends on how you spend your money. Put compound interest to work for you by starting to invest now. The sooner the better!

There are two important keys to understanding compound interest.

The first one is that you must start now. Even though you may not be making a lot of money, it doesn't matter. It's like the example of the magical penny. All it takes is a little money "compounded over time" to grow into great wealth.

The critical point is that it doesn't matter what you earn— The fact is, the sooner you start saving and investing, the greater your wealth will be long-term.

The second most important fact is that you must invest whatever you have even if it's a small amount. All great wealth starts out with a little bit of money. The key is to begin investing with whatever you can save.

These are two major secrets of wealth-building that the rich understand and the poor just don't "get!"

To demonstrate how incredible this philosophy of compound interest is and how saving small amounts of money compounded over time will create great wealth, here's an eye-opening example:

Do you realize that if you were 20 years old and you saved just $2 a day or $60 every month for 45 years and this money compounded at the rate of 10%, by age 65 you would have $634,191.35. The most important thing to remember is that you must religiously save this amount every month. But it's <u>only</u> $60 a month and that should be easy!

Imagine $634,191.35 just for saving $60 every month!

JUST THINK HOW MUCH GREATER YOUR WEALTH WOULD BE IF YOU HAD EARNED MORE MONEY; SAVED EVEN MORE MONEY AS YOU GOT OLDER; AND YOU WERE TO ABLE INVEST EVEN MORE!

Here's something even more incredible to consider:

In this example, we were only using 10% as our compound interest rate. The fact is that's only the historical average of the S&P 500. Just think what would happen if you were to double that! You're probably thinking—WOW! That seems unbelievable. The fact is there are many top money managers that have been averaging 20% rates of investment returns or more for the last five years.

THAT DOESN'T EVEN TAKE INTO ACCOUNT A REAL **HOT** COMPANY WITH RECORD PROFITS WITH NO LIMITS IN SIGHT AND EXPERIENCING SOARING STOCK PRICES — AND IMAGINE IF THEY SPLIT THEIR STOCK SEVERAL TIMES. THIS IS ONE EXAMPLE OF HOW INCREDIBLE FORTUNES ARE MADE IN THE STOCK MARKET. YOU CAN'T WIN IF YOU DON'T PLAY AND YOU CAN'T PLAY IF YOU DON'T PAY. THE FACT IS: THERE IS MONEY TO BE MADE IN AN UP MARKET AND MONEY TO BE MADE IN A DOWN MARKET. YOU MUST BECOME KNOWLEDGEABLE ENOUGH TO HARNESS THE POWERS OF COMPOUND INTEREST AND INVESTING. THIS IS NOT THE TIME TO CLAIM "IGNORANCE IS BLISS!"

Start learning how to invest at an early age.

Start investing at an early age.

The following chart is a great example of why young people need to start saving at an early age.

Early Al
Investment Return 10%

Age	Savings	Investment Return	Balance
22	1,200	120	1,320
23	1,200	252	2,772
24	1,200	397	4,369
25	1,200	557	6,126
26	1,200	733	8,059
27	1,200	926	10,185
28	1,200	1,138	12,523
29	1,200	1,372	15,095
30		1,510	16,605
31		1,660	18,265
32		1,827	20,092
33		2,009	22,101
34		2,210	24,311
35		2,431	26,742
36		2,674	29,417
37		2,942	32,358
38		3,236	35,594
39		3,559	39,154
40		3,915	43,069
41		4,307	47,376
42		4,738	52,113
43		5,211	57,325
44		5,732	63,057
45		6,306	69,363
46		6,936	76,299
47		7,630	83,929
48		8,393	92,322
49		9,232	101,554
50		10,155	111,710
51		11,171	122,880
52		12,288	135,169
53		13,517	148,685
54		14,869	163,554
55		16,355	179,909
56		17,991	197,900
57		19,790	217,690
58		21,769	239,459
59		23,946	263,405
60		26,341	289,746
61		28,975	318,720
62		31,872	350,592
63		35,059	385,652
64		38,565	424,217
65		42,422	__466,638__

Dan Delay
Investment Return 10%

Age	Savings	Investment Return	Balance
22		-	-
23		-	-
24		-	-
25		-	-
26		-	-
27		-	-
28		-	-
29		-	-
30	1200	120	1,320
31	1200	252	2,772
32	1200	397	4,369
33	1200	557	6,126
34	1200	733	8,059
35	1200	926	10,185
36	1200	1,138	12,523
37	1200	1,372	15,095
38	1200	1,630	17,925
39	1200	1,912	21,037
40	1200	2,224	24,461
41	1200	2,566	28,227
42	1200	2,943	32,370
43	1200	3,357	36,927
44	1200	3,813	41,940
45	1200	4,314	47,454
46	1200	4,865	53,519
47	1200	5,472	60,191
48	1200	6,139	67,530
49	1200	6,873	75,603
50	1200	7,680	84,483
51	1200	8,568	94,252
52	1200	9,545	104,997
53	1200	10,620	116,816
54	1200	11,802	129,818
55	1200	13,102	144,120
56	1200	14,532	159,852
57	1200	16,105	177,157
58	1200	17,836	196,193
59	1200	19,739	217,132
60	1200	21,833	240,165
61	1200	24,137	265,502
62	1200	26,670	293,372
63	1200	29,457	324,029
64	1200	32,523	357,752
65	1200	35,895	__394,847__

Pete Perseverance
Investment Return 10%

Age	Savings	Investment Return	Balance
22	1200	120	1,320
23	1200	252	2,772
24	1200	397	4,369
25	1200	557	6,126
26	1200	733	8,059
27	1200	926	10,185
28	1200	1,138	12,523
29	1200	1,372	15,095
30	1200	1,630	17,925
31	1200	1,912	21,037
32	1200	2,224	24,461
33	1200	2,566	28,227
34	1200	2,943	32,370
35	1200	3,357	36,927
36	1200	3,813	41,940
37	1200	4,314	47,454
38	1200	4,865	53,519
39	1200	5,472	60,191
40	1200	6,139	67,530
41	1200	6,873	75,603
42	1200	7,680	84,483
43	1200	8,568	94,252
44	1200	9,545	104,997
45	1200	10,620	116,816
46	1200	11,802	129,818
47	1200	13,102	144,120
48	1200	14,532	159,852
49	1200	16,105	177,157
50	1200	17,836	196,193
51	1200	19,739	217,132
52	1200	21,833	240,165
53	1200	24,137	265,502
54	1200	26,670	293,372
55	1200	29,457	324,029
56	1200	32,523	357,752
57	1200	35,895	394,847
58	1200	39,605	435,652
59	1200	43,685	480,537
60	1200	48,174	529,911
61	1200	53,111	584,222
62	1200	58,542	643,964
63	1200	64,516	709,681
64	1200	71,088	781,969
65	1200	78,317	__861,486__

The information in these three charts is based on saving only $25 a week or $100 a month or a total of $1,200 a year. The first chart is for "**Early Al**" who saved $1,200 a year for only eight years and then never saved another penny the rest of his life. At age 65, he will have accumulated through saving and investing $466, 638. That's incredible—just by saving $9,600 over eight years and investing at a minimum rate of return of only 10%. It's amazing how time can grow money—even a little bit of money!

The second chart is for "**Dan Delay**" who frolicked his early life away and then decided to get serious about saving at age 30. He saved $1,200 a year over 35 years for a total investment of $42,000 but could only grow it to $394, 847! Still great money, but when you compare the two, you can see how important it is to start saving right away— you get a head start that's almost impossible to make up later.

Then, the final chart is for "**Pete Perseverance**." It shows that if you start early and never give up saving, you can amass an incredible fortune of $861, 486—almost a million dollars! <u>Just by saving only $25 a week or $100 a month.</u>

Just think how much you can accumulate if you save even more money. Or if your interest rates exceeded 10% a year.

Remember, it's not what you earn that can make you a fortune, it's what you save and invest that's so critically important. Because in this example, $1,200 is only 10% of a $12,000 annual income!

This example really shows: the awesome power of compound interest, how important it is to save small amounts of money, and the importance of investing over long periods of time.

Here are the most important questions you should ask—

1. How much am I earning?
2. How much am I saving?
3. How much am I investing?

WEALTH NEVER COMES FROM HOW MUCH YOU EARN. WEALTH ONLY COMES FROM THE SIZE AND QUALITY OF YOUR INVESTMENT PORTFOLIO.

CONCERNED THAT LIFE HAS PASSED YOU BY?

Let's say you are **45 years of age** now and you are just getting your life together—is it too late to start investing?…**NO!**

For the purposes of this example, let's say you are earning $40,000 a year.
If you were committed to saving 10% or $4,000 a year, (that's only $11 a day) and invested it at the same 10%, by the time you were 65 you would have a cool $250,000 invested into a nice little nest egg!

KEY LESSON: *It's never too late to start investing!*

The Savings Account Mistake

You must beat inflation! If you want to retire rich, the worst place you can put your money is in a savings account. A bank savings account will only pay you between 3-5% or less. That barely keeps up with the rate of inflation. In the past 50 years in America, we have averaged a 3-4% rate of inflation. It's very clear—if you are going to grow your savings into healthy investments, you can't do it by putting your money into a bank savings account.

Savings accounts are good while you are accumulating enough money to put into your investment portfolio.

Real wealth is measured by the growth rate of your investments.

Most people consider being able to pay their bills "managing their money." While commendable, it is also very tragic, because correct money management includes investing to beat the rate of inflation and ultimately, growing your money into fabulous wealth.

Learning how to be wealthy requires lifelong
"wealth-building" thinking.

Lifelong wealth-building requires "RISK."

Nothing is certain except the past.
— Seneca

Just like any other success, the people who cannot force themselves out of their comfort zone of security to take on some risk will never experience the rewards of financial success. That's probably why the bottom 60% of Americans do not own stock and the top 10% of the wealthiest people all own stock.

Saving your money in a bank because you think it's safe and secure is really long-term financial suicide because you are not even beating the rate of inflation.

WISDOM KEY

The concept of investing is to buy with your savings an investment, which will grow in value over a long period of time, with a rate of growth that is greater than the rate of inflation. While time and compound interest are your allies in growing your money—inflation is your worst enemy.

With inflation averaging between 3-4%, it is very important to invest your money where you are getting a rate of return that is greater than inflation. There are many investment considerations: new business ventures, bank savings accounts, bank certificates of deposit, real estate, gold, municipal bonds, U.S. Treasury bonds, IRA's, Keogh Retirement Plans, individual stocks, and stock mutual funds, just to name a few.

If your company has a retirement plan like a 401K and they match (to some extent) your investment, this is the easiest place to start. The best thing you can do is maximize your investment in this program. But, if the company does not match—then you must diversify.

Investments such as real estate or new business ventures are tricky. Don't get involved unless you know absolutely what you're doing. In new ventures, only get involved if you have some controlling interest, or if you're an expert in the field, or if the company principals are regarded as experts with proven track records.

For new investors, take 10% of the money you set aside for long-term investment and put it in individual stocks, or stock mutual funds, or index funds recommended by a proven professional.

Many people are afraid of the stock market because of the sensationalism created by newspapers when the stock market takes periodic dives. The fact is that the stock market has outperformed all other investments over time. Since the beginning of the stock market, the Standard & Poor's average gain over time, including all major market crashes, has been 10-12% yearly.

The most important concept to remember is that smart investing is created over long periods of time where gains and declines are averaged out.

Today, the government has implemented safety procedures to guard against a catastrophic stock market crash. And banks are guaranteed by federal insurance. So a national financial collapse, such as the 1929 crash, probably will never happen again.

Huge market swings are more commonplace today with the introduction of the daily investor or "day trader," who is investing over the Internet and the rapidity at which "market changing information" reaches the individual investor.

Historically, we find that expansion periods seem to last about five years—with the first and last years ramping up or down followed by one year of major decline. However, despite this "perceived" volatility, the market keeps gaining. I can remember in 1975 when the Dow Jones first broke through 1000. Now it is near 8,000.

While nothing is certain, the one thing we do know, based on historical trends, is that despite all the daily stock market dips and downturns, the stock market always has come back even stronger.

Your decision to invest should be determined by:

1. **Your comfort level of risk**
2. **Your knowledge of what you are investing in**
3. **Your financial goals**

WISDOM KEY

Security is an interesting concept—there is none. But to a degree, you can achieve some level of comfort or security by taking risk. This is the paradox of risk—wealth-building *cannot* happen in the comfort zone of security.

TOTAL SECURITY IS ACHIEVED ONLY WHEN YOU HAVE NO DEBT!

Bulls make money. Bears make money.
But hogs and lambs get slaughtered!

The moral is: don't be a hog by being greedy
and don't be a lamb that's too timid
to make a decision or take risks.

Being a hog or a lamb will get you killed in the market!

All investment strategies will include risk.

Remember: the greater the yield—the greater the risk.

WISDOM KEY

Don't risk what you can't afford to lose. Investment money should always be money that you won't need for five years. It's best to limit your stock investments to exchange-listed stocks. All stocks will have peaks and valleys—that's why you want to invest in good companies with great products and competent leadership.

Even good companies will have bad years and the stock will decline. However, if the public believes in the product and continues to buy, strong competent leadership will generally be able to turn the financial picture into a healthy one again and make the stock a buying opportunity.

Investments or risk-taking should be based on knowledge, patience, and common sense.

Your investment strategy. Always diversify your risk by making sure your hard-earned fortune is not wiped out by one bad investment. Never put all your investment eggs in one financial basket. Betting on one company's stock is not good advice.

Spread your risk. Invest in several good stocks you know well or companies that make products you use and believe in. Another option is to invest in stock mutual funds. A stock mutual fund is a collection of stocks from different companies managed by an investment professional who specializes in a particular field, such as restaurant stocks, bank stocks, Internet stocks, high-risk growth stocks, or foreign company stock investments, etc.

Your investment goal. Your minimum investment goal should be 15%. Inflation will wipe out 5%, so that leaves you with a 10% return on your money.

Rules for the Beginning
"Mover & Shaker!"
(Someone just starting to build a financial empire!)

Rule Number One: Money is attracted to money! It takes money to make money.
However, the exception is: If you are just starting out in life or you are starting over
after some major failure, your ability to "get in on the action" will be difficult at first.
But don't lose hope because money is always attracted to Top Performers! The only way
you are going to overcome not having money is to be recognized as being an industrious
hard worker with solid character and honorable ethics. In order for you to stand head-
and-shoulders above everyone else, you need to outwork and outperform everyone else.

**Rule Number Two: Money will always go to hard-working people who can be
trusted.** People need to depend on you. They need to trust you. Your honesty and
integrity will attract the attention of the "movers and shakers." You will become so
valuable to the success of the operation that they will want to cut you in on the deals,
just to ensure their success!

Rule Number Three: Money is always building partnerships. As a result of your
industriousness and ability to be trusted, you will be invited in on the "deals" and be
included in investment opportunities, initial public offerings, and partnerships in new
business ventures.

Putting your investment strategy together.

Hire a professional financial advisor. Unless you are thoroughly competent in a
chosen investment field such as new business start-ups or real estate investing, it is
important that you hire a trained, professional, financial advisor to assist you in your
investment decisions.

Professional advisers have studied and trained for the rigors of investing. This is what
they love to do. When you hire someone who eats, breathes, and dreams about what they
love to do, they are going to be very passionate when it comes to creating your success.

As professionals, they put in long hours every day studying investments. Their success
depends on how successfully they grow and protect your money.

Don't lose sleep worrying about your investments. Let a professional investor
worry about your money. You need to concentrate on what you do best and focus all
your energies in doing what you love to do. However, remember…

**Nobody cares more about your money than you do.
Make sure you are responsible for it and how it is being spent!**

Do not use a stockbroker or an insurance agent as your financial advisor. A financial advisor whose fees are tied to your actual investments may not always base decisions on your best long-term interests. Do your homework and find a good financial advisor. Get recommendations from wealthy people you know and respect or ask your banker, lawyer, stockbroker, or Certified Public Accountant for referrals. Don't hire a "new" professional financial advisor. Find one with a successful track record.

Never put your money into anything that eats or depreciates. When you are just starting out, don't put your hard-earned money into things that are just for show and are going to rapidly depreciate and require upkeep. Cars, boats, snowmobiles, jet skis, motorcycles, and trendy clothes are bad investments. Don't rent or lease things that depreciate. It's better to own them for income tax depreciation purposes. Things that eat are expensive—this includes pets and children!

CHILDREN WILL BE YOUR GREATEST EXPENSE. IF AT ALL POSSIBLE, TRY AND PLAN FOR THESE WONDERFUL ADDITIONS TO YOUR FAMILY.

Once you decide to have children…you need to financially plan for their education, feeding, and medical costs. Instead of having your children become a drain on your family budget, train them early to be responsible for paying their own way. Encourage them to be fiscally responsible and have them start investing at an early age for their own future.

Investing is for the long term. Be prepared for the long haul. While there are exceptions and some people have struck it rich overnight, for the majority of us our wealth is going to happen over a long period of time. You need to have realistic expectations that wealth is created slowly over time. Patience and discipline are your greatest friends in building your fortune.

IF SOMEONE TRIES TO CONVINCE YOU THAT THEY CAN MAKE YOU A FORTUNE OVERNIGHT, VIEW THEM WITH DISTRUST AND RUN FROM THEM!

"Get-rich-quick" thinking is not good. Wealth is a powerful resource—one that has to be used. It takes responsibility, discipline, and knowledge for you to be given the right to <u>manage</u> money. Notice I didn't say <u>have</u> money. Nobody just "has" money. You are either using it or you are losing it. Because money is energy, it must be either grown or spent—it never stays idle.

Simple Important Rules Before You Start Investing

- Never invest what you cannot afford to lose.
- Never borrow to invest.
- Beginning investors should set up a cash account, not a margin account.
- Be prepared to leave your money invested for a minimum of five years.
- Hire a financial planner on a fee-for-service basis. Do not buy your investments from your financial planner.
- Do not use your stockbroker or insurance agent as your financial planner.
- Do your homework. Only invest with money managers who have successful track records.
- Your team of advisors should all be in agreement with your investment strategy. This team includes your accountant, financial planner, stockbroker, lawyer and possibly your banker.
- Don't buy stock on "tips" you hear from people you don't know.
- Never buy an investment over the phone from someone you don't know.
- Have realistic expectations. "Getting rich quick" is immature thinking when it comes to long-term investments.
- Limit your investments to what you can control.
- You must have an investment strategy that includes a "buy" strategy as well as an "exit" strategy.
- You must have Stop-Loss Orders on your stocks to protect your investment. A Stop-Loss Order is a number (let's say 8% or 10%) below your purchase price at which you are unwilling to accept additional losses.
- You must remove emotions from your investment decisions. Never fall in love with a stock.
- Keep a majority of your stock investments to exchange-listed stocks.
- Make sure your hard-earned fortune is not wiped out by one bad investment. Diversify your risk by diversifying your investment portfolio.
- Don't follow your investments on a daily basis.
- Don't let the ups and downs of the market make buy or sell decisions for you.
- Check your long-term investments every three months or at least twice a year.
- Stick to your investment strategy without fail.

How to Pick a Stock

First, you must learn what influences a company's profitability, its growth prospects, and the value of a stock (which may be influenced by factors that have nothing to do with the company). There are four major factors you must consider before investing in a company's stock: The Overall Economy, The Global Stock Markets, Sectors, and Industries. Most novice investors get this backward—they spend all their time and energy trying to find a company to invest in rather than understanding the big picture first.

THE ECONOMY—The health of our economy is what drives business. Just like everything else, it has its ups and downs. This is the Universal Law of Timing, Cycles, and Seasons. Throughout history we have seen a cycle, on average, of five years of growth and expansion and one or two years of contraction. Understanding which cycle we are in will have a lot to do with determining our investment decisions.

There are five key indicators that affect the economy: Interest Rates, Gross Domestic Product, the Inflation Rate, Consumer Spending, and Leading Economic Indicators. These economic indicators include: consumer spending, unemployment claims, new jobs created, building permit applications, inflation rate, and the nation's money supply, to name a few.

The stock market's movement and the vitality of a sector determine 80% of a company's price. Get this right and you are ahead of the game!

THE STOCK MARKET—50% of a stock's price can be attributed to "market movement." The stock market is made up of the New York Stock Exchange, NYSE or more commonly known as "The Big Board;" the NASDAQ, where most of your new company start-ups are placed; and the AMEX. The Indexes include: the Dow Jones Industrial Average, The Standard & Poor's 500, and the Russell 2000. Then there are the stock exchanges of other world markets like Japan and the Euro-markets, which can affect our national markets.

SECTORS—30% of a stock's price can be attributed to the "vitality" of a sector. There are eleven sectors: Technology, Energy, Capital Goods, Basic Materials, Communication Services, Consumer Cyclicals, Financials, Utilities, Healthcare, Transportation, and Consumer Staples.

The vitality of a sector is fairly simple to understand. For example, the Transportation Sector (at the time of this writing) is a fairly weak sector because everyone has a car. Technology will be a relatively strong sector because not everyone has the latest technology. Right now, Healthcare is a strong sector because we are on the verge of discovering how to use DNA to bio-genetically design medicines to a specific person's needs. The Financial Sector is a strong sector because right now people are just figuring out how to invest in the stock market using the Internet. For the first time in history, you don't have to be wealthy to have a Wall Street connection and to be an investor.

INDUSTRIES—Each sector is divided up into major industries. For example, The Transportation Sector includes: the Automotive Industry, the Railroad Industry, and the Airline Industry. The Technology Sector would include: Software, Hardware, Electronics, Semiconductors, etc.

Understanding which sector is **HOT** will help you in determining which industry has the best prospects for growth. **Hint:** <u>A key indicator is to determine where institutional money is flowing.</u> An institution might be a big bank or the teachers' retirement fund, where money managers have tens or hundreds of millions to invest.

COMPANY STOCKS—Picking a stock will be determined by your asset allocation strategy. For example, your long-term growth "buy and hold" stocks probably will come from the NYSE market. Since technology is a strong sector, you would then determine that software is the strongest industry in the technology sector because hardware has become a commodity. Once you have determined that software is the strongest industry, you next want to pick the strongest company in the software industry, which would be Microsoft.

Your momentum stocks for short-term profit most likely will come from the NASDAQ market. Momentum stocks require greater due diligence because of the increased risk factor. They also require constant watching for the next innovation that might wipe out your company's product or service. After determining that technology is still a strong sector all the way around, you might determine that communication companies are your best investment. Your next move would be to determine the one company that is a market leader with the best prospects for long-term growth.

What factors do you look for in determining the strength of a company?

- **An awesome product with huge market potential**
- **Experienced management team with high stock ownership**
- **Accelerating revenue growth of at least 25% from the same quarter over last year**
- **Accelerating earnings growth of least 25% for the past three years**
- **Return on Investment (ROI) or Return on Equity (ROE) of at least 20%**
- **10% net margins or better**
- **Relative Price Strength of 80 or higher—this means this company is in the top 20% of the industry performers**
- **Strong Research and Development**
- **Market leader with minimal competition**
- **Strong employee culture**

Other Tips:

- Your "buy and hold" stocks should not be under $15 a share. The best performing stocks over the past 45 years have been $28 stocks. Market leaders with a future simply do not trade under $15.
- Buy stocks on the strength of the company and not on the dollar price per share. Beginners often choose a lower-priced stock because they think they can afford it. But a higher-priced stock may indicate the value of a successful company with a future. Institutions generally will not buy stocks of smaller companies. If an institution is buying a particular stock it is because their due diligence has determined the prospects of this company's future is very good. Institutions include pension funds, financial institutions, and mutual funds. Follow the big boys.
- Heavy volume trading may indicate that institutions are investing in a stock.
- Major gains are made when a company's stock has held steady while quarterly sales, profits, and ROE have all been improving. This is a stock that is ready to "break loose." Especially if this company is a market leader or soon will become a market leader.

How many individual company stocks should you own?

If you only have a little money to invest, buy just a few stocks. If you have substantial investment dollars, you will want to diversify your portfolio.

You don't need to own a lot of stocks. Pick out a few good high-quality companies that are market leaders. Only pick companies with products and services that you understand. You cannot effectively manage a large number of stocks.

Up to $5,000	2 stocks
$5,000 to $10,000	2-3 stocks
$10,000 to $20,000	3-4 stocks
$20,000 to $50,000	4-5 stocks
$50,000 to $100,000	5-6 stocks

How to Protect Your Stock Investments

(Oh my God! I wish I had known this when I first started investing!!)

1. **Always cut your losses by placing a Stop-Loss Order at 10% below your purchase price.** If the stock is a good company with a good product, consider buying back in at the bottom.

2. **You must have a "buy" strategy and you must have a "sell" strategy—and stick to it!** If your goal is to get a 15% return on your money, sell the stock when it reaches your goal. However, if the stock is gaining momentum and trending upward, keep raising your Stop-Loss Order at 8% below the day's high. If the stock doubles in price, consider selling enough to get your original investment back and let the rest ride and look for another stock for your original investment dollars.

3. **Always sell your losers first and not your profit makers.** Many people sell their profit makers and then hang on to their losers, hoping they'll make a comeback—not wise.

4. **Learning how to become successful at investing takes time, and *you will lose money!*** It will take several years for you to gain competency and feel comfortable picking stocks. In the beginning, any losses should be considered as the cost of your learning experience. Don't be emotional. Consider your loss as tuition to the Millionaire's Academy. It is no different than investing in your financial education.

Once you have formulated an investment strategy—stick to it!

5. **Advice for the "buy and hold" investor—don't let market movement make "buy and sell" decisions for you.** People who make fortunes in the stock market are the ones who have invested in good companies and have kept their investments for the long haul.

6. **Don't worry daily over your investments.** You need to know what is happening to your investments, but you shouldn't be following them every day. Constant attention and daily monitoring will only worry you and cause you to react to daily market swings.

7. **Review your investments every three months or at least once every year.** If you have chosen good companies with good leadership, the best thing to do is nothing. Remember, results happen over time.

People focus on what the market is doing, when the market is focused on tomorrow.

The "once in a lifetime" opportunity.

These are the opportunities that are too good to be true or the "really hot deals" that you just can't afford to pass up. From time to time, a friend or relative will come to you with an unbelievable money-making opportunity.

MY BEST ADVICE FOR YOU IS TO "RUN FOR THE HILLS" FROM ANYONE WHO TELLS YOU THAT HE CAN MAKE YOU A TON OF MONEY OVERNIGHT!

Look, if you haven't got the money, you can't do it! No matter how good it seems, don't sit there and listen to them. All you are doing is torturing yourself. Don't let greed influence your decisions. Tell them the truth—you can't afford it—period.

The most important lesson to be learned here:

Unless you are prepared to lose everything, or you have enough spare cash lying around, you can't do it. It's just that simple. You must learn that this won't be your last great opportunity. There always will be other opportunities. And you can't be part of every one that comes along. If it's too good to be true, it probably is!

However, Cash Is King! When a real opportunity does come around, this is the time you want to have "ready cash" that does not affect your lifestyle and previous commitments. Typically, deals like this require a greater risk but the rewards are tremendous. But again, if you don't have the cash—don't even think twice about deals like this. You can't afford risking your family's future.

Get conservative in your old age. As you grow older and you achieve a comfortable level of wealth, your investment portfolio should become more conservative—because you have less time to overcome the ups and downs of the stock market. However, if you started investing late in life, you may have to settle for a higher risk to achieve your investment goals by retirement. These decisions are all based on how comfortable you are with "risk-taking."

Your retirement investment accounts need to be averaging a conservative 10% at the minimum for you to beat the 3-4% rate of inflation and for you to take a maximum of a 5% retirement withdrawal.

Dollar Cost Averaging, or Stock Averaging Over Time

Once you have determined a stock investment plan, you must faithfully stick to it, whether the market is up or down. It's true that ideally you want to buy low and sell high, but remember, your investment strategy is to create wealth over time. The key words are "over time." Dollar Cost Averaging, also known as Stock Averaging Over Time, is critical to understand because the average person has the wrong concept of buying stock. When the stock market is rising, they want to buy. When the stock market is falling, they want to sell and get out.

Here's the problem with this philosophy. Let's say the price of a can of soup, normally $1.50, is rising to $2.00 a can—is this a good time to buy cans of soup? NO! Let's say the price of soup starts falling to $1.00—is this the best time to buy soup? YES!

The best time to buy soup is when the price is falling! In fact, I would go out and buy all I could, especially if it's good soup. The same philosophy holds true with buying stocks in a good company with good leadership even if the market is declining—the questions you need to ask are: "Is the company still good? What about the quality of its leadership and products? Will the consumer always buy this company's product?" If the answers are yes to these questions, then you need to keep on investing.

Buying a good company's stock when the price of the stock is falling is a good investment. But if the company is having leadership problems and consumers are no longer interested in the products, then it's time to sell this stock.

Sometimes the market falls for reasons that have nothing to do with the company itself. The market may rise because there is a new leader in Russia, or it may decline because the President had an affair with an intern!

The point is, you can't make decisions based on market gains or declines. Your investment decisions need to be based on the company, its leadership, its financial performance, and its products.

IMPORTANT THOUGHT...

If you only bought stock when the stock price of the company was rising— you would not own very much stock.

This is the concept of dollar cost averaging. Every year, you must stick to your investment strategy and invest faithfully. Some years when the price of the stock is up, you will be able to buy less stock. During the years when price of the stock has declined, you will be able to buy more stock. For example:

Year	Stock Price	Shares Bought	Total Invested
Yr. 1	$4.00	600	$2,400
Yr. 2	$6.00	400	$2,400
Yr. 3	$8.00	300	$2,400
Yr. 4	$10.00	240	$2,400
Yr. 5	$6.00	400	$2,400
Yr. 6	$8.00	300	$2,400
Yr. 7	$12.00	200	$2,400
Yr. 8	$16.00	150	$2,400
Yr. 9	$22.00	109	$2,400
Yr.10	$24.00	100	$2,400
Ending Price	**Total Shares**	**Total Invested**	
$24.00	**2,799**	**$24,000**	

$24 x 2,799 shares = $67,176 on a $24,000 investment!

Compare this to putting your money in a bank savings account that pays only a 3% compounded interest rate. The same $24,000 invested at a compounded 3% interest rate over 10 years would only grow to $32,253 compared to stock averaging results of $67,176!

This example demonstrates that "stock averaging investing," whether the market is up or down, is clearly a better investment than just putting your money in a bank savings account.

In dollar cost averaging, don't keep buying the same stock if it is showing a consistent downward trend. Pick a different stock immediately. Remember to always set your Stop-Loss Order at 10% of the price you paid for it. Even in dollar cost averaging, consistency is the key word. If the stock you picked is too volatile, you may have picked the wrong stock.

GET OUT!

The Rule of 72 is a simple formula, which is used to determine how long it will take to double your money according to your interest rate goal. This rule demonstrates how even small rates of return can affect your investment portfolio. Simply, 72 divided by your interest rate equals the number of years to double your money. When dividing, only use the number—not the percentage. For example: 8% becomes 8, so to double your money at 8% the equation would be, $72 \div 8 = 9$ (years).

72 divided by 1%= 72 years to double your money.
72 divided by 8%= 9 years to double your money.
72 divided by 10%= 7.2 years to double your money.
72 divided by 12%= 6 years to double your money.
72 divided by 20%= 3.6 years to double your money.

For example, if you invested $10,000 at a 10% interest rate, it would take you 7.2 years to double your money to $20,000. $10,000 invested at 12% would take you 6 years to double your money to $20,000.

This rule is similar to the Rule of 72 in the way you formulate how long it will take you to "triple" your investments.

116 divided by 1%= 116 years to triple your money.
116 divided by 8%= 14.5 years to triple your money.
116 divided by 10%= 11.6 years to triple your money.
116 divided by 12%= 9.6 years to triple your money.
116 divided by 20%= 5.8 years to triple your money.

Investment Decisions Regarding Your Home

Get your priorities straight! After high school, you should be saving for your first home instead of trying to buy a fancy expensive car that only depreciates and costs money to maintain.

Our First Home

Your Number One financial goal should be to buy your first home. Once you are paying rent, it is very difficult to save enough money for a down payment.

You should be hell-bent on saving every penny you can get your hands on, even if you have to convince your sweetheart to skip the big wedding and expensive honeymoon. Take the money you save and put it immediately toward a down payment.

WISDOM KEY

> **Your first home will be the most important investment you will make in your life.** There is nothing worse than paying rent or mortgage payments on someone else's investment. Make owning your first home your number one financial goal.

All new homebuyers should take a real estate license course. This is a required course for all real estate agents before they can apply to get a license. Even if you never plan on selling real estate, this is the best thing you could do to learn about the most expensive investment you will ever make—your first home.

This course is usually held in the evenings, takes about one to two weeks and usually costs about $500. What you learn about home buying and selling will be invaluable to you in looking for your own first home. You will learn about the different ways to finance a home mortgage, how to inspect a home for flaws and repairs, how to determine if the home you are interested in is a good investment, state laws governing real estate sales and how the laws relate to you. Take this course. It's priceless!

Your home will be your most expensive investment as well as your best interest deduction on your taxes.

Do not buy townhouses or condos. Don't be lulled into some sales pitch of affordability. Generally, it's more difficult to find buyers when it comes time to resell. Have patience and keep saving until you can buy your first real "stand alone" home.

YOUR GOAL: Have your mortgage paid off by the time you retire.

PLEASE NOTE: I said by the time you retire—not before you retire. Contrary to what some people think, paying off your mortgage as quickly as you can is bad advice. Do not pay off your mortgage ahead of schedule. It's the cheapest money you can borrow. In the interim, if you are able to save extra money or earn extra money, put it into long-term investments that can take advantage of compound interest rates and create real wealth.

Never pay more than required. Never double up on payments on your home mortgage when you have other high interest debts. You do not want to be "house rich" and "cash poor."

Most wealthy people have carried large mortgages on their homes. You would think that wealthy people would pay off their homes first. The fact is they don't. Wealthy people understand the value of carrying large mortgages at low rates and the value of investing their extra money into high-yield, long-term investments that grow at above-average rates of return. Here's the question that you need to understand: "Why pay off a 7% mortgage when the stock market is averaging 10% returns or higher?

TRYING TO PAY OFF YOUR HOUSE EARLY IS LIKE PUTTING YOUR MONEY INTO A "PIGGY BANK"— IT DOESN'T EARN INTEREST AND THAT DOESN'T EVEN TAKE INTO CONSIDERATION THE TAX CONSEQUENCES.

The interest on your mortgage is tax deductible—so why pay it off? Instead of making extra payments on your house, pay off your 18% credit card interest, which is not tax deductible.

If you have extra money, put it into investments you can cash in or borrow against in times of financial crisis. If you lose your job, your bank will not lend you money against your home. This is very ironic—because here you thought making extra payments on your house would benefit you in times of crisis.

The fact is—you have become "house rich" and "cash poor."

You do not impress anyone by making extra payments on your home mortgage. Your banker will not care if you have made extra payments when you are behind on your house payments during a financial crisis. You are better-off having investments that you can cash in to help overcome the crisis.

In reselling, the balance of your mortgage has no effect on the value of your house. It still sells for the same price.

Here's another thing to consider: Your house is not an investment that you want to sell. Just because you have value in your house, it is not wise to borrow on it and increase the payments. Additional money paid against your mortgage will not raise the value of your home. You'd be better-off placing your money in a stock investment where compound interest will grow your money exponentially and be there when you need it.

Do not place second mortgages against your home unless you can immediately pay off this second mortgage. Consider a second mortgage on your home only in extreme life or death emergencies.

There is no advantage to paying off your mortgage ahead of schedule. Plan to have your mortgage paid off by the time you retire. In the interim, if you are able to save extra money or earn extra money, put it into long-term investments that can take advantage of compound interest rates and create real wealth.

When *should* you pay off your mortgage ahead of schedule? The only time I would recommend paying off your home mortgage is if you are near retirement age and you have received a large amount of money (inheritance, a surprise lottery win, early retirement payoff). Definitely pay off your mortgage in these circumstances.

Rule of thumb regarding home mortgages. The total of your debts, including your home mortgage, should never exceed 30% of your income. If you are following the 10-10-10-70 financial plan, this 30% will be allocated to the 70%; this will leave you 40% for all other expenditures or expenses.

CAR LOANS
The Bottomless Money Pit

Next to your home, cars are generally your second biggest expense until your children go to college.

Cars are your biggest depreciating asset, and will cost you money!

THE BIGGEST MISTAKE MANY YOUNG PEOPLE MAKE, IS TO DREAM ABOUT OWNING A FANCY NEW CAR.

Don't sabotage your financial future by driving a car you can't afford to pay for in cash!

Never borrow money to buy a depreciating asset. The hardest thing to do is save up enough money to pay for your car in cash. But in the long-run, this is the best way to stay out of debt. Unless you are wealthy, never buy new cars; always buy a car that is at least one year old. You lose 30% of a new car's value just by driving it out of the show room. Then you lose 20% of the car's value in the second year, another 20% of the value in the third year, and about 10% every year after that. If you do buy a new car, fax your bids to the dealer. You will generally get a lower price if you don't have to play give-and-take with the salesmen and their Sales Manager.

Buy a good used car and drive it as long as you can. Don't worry about what the neighbors think. Take good care of your car. Keep it clean and in good repair. It's amazing how much better a car seems to drive when it is clean. The most important thing you can do for your car is to change the oil every 2,500 miles even though the car manual says 3,000 miles. If you can keep the oil clean, you can drive the car forever.

Driving a nice, shiny new car will cost you a fortune!

Compare the car-buying habits of these two families:

The Havenots buy a new $25,000 car every three years. They pay 10% down and finance the rest at 8%. The car has lost 40% of its value after three years when they trade it in. They spend $500 a year for repair and maintenance.

The Havemores buy a "new used" $15,000 car every six years for cash. They spend $1,000 for repair and maintenance every year, for 10 years.

To demonstrate how expensive it is to drive a new car, calculate the total car payments in the Havenots' scenario and the Havemores' scenario. Next, take the amount the Havemores saved and invest it over 40 years at 10% interest...

What's the difference?

$1,000,000

> If the average family did nothing else but buy used cars instead of new cars and invested the difference, at the end of 40 years they could retire very wealthy with $1,000,000!

WISDOM KEY

A new car is the worst "investment" a family can make.

➢ **Don't waste $1,000,000 of your family's future by driving new cars.**

➢ **Unless you can walk into a showroom and plunk down the entire sales price in cash, don't buy new cars.**

LET'S SUM THINGS UP!

What does this mean to me?

1. **Money is energy.** It must always be kept moving or you will lose it. Money is attracted to positive attitudes and industrious work ethics.

2. **There is no such thing as a free lunch.** There are no "get-rich-quick" shortcuts to becoming wealthy. But anyone can become wealthy over time.

3. **You must believe that you deserve to be wealthy.** Becoming wealthy is an attitude. Develop "prosperity consciousness!"

4. **Wealth does not come from what we earn but from the growth of our investment portfolios.** You don't have to be a financial genius, but you will have to work at understanding your investments and where your money is going.

5. **Wealth requires responsibility and accountability.** Budgeting and keeping track of your money are prerequisite habits you must master before you become good at saving your money. No matter how much you earn, the key to all great wealth is the discipline of saving and investing. The key is to start right now—the sooner the better.

6. **Anyone can become wealthy, regardless of what he or she gets paid.** Consistent savings of small amounts of money, invested over time, will result in exponential fortunes through the power of compound interest.

7. **You must "give it to grow it!"** One of the greatest secrets of wealth is that the more you give away to help make this world a better place, the more abundantly it will be returned to you. This is God's unconditional guarantee! However, if you don't tithe and give to charity, don't expect God's help. It's just that simple.

CALL TO ACTION:

1. Get out of debt and start living debt-free. Commit to saving something from every paycheck.

2. Learn how to think about and handle money the right way. Write down your financial goals and create a budget. Know where your money is going!

3. Start saving, investing, and tithing. Learn how your generosity primes your wealth, just as a little water primes a pump.

WHAT YOU CAN ACCOMPLISH:

A commitment to savings and investing can reward you with all the wealth you will ever need to live a rich and fulfilling lifestyle. You will never have to worry about paying bills. You can give your family a great lifestyle filled with opportunity. With wealth, you can fulfill your life's higher purpose of making a positive difference in the world. That's what this book is all about—bettering the world by bettering YOURSELF.

Sources & Inspiration

The information in these books is powerful. I urge you to buy these books and read them over and over again until they become part of your daily life.

George S. Clason, *The Richest Man In Babylon,* (Signet Books, New York, N.Y. 1988)

J. Paul Getty, *How To Be Rich,* (Jove Books, New York, N.Y. 1965)

David Chilton, *The Wealthy Barber,* (Prima Publishing 1997)

Robert G. Allen, *Creating Wealth,* (Fireside Books, New York, N.Y. 1986)

Robert G. Allen, *Multiple Streams Of Income,* (John Wiley and Sons, Inc., New York, N.Y. 2000)

Robert T. Kiyosaki with Sharon L. Lechter, *Rich Dad, Poor Dad,* (Warner Books, New York, N.Y. 2000)

Bill and Mary Toohey, *The Average Family's Guide To Financial Freedom,* (John Wiley and Sons, Inc., New York, N.Y. 2000)

Thomas J. Stanley and William D. Danko, *The Millionaire Next Door,* (Longstreet Press, Marietta, Ga. 1996)

Suze Orman, *The 9 Steps to Financial Freedom,* (Crown Publishers, New York, N.Y. 1997)

Grady Cash, *Spend Yourself Rich,* (Financial Literacy Center, Kalamazoo, Mich. 1998)

Ric Edelman, *The New Rules Of Money,* (Harper Collins Publishers, New York, N.Y. 1999)

Ric Edelman, *The Truth About Money,* (Harper Collins Publishers, New York, N.Y. 1998)

Tod Barnhart, *The Five Rituals of Wealth,* (Harper Collins, New York, N.Y. 1995)

Brooke M. Stephens, *Wealth Happens One Day at a Time,* (Harper Business, New York, N.Y. 1999)

Robert J. Garner, Robert B. Coplan, Martin Nissenbaum, Barbara J. Raasch, Charles L. Ratner, *Ernst & Young's Personal Financial Planning Guide,* (John Wiley & Sons, Inc., New York, N.Y. 1999)

Peter Lynch and John Rothchild, *Learn To Earn,* (Fireside Books, New York, N.Y. 1995)

William J. O'Neil, *24 Essential Lessons For Investment Success,* (McGraw-Hill, New York, N.Y. 2000)

William J. O'Neil, *How To Make Money In Stocks,* (McGraw-Hill, New York, N.Y. 1988)

Sandy Botkin, *Tax Strategies For Business Professionals,* (Self-Published, The Tax Reduction Institute, Germantown, Md. 2001)

Janet Bodnar, *Kiplinger's Dollars & Sense for Kids,* (Kiplinger Books, Washington, D.C. 1999)

Stawski Kids, *Parents & Money,* (John Wiley & Sons, Inc., New York, N.Y. 2000)

Investor's Business Daily, *Guide To The Markets,* (John Wiley & Sons, Inc., New York, N.Y. 1996)

I also highly recommend subscribing to the Investor's Business Daily newspaper.

Building Your "University on Wheels"
Audio Success Library
The following audio books can be purchased at any Barnes & Noble,
Border's book store or on-line at Amazon.com.

The Magic of Believing
Claude M. Bristol

Success and the Self-Image*
Zig Ziglar

How To Be A Winner
Zig Ziglar

The Art of Exceptional Living*
Jim Rohn

Live Your Dreams*
Les Brown

It's Not Over Until You Win!
Les Brown

Dare To Win
Mark Victor Hansen/
Jack Canfield

Celebrate Life
Leo Buscaglia

Success Is A Choice
Rick Pitino

The Winner Within
Pat Riley

The One Minute Millionaire
Mark Victor Hansen and
Robert G. Allen

The Psychology of Achievement*
Brian Tracy

Maximum Achievement
Brian Tracy

Unlimited Power
Anthony Robbins

Awaken the Giant Within
Anthony Robbins

The Power of Positive Thinking
Dr. Norman Vincent Peale

The Pursuit of WOW!
Tom Peters

Being Your Own Boss
Denis Waitley

Life Strategies*
Phillip C. McGraw, Ph.D.

The Magic of Thinking Big
David J. Schwartz, Ph.D.

The Generosity Factor*
Ken Blanchard and
S. Truett Cathy

How To Build a Network of
Power Relationships
Harvey MacKay

* Recommend listening to first...Put the pure, the clean, the powerful, the positive into your mind!

For a more complete list of inspiring authors and speakers call the following company for a catalog. I highly recommend everything they inventory! Nightingale Conant 1-800-525-9000

Yes, the American Dream
no longer has to be just a dream...

How will they write your legacy?

Believe in yourself...God does!

The Magic is in You!

You Are A Winner!

"Famous Dave's" Award-Winning Cookbook...

Backroads & Sidestreets

The Legend of Famous Dave

For over 30 years, "Famous Dave" Anderson has traveled the backroads and sidestreets in search of the best tasting recipes from America's Best Roadhouses, Blues Joints, and Northwoods Lodges. These are the "Best of the Best" award winning recipes your grandmother wished she could get her hands on! Discover the legendary $1,000,000 hickory smoked rib recipe that launched a national BBQ company, the secrets to making the best southern fried chicken, how to make the perfect lemon meringue pie, and extraordinary sticky buns as big as your head.

Famous Dave's Backroads & Sidestreets
wins **"Award of Excellence"** for being the
"Best Bar-B-Que/Grill Cookbook in America"
by the prestigious National Barbecue Association

Check Out Dave's LifeSkills Center for Leadership

All profits from the sale of Backroads & Sidestreets go to the LifeSkills Center for Leadership, a non-profit foundation whose mission is to work with at-risk children by *"Turning Today's Challenges into Tomorrow's Opportunities."* To learn more visit: **www.lifeskills-center.org.**

Visit Famous Dave's, Home of the World's Greatest Barbeque

To learn more about Famous Dave's BBQ or to find the restaurant nearest you visit: **www.famousdaves.com.**

To Order Your Copy of "Famous Dave's" Backroads & Sidestreets

Contact your local bookstore or visit them online.

Thanks For Your Support!

Famous Dave